SHAKESPEARE
AND THE RIVAL TRADITIONS

Shakespeare
and the Rival Traditions

by ALFRED HARBAGE

BARNES & NOBLE, INC.

New York

Publishers • Booksellers • Founded 1873

First published, 1952 by The Macmillan Company

Reprinted, 1968

by special arrangement with

The Macmillan Company

L. C. Catalog Card Number: 68-23759

Printed in the United States of America

To

Oscar James Campbell

Contents

Introduction

THE number of works about Shakespeare, although depressing to everyone who proffers another, seems less monstrous when weighed with the circulation of his own. Editions continue to flow from scores of presses, presumably to be read, and translations to appear in scores of languages, including Afrikaans, Kirghiz, and Azerbaijani. More impressive, because less indebted to academic endeavor, is the currency of these works in the theatre. Some have had a continuous stage history for the three and one-half centuries of their existence, and are now played more frequently than ever before. In this open contest, ruled by hard economic laws, Shakespeare is still winning against all contenders, even George Bernard Shaw. He is the favorite playwright of the strange new Russia. He was performed in Berlin on the eve of its fall. Anecdotes thrive upon this Shakespeare-Imperialism. The recent failure of *King Lear* on Broadway was reputedly predicted, on the ground that the play, although long a favorite in the Yiddish theatre, would never go in English. I recall how at one of my lectures a young oriental forsook the usual shyness of her race and sex to demur at my statement that *Macbeth* was still wholly intelligible throughout "Western" civilization, conveying as she did so a sense of her private opinion that its author was really Chinese. My literary correspondence is not wide, but I once received in the same mail two letters on fairly abstruse Shakespearean questions, one from Bulgaria and one from Iran.

It is not quite right to say that the excitement has all risen since Shakespeare's death. In his lifetime his work excited those it was designed to excite, the frequenters of certain large arenas in Shoreditch and Southwark. There were even brave voices opposing the set of correct critical opinion by suggesting that it would interest posterity. Season and circumstances were right for the growth of great drama. If the tree missed pruning by the belletristic élite, it also escaped pollarding: it was allowed to spread its foliage wide and thrust its roots deep in search of its own proper sustenance.

What was the nature of that sustenance, and of the other accidents of growth? Since the last secret of genius must always elude us, this is the greatest question about Shakespeare we have some hope of answering. A number of men for a number of generations have collaborated in the attempt. If they have seemed sometimes to be looking too long and intently at objects too small, the circumstances are largely to blame. Elizabethans did not trouble to write the history of their stage and the lives of their playwrights, or even to print carefully and punctually the texts of their plays. Envious and calumniating Time came near to putting into his wallet as alms for oblivion the whole wonderful record. We should remember that Edmond Malone in the eighteenth century risked becoming a figure of fun by concerning himself with details that are now the stock in trade not only of Shakespeare's popular biographers but even of his theatrical producers. It is fortunate that there have been men willing to deal with minutiae, the scattered records accidentally preserved, and doggedly deny that we may resolve all mysteries by declaring that Shakespeare was not Shakespeare but somebody else, or by relying solely on our oracular gifts, with the plays used like the ink blots in the Rorschach test. These men have rescued a history.

A latent sense of guilt has inspired these defensive opening remarks. Partisan winds have been blowing cold on literary historians. Stiff questions are asked on the floor of the House of Letters. They go something like this: If you wish to write about Shakespeare, why not write about *Shakespeare*—instead of his *Theatre* or his *Times*, his this or his that, including his lesser contemporaries who, whatever they were, wanted much, God knoweth, of being other Shakespeares? It is a charge of irrelevance; and, to the extent that it is justified, we must bow our heads in submission: the goodness of our intentions cannot exculpate us, nor our long-watch'd labors and pinching throes. I feel especially exposed as I submit this volume.

Although naturally persuaded of my own instinct for the essential, I am acutely aware that I have discussed the earnings of actors who trudged England's roads before Shakespeare was born, the seating capacity of theatres where his plays were *not* performed; that I have analyzed the Renaissance idea of chastity instead of the character of Cleopatra, the preachment on Election in the *Book of Homilies* instead of the imagery of *Hamlet*. Why does such matter appear in my book? The partisan winds are salutary in that they make me wish to say directly, what I am trying to do and how I am trying to do it.

My aim is to present a new synthesis of the facts about Elizabethan theatres and the content of Elizabethan plays, as a means of defining Shakespeare's materials and intentions. Although the whole of English Renaissance drama until the date of his last play falls within my purview, I am not writing its history in the usual sense. My book is not a descriptive chronicle or a critical survey. It contains no biographies of authors and no synopses of plays. Its organization is not chronological. I am concentrating upon the single central problem: How did the Elizabethan theatrical industry organize itself in order to serve its clientele, what was the view of life which this clientele brought into the theatres, and how was this view of life reflected or refracted in the plays? I know that the claim that one is adding to the understanding and therefore appreciation of Shakespeare is both bold and conventional, that his plays need no prop, and that those who do not understand and appreciate them already are not apt to be saved by a book. But I also know that those whose interest in Shakespeare has survived beyond the period specified by their academic masters have no aversion for the peripheral. In my experience they have proved humblingly grateful for any attempt, however feeble, to outline his assumptions, to indicate the doubts and certainties in *his* day, to suggest what he was *like*. To suggest what he was like, with the inevitable complement, what he was *not* like, is to invoke history.

What will seem to be the chief novelty of my book is its insistence upon the duality of Elizabethan drama. I have preserved, throughout, the distinction between the drama of the public theatres, where Shakespeare was placed, and the drama of the private theatres, where he was not. The method has the value of throwing into relief the Shakespearean assumptions by constant reference to their negative as cultivated in a dissident coterie. I am actually presenting, by a process of fragmentation, just two plays—the popular play and the coterie play. I have toyed with the notion of calling the first the *archetype*, with the ideals it embodies *myths*, and the second the *anarchetype*, with its separatist and disintegrative features *contramyths*; but I feel inexpert and self-conscious in using such language and must confine my sortie to the present remark. My emphasis throughout upon the two dramatic traditions is so great that I need dwell no further on the subject now; but I am hopeful that future discussions of Elizabethan drama will be influenced by the distinction made. We would not think of regarding as a single entity the various audiences and reading publics of the present day, as if the art of the theatre, the screen, the popular weekly, and the literary quarterly was quite homogeneous. Confusion is bound to result from ignoring equivalent distinctions in Shakespeare's day.

I am concerned with the substance and sentiment of the drama rather than its artistic technique; and while I feel the force of the objection that the two things are, or ought to be, inseparable I have seen no alternative to my limitation of aim. As it is, I have felt in writing each chapter that I was trying to fit a thousand pieces into a box that would hold a hundred, that the problem of selecting and ordering such complex material was too much for me, that I was neglecting constantly the need for explanation and qualification—in a word, that I was producing the token of a book I wished I had the power to write. I have often envied those who could devote a volume to a single play or an essay to a single passage. I recognize as well as anyone is likely to do that in the ruthless succession of my categories and contrasts the Shakespearean essence is lost. I believe, however, that it is only momentarily lost, and that, although my discussion may not be criticism, it has something to say to critics.

All but the most apocalyptic of critics seem willing to concede historians a place at least as humble servitors in the study of literature. As I take my place among the sons of Martha, I recall that in my earlier *As They Liked It*, I may sometimes have seemed to be

aspersing historical methods. If so, I herewith recant. I trust, however, that no one who happens to know that book will suppose that
I am denying here what I affirmed there, that Shakespeare is an
artist and not a moralist; rather I am describing the happy situation
in which the artist need only be moral—in which he may concentrate
upon means, having reached with his audience a harmonious agreement about ends. At the risk of seeming to stress unconscionably the
importance of my views, I must try to distinguish between what I
was doing then and what I am doing now. In *As They Liked It* I was
dealing with an aesthetic-psychological phenomenon. I was trying
to illustrate how Shakespeare induced pleasurable excitement by art-
fully suspending issues, keeping ideas of good and evil in apparent
flux, offering simultaneously both perturbation and reassurance. Reassurance is currently out of fashion, and to several of my reviewers
I seemed to be finding more of it in the plays of Shakespeare than
was quite respectable. Distinguished by reprobation in no less a place
than a leader in the *Times Literary Supplement* was my opinion that
Shakespeare did not require his audience to sacrifice to two hours'
entertainment the truths they lived by, and to accept in their place
the idea that life is a tale told by an idiot or that clouds of glory
trail in the Boar's Head Inn. However I am of the same opinion still:
that it is the underlying philosophical stability of the Shakespearean
world that renders the surface instability so pleasurable.

Although far from devoted to the image of a skeptical, enigmatic,
or repining Shakespeare, Professor Elmer Edgar Stoll, for reasons
of his own, submitted my views to courteous rebuke, along with
those of S. L. Bethell. I had not yet read Mr. Bethell's book, but I
did so now and, understandably perhaps, with great enthusiasm. The
readiness of this critic to discuss Shakespeare's plays in terms of
current motion pictures and musical comedies (most "Elizabethan"
of our forms of art) delighted me, and does so still. Allowing for a
"multiconscious" response to their complex art, Mr. Bethell per-
mits the plays to remain as they are, and applies no externally derived
and hence flattening principles. Great works of popular literature
establish their own criteria and are best understood where most beloved. But the approach of Mr. Bethell and, if he will accept the

alliance, of myself assumes a rock-bottom of agreement between artist and audience. They could move about so freely together only because the ground underfoot was so firm. The plays required the utmost in spontaneity of response—complete trust in their ethical postulates as well as complete submission to their artistic conventions—and could have been written only for an audience secure in the knowledge that it would not be betrayed. To bring this matter to a close: in *As They Liked It*, I tried to describe Shakespeare's methods of manipulating moral substance so as to produce the maximum in dramatic effect; in the present book, I try to define what that substance was. So that I may not seem merely to be imposing my own predilections upon Shakespeare, I contrast his code with its contemporary rival and proceed by demonstration.

Perhaps the success of a book like the present must be measured less by how many readers it persuades than by how few it repels. The most valid objection to the historical treatment of works of art is that it tends to render the works themselves mere *history*—to fix them in their own time and divorce them from ours. The most valid objection to the treatment of an artist's "philosophy" is that it tends to wrest the artist from those who feel no loyalty to the principles revealed. Obviously both objections presume some defect either in the principles themselves or in the analyst's sense of them.

If the Shakespearean principles are not basically obsolete, there should be no danger in examining them. Actually, they are more apt to seem obvious than obsolete. It is the attempt to avoid the *obvious* that makes so much recent Shakespearean criticism so mystifying. Certainly each generation must have the privilege of seeing in its own light the works of art of the past; but the new light must be a supplement and not a substitution: the light of the artist's own age cannot safely be excluded. Some of our twentieth century criticism is written under an oddly flickering flame; and, although often rich in stimulating insights, it can have a blighting effect upon those without maturity to weigh and consider. When our questing youths speak of the *Wasteland* qualities of this play, the pagan ritualism in that, the incestuous motivation of a third, or the hilarious satire upon valor and chastity in a fourth, while having missed the gist of all, one wonders what they have been reading, or by whom they have been indoctrinated. In simple fairness to them, we must let them see in Shakespeare a little less of Frazer and Freud, and a little more of Erasmus. There would be less religiosity in the criticism, less moralizing without reference to any identifiable morality, less of the confusedly edifying, if there were more respect for Renaissance principles as such and more trust in Shakespeare's own wisdom and tact. The most modish treatises upon Shakespeare are riddled by the covert assumption that, as a thinker, he is in need of assistance.

Rightly considered, the principles to which Shakespeare subscribed are no more exclusive than obsolete. His plays are religious at core, but they do not probe the tender area of rivalry in theologies. To their religious core I have applied the term "Christian humanism"; but if this were taken to imply that persons of non-Christian faiths are denied full rapport with them, the acceptance of the plays in the world about us would supply prima facie proof that the implication was false. In the month of the present writing, a Jew, a Catholic, and a Protestant among the New York state board of regents collaborated in the composition of a prayer proposed for use in the public schools, and the University of Notre Dame stood as host to a Jew, a Hindu, a Moslem, a Confucianist, and a Buddhist, each expounding according to his tradition the Natural Law as bond between Man and his Creator. These men, and the multitudes articulate through them, are religious in the sense in which Shakespeare's plays are religious. If Shakespeare himself was religious in an additional sense, as he may well have been, he was not aggressive about it.

To extract particular "lessons" from the plays and to designate particular characters as didactic "spokesmen" does violence to an artistic idiom that cannot be transposed. The moral exegesis always seems crude, *morally* crude. The exegete is constrained to offer as evidence the details of the façade, whereas the morality resides in the foundation and framework. Its fundamental and pervasive character renders absurd the periodic attempts to deny its existence. Although Shakespeare was preeminently the entertainer, that "master of the revels to mankind" who made Emerson momentarily uneasy and

Tolstoy strangely unfair, he is not open to the charge of frivolity. He had probably forgotten what was in some of his plays by the time he came to write some of the others, and our grim earnestness about all would have left him bemused; still he and his audience had the inestimable advantage of believing in something. His artistic accomplishment was conditioned by that fact. To argue the point if there were no longer anything available in which to believe—nothing to supply art with foundation and framework—would be useless, even morbid and cruel. But the assumption that the twentieth century has dissolved all the verities seems a little hasty to judicious minds. The plaintive cries for a "new formulation," as if all the old ones were long since spent, return a hollow echo in the corridors of history: the process of formulation has been continuous, and has never been visibly affected one way or another by mere wistfulness. The audience-artist relationship, and the common pool of principles, will be the subject of my conclusion. The one thing that seems to me more fascinating than Shakespeare is the possibility of producing his like again; and in moments of elation I have hoped that my book would seem relevant to our literary situation today. My concluding plea for the art of the wider audience, on the authority of the Shakespearean precedent, may itself seem a little wistful, but I trust it will be charitably interpreted as something other than a display of inverted snobbery.

What follows concerns tactics. Everyone who has worked with Elizabethan drama knows how slippery the footing, how difficult to determine simply who wrote what when—with what hazards for honest impulses, what opportunities for dishonest ones. I have tried to minimize the hazards (and opportunities) by letting no important point hinge upon a disputable decision about date and authorship, and by eliminating from discussion all plays that cannot be assigned upon some kind of objective evidence either to one repertory or to the other. An abundance of plays remain to let me create—I must use the terms once more—my *archetype* and *anarchetype*. In quoting and citing all plays I have tried to convey a true impression and not, by the judicious selection of uncharacteristic details, to perpetrate a fraud. Only the plays of Shakespeare are treated allusively. Illustrations from the others are self-sustaining, and normally require for their understanding no familiarity with their context. In the treatment of the ideals—religious, humanistic, sexual, familial, communal—the definitions derive originally from the plays themselves, although I dwell first in each chapter upon the background in the thought and customs of the age. These introductory discussions are summary and unlearned. I have not sought to supply the *locus classicus* of the expression of any idea, but to find my text, whenever possible, in the most familiar places—Starkey, Hooker, the homilies, and the like. The subtopical arrangement of the relevant chapters should prove useful in indicating why Shakespeare may appear both Catholic and antipapal, ribald and chaste, aristocratic and egalitarian, or similarly contradictory.

My book is documented throughout, but contains no footnotes in the sense of additions to or deductions from the text. The note numbers on the pages may be ignored unless the reader is interested in the source of a quotation. I have supplied the act, scene, line reference for quotations from Shakespeare (all drawn from the Kittredge text), and the act, scene reference for others, unless plays are undivided, in which case I have supplied the line or page reference in the editions used. Whatever the editions, I have modernized the punctuation and spelling.

I have not included in my book-list any works other than those cited in documentation, even though countless relevant works are uncited. In the case of monographs dealing specifically with certain of my subtopics—the attitude toward foreigners, the treatment of children, and the like—the omission may appear callous. Although the conclusions of some of these monographs seem to me partly vitiated by the failure of their authors to distinguish between popular and coterie attitudes, that is not my reason for failing to mention them. Some I have absorbed unconsciously, some I have forgotten, and some I have not read. My book touches upon so much, that a list of all related works would have to be a bibliography of the Elizabethan drama and age. The constant recurrence of the names of Sir Edmund Chambers and Sir Walter Greg in my documentary notes is eloquent enough. If I have been able to devote little space to thanking my predecessors, fortunately I have also been able to devote little space to reproving them.

I wish to thank for their assistance in putting this book through the press my wife, and my friends Professors Matthias Shaaber and Allan G. Chester. I wish there were some way of thanking all those men whose works fail to appear in my book-list, yet have given me great pleasure and a sense of kinship. When I was assembling the list from my documentary notes, I was astonished to notice that I had cited no works by the guides of my youth, the late Felix E. Schelling and Edward P. Cheyney. I can only conclude that I have assumed that whatever was theirs is mine. No doubt I have done likewise in the case of other authorities. Let me now gratefully acknowledge the aid of all the collaborators, living or long-since dead. The more among the living who will recognize the views of this book as their own, the better I shall be pleased.

Part One

TWO THEATRES

I

Theatre of a Nation

IT is a peculiarity of the English Renaissance stage that it was never taken for granted. The great London theatres were already famous, Alleyn was performing in *Tamburlaine,* and Shakespeare's years were nearly half spent when the occupation of an elegant stranger astonished Robert Greene. "A Player!" quoth he, "I took you rather for a gentleman of great living, for if by outward habit men should be censured, I tell you you would be taken for a substantial man."[1] This note of surprise that players should prosper had been sustained in English voices at least for ninety years. A fifteenth century predecessor of Greene had written,

> There is so much nice array
> Amongst these gallants nowaday,
> That a man shall not lightly
> Know a player from another man.[2]

Even more intransigent than the wits were the spokesmen of church and state; they persistently viewed the stage as an abnormality and recorded only crises, so that we gain the impression that for two centuries theatrical activity was just emerging from rude origins or just verging on collapse. The whole story, however, contrasts remarkably with its episodes, as conveyed by royal proclamations, civic ordinances, proceedings in chancery, and public or private slurs; and what we see if we look patiently is that Medwall's "gallants" and Greene's

3

"unsubstantial" man were part of a large, lucrative, and relatively stable industry.

Actors were not viewed as an excrescence by the people generally. Their great-grandsires, by Shakespeare's time, had seen the playbills and heard the drum announcing the arrival of bands of strollers; these were part of the landscape, like carriers and canalmen, only gayer to the eye and associated in the mind with more exciting commodities. From the mid-fifteenth to the mid-seventeenth century, they were integral to the life of the nation, and brought drama to a larger percentage and a truer cross-section of a national population than any comparable group of record. We must begin with a portrait of these actors of England, and their amazingly inclusive clientele.

Professional acting, as precipitated by the ferment of the fifteenth and early sixteenth centuries, was not localized in origin or restricted in personnel. For generations clerks and craftsmen had been performing as amateurs throughout the land in the religious and allegorical drama sponsored by trade guilds and other organizations. When any group of men banded together of their own initiative and performed for profit, they must be considered as professionals, even when their activity was only supplementary to some other means of livelihood. Such groups might be made up of brother guildsmen, village neighbors, fellow servants from a manor house, the "waits" or musicians of a town, or result from some purely fortuitous combination of individuals. Minstrels, of course, appear in the record; but there is no evidence that they dominated the new craft, although they may have contributed some of its organizational features. As early as 1464 "players in their interludes"[3] are distinguished from minstrels among those exempt from the restrictions of the Act of Apparel, and in 1469 the minstrels are complaining of the competition in the field of entertainment offered by "rude husbandmen and craftsmen."[4] Talent for acting, real or assumed, might burgeon anywhere: a Paston letter of 1473 laments the loss of the horsekeeper, W. Woode, who for three years had been playing "Saint George and Robinhood and the Sheriff of Nottingham."[5] Even the most élite troupes were recruited from craftsmen. In 1528–1529

George Maller, a King's Player, was accepting for a consideration servants who wished to learn to act in the hope of themselves becoming King's Players. One of these was Thomas Arthur, a tailor. Since Maller himself was designated a glazier, we have the arresting instance of a glazier training a tailor in the art of acting for royal spectators. Although Thomas Arthur was described by his master as "right hard and dull to take any learning, whereby he was nothing meet or apt to be in service with the King's grace to make any plays or interludes before his highness,"[6] nevertheless, with three fellow aspirants, he toured the provinces with considerable success.

Tokens of recruiting from standard crafts continue to the end. James Burbage, famous actor and father of the more famous Richard, was "by occupation a joiner, and reaping but a small living by the same, gave it over and became a common player in plays."[7] Ben Jonson's career on the stage was preceded by bricklaying and soldiering; Shakespeare's, in all probability, by fashioning gloves. Sir Oliver Owlet's Men in Marston's satire of 1599[8] are made up of a fiddle-string maker, a beard maker, a peddler, and a poet; and, although at the moment they fall somewhat short of professionalism, the carpenter, weaver, bellows mender, tinker, joiner, and tailor who perform Shakespeare's "Pyramus and Thisbe" are, in their pristine walks of life, not unrepresentative. In early times a displaced priest, and in later an unpreferred graduate of the university, might become a professional actor. Gosson in 1582 says with his usual acerbity, "Most of the players have been either men of occupations which they have forsaken to live by playing, or common minstrels, or trained up from their childhood to this abominable exercise and have now no other way to get their living."[9] By Gosson's time an increasing number in the craft were superannuated singing boys or had been bred up as learners in the acting companies; nevertheless, even in later Stuart days, an actor's burial record sometimes describes him as a clothworker, or his will proclaims him a grocer, weaver, or pewterer,[10] thus commemorating his abandoned trade or the normal occupation of his parents and relatives. English actors were not, like earlier mimes, a distinct and disreputable caste, but venturesome recruits from the working classes, linked by familiar occupations and family ties to the bulk of the population. Persons of gentle birth would wish to avoid the craft, but gentility could be achieved by conspicuous financial success in it; and Shakespeare was but one of half a dozen in his company who died bearing coats of arms. Here was a new hierarchy, with the old epithets about rogues and vagabonds applicable only to the inebriate hirelings and sharking strollers at its lower extreme. Charges of licentiousness by enemies of actors and exhortations to strict living by their friends, as appropriate to men who live in the world's eye, suggest uniform notoriety; but the leaders were householders, parish officers, and churchwardens: stoutly bourgeois, they reared large families and acquired land.

The troupes were organized as business partnerships, ultimately stabilized by bond and contract. Although nominal association with a noble or royal household became increasingly obligatory, the earliest companies on record were not so associated. In 1427 interludes were performed before King Henry VI by the Players of Abington, evidently a town troupe, and by Jack Travail and his Companions, evidently minstrels of the road.[11] Between 1492 and 1509 the companies of various noblemen performed at the royal court, but so also did the Players of Wymborne Minster, the Players of London, the Players of Mile End, and the like.[12] The records of performances at Ipswich in the 1560's reveal the heterogeneous character of dramatic companies before a statute of 1572 legislated against those not licensed by two justices of the peace or "belonging to any baron of this realm or . . . any other honorable personage of greater degree."[13] Fees for town performances were paid to Mr. Dennyes' Players, Father Romsey, Peter Moon and his Company, James Candler and his Company, Martin the Minstrel and his Company, the Town Players, "certain players of Lincolnshire," and "certain strange players."[14] At Exeter in 1556 payment was made for a play presented by "a man and his four sons."[15] Town troupes, their members enjoying status as dwellers in the community rather than as nominal servants of lords, endured long after the statute. The town fathers of Norwich exercised their local prerogative on February 4, 1576:

This day the whole company of the waits of this city did come into this court and craved that they might have leave to play comedies . . . interludes . . . and tragedies which shall seem to them meet, which petition by the whole consent of this court is granted to them, so far as they do not play in the time of divine service and sermons.[16]

The players of Penrith were still active in 1622; the Players of Warwick, in 1624.[17] Such companies were relatively stationary. To move about freely, the actors needed credentials from lords; but these seem to have been easily obtained, the documents in some cases acquiring the elastic and transferable character of an indulgence.

To the year 1469 belongs our first notice of a troupe organized in the fashion that was to become generally sanctioned: the Players of the Earl of Essex.[18] By the end of the fifteenth century there were companies bearing the name of Gloucester (who as Richard III was to prove a boon to actors yet unborn) as well as of Oxford, Derby, Shrewsbury, Northumberland, Arundel, King Henry VII, and Prince Arthur. Early in the sixteenth, additional companies bore the names of Norfolk, Buckingham, Wiltshire, Ferrers, Clinton, and others.[19] The relation of the acting companies to royal or noble patrons is important as a token of the inclusiveness of their associations, but should not obscure the fact that English Renaissance drama and its achievements stem from the hosts of commoners willing to pay for it. As late as 1581 the will of Alexander Hoghton of Lea in Lancashire indicates that he kept and costumed actors as a regular household expense, and expected that his heirs might do so.[20] There must have been many similar instances; but in the case of the important companies the lords neither boarded nor paid the players, but simply sponsored their self-supporting activities. They did so partly because of their surviving feudal paternalism, partly because they liked plays, and partly because other lords did so and a company of actors advertised one's existence.

The role of patron cost little or nothing. The King's Players between 1494 and 1556 were paid an average of £3. 6s. 8d. each per year, in addition to their earnings from actual performances at court or elsewhere; but their case is unusual. What a company could normally expect from its lord was a document declaring that its members were his servants and should be respected accordingly, occasional intercession on their behalf if they got into trouble, a payment when they performed before him (such as they would receive in similar circumstances from any other lord), and, occasionally, a "badge" or livery—an allowance of cloth so that they might wear the colors of his house. The actor as unpaid servant came on the scene quite early. Although Northumberland was patron of a company, no provision for it appears in the detailed audits of his huge household. The reason is suggested by an entry of 1512 concerning the three minstrels he maintained, players upon the tabor, the rebec, and the lute, "to be paid in household *if they have it not by patent or warrant*"[21]—that is, presumably, to receive wages only if they were not earning fees as itinerants visiting other lords, as the minstrels of other lords were earning fees by visiting Northumberland. Evidently the Earl's players "had it" by patent or warrant only. In the time of Marlowe and Shakespeare, the Lords Leicester, Oxford, and Derby took as much personal interest in their companies as any, but not enough to prevent each from being a purely commercial organization detached from the actual lordly household. Leicester performed very real services for the troupe bearing his name, yet a letter sent him in 1572 by James Burbage and his fellows includes the reassuring note, "not that we mean to crave any further stipend or benefit at your Lordship's hands but our liveries as we have had, and also your honor's license to certify that we are your household servants . . ."[22]

It was the custom of Northumberland to double his fee to a visiting troupe if its patron was "his special Lord and friend and kinsman,"[23] and the mayors of towns were sometimes impressed by the prestige of a company's "lord"; but normally the importance of companies cannot be gauged by the importance of their patrons. Their ability to cohere, and to attract the right actors and playwrights, determined their fate. A number of very poor companies boasted very great patrons. Queen Elizabeth's Men, so eminent in the 1580's, sank into an obscure provincial existence after the death of the beloved Richard Tarleton and the rise in a rival troupe of Edward Alleyn playing in the dramas of Marlowe. Richard Burbage and William Shakespeare proved to be a matchless team, and their company ascended in spite of the frailty of its lords. It became the King's Company in 1603 because it was already the best; it owed none of its eminence to the royal touch.

The number of actors in the earliest troupes seems to have been standardized at four: such is the number given in records of Essex's Men, Gloucester's Men, King Henry VII's Men, and the Players of Coksale before 1494,[24] and of Norfolk's Men and Thomas Arthur's Company a few decades later.[25] In the Shakespearean era, whenever troupes of actors are introduced into plays, with an archaic or rustic effect as the aim, the actors are usually four in number. At Elsinore "Enter four or five Players," including his ladyship boy, nearer heaven by the "altitude of a chopine" since Hamlet last saw him. In *Sir Thomas More* the action is set in the early sixteenth century, and the company consists of four men and a boy; in *Histriomastix* the company consists of four men including the poet. Originally the women's parts must have been taken by a man, the slightest of the four. It seems likely that the assignment of such parts to a boy accompanying the troupe as a learner was an early phenomenon, but there is no certain evidence of his ladyship's presence until well along in the sixteenth century. The growth in the size of the companies may be readily traced. Between 1494 and 1552 the number of King's Men increased from four to eight. The size of the troupes visiting Southampton in 1576–1577 is fortunately noted in the town records: Lord Clinton's Men and Sir Richard Bartlett's Men, six each (the same number as Prince Edward's Men in 1538); Delaware's, Worcester's, and Stafford's Men, ten each; Bath's Men, eleven; and Leicester's, twelve.[26] In this connection it may be noted that such plays and interludes as were published in the 1560's and 1570's, with the casts prearranged for doubling or with a general note of how many actors may "well and easily play" them, usually presuppose a diminutive troupe—one of a number of indications that most of the published pieces do not properly represent the repertories of the more progressive companies of the time: *Impatient Poverty, Lusty Juventus, Mary Magdalene, Longer Thou Livest the More Fool Thou Art, New Custom,* and *Tide Tarrieth No Man* are all for the old standard number of four actors; *Trial of Treasure* and *Like Will to Like*, for five actors; *King Darius, Horestes, Common Conditions,* and *Conflict of Conscience,* for six actors; *Enough Is As Good As a Feast,* for seven actors; and *Most Virtuous and Godly Susanna, Patient and Meek Grissill,* and *Cambyses,* for eight actors. In Shakespeare's own period the number of members of the leading London companies was normally ten; but these companies—Chamberlain's-King's, Admiral's-Prince's, Worcester's-Queen's—employed often an equal number of lesser actors or "hirelings" besides musicians, stage hands, fee gatherers, and the like, and were also training and presenting in their plays five or six boys, so that from thirty to forty persons[27] were making a living from each enterprise, not to mention those profiting from ownership of the theatres which the companies rented. The players had come a long way since 1465, when Sir John Howard was paying the four-man troupes two shillings for performances at Stoke-by-Nayland.[28]

The capital investment of the pioneer companies, and those in the provinces later, was not great. Cervantes speaks of the early Spanish strollers, associated like the English in groups of four men, carrying their costumes in a sack and acting on improvised stages:

> There were no figures which arose or seemed to arise from the center of the earth through the hollow of the stage, which at that time consisted of four or five benches arranged in a square, with four or five boards upon them, raised about four spans from the ground. . . . The furnishings (*adorno*) of the stage were an old woolen blanket drawn by two cords from one side to the other, which formed what is called a dressing-room (*vestuario*).[29]

How well the description fits English conditions on the road is indicated by the provision made in town halls for the sample performance traditionally given by visiting players before the mayor and corporation. Workmen were paid a few pence for setting up and taking down a stage of "barrels and timber" or "tables, trestles, and forms" or "twelve long poplar planks."[30] When the company moved over to the local inn yard or other authorized spot for performances before the lesser townsfolk, the change was only to a different set of trestles and planks or a level patch of mother earth. In early years the church was not uncommonly used, and a few communities boasted a town stage with scaffolds for seating.

For costumes the players would carry a few all-purpose garments. John Rastell, amateur of the drama, possessed a particularly grand set of playing suits in the 1520's, made by his wife, the sister of Sir Thomas More, and a tailor, who assessed their value at twenty shillings each.[31] The lot included "a woman's garment of green and blue sarcenet, checked and lined with red buckram," a garment "for a priest to play in, of red saye," another "with Roman letters stitched upon it," one "of red and green saye, paned and guarded with gold skins and lined with red buckram," and "a short garment of gold skins and fustian, of Naples black, and sleeved with red, green, yellow, and blue sarcenet." Besides additional caps and cloaks, there were a hundred-odd yards of green, yellow, blue, red, and silvered cloth suitable for hangings. Rastell had acquired the garments for humanistic experiments with drama upon his own private stage, but they proved so desirable that, during his absence from London, one Henry Walton, to whom he had entrusted them, hired them out to professional companies playing about the city. They were used on occasion by the King's own company, and, all told, about forty times a year, so that Rastell became inadvertently the first recorded costumier and complained bitterly at law when he recovered his property badly frayed. The town of Chelmsford, Essex, in 1562–1563 acquired costumes for a play of the old biblical type, and hired them out profitably for a decade following to players in many neighboring towns, to individual impresarios, and once even to the company of the Earl of Sussex.[32] It was an age of scarcity, and one costume per troupe member must have seemed ample in early times. With rosettes on their slashed shoes and as lavish a display of color as they could manage, the actors competed in gaudiness with the gaudy styles of the day. The twenty shillings value per garment named in Rastell's suit was vigorously contested, and the garments owned by the actors themselves would not have approached that value. Still, "tempora mutantur," as the actor said who accosted Robert Greene, and who valued his own share of playing apparel at two hundred pounds.[33] There is the familiar instance of Worcester's

Men in 1602 paying £6. 13s. for the gown worn by Mistress Frankford in *A Woman Killed with Kindness*—13 shillings more than Heywood was paid for the play.[34]

The companies traveled in ways varying with their dignity and prosperity. Often they simply walked, with playing packs on their backs or on a single pack horse. Sometimes they used a wagon. Ben Jonson himself is sternly reminded in 1601 of how once he ambled "in leather pilch by a play-wagon in the highway and [took] mad Jeronimo's part to get service among the mimicks."[35] Many of the provincial companies walked their circuits until the end, but a London company like Shakespeare's, even though once mocked by Jonson as forced "to travel with pumps full of gravel . . . after a blind jade and a hamper,"[36] would have made its occasional tours in a far different way. Studioso, the embittered scholar of *Return from Parnassus*, gives us the picture in 1601:

> England affords those glorious vagabonds
> That carried earst their fardles on their backs
> Coursers to ride on through the gazing streets,
> S[w]ooping it in their glaring satin suits,
> And pages to attend their masterships.[37]

Tall and personable by professional selection, the actors had a special aptitude for wearing fine clothes and showy rapiers. When the King's Men swept into Oxford in 1606, with *King Lear* recently added to their repertory, they must have made a splendid cavalcade. Still, for their official performance in the town hall, they received only the modest sum of one pound;[38] and they must, in the old fashion, have posted bills and sent abroad their crier with drums and trumpet, to announce their presence and whereabouts to the general public.

To some extent the medieval tradition of free hospitality to wandering minstrels was carried over into the new age of professional acting; it is certain that when the troupes played in the manor houses that dotted England, they received food and lodging as well as money. In illustration we find records like the following from Knowsley Hall, Lancashire, in 1587, with its touching anticlimax: "On Thursday . . . my Lord of Leicester's Players played; on Friday they played again . . . and on Saturday they departed away, and Mr. Sorrowcold a preacher came."³⁹ Town records frequently mention the expense of a collation as well as a fee for the performance before the mayor. At inns the mere presence of the actors with their ability to attract custom may have gone part way toward discharging their score with the host; and it must have been a poor village that could not exchange at least subsistence for their talents. Dekker twits the strollers for traveling "upon the hard hoof from village to village for cheese and buttermilk."⁴⁰ It appears likely that most of what the players on the road gathered in cash was retained as profit, except for such sums as were set off against the dilapidation of garments and the acquiring of new play texts not created by themselves.

These actors brought drama to scores of towns, from the Channel ports to the border of Wales, from St. Ives near the southwestern tip of Cornwall to Newcastle in the North. Their discernible traces cover England like lace, even though the records were casually kept, have been mostly destroyed, or lie still undisturbed in the dust of provincial archives. In many instances, an acting company is known to us only through a memorandum of payment in some town chamberlain's accounts, representing a single performance in a single place; yet that company may have lived the normal span of years and added its thread to the close web of theatrical activity. We know that the Earl of Wiltshire's Men performed in Wallingford in 1515, the Earl of Bridgewater's in Plymouth in 1544–1545, and the Earl of Montgomery's in Coventry in 1610–1611;⁴¹ but, of these particular companies, nothing more. In the spring of 1633 a pick-up troupe, including one that did "nothing but drive the horse and beat the drum" and another that received "nothing but meat and drink," was swinging through the Midlands—Leicester, Market Bosworth, Stanton, Solihull, Meriden, Coventry, Kineton—five weeks in Leicester, three days each in little Solihull and Kineton, and, second-rate though it surely was, in the halls of Sir Thomas Lucy of Stratford and of Sir William Spencer of Wormleighton. Of this itinerary we should know nothing had not the company come to grief in Banbury for using a tampered license.⁴²

How early the extensive activity of the players began is not generally realized. The Northumberland household accounts of 1511–1512 mention 33s. 4d. "for rewards to players for plays in Christmas by strangers in my house."[43] Since the reward was "by estimation" 22d. per play, we get for this Christmas season twenty plays, acted by perhaps as many as ten different troupes. After leaving the Northumberland house, these would fan out through Yorkshire. Between 1536 and 1538 Thomas Cromwell, prospering as Lord Privy Seal, paid for performances in his household given by players of the King, the Queen, the Lord Chamberlain, the Lord Chancellor, the Lord Warden, and the Lords Exeter, Cobham, and Suffolk.[44] The number of companies steadily multiplied. The records compiled by Professor Murray indicate the existence between 1558 and 1642 of at least one hundred and fifty distinguishable troupes whose known activity was confined to touring the provinces. During Marlowe's and Shakespeare's play-writing careers, the town of Coventry was visited by an average of seven or eight different companies a year.[45] Recorded visits to such places as Coventry, Bristol, Ipswich, Leicester, and Bath, where records are fairly abundant, mean unrecorded visits to the small towns and villages near by. The troupes were required to keep moving. They might perform in the household of their nominal master, but evidently with no greater frequency than in that of some other lord. Normally, they were on the road, retainers *in absentia*.

The abundance and mobility of the companies are especially striking in view of the light population of England. According to the best guesses that can be made of a population untabulated by census, at no time before 1613 did the residents of the average town exceed two to five thousand, of the few large provincial cities ten to twenty thousand, of prodigious London one to two hundred thousand, and of all England four to five million.[46] In a word, the whole English-speaking world served by such abundant theatrical activity was no larger numerically than half the metropolitan area of modern London or New York. The latter are the theatrical centers of our present English-speaking world; but, compared with Elizabethan England, they appear apathetic. In the year of *Hamlet*, Londoners could attend a new play every week; but even in Bath, as has been estimated, the townsmen could attend fifteen to twenty plays a year.[47] There were few places in England where a man with the necessary pennies and inclination could not attend a dozen. Small communities near the main roads must have suffered not from too few performances, but from more than their economy could well afford.

The audience was national in the most literal sense. It has been mentioned that the earliest recorded troupe bearing the name of a lord was Essex's Men of 1469. At the moment we meet them they are performing, characteristically, not before Essex but before the burghers of a country town.[48] The place is Malden, and their reward five shillings. We hear of them again in 1482 when a performance in Stoke-by-Nayland brings them twenty pence from Lord Howard, and in 1494 when a court performance before King Henry VII brings them a full pound.[49] To town hall, county house, and royal court we must add roadside inn, village green, and city street, letting all form a composite in our minds if we are to visualize the "theatre" of this band of players. One day they act before king and nobles in the glitter of a royal banquet hall; another, before the equally formidable corporation and mayor of a town sitting in state with their wives; another, before the family and retainers of a manor house (numbering sometimes several hundred people); another, before a London throng; another, before wide-eyed villagers—the same actors, performing, so far as we can determine, the same plays. Ultimately, as we shall see, a very few of the very best companies became domiciled in London; but even these retained their contact with the road. In August and September of 1597, Shakespeare's own company played from Dover to Bristol, one hundred and sixty-eight miles apart, including in their itinerary such unpretentious places as Marlborough, Faversham, and Rye.[50]

Much of our knowledge of the size and composition of audiences, and of the development of London as the hub of the national theatre, must derive from the records of company incomes viewed in relation to the prevailing rates of theatrical admission. Precautions must be taken lest the sums mentioned appear meaningless or absurd. At no time in the centuries under survey did the average daily wage of skilled craftsmen in England exceed a shilling a day.[51] In the fifteenth and early sixteenth centuries, and outside the larger cities thereafter, it was considerably less. Taking the shilling as our standard, however, we are able to view Renaissance sums of money in terms of percentage of income, and arrive at modern equivalents more reliable than those obtained after multiplying by arbitrary figures from six to twenty according to the whim of the moment. It is always possible to ascertain the modern average daily income as it varies from place to place or year to year, and to be acutely conscious of one's own; then when we hear of the Elizabethan spectator spending a penny, or one-twelfth his daily income, we can aid our imaginations by substituting one-twelfth the modern daily income; or when we hear of a company receiving a fee of one pound, we can substitute twenty times that modern daily income. The actual arithmetical process need not be completed. The Oxford town reward of one pound to the King's Men in 1606 was mentioned above as small, but when we reflect that twenty craftsmen of Oxford would have had to work from dawn to dusk to earn an equal sum, and support with it their collective dependents, it begins to seem larger. At popular rates of admission, the company would have had to entertain several hundred to collect this pound at their regular pitch.

The most revealing early record of the financial side of the drama occurs midway in *Mankind*, a morality play of about 1475 which bears all the signs of having been acted by professional players in a public place. At a tense moment in the performance the audience is informed that a collection will be taken before further delights are shown. The character Now-a-days speaks disdainfully of groats, pence, and tuppence, and suggests that gold royals must be forthcoming before the play will continue, whereupon the character New-Guise says, "Not so! Ye that may not pay the t'one, pay the t'other!"[52] How wonderfully enduring are all human subterfuges! That either "the sovereigns that sit" or "the brethren that stand right up"[53] would pay a royal (ten shillings) at such a performance was, of course, unthinkable; still, mention of the sum might induce a number to offer a penny instead of the contemplated groat. Actually it was the penny that became the standard unit of theatrical exchange. Whenever possible, it was collected before the performance began. In 1567—that is, before we are accustomed to thinking of theatres as such—we hear of the hired men that stand "at the gate with a box (as the fashion is), who took of every person that came in a penny or an half-penny at the least."[54] In 1579 Gabriel Harvey wrote to Edmund Spenser of "the Theatre or some other painted stage whereat thou and thy lively copesmates in London may laugh their mouths and bellies full for pence or two-pence apiece";[55] and in 1599 Thomas Platter, after mentioning the yards and galleries of the Bankside theatres, described the perfected system of admission:

> . . . Whoever cares to stand below only pays one English penny, but if he wishes to sit he enters by another door, and pays another penny, while if he desires to sit in the most comfortable seats which are cushioned, where he not only sees everything well, but can also be seen, then he pays yet another English penny at another door.[56]

No estimate can be made of what the actors of *Mankind* collected, or of the number in their audience, but certain figures relating to the itinerant stage in general invite interpretation. We have noticed that in 1512 Northumberland was paying twenty pence to each of the many acting troupes who performed in his hall. In 1522–1523 he systematized his rewards at a higher level: "My Lord useth and accustometh to give yearly when his Lordship is at home to every earl's players that come to his Lordship betwixt Christmas and Candlemas . . . ten shillings."[57] The rate, for that time, was generous. The payment of twenty pence or even less for a performance in a manorial hall during the fifteenth and early sixteenth centuries was not uncommon. At Malden the players were paid for their town-hall performances sums rising from fourteen pence in 1540 to five shillings in 1562.[58] When the Queen's Men played *The Market of Mischief* at the town hall of Norwich in 1546, six shillings, four pence, "was gathered among the people there," and enough added from civic funds to bring the total to ten shillings.[59] At Leicester this system of supplementing a collection was practiced frequently from 1556 onward into the seventeenth century, but the total aimed at was a pound or more.[60] A great variety of sums appear in town records, reaching as high as two pounds in isolated instances; but through the long history of provincial acting the "normal" payment for the official performance before mayor and leading burghers was ten shillings or a pound. The normal payment before the households of the greater landed gentry was probably also ten shillings or a pound. When, in 1599, the Steward in *Histriomastix* offers Sir Oliver Owlet's Men four angels (two pounds) for a performance in the hall of Philarchus, the rarely reached zenith of such payments is represented, and when the actors refuse to perform even for eight royals, the arrogance of these "proud statute rogues" is, of course, an enormity.[61]

Tudor habits of expenditure are impressive in their consistency and hard logic. The reward to London companies for a performance at court, reaching in Shakespeare's time ten pounds, was about equal to what the actors would have earned at a successful public performance. The ten shillings to a pound rewards for special performances in the provinces probably represent the average take at public performances in the localities in question. Some confirmation of the assumption exists in the several instances in which the total gate at such performances is mentioned—"some forty shillings gathered"[62] in *The Merrie Conceited Jests of George Peele*, about 1607, and "they scarce had twenty shillings audience at any time for a play in the country"[63] in *Ratsey's Ghost*, 1606. The public performances may have been slightly more profitable than those in common hall and manor house. To prevent a drain on local economy, the town officials limited the duration of visits. At Canterbury no single company could play more than two days in any one month; in 1588, at Norwich, Leicester's Men were given two pounds subsidy on condition that they would play publicly only twice; and in 1617 the Queen's Men were allowed but three days.[64] Two or three performances per visit were what the officials wished, and four to six probably what they had to put up with. When Walton was hiring out Rastell's costumes in the 1520's, he charged eight pence for their use in "interludes in the winter" and two shillings or more for their use in "stage plays in the summer."[65] The distinction between interludes and stage plays here rests obviously not on the nature of texts but on the auspices of performance, with the stage plays out-of-doors and public—and perhaps sufficiently more profitable to justify the greater charge for the costumes. However, the point cannot be pressed, a different reason for the higher charge for public performances suggesting itself in another record relating to costumes. In 1572 Thomas Giles protested against the habit of the Yeoman of the Revels of hiring out court costumes to common actors,

by reason of which common usage, the gloss and beauty of the same garments is lost and cannot so well serve to be often altered and to be shewed before her Highness as otherwise it might and hath been used; for it taketh more harm by once wearing into the city or country where it is often used than by many times wearing in the court, by the great press of people and foulness both of the way and weather, and soil of the wearers who for the most part be the meanest sort of men.[66]

There is something almost symbolic of the age in the fact that a playing garment that had glistened at court might appear at a wayside inn, and might be donned again by your sweet courtier after covering the back of the "meanest sort" of man. The "great press of people" mentioned in the document is suggestive, but few communities outside London afforded premises where more than two pounds could have been efficiently collected. For the take at an inn to reach this figure, between three and four hundred people must have crowded in.

We can picture the galaxy of companies playing before town-hall, manor-house, inn-yard and village-green audiences, ranging in size from a few score to conceivably half a thousand, but averaging out at a few hundred. Such companies, even the most successful of them, could scarcely have cleared, week in and week out, more than a pound a day—a twenty shilling profit to be shared. Rarely was anything shared equally in this era of nice prerogative, so that the leading players may have earned four shillings, the lesser players one. With the full later-day complement of ten men, the high average earnings would have been two shillings per man—double what ordinary craftsmen received but not a spectacular income. About 1606 we hear that "the very best" of provincial actors "have sometimes been content to go home at night with fifteen pence share apiece."[67] The four players who revolted from George Maller in 1528–1529 were said to have made thirty pounds on their tour.[68] Possibly they did; but, if so, they would have been wonderful venturers, able to look down their noses at the voyagers to New-found-land. There was small chance that actors who remained on the road would grow rich, and no evidence that any of them did.

However, there was *London*. It is sometimes assumed that, before the building of the Theatre in 1576, there was too little commercialized acting in London for it to constitute a legislative problem;[69] but the assumption will not bear scrutiny. By 1576 acting had been highly commercialized for a century, and for nearly that length of time the commerce had been abundant in London. We may point to the initial probabilities in the case: with the provinces teeming with theatrical activity, the more densely populated area of the capital would never have been neglected. There is more direct evidence. The playing garments of Rastell must have been hired out their forty times a year in the 1520's to some purpose. The many companies enumerated above playing at Cromwell's house in the 1530's, and the additional ones playing at Whitehall from the beginning of Elizabeth's reign—Queen's, Leicester's, Warwick's, Rich's, Lane's, Sussex's, Clinton's—cannot be supposed, in view of the nature of company methods in general, to have played only in banquet halls. Actually the companies mentioned at court represented only a selection of the best of those visiting the city. Theatrical activity had become a legislative problem certainly by February 6, 1545, when a city proclamation forbade playing in London

unless it be in the houses of noblemen, or of the Mayor, Sheriffs, or Aldermen of the same his highness' City for the time being, or else in the house of gentlemen, or of the substantial and sad commoners or head parishioners of the same City, or in the open street of the same City as in time past it hath been used and accustomed, or in the common halls, fellowships, or brotherhoods of the same City . . .[70]

A surprising number of places where plays *could* be acted is listed, including the interesting item, "the open street of the same City as in time past." Notably absent is mention of the city inns, which we may presume were aimed at in the proclaimed injunction against playing in "divers and many suspicious, dark, and inconvenient places." We may deduce that by 1545 the players were already intrenching themselves in the inns, with the Lord Mayor and Aldermen in fear of the consequences. The point of view of the officials is understandable. At places like Coventry and Canterbury, the actors would play a few days and move on. At London they might become fixtures—with troublesome consequences to those responsible for good order and a stable economy. What the officials did was to fight a rear-guard action, making rulings highly restrictive or prohibitive at the same time that they were yielding ground under popular pressure. Bath's Men were arrested in 1546 for "playing lewd plays in the suburbs of London,"[71] and Oxford's in 1547 for playing in Southwark during the singing of the dirge for King Henry VIII;[72] whether their offenses were aggravated by the use of inns, we do not know. A Lord Mayor's precept of 1555 specified that "taverns, alehouses, and other victualing houses" must not harbor playing;[73] nevertheless they did so, as continued official references to them prove. The earliest mentions of particular inns in the metropolitan area occur in 1557, when John Rough and others assembled at the Saracen's Head in Islington for Protestant worship "under the color of coming to see a play,"[74] and when *A Sackful of News* was performed at the Boar's Head without Aldgate, to the vexation of the Privy Council.[75] In a letter of 1564 Bishop Grindal exhorted Cecil to act against the players and also "the houses where they play their lewd interludes."[76] In 1567—that is, nearly a decade before James Burbage erected the Theatre—the Red Lion Inn at Stepney was provided with regular scaffolds so that spectators might view such plays as *The Story of Samson*.[77]

It is clear that London had theatres before the "first" theatre was built. That the conversion of the Red Lion Inn was no isolated case is proved by an act of the common council of London in 1574, which mentions the "inordinate haunting of great multitudes of people . . . in great inns having chambers and secret places adjoining to their open stages and galleries."[78] In 1578 John Stockwood said in a sermon at Paul's Cross:

Will not a filthy play, with the blast of a trumpet, sooner call thither a thousand than an hour's tolling of a bell bring to the sermon a hundred? . . . if you resort to the Theatre, the Curtain, and other places of plays in the city, you shall on the Lord's day have these places, with many other that I cannot reckon, so full as possibly they can throng. . . . For reckoning with the least, the gain that is reaped of eight ordinary places in the city which I know, by playing but once a week (whereas many times they play twice and sometimes thrice) it amounteth to 2000 pounds by the year.[79]

Stockwood was a public man making a public utterance; his words cannot be discounted like those of some satirical pamphleteer. The word "filthy" represents his opinion, but the rest represents the facts. The activity described could have existed only after long and steady growth. The Theatre had been built two years, the Curtain one year, before the sermon, but Stockwood knew of six other regular playing places—probably Blackfriars and Paul's, to be discussed in the following chapter, and four adapted inns—besides other occasional playing places that he could not "reckon." There is mention of inn-yard playing in London long after the regular theatres had appeared; indeed the Crosskeys Inn, the Bell Inn, and the Bull Inn along the artery of Gracechurch-Bishopsgate Street, bisecting London and leading to the Theatre and Curtain in Shoreditch, suggest a conveniently located and generally recognized theatrical "district." Henry Chettle slyly notes the fact as irritating to certain commercial interests in the city: if the theatres were suppressed, "the flock of young people would be equally parted. But now the greatest trade is brought into one street . . . by Shoreditch to Hackney."[80] In 1578, then, London audiences were mentioned in terms of thousands of people and theatrical receipts in terms of thousands of pounds; yet we are still only midway in a period of growth.

Such inns as were conveniently placed and possessed suitably large yards had the disadvantage of being goods depots, encumbered with carrier carts and pack horses half the days of the week.[81] This fact, and the antagonism of civic officers, induced the erection of special buildings in Shoreditch, the Bankside, and the northwest suburbs where, ultimately, plays could be performed every afternoon except on Sundays and during certain weeks of Lent or heavy visitations of the plague. These open amphitheatres became the most graphic monument to the theatre of the nation. Between 1576 and the year of Shakespeare's death, nine such structures were built or rebuilt—the least of them, in Stockwood's term, "gorgeous." Rarely were more than three of these public theatres operating at one time; but since each could accommodate in all likelihood from two to three thousand spectators, and since London was by modern standards a small city, their existence seems miraculous enough.

Still remembering the great value of the shilling and pound in terms of Renaissance incomes, we may note how heavily the theatrical industry in London was capitalized.[82] The Burbage Theatre was built at a cost of about £666 in 1576, the first Globe for between £400 and £600 in 1599, the second Globe for £1,400 in 1613, the first Fortune for £520 in 1600, the second Fortune for £1,000 in 1622. An abortive attempt of James Burbage to erect a regular theatre in Blackfriars after 1596 cost him £600 for the premises and £300 for alterations. The Boar's Head Inn, used briefly for a theatre after 1600, had its yard converted at a cost of £360;[83] and in 1613 the Bear Garden was converted to the Hope for £320. Equally large sums must have gone into the building of the Curtain, the Swan, and the Red Bull. Expensive though they were, the rental yielded by the buildings was disproportionately large: the owners' clear profit from the Theatre seems to have been modest, as little as £100 a year; but, at least in contemporary allegations, the first Globe yielded £420 to £560 yearly; the second Globe, still more; and the Red Bull between 1612 and 1619, £540 a year.[84] The most reliable information refers to the Rose, built by Philip Henslowe in 1587 at a cost of about £816. A decade later the owner was receiving as rental an average of 30.16 shillings every day the theatre was used.[85] It was commonly used as often as 230 days a year, thus yielding in a good year gross returns of £346 on the original £816 investment!

We have been dealing only with theatre rentals, not with total theatrical receipts. The thirty shillings, odd pence, that came to Henslowe after each performance overmatches the total sum earned by a company playing before officials in provincial towns; but it represented only a fraction of a total London gate. During most of the first decade of Shakespeare's career, his own company, the Lord Chamberlain's Men, and their rivals, the Lord Admiral's Men, were the fixed London companies, with others making only sporadic incursions; during the second decade of his career there were three major public companies. The old rivals occupied respectively the Globe and the Fortune; the third company occupied the Rose, Boar's Head, and Curtain until finally it moved into the newly built Red Bull. It was the least among the three, but it was grossing eight to nine pounds per performance.[86] A considerable body of scattered evidence shows that eight to nine pounds is a moderate estimate of the average daily take of each of the three leading companies at the turn of the century. It is little wonder, in view of the thriving industry the theatre had become, that the ablest men connected with it grew prosperous. The Henslowe-Alleyn fortune, representing the reward of the combined talents of a leading actor and an astute theatrical investor, was large enough to be impressive in any age: £10,000 of it went into the founding of the College of God's Gift at Dulwich. The profits of their great rivals were more equitably distributed. Shakespeare retired a moderately wealthy man; Richard Burbage died worth reputedly £300 a year in land; and in 1620 one John Witter complained that he was "not of ability and power to contend in law with . . . John Hemmings and Henry Condell, who are of great living, wealth, and power, and have many more mighty and great friends than your said subject."[87]

The money that has been clinking in our sentences is important simply as evidence of public support of the drama. Rival companies playing daily through most of the year, and gathering sums of eight or nine pounds an average performance, mean hosts of playgoers. The pounds broken down into penny, twopenny, and threepenny bits represent people. I have tried to describe these people elsewhere—the number, social composition, behavior, and responsive capacity of the people in Shakespeare's audience.[88] The indications are that in the first few years of the seventeenth century, the time of Hamlet and Lear, the London area of about 160,000 people was sending eighteen to twenty-four thousand spectators weekly to see the plays, providing an audience at each of the three active public theatres of slightly more than a thousand on ordinary occasions, and from two to three thousand on holidays and at premières. The estimate is bound to arouse incredulity; but, when estimates are made, specific figures must be named, such as conform with what knowledge we possess. The exact figures need not be defended in the present case, but they should not be altered to taste—and the salient fact must remain, that Shakespeare's audience was an audience of the many. It was composed of human beings like ourselves, with craftsmen and shopkeepers predominating, but with the gentry and nobility well represented, the selective principle consisting simply of possession by each spectator of some spiritual vitality, some trace of the contemplative mind—in a word, susceptibility to the appeal of dramatic art.

In the Middle Ages, London had not been notable above other places for the kind of drama prevalent; indeed smaller centers like York and Coventry boasted richer dramatic traditions. London, the industrial capital of the nation, became the hub of theatrical activity when theatrical activity became an industry. Not the royal household near by, nor the courtiers clustered there, but the concentration of population was the lodestone. Only at London was there the audience-accessibility that would permit of successive performances in fixed stands. To strollers packing their gear in the country towns, it must always have appeared as Mecca. But to establish itself in London, a company was forced to win a nation-wide competition. It is at this point that the advantage of viewing the English Renaissance stage in the large should appear. A performance by Shakespeare's fellows at the Globe was no trivial or isolated thing but part of a long tradition, vitally related to activity in every shire of the land. It is amusing to hear Shakespeare designated as a mere Stratfordian and actor. Stratford was England, and to be an actor in the Chamberlain's-King's Company was a rarer distinction, less mechanically achieved, than to be a peer of the realm. If the glover's son had accomplished nothing more, he would still qualify as a more remarkable man than Oxford.

A homely analogy may be used. As we watch a major-league base-ball team in action, the conviction is borne in upon us that at no other time anywhere could a group of men do the particular thing that these men are doing better than they are doing it. This is *excellence*. And then we recall that a multitude of men and boys have been playing ball on city streets, town lots, and country meadows, and thousands of school, neighborhood, town, and industrial teams have contributed players to dozens of minor leagues. The men on the field before us have survived a great sifting process and are doing to perfection what, in this particular kind, a whole people wants to see done. A people does best what it does most, and genius stands at the apex of a broad-based pyramid.

If the analogy seems to attribute to the Elizabethans the dread competitive efficiency of modern America, or to identify the dexterity of Elizabethan performers with the quality of some of the plays they performed, the exaggeration is in the direction of truth. Much book learning went into *Tamburlaine*, but the mold was pro-vided by ruthless Cambyses and the invincible knights who had walked the stage in Marlowe's boyhood. Marlowe in Canterbury, Greene in Norwich, Shakespeare in Stratford had seen the strollers perform. Whatever the defects of the plays written by "riming mother wits," they were a spontaneous expression of the mimetic impulse, and shaped to the understanding and tastes of the spectators. Nurtured on a living drama, the instinct of the playwrights was to keep it living—the projection of a living audience. A conceit of the epilogues is that cries of approval and clapping hands will waft a play to port. Shakespeare's plays sailed full-bellied with the wind. The general public has left us no sign that its interest in playing and its interest in plays were separate; to a degree now inconceivable the dramatic experience was pure, and Shakespeare's plays like the men who performed them were recognized as champion. Certainly so far as their content is concerned, anyone who maintains that they were beyond the grasp of their audience, or moved, in any particular, counter to the dreams, aspirations, or conscience of the common people of England in the time of their creation, has taken upon him-self a tremendous burden of proof.

Nevertheless—and it is one of the most striking facts in cultural history—within a few decades of bringing the stage to its peak as a national institution, the nation resolved to extirpate it. When in 1642 Parliament ordered that "public stage plays shall cease and be forborne," it was expressing the will of the majority of the very people who had supplied the matrix for Tamburlaine, Faustus, Shylock, Falstaff, Hamlet, Rosalind, and Lear. To say that Puritanism had triumphed is to oversimplify. To an extent that has never been recognized, the popular drama at its height expressed many of the attitudes we associate with Puritanism, and its period of hardiest growth had been synchronous with that of the bitterest and most sustained attacks by the clergy. The people followed only when led in the direction they wanted to go. The forces which effected the rift between plays and the populace, not repaired for centuries, will be treated in later chapters. Brief mention may be made here of a few external symptoms.

When James Burbage built the second Blackfriars in 1596, he intended it certainly for Shakespeare's company. It was a move toward taking the drama indoors, toward imitating the methods of the theatre of a coterie, and must mean that the Burbages had seen omens in the sky. In 1609 Blackfriars was actually occupied by the company and soon became their more important theatre. Thereafter, the new theatres built were enclosed and were in the neighborhood of Fleet Street and Drury Lane. When Henslowe adapted the Hope on the Bankside in 1613, he was evidently planning a straddle for the Lady Elizabeth's Men between Whitefriars, a "private," and the Hope, a "public," theatre, in imitation of the straddle of the King's Men between Blackfriars and the Globe. Actually the Red Bull of 1605 was the last of the new, truly public theatres—built far out in Clerkenwell for a company which seems to have had no expectation of patronage by the gentry. Some time before 1642, Blackfriars, the Phoenix, and Salisbury Court—all fashionable enclosed houses—have become the important theatres; and the Restoration picture of the drama as a diversion of the leisured classes has been blocked out. Whether the players are abandoning the people, or the people are abandoning the players, or there is a divorce by mutual consent, the signs of change are unmistakable. And something is happening in the provinces roughly parallel to the change in London. It is not always easy to determine whether the towns are taking action for old economic or new moral reasons, but it is observable that such places as Exeter, Dover, Barnstaple, Canterbury, and Plymouth, although welcoming the actors at the beginning, wanted no more of them at the ending of the first decade of the seventeenth century.[89] The provincial theatre did not wholly wither away before 1642, and in London the Fortune and Red Bull were not wholly deserted; but the trumpet of the theatre of a nation was no longer quickening the beat of a million hearts.

II

Theatre of a Coterie

WHEN Rosencrantz tells Hamlet that "an aery of children, little eyases, . . . berattle the common stages—so they call them," and Hamlet remarks that they may themselves grow to be common players and find their writers have done them wrong to make them "exclaim against their own succession,"[1] of course the *common* stages and *common* players belong to the theatre of the nation. The "aery of children" belongs to a theatre of a coterie. The traditions of the two are as distinct as the size of their actors. The wandering minstrel and Corpus Christi actor standing in the far vista of the one tradition are replaced by the courtly reveler and academic amateur in that of the other. Although both theatres have long been commercialized by the time of *Hamlet*, it is little wonder that their relative social standing should be a sensitive point, with the writers for the "little eyases" sticking upon their gentility.

The efflorescence of academic drama in the sixteenth century and the elaboration of medieval reveling at the Tudor court need not be reviewed. Much "private" drama remained truly private. The play-acting at the universities, the inns of court, and most of the grammar schools, as well as that species of courtly mumming that developed into the literary mask, continued through the sixteenth and seventeenth centuries to be an academic or social indulgence and an expense to those who fostered it. An occasional college author or actor might receive preferment or a cash award, and professional entertainers were paid to help with the masks, but there was no paying audience as a shaping influence. It is with the professional offshoot of these amateur theatricals that we are concerned.

Leanings toward commercialization are discernible among grammar-school masters, a class of men necessitous by definition; and a brief note on their activity will serve to introduce an account of the all-important role played by the masters of boy choristers. It has been mentioned that Thomas Cromwell was often entertained by adult troupes of actors during the days of his ascendency.[2] In 1538, we find also a payment of twenty-two shillings, six pence, to "Mr. Hopton's priest for playing before my Lord with his children," and five pounds to Mr. Nicholas Udall, "the schoolmaster of Eton for playing before my Lord."[3] Some years later the Eton boys earned another master £6. 13s. 4d. for a performance at court; but no other appearances under Udall are recorded. However, in 1554, when he was teaching boys in the household of the Lord Chancellor Bishop Gardiner, the Revels Office received a directive from Queen Mary to provide costumes whenever needed because "our wellbeloved Nicholas Udall hath at sundry seasons convenient heretofore shewed, and mindeth hereafter to shew, his diligence in setting forth of Dialogues and Interludes before us for our regal disport and recreation."[5] Obviously this educator doubled in the role of paid producer whenever he could. Better placed than Eton for serving the market of court and city was Westminster School, with the added advantage of having choristers among its pupils. The choirmaster, John Taylor, was paid for the services of Westminster boys in several of the Lord Mayor shows in the sixties, while the school players performed before the Society of Parish Clerks in 1562 and before the royal court at intervals between 1564 and 1574.[6] They then yielded place to the boys of the recently founded Merchant Taylors' School. Sir James Whitelocke tells how he was taught in that "famous school" by Richard Mulcaster: ". . . yearly he presented some plays to the court, in which his scholars were only actors, and I one among them, and by that means taught them good behaviors and audacity."[7] The benefits to the scholars were matched by the benefits to the master; Mulcaster received the regular fee of the

professional troupes on each of the six occasions between 1573 and
1583 when he brought his boys to court.[8]

The Merchant Taylors' boys also acted before paying audiences
in the city. In March, 1574, the masters of the company, because of
"the tumultuous disordered persons repairing hither to see such
plays as by our scholars were here lately played," decreed "that
henceforth there shall be no more any plays suffered to be played
in this our common hall, any use or custom heretofore to the contrary in any wise notwithstanding."[9] The seat of the grievance was
that "the masters of this worshipful company and their dear friends
could not have entertainment and convenient place as they ought
to have had"—Mulcaster having adopted the dangerously democratic penny admission charge and thus drawn in the general public.
When the hall was denied him, he may have used his own lodgings or
the school for his theatre. The court performance of *A History of
Ariodante and Genevora* in 1583 involved charges to the Revels
Office "for carriage of stuff to Mr. Mulcaster's and back again."[10]
Spenser's schoolmaster was native English to the core, and if any
of the Merchant Taylors' School plays had survived they would
probably prove that the Mulcaster line was more popular than genteel.

A few records of grammar-school plays in public performance
relate to the provinces. In 1546 Ralph Radcliffe's school at Hitchen
was regaling the community with plays on Chaucerian as well as
religious themes;[11] and in 1565–1568 the appearance of professional
troupes before the Mayor and Corporation of Plymouth was varied
by four performances, paid for at regular rates, by the schoolmaster
and children of Totnes.[12] But such experiments, in London or elsewhere, were bound to be short-lived. Grammar-school boys could
not be exploited extensively as actors because the academic regimen
had been designed to leave little surplus time and energy; moreover,
the lives of the boys remained in the control of their parents, solid
citizens who knew what schools were for. The theatrical activities of
a Udall or a Mulcaster are, on the whole, less representative than the
more sporadic and disinterested ones of a Holofernes or a Parson
Evans.

With child choristers the case was different. It is with odd sensations that we now read the old commissions authorizing choirmasters to "take up" singing boys for the royal chapels, even before the privilege was abused and, in individual cases, boys "in no way able or fit for singing" were, in effect, kidnaped, handed dramatic roles, and "commanded to learn the same by heart."[13] The lot of the mildly disciplined modern choirboy gives us no notion of that of the Renaissance chapel child—divorced from his parents, huddled up in lodgings, and worked to what must often have been the limit of physical endurance. A whole world of life behind scenes opens up to us in the terse record of a payment when the Children of her Majesty's Chapel climbed from their barge and wherries after overnight attendance at the bright festivities of Hampton Court: "To Thomas Totnall, for fire & victuals for the children when they landed, some of them being sick & cold & hungry."[14] The year was 1574; the day, Ash Wednesday. The education of the children, and their fate after their voices broke, were of some concern to those they served, and at least one master remembered his boys in his will; but the fact remains that the choristers were unpaid and exactingly drilled child laborers. They were selected in the first place for beauty and musical talent, and were expected to wear a revels garment as gracefully as a surplice. The masters were equally versatile, composers of secular as well as sacred music, impresarios, pageanteers, and poets. It was inevitable in an age of drama that an institution that provided producer and performers ready-made should create a theatre.

The chapels of the great nobles were performing plays at the very beginning of the sixteenth century. Between 1511 and 1522 the almoner of the Earl of Northumberland was provided with a servant "for writing of the parts" when he proved himself a "maker of interludes," and an extra reward of ten shillings or a pound was given for dramatic offerings by his singers.[15] The children of Oxford's chapel performed at court in 1506;[16] and nine boys with their master, evidently representing the chapel of the most famous Earl of Oxford, received a fee for a performance at Bristol in 1581.[17] The burghers of Norwich were entertained by the chapel children of the

Duke of Norfolk in the Christmas seasons of 1564 and 1565, and showed their appreciation in terms of shillings and pence.[18] No doubt there was much more such activity than can now be traced; and in some instances the adult actors of popular troupes must have served their apprenticeship in the chapels of their lords.

The chorister drama that evolved into a regular theatrical industry, rivaling the popular stage, centers in the three chapels belonging to or closely associated with the royal court. The Chapel Royal, serving the monarch at Whitehall or moving with the household to other seats, included besides its adult personnel twelve singing boys and their master. A separate royal establishment at Windsor included at first six and finally ten singing boys and their master. The "song school" of St. Paul's Cathedral, an establishment distinct from the grammar school, consisted of ten singing boys and their master. Although the first function of the Paul's boys was to sing in the cathedral service, they assimilated characteristics of the household choristers long before Elizabeth's reign and became formidable rivals of these in purveying dramatic amusement to the gentry. In all three groups the master was provided with a living and the boys with their subsistence, so that all monetary rewards for acting plays must be considered as special perquisites of the masters and the *vera causa* of juvenile professionalism.

The actor in the coterie theatre was little more than a chattel and not, as in the popular theatre, the very keystone of the structure; therefore little need be said of his social relationships and destiny. Until the period 1599–1613 his age was approximately eight to thirteen, about the same as that of the boys attached to the popular troupes as learners and actors of the female roles. He possessed a trained alto or soprano voice, a true ear, and a knowledge of musical notation. He was able to read and received, at least in theory, the training in Latin grammar of the boys in regular schools. Although usually from a humble household, he might proceed to the university and even become in later life a "gentleman" of the Chapel. More commonly, no doubt, he sought a place as a regular actor, or simply found himself adrift, deploring the childhood gift that had denied him apprenticeship in a regular trade. The five or six boys in the chapel of the Earl of Northumberland were designated "triballs" and "meanys" or first and second trebles, and they sang with the basses, "standing tenors," and "counter-tenors" of the gentlemen of the chapel. Before chorister acting became completely commercialized, the adult singers sometimes acted with the boys; and, although this practice did not endure, chorister casts were not uniformly juvenile. The masters and actor-managers of the children may sometimes have performed parts, and boys remained with companies after ceasing to be boys. Such was certainly the case in the "chapel" company assembled at Blackfriars in 1600. Of the boys conscripted, Salmon Pavy was ten, Nathan Field twelve; and although Pavy died at thirteen, famous for playing old men—"Sure the Parcae thought him one, he played so truly"—Field was still with the company (and writing plays) when in his early twenties. In a postscript to *Sophonisba* in 1606, Marston referred to the company as "youths"; and the term was fairly common. Chapel boys no doubt were more precocious than even the average Elizabethan child, and their activity was sophisticating. Certainly Nathan Field's educational experience was unique. When he was not getting his lines for the high-flavored plays at Blackfriars, Ben Jonson was guiding his classical studies, reading him "the Satires of Horace, and some Epigrams of Martial."[19]

Since the coterie companies were limited in effect to two, it will be possible to depart from the method of giving a composite account used in the case of the adult troupes, and, instead, to sketch the history of each. The Paul's boys had been performing at court for fees probably since 1534 under John Redford, and certainly since 1551 under Sebastian Westcote.[20] John Heywood, court musician and interludist, had been associated with both masters, and in the first years of Elizabeth's reign a play was performed at Nonsuch by "the children of Paul's and their master S[ebastian], Mr. Phillips and Mr. Heywood."[21] If all the facts were known, the most consistently successful producer of chorister drama might well prove to be Sebastian Westcote. He was a stubborn Catholic, presenting us with the anomaly of a noncommunicant vicar choral of St. Paul's Cathedral during twenty-four years of a Protestant reign—protected, possibly because of his theatrical usefulness, by that watchdog of Protestantism the Earl of Leicester himself. Westcote never gave more than the minimum of ground necessary to retain his post. That he was possessed of some histrionic talent is attested by his hapless antagonist, Bishop Grindal, who by 1563 had begun to fear "lest his humility in words be a counterfeit humility, and his tears crocodile tears, although I myself was much moved with them at the first."[22]

It was a privy-council matter that "one of Sebastian's boys, being one of his principal actors, is lately stolen and conveyed from him"[23] in December, 1575, the very month in which the court of aldermen of London was expressing indignation "that one Sebastian that will not communicate with the Church of England keepeth plays and resort of the people, to great gain and peril of the corrupting of the children with papistry."[24] He had become fairly opulent by the year of his death, 1582, and was able to leave bequests to a number of relatives, to choristers past and present, and to half a dozen household retainers, including "Shepard that keepeth the door of plays."[25] To one Edward Cooper, "the innocent in my house," he left £6 13s. 4d., a sum identical with the basic court fee for dramatic performances; perhaps we may deduce that Cooper was considered amusing. There is no mention in the will of playbooks or costumes, these probably having already passed to the young scrivener, Henry Evans, who was Westcote's friend and the overseer of his will and appears as a figure in the activities of boys' companies at both the first and the second Blackfriars theatre which will be described below. The practice of the choirmasters to enlist secular aid in their dramatic ventures seems to have begun early.

We have little information on the nature of the theatre used by the Paul's boys. Most likely it was a hall in the building serving as the "song school" and residence of the master. Westcote's will mentions a gatekeeper as well as a doorkeeper, while the number of permanent inmates of his household implies a sizable establishment. In 1608 the theatre is described as "near St. Paul's church, then being in the hands of one Mr. Pierce but then unused for a playhouse,"[26] and the location, near the book mart and the Blackfriars residential district, as well as convenient to the western suburbs and inns of court, may be considered as ideal. Its convenience to the London literati is suggested by Nashe in 1596: "We need never wish the plays at Paul's up again, but if we were weary with walking and loth to go too far to seek sport, into the arches [of St. Paul's Cathedral] we might step and hear him [Gabriel Harvey] plead, which would be a merrier comedy than ever was old Mother Bombie."[27] Westcote's success in having his productions selected for court performance suggests that his playhouse was operating for most of the three decades of his mastership, even though we must wait until 1575 for certainty that he was keeping "plays and resort of the people, to great gain."

The Paul's boys united with the rival Chapel children at Blackfriars for the years following Westcote's death, 1582 to 1584; but by 1587 they had been reestablished in their own theatre by Westcote's successor, Thomas Giles, who with John Lyly as his chief dramatist presented plays until 1590, when the company was suppressed for its scandalous zeal in satirizing the Marprelates. After nearly a decade of silence, we hear, in a newsletter of November 13, 1599, that "My Lord Derby hath put up the plays of the children in Paul's to his great pains and charge."[28] Derby's part in the revival remains obscure, but the Paul's boys became aggressively active until 1606. When they got into trouble, their current master, Edward Pierce, would coolly refer complaints to his secular arm, Thomas Woodford;[29] and before the venture was over, at least one other professional showman, Edward Kirkham, who slipped in and out of theatrical companies as he saw opportunity, was described as "one of the masters of the Children of Paul's."[30] In 1607–1608 a company called the Children of the King's Revels was performing in a new theatre in the Whitefriars priory buildings under the aegis of an actor-manager in partnership with an assortment of aspiring playwrights, theatrical speculators, and their victims.[31] The coincidence of dates, with the fact that Thomas Woodford was one of the prime movers, suggests that this phoenix had risen from the ashes of Paul's. If anything were needed to demonstrate the commercial exploitation of boy actors, the frenetic financing of the short-lived King's Revels Company would serve. After the collapse of the company, there seems to have been some threat that theatrical activity would revive at Paul's; but in 1609 Master Edward Pierce accepted the £20 a year to keep his theatre closed offered by the companies then holding Blackfriars and Whitefriars, and English drama withdrew permanently from the protective shadows of the Cathedral.

The early successes of the Paul's boys may best be discussed in connection with the career of the more famous troupe, the Chapel Royal boys. Between 1517 and 1521 William Cornish, master of the household chapel, presented his children in an interlude at court once or twice a year and received the regular playing fee of £6 13s. 4d.[32] Similar payments are recorded to Cornish's successors, William Crane, Richard Bower,[33] Richard Edwardes, and William Hunnis or his coadjutors Richard Farrant, Henry Evans, and John Lyly, so that from at least 1517 to at least 1584 dramatic activity by the chapel children was practically continuous.[34] In the mid-seventies, when the normal fee to popular troupes performing at court rose from £6 13s. 4d. to £10 per performance, the fee paid the children rose likewise. Most of the masters were at least occasional playwrights, while several of them achieved fame. As a separate dramatic organization between 1567 and 1577, the boys of the second royal chapel, at Windsor, had been appearing at court under their master, Richard Farrant. The coalition of the Windsor and the Chapel Royal boys in 1577, and the joint venture of Farrant and Hunnis in establishing a theatre in the Blackfriars priory buildings was, in all likelihood, suggested by the increasing success of their rivals, the Paul's boys. Between 1559 and 1582, the year of Westcote's death, the Paul's boys received fees for plays at court twenty-eight times as compared with the twenty-three times of the Windsor and Chapel Royal boys combined, with their superiority especially marked before the latter acquired Blackfriars. In the same period the total number of court performances by the popular adult troupes was fifty-nine, with no single troupe approaching the record of the Paul's boys. These figures have considerable bearing upon theatrical conditions in London proper.

Play productions were selected for court on a competitive basis, with the Revels office conducting tryouts and showing little deference to the livery of the actors, royal or otherwise. Proficiency was demanded, and it could not be acquired at the court itself; therefore a series of court performances by any company indicates that it had engaged in dramatic activity elsewhere. It has been suggested that the boy actors acquired theatres, called "private" houses, as a piece of opportunism resulting from a loophole in an Act of the common council of London, December 6, 1574, which strictly regulated performances at inns where money was collected at the gate but granted latitude in the case of performances in private houses on the occasion of weddings or other festivities.[35] It is true that the term "private" became associated with the playhouses of the child companies; but dating such playhouses from the Act of 1574 involves the same kind of error as dating the London activity of the popular troupes from the erection of Burbage's Theatre in 1576. The Act of 1574 was little different from the proclamation of City policy in 1545,[36] and little more effectual, so that it must not be considered epoch-making. Actually it was six months *before* the Act that Mulcaster's boys were ending their career in Merchant Taylors Hall; the performance by boys before city audiences could have been no new thing. That London performances were considered as the natural prerequisite to court performances is indicated by a letter from the privy council to the Lord Mayor in 1578, requiring him to allow six companies, Sussex's, Essex's, Warwick's, and Leicester's Men, and the Chapel and Paul's boys, "to exercise playing within the City" because "the companies aforenamed are appointed to play this time of Christmas before Her Majesty."[37] The "private" play-house, where choristers "exercised" before paying members of the more opulent London and Westminster public, may date from a period even earlier than Elizabeth's accession.

The two chapel masters were less strategically placed than West-cote at Paul's, with the home base of the one at Windsor and of the other at East Greenwich.[38] It does not follow that they had no opportunity of "exercising" their boys before paying audiences. An alleged attack of 1569 upon Sabbath performances "in Her Majesty's chapel" itself is now held suspect,[39] but Richard Edwardes' fame as a dramatist could not have derived from his single printed play and the few recorded performances before Queen Elizabeth and the Members of Lincoln's Inn. Five years after his death in 1566, he was still serving as an illustration of London small talk—"a good wit, and a good poet, and a great player of plays."[40] The royal choristers could have been brought to perform in wealthy households, or their masters could have found lodgings with halls capacious enough for a temporary stage. One of the obligations of the master of the Chapel Royal was to find quarters for his boys near Whitehall when the Queen was in residence.[41] But whatever Edwardes, Hunnis, and Farrant may have attempted early in the reign, it is certain that Westcote's situation at Paul's must have seemed enviable. It is not surprising then that in 1576–1577 Farrant should have combined with Hunnis and leased tenements in Blackfriars not far from the Paul's theatre. The complaint of Farrant's landlord will describe the project sufficiently for the moment: "Farrant pretended unto me to use the house only for the teaching of the Children of the Chapel, but made it a continual house for plays to the offense of the whole precinct, and pulled down partitions to make that place apt for that purpose."[42] For five years the two companies of boys, Paul's and the Chapel-combination, competed in close proximity. In 1582 Stephen Gosson mentions their theatres casually as fixtures in the London theatrical world: "But in plays, either those things are feigned that never were, as *Cupid and Psyche* played at Paul's and a great many comedies more at the Blackfriars and in every playhouse in London, which for brevity's sake I overskip."[43]

The tendency of chorister companies to escape from the fostering chapels and come under secular control is illustrated by the complex maneuvering at Blackfriars from 1580 to 1584.[44] Farrant died in 1580, and the lease to the theatre held by his widow passed first to Hunnis in partnership with one John Newman, then to the scrivener Henry Evans, who had been associated with Westcote at Paul's, and then to the Earl of Oxford, who conferred it upon John Lyly. Between 1582 and 1584 the company seems to have been made up of a combination of Chapel Royal, Windsor, and Paul's choristers or ex-choristers with recruits from the chapel of the Earl of Oxford— in a word, just a company of professionally managed juvenile actors enjoying the privileges, through Hunnis, of association with the royal household. Sometimes, toward the end, they were dubbed the "Earl of Oxford's Children." The lease to Blackfriars was lost in 1584, and Lyly, as has been noted, shifted his activity to Paul's theatre in 1587. In the period after 1584 Evans or Hunnis staged occasional plays with the boys of the Chapel Royal although we do not know of any theatre at their command. There is no reason to doubt that *The Wars of Cyrus* and Marlowe and Nashe's *Tragedy of Dido* were, as their title pages state, "Chapel" plays, although both, in their present versions, must date later than 1587. The history of the company is obscure, however, until after the Paul's boys, suppressed in 1590, were "up again" in 1599.

On September 2, 1600,[45] the ubiquitous Henry Evans rented for £40 a year the "second" Blackfriars theatre, constructed by James Burbage in 1596 for the use of adult actors but left standing idle because of protests from wealthy residents of the precinct. With his son-in-law Alexander Hawkins and one James Robinson, Evans formed an alliance with Nathaniel Giles, the successor of William Hunnis as master of the Chapel Royal. Armed with Giles's commission to take up singing children, this "confederacy" proceeded to recruit a company with undisguised ruthlessness. When Thomas Clifton, a boy of thirteen, was "seized" in Christ Church cloisters, his father, who happened to be a man of influence, not only retrieved the lad but created a stir that led to a hearing in Star Chamber.[46] Evans temporarily and Giles permanently faded into the background as a matter of prudence, and within a few years the company had lost even its nominal identity with the Chapel. After 1603 its name alternated between "Queen's Revels Company" and "Revels Company" as its notoriety inspired successive periods of official tolerance and censure. From the outset it was a strictly commercial venture. In its first few years, three new speculators bought into the enterprise, Edward Kirkham, Thomas Kendall, and William Rastell; and a syndicate of shifting membership and quarrelsome habits governed its troubled destiny at Blackfriars until the latter part of 1608, when the lease to the theatre was regained by the Burbage family for the use of the King's Men. The company then played at Whitefriars and elsewhere until 1613, when most of its actors seem to have been absorbed into the Lady Elizabeth's Men. Three of the boys among the original troupe ultimately became King's Men, Nathan Field's opportunity coming possibly because of the withdrawal from membership by William Shakespeare.

It has been noted how the King's company, by extending its activities to include performances at Blackfriars as well as the Globe, became ambidextrous and altered the pattern of London theatrical attendance; but it did not become primarily a coterie company until some years after the period with which we are concerned. Even the latest of the plays that Shakespeare himself wrote or collaborated upon, *Henry VIII* of 1613, had its opening at the Globe; and when the theatre burned down upon that occasion, it was rebuilt at great expense. That there were two distinct theatrical traditions in England, signalized by two distinct kinds of theatre, until the date of Shakespeare's retirement is sufficiently clear. To recapitulate—there were operating in the London area, synchronously with innyard and regular amphitheatre playhouses of the popular troupes, certain smaller playhouses of chorister or pseudo-chorister actors: probably one with at intervals two from the beginning of Elizabeth's reign in 1558 until 1575, certainly one from 1575 to 1577, certainly two from 1577 to 1582, certainly one from 1582 to 1584, possibly one from 1584 to 1587, certainly one from 1587 to 1590–1591, probably none from 1590–1591 to 1599–1600, certainly two from 1599–1600 to 1608, certainly one from 1608 to 1613. It has been an arduous journey to this conclusion, but a necessary one.

The unroofed circular pit of the typical public theatre attested its descent from the innyard, animal-baiting arena, and mere plot of ground where medieval throngs had gathered about a pageant wagon. The roofed rectangular auditorium of the typical "private" theatre attested its descent from the banqueting halls of the wealthy or academic. The private playhouses were artificially lighted and heated, and provided throughout with seats. The original vocation of the masters and actors was reflected in the extensive use of music—a concert of an hour's duration before the play began, a variety of instrumental and vocal renderings between the acts, and the

abundant use of songs and "mood music" within the plays themselves,[47] although in this last particular we find less distinction from
practice at the popular theatres than we might expect. After 1600
the methods of staging at the popular houses seem to have maintained also at Blackfriars and Paul's, the texts of their plays providing abundant evidence of action shifting between outer, inner, and
upper platforms unhampered by scenery; however, in the texts surviving from the earlier period, the concentration of locale suggests
that the masters may have employed scenery—either the fixed sets
in perspective associated with the "Serlio stage" or, more probably,
the disjunct though practicable canvas houses of the "simultaneous
setting" employed at the Hôtel de Bourgogne in Paris and supplied
by the Revels Office for play productions at Whitehall. That the
actors were juvenile is reflected in nearly every *dramatis personae*:
their writers were not forced to restrict the number of women and
pages in the stories. But among the distinguishing features of the
"private" theatres none thus far mentioned had a fraction of the influence, in giving their plays their peculiar quality, of the fact that
the audience was a coterie. These theatres catered to the few. The
number and nature of these few must be our chief concern.

Four classes of evidence aid us in estimating the number of patrons of the chorister troupes: the size of their theatres; the yearly
number of performances; the prices of admission; and the profits
or lack of profits among the masters or syndicates in charge. Need-
less to say, the evidence is all fragmentary; but its cumulative weight
is considerable. The less dreary of the matter follows, with supplementary data relegated to Appendix A.

The lease of chambers in Blackfriars obtained by Richard Farrant for the chapel theatre erected in 1576–1577 reads in part:

> . . . and the four other chambers or rooms residue of the said, six
> upper chambers do contain, in length one-hundred-and-ten foot, and in
> breadth from the east to the west part thereof twenty-two foot of assize,
> of which four chambers last recited one of them is seeled with wainscote
> on the east part, south part, and a part of the west, with a great round
> portal contained within the same chamber . . .[48]

Let us assume that a platform was erected in the wainscoted southern chamber, and an arras hung across its interior "great round portal." A stage and backstage tiring house would thus have been provided. With partitions removed from the remainder of the suite (as the landlord's complaint proves them to have been) an auditorium twenty-two feet by, let us say, seventy-five feet would be available. Allowing a two-foot-wide central aisle along the length of this auditorium, and three and three-quarters square feet of space per seat in the sections at either side, four hundred spectators could have been accommodated, facing each other in rising tiers of benches as at court masques. This reconstruction is purely hypothetical, its only value being that it gives us the *maximum seating capacity* of any conceivable adaptation of the Blackfriars premises. No dimensions survive for Paul's, but the case may be put thus: since Farrant's Blackfriars, accommodating four hundred spectators or fewer, had been built in proximity to and emulation of Paul's, the latter also, in all likelihood, accommodated four hundred spectators or fewer. It is difficult to imagine any section of a song school and residence holding more, although provision for that many was contrived at Davenant's residential Rutland House theatre in 1656.[49] The "second" Blackfriars, originally designed by James Burbage for the Chamberlain's Men, provided for tiring house, stage, and spectators an interior sixty-six feet long, forty-six feet wide, and sufficient height for galleries. Its total seating capacity was certainly less than nine hundred and possibly less than seven hundred. The Whitefriars playhouse may have been of equal or greater size, but the point is of minor significance; only for a brief interval in 1607–1608 were Blackfriars and Whitefriars used concurrently by chorister companies.

Now if, as is at least conceivable, 800 seats were available in the two private theatres following the year 1577, and 1,300 in the two following the year 1600, we could scarcely conclude on the basis of capacity alone that these were the theatres of the *few*, even though, as is almost certainly the case in either period, the combined audience capacity of the active public theatres was six times as great. Capacity is significant only in relation to frequency of use.

But observe: the large open-air theatres were used daily during a long season, while the smaller enclosed theatres were used only weekly during a short season—a fact that has never been adequately stressed.

On Saturday September 18, 1602, Philip Julius, Duke of Stettin-Pomerania, visited Blackfriars and described the "wöchentlich" performances there.[50] In 1611 Prince Otto von Hessen-Cassel alluded to Whitefriars and mentioned that the boys "play about three oclock, but only from Michaelmas to Easter."[51] Confirmation is available. On April 20, 1602, three of the entrepreneurs of the Chapel company agreed to pay Henry Evans eight shillings "every week weekly on Saturday . . . when and so often as any interludes, plays, or shows shall be played, used, showed, or published in the great hall and other the rooms situate in the Blackfriars, London,"[52] and, in litigation of 1608, one of the points in dispute was whether there had been a performance on Saturday June 16, 1604. Performances were certainly *wöchentlich*. As regards the length of the season, there is also confirmation. Samuel Daniel as the nominal censor of the Blackfriars company after 1604 was guaranteed £10 a year "if the said children should play or make any shows, either publicly or privately, the full time of six months in every year."[53] Since the recorded performances of Saturday September 18, 1602, and Saturday June 16, 1604, fall outside the Michaelmas to Easter period specified by Prince Otto as the Whitefriars season, the Blackfriars season during the years in question must have been interrupted by Lent and perhaps the vacation between Michaelmas and Hilary term to bring it down to the six months mentioned in Daniel's contract. At Paul's *The Old Joiner of Aldgate* was being played periodically during Hilary term, 1603, specifically on Monday February 28.[54] Although an Induction to one of the Paul's plays mentions "six penny fees all the year long,"[55] the reference is only to a theatrical season as distinct from a single legal term, and does not alter the probability that at Paul's, too, there were only weekly performances for six months of the year—with the playing day evidently Monday instead of Saturday. That the limited number of performances indicated above was characteristic of the enclosed theatres might have been inferred: the boys would have been incapable of the continuous repertory performances that astonish us even in the case of the adult actors of the popular troupes; moreover, except in the cool months their theatres would have been intolerably close.

In 1601, the probable year of *Hamlet*, the two private and three public theatres in London had, so far as we know, full seasons. If the private theatres were taxed to their combined capacity, placed at the highest possible estimate of 1,300, at each of the twenty-seven weekly performances, their total admissions would have been 35,100. If the public theatres were taxed to somewhat less than half of their combined maximum capacity, with 3,750 spectators on two hundred and thirty days of performance, *their* total admissions would have been 862,500.[56] The ratio of attendance at private and public theatres would have been 1 to 24.6. The actual ratio, however, was probably nearer 1 to 50, as a further scrutiny of the facts will show.

Although the private theatres were much less heavily capitalized than their rivals and had fewer charges against income, they were in perpetual financial straits even with high prices of admission. The only possible explanation is slim attendance. No admission fee so small as a penny is ever mentioned in connection with chorister drama. In 1589 fourpence is named as the admission at Paul's,[57] but in that year William Darrell paid sixpence.[58] In 1602 Duke Philip names one shilling as the price of admission at Blackfriars;[59] and in 1611 Otto von Hessen-Cassel remarks (in princely fashion) that at Whitefriars "the price is only half a shilling, but for the better places half a crown."[60] Sixpence and a shilling are the sums most commonly mentioned, but eighteenpence also appears in the record, so that the price range, at least after 1600, seems to have been six times that of the onepenny, twopenny, threepenny range of the public theatres. An allusion to the "twelvepenny-stool gentlemen"[61] may mean that a shilling above the ordinary maximum was charged for a stool on the stage—which would bring the range up to Prince Otto's high figure of half a crown. No doubt most places cost a shilling, with the sixpenny places stigmatizing their occupants as genteel "groundlings." Jonson sneers at

the shop's foreman, or some such brave spark,
That may judge for his sixpence[62]

and actually speaks of the "sixpenny mechanics" of a later Blackfriars audience as "the faeces or *grounds* of your people, that sit in
the oblique caves and wedges of your house."[63] The social implications of the high admission charges will be touched upon later.

With such prices prevailing, a private theatre would have been
a bonanza if filled once a week for twenty-seven weeks as hypothe-
sized above, especially the second Blackfriars had it had the capacity
of 900 seats used in obtaining our tentative ratio of 1 to 24.6. It would
have grossed over £1000 a year, with only £40 due in yearly rental
and with actors too young to demand shares. That it ever grossed
even £500 a year is extremely doubtful. It is significant that in the
whole history of chorister drama Sebastian Westcote is the only
master who indubitably prospered. Six years after the first Blackfriars opened, William Hunnis petitioned the royal household for
an increase of sixpence a day apiece "for the children's diet" and
gave a melancholy picture of himself and his predecessors—all play
producers: "The burden hereof hath from time to time so hin-
dered the masters of the children, viz. Mr. Bower, Mr. Edwardes,
myself, and Mr. Farrant, that notwithstanding some good helps
otherwise, some of them died in so poor case and so deeply indebted
that they had not left scarcely wherewith to bury them."[64] John
Lyly ended his association with the enterprise in debtors' prison.

Considerable sums of money are mentioned in the litigation among
the partners at the second Blackfriars and at Whitefriars, but the
sums mostly represent hypothecation: new partners hopefully
bought their way in only to find the assets intangible. Partnerships
at these theatres tended to wind up in a scramble for the costumes.
In 1608 plague and trouble with the authorities had added to the
woes at Blackfriars; and Henry Evans later testified that one of the
partners, Edward Kirkham, wanted to wind the business up, stating
"that he would deal no more with it, for it was a base thing, or used
words to such or very like effect."[65] Evans's most valuable asset
proved to be the lease to the theatre, wanted by the King's Men,
and, to Kirkham's chagrin, he disposed of it for a seventh interest

in such rental as they would pay. Although the earnings at Black-friars between 1600 and 1608 are named by litigants from time to time, the problem is less to interpret the sums than to identify the hardier liars. The probability that emerges is that the net annual earnings were about £200 before 1606 and about £300 thereafter, indicating a gross nearer £500 than £1,000, and a weekly number of spectators nearer 450 than 900. It would probably be safe also to halve the 400 weekly attendance assumed as a maximum at Paul's. Their project after 1599 was less ambitious than that of the Chapel company, and their collapse earlier. It has been previously noted that Edward Pierce was finally willing to trade any prospective earning powers of his theatre for a payment of £20 a year. The sensational nature of the chorister plays from 1600 to 1613, and possibly of some before 1590, must be partly attributable to the difficulty of recruiting audiences to see boys perform at the prices charged.

To sum the matter up, it appears likely that in the year of *Hamlet* eighteen to twenty-four thousand spectators a week through nine or ten months of the year were patronizing the Chamberlain's Men at the Globe, the Admiral's Men at the Fortune, and Worcester's Men at the Boar's Head or Rose,[66] compared with six to seven hundred spectators a week through six months of the year patronizing the Chapel boys at Blackfriars and Paul's boys at their song school. The nature of the evidence requires methods of estimate so speculative that no one would wish to defend the exact figures proffered. Whatever their normal practice, the boys may sometimes have acted more than once a week and more than six months a year; the men sometimes curtailed their long season and suffered through slack periods. Nevertheless, even if we doubled the attendance figures given for the boys and halved those for the men—and only legerdemain could effect a more drastic revision—the distinction in size between the two clienteles would still remain great enough to retain all its significance.

We are, of course, confronted with an anomaly. Why, if the popular companies were doing so well, did the chief of them in less than a decade after 1600 begin to abandon its purely popular methods? Why, by 1642, were all the major theatres "private" ones? We might reply that the period of greatest efflorescence and the period of dissolution have coincided in the case of other human institutions, but we can do somewhat better than that. What was happening in the theatres was part of a national revolution. The sector of the population which we customarily call Puritan must have been increasingly reluctant to go to the theatres, and the actors may have felt compelled to insure their own future. We need not assume that they did so without regret; those members of their audience who took religion so seriously may have been somewhat above the average in sensibility.

The year of *Hamlet*, all things considered, may not be the best choice for illustrating the supremacy of the popular troupes. It was in that year that the boys, still something of a novelty after their recent revival, were whipping up attendance by attacking the men. Jonson gives us the picture from the boys' point of view, when he makes an actor from the Globe say, ". . . This winter has made us all poorer than so many starved snakes: nobody comes at us, *not a gentleman*."[67] Hamlet himself asks, "Do the boys carry it away?" and Rosencrantz replies, "Ay, that they do, my lord; Hercules and his load too." Of course, if the load of Hercules were actually being carried away, Shakespeare could scarcely have afforded to make the joke. The leadership of his company is curiously conceded in a Paul's play of 1605. A character named Bellamont, but pretty clearly intended as Chapman, affirms that he will see no one while he is working on his play:

> *Servant.*
> Not a player?
>
> *Bellamont.*
> No, though a sharer bawl;
> I'll speak with none; although it be the mouth
> Of the *big company*, I'll speak with none; away![68]

That the "big company," secure in its thousands, ever looked with indifference at the hundreds drawn in by the boys, we cannot by any means assume. Those hundreds paid high rates; and, quite apart from any restiveness the King's Men may have sensed among their humbler but increasingly scrupulous patrons, they would cannily have recognized that the hundreds might be augmented in a properly manned and managed high-price theatre. At the moment, however, our task is to determine who those hundreds were.

The most unassailable answer is that they were the ones who could, or thought they could, afford to pay sixpence or a shilling to see a play. This eliminates all but a small fraction of the population. That a shilling was a large sum of money becomes apparent after even the most fleeting glimpse into the private life of the times. One need only observe the almost desperate concern of Samuel Daniel, reputable gentleman and respected poet, over the payment of the five shillings weekly due him or his assigns from the patentees at Blackfriars in order to acquire a respect for Elizabethan silver.[69] Among the most available "gentry"—the younger sons in service, the students at the inns of court, the tutors or literary men associated with wealthy households, the inactive captains, the foreign tourists, the provincial gallants sojourning in London—those individuals with more than a few shillings a week to spend on luxuries must be considered exceptional. A relevant remark on their resources in connection with one kind of luxury is made by the bawd in Marston's *Dutch Courtesan*: ". . . who helped thee to thy custom, not of swaggering Ireland captains, nor of two shilling inns a' court men, but with honest flatcaps, wealthy flatcaps, that pay for their pleasure the best of any men in Europe, nay, which is more, in London . . . ?"[70] The ones who could spend sixpence or a shilling on a play without a sense of extravagance were few indeed, and, in spite of Marston's allusion to opulent "flatcaps," included no ordinary workingmen.

There are modern instances of workingmen willing to pay a half-day's or a full day's wage for a single admission to a spectacle, but the spectacle is always a world-series ball game, a championship boxing match, or the like, never anything of a type that can be had elsewhere at cheaper rates. Wage earners do not purchase orchestra seats in our modern theatres, the cost of which in percentage of income is equivalent to the lowest admission charge at Blackfriars and

Paul's; indeed they rarely go to our theatres at all, but are content
with the motion pictures. A workingman at the coterie theatres
would have been something of a marvel, like Jonson's brave "shop's
foreman," unless he was there through interest in a particular scandal. When *The Old Joiner of Aldgate* was played at Paul's in 1603,
John Howe, the old joiner himself, attended. He was only a barber,
but he was doing well for himself at the time as marriage broker for
his heiress daughter. He took the play philosophically: ". . . for
that kings had been presented on the stage, and therefore barbers
might." Flaskett, one of the daughter's suitors, was also in the play
and in the audience, but the Reverend Dr. Milward, who had snared
the prize, aloofly stayed away: ". . . there was not anything in the
. . . playbook that touched him at all."[71] The exclusion by economic
means of the craftsmen, shopkeepers, and their families, who con-
stituted the bulk of the audiences at the other theatres, was indeed
a chief *raison d'être* for Blackfriars and Paul's:

> *Sir Edward Fortune.*
> I saw the Children of Paul's last night,
> And, troth, they pleased me pretty, pretty well;
> The apes in time will do it handsomely.
>
> *Planet.*
> I' faith, I like the audience that frequenteth there
> With much applause: a man shall not be choaked
> With the stench of garlic, nor be pasted
> To the barmy jacket of a beer-brewer.
>
> *Brabant Junior.*
> 'Tis a good gentle audience . . .[72]

The gentility of the audience in Lyly's time is attested to in prologues assuring the "gentle gentlemen"[73] that the author shuns "the
vulgar," or places his "studies before gentlemen,"[74] but the note is
struck most insistently after the reopenings in 1599–1600. In four
successive plays at Paul's, Marston speaks of "the gentle front of this
fair troop, select and most respected auditors," the "gentle presence
and . . . calm attention of choice audience," "this choice selected
influence," and "kind gentlemen and most respected auditors."[75]
Jonson's earliest term for the patrons of Blackfriars is "this fair so-

ciety."[76] The refinement of the clientele was impressed upon foreign visitors, as evidenced in the diary of Duke Philip Julius of Stettin-Pomerania:

Those who wish to see one of their performances [at Blackfriars in 1602] must give as much as eight shillings in our money [i.e. Stralsund—one shilling English], but there are always a good many people present, many respectable women as well, because useful argumenta, and many good doctrines, as were told, are brought forward there. They do all their plays by [artificial] light, which produces a great effect. For a whole hour before [the beginning of the play] a delightful performance of instrumental music is given on organs, lutes, pandores, mandolins, violins, and flutes; and a boy's singing *cum voce tremulo* in a double bass [*sic*—in einer Basgeigen] so tunefully that we have not heard the like of it in the whole journey except perhaps the nuns of Milan did it better.[77]

Prince Otto's reference to "die beste cumpani in Lunden"[78] in his description of Whitefriars in 1611 may apply either to the performers or to the audience.

A distinction should be made between occasional patrons like Duke Philip and Prince Otto, and the habitués. No doubt foreign guests were taken to these theatres as to all the sights in London; and country gentlemen in town at term time would naturally seek out the latest thing in entertainment. William Drummond was a romantic youth whose literary idols were Sidney, Spenser, and their idealistic and mellifluous successors, yet during his visits to London in 1606 and later he picked up a number of the amatory and satirical works currently in the bookstalls, including the plays of Marston.[79] To have even six or seven hundred spectators a week, Blackfriars and Paul's must have been visited at least once in a while by most of the resident and visiting gentry. Not all of these liked what they found there: Jonson alludes to the one with "more beard than brain" who "prunes his mustaccio, lisps, and with some score of affected oaths, swears down all that sit about him, 'That the old *Hieronimo*, as it was first acted, was the only best and judiciously penned play of Europe.' "[80] But the majority, while perhaps somewhat bemused by the sophistication of the plays, and disinclined to take them as steady diet, might, like the occasional night-club visitor today, have been less pleased if less disconcerted.

The habitué gave these theatres and their plays a special coloration, and makes the use of the term "coterie" inevitable. Presumably
it was a taste too cultivated for popular fare that marked him out.
Lyly had expressed his faith that the superior rank of the spectators
was evident not only in their "fair front" but in their superior dè-
portment and critical acumen, with references to "precise judgments" and "wonted courtesies";[81] but it remained for Ben Jonson,
in the prologue to his first play at Blackfriars, to elaborate the theme:

> If gracious silence, sweet attention,
> Quick sight and quicker apprehension
> (The lights of judgment's throne) shine anywhere
> Our doubtful author hopes this is their sphere.
> And therefore opens he himself to those;
> To other weaker beams his labors close:
> As loth to prostitute their virgin strain
> To ev'ry vulgar and adult'rate brain.
> In this alone his Muse her sweetness hath,
> She shuns the print of any beaten path;
> And proves new ways to come to learned ears—
> Pied ignorance she neither loves nor fears.
> Nor hunts she after popular applause,
> Or foamy praise that drops from common jaws:
> The garland that she wears, their hands must twine
> Who can both censure, understand, define
> What merit is.[82]

In his usual fashion, Jonson tried to quell with satire anyone who
might not be suitably impressed. In the induction a supercilious fop
speaks between puffs on his tobacco pipe:

By this light, I wonder that any man is so mad to come to see these
rascally tits play here. They do act like so many wrens or pismires, not
the fifth part of a good face amongst them all. And then their music is
abominable, able to stretch a man's ears worse than ten pillories, and their
ditties most lamentable things, like the pitiful fellows that make them—
poets. By this vapor, an 'twere not for tobacco, I think the very stench of
'em would poison me; I should not dare to come in at their gates. A man
were better visit fifteen jails or a dozen or two hospitals than once adventure to come near them.[83]

So far as we can determine, London as yet had no social milieu in which the mere fact of being a poet, critic, or publisher conferred prestige. Intellectual life seems to have been dominated, at least in secular circles, by the legal profession. The first club of "wits" of which there is record—the Sirenaics, who met periodically at the Mermaid in 1612 and possibly earlier—was composed mainly of minor government officials and lawyers.[84] John Donne was associated with this group, and it is barely possible that Ben Jonson was; but Shakespeare certainly was not. No popular writer, indeed no poet as poet, would have found a welcome in this rather hard-headed assembly. When Jonson's offerings failed to meet uniform approval, so that capricious gallants and self-assertive lawyers and military men seemed to him to preponderate over "learned ears," he proceeded, in Marston's words,

> To crack rude scorn even on the very face
> Of better audience.[85]

Not everything that drew Jonson's scorn deserved it; but there are numerous indications that the coterie audience was not invariably courteous and discerning, and that its smart and sensation-seeking elements were at least as conspicuous as its learned ones. For vignettes of members of the London leisured class we have no choice but satirical ones. Everard Guilpin describes Gnathe, who

> lies in bed 'till noon,
> Then, all high-stomached riseth to his dinner,
> Falls straight to dice, before his meat be down,
> Or to digest, walks to some female sinner.
> Perhaps fore-tired he gets him to a play,
> Comes home to supper, and then falls to dice,
> There his devotion wakes 'till it be day,
> And so to bed, where unto noon he lies.[86]

One cannot read the early verse of John Donne without a sensation that the author was tasting the society and perhaps the pleasures of the Gnathes, with a consequent revulsion of feeling. An audience of Donnes might seem good enough for anyone, but we may guess that in and about the inns of court were many who shared

Donne's mood with something less than his genius. Marston himself, one of the most persistent writers for the boys, was in some ways a grotesque duplication of Donne. Something about the attitudes of the coterie audience may be learned from the personalities of its writers, several of whom were recruited from it. The subject will be mentioned in a later chapter, but a word may be inserted here about Edward Sharpham. He was a man about town who died in 1608 after displaying his wit in two lamentable plays for the boys. Besides the "sums of money due and owing" him, his will mentions only personal apparel—the accoutrements of a gallant. There are the pale carnation stockings, the rapier hatched with silver, the girdle and hangers trimmed with silver, and so on. In one of Sharpham's plays there is a satirical reference to "half-lined cloak citizens,"[87] and in the other to a gentleman whose cloak is not lined through but "a good depth in."[88] A garment de rigueur is itemized in the will: "my damson-colored cloak lined through with black velvet."[89] Such was Sharpham's white plume.

A wry allusion to a clientele of gentlemen occurs in the induction to John Day's Isle of Gulls, a Blackfriars play of 1606, when one of the stage-stool spectators says, "Well, I'll sit out the play . . . but see it be bawdy or, by this light, I and all my friends will hiss," and the boy-prologue replies, "You should not deal gentlemen-like with us else." A few years later the audience is described as

> Compos'd of gamester, captain, knight, knight's man,
> Lady or pusill that wears mask or fan.[90]

With the increasing tendency of those who could afford it to gravitate to London, the fashionable set and its hangers-on became more and more numerous. Its mixed nature in 1609 is suggested in Jonson's prologue to Epicoene, which promises cakes

> fit for ladies: some for lords, knights, squires;
> Some for your waiting-wench, and city wires;
> Some for your men and daughters of Whitefriars.

Henry Fitzgeffrey's "Notes from Black-Friars" belongs to a period after the theatre had been taken over by the King's Men; but he is interested chiefly in the habitués of "gallants' row," and his observations are relevant: there are writers, including "crabbed Web-sterio," the soldier Sir Island Hunt, the ladies' man Dandebrat, a Cheapside dame, a prodigal, a woman of the "masculine gender," an overdressed dandy, and a young lady with a yellow fan.[91] We get the impression less of those who can "censure, understand, define what merit is" than of idlers on parade, and, despite the afternoon playing time, an atmosphere of "night life." Fitzgeffrey, of course, is a satirist, and we must never forget the necessary discount.

The private theatres were completely *urban* with all the term implies, and not, like the public theatres, the urban centers of a nation-wide activity. A carter, bargeman, farmer, or discharged halberdier in London would have felt at home in the Rose, the Fortune, or the Globe: the building would be awe-inspiring, but he might have seen these players or this very play right in his native shire. The Black-friars and Paul's companies lacked this contact with England out-side the metropolis. The few records of their performances in the provinces come after the collapse of each London venture, and rep-resent the attempts of managers to eke out a livelihood with rem-nant troupes. The Chapel company appeared at Norwich and Leicester after the loss of the first Blackfriars, the Paul's boys at Gloucester after their inhibition in London in 1590, and the "Rev-els" company at various towns after the split among the managers of the second Blackfriars in 1608.[92] There is nothing equivalent to the road tradition that gave the adult actors the whole population as their potential audience; consequently, the national spirit was never the shaping influence upon coterie plays.

The distinction between the audiences of the two kinds of thea-tre is not a distinction between plebeians and patricians, but between a general public and a coterie. The milieu of the private playhouses was not "lordly." Lords are no more apt to appear in the orbit of the boys than in that of the men. Leicester, Oxford, and Derby gave protection to chorister groups as part of their general activity as patrons, but they conferred their livery upon popular troupes as well. Derby, named as patron of the revived Paul's boys in 1599, was said in June of that same year to be "busy penning comedies for the common players,"[93] while his Countess was petitioning Secretary

Cecil that her husband's men be not "barred from their accustomed playing . . . for that my Lord, taking delight in them, it will keep him from more prodigal courses."[94] As performers, the popular actors continued to have, as always, entrance into the court and the manor houses of the realm; and their London theatres attracted their share of lords. When Jonson alludes to "pied ignorance" or to the "vulgar and adult'rate brain," he is expressing distaste for the inclusiveness of the audience of the public playhouses, and the preponderance of plain people in that audience. Actually it incorporated the audience of the private playhouses. The latter was a sector of the London playgoing public, which isolated itself on particular occasions and required plays calculated to its particular meridian. So far as the majority of its members can be placed in any familiar structure of society, they were the precariously well-to-do. Only a tiny minority of them, even in Lyly's time, could have been officially courtiers, but their eyes were turned toward Whitehall. They enjoyed gossip about the court and satire upon its members, particularized if possible but generalized if not. They certainly squinted at Eastcheap, where, none the less, the family prosperity of some of them had originated. The coterie audience was an amalgam of fashionable and academic elements, socially and intellectually self-conscious. Of the "publics" available in England at the time, it was the most *avant-garde*, the most sophisticated, the most interested in art as art. One can picture the young Elizabethan intellectuals fingering the newer things in the bookstalls before dropping into the nearby theatre: many of them must have come from the direction of Gray's Inn, Lincoln's Inn, the Middle and Inner Temples, and the lodging houses in Westminster, or along Fleet Street and the Strand.

In some ways the little theatres then resemble certain of the little magazines now—in the sense of self-righteousness among the writers, in the proud refusal to go along with popular tastes, even in the financial frailty. The theatre of the many was an actors' theatre—a theatre of craftsmen-sharers who gauged what the people wanted and commissioned authors to produce it. Landlords sat down with actors and dramatists to discuss such matters at local taverns. Authors, unless they were actors, had a minor place in these councils.

The theatre of the few, although the managing syndicates were just as financially avid, was more nearly a musicians' and authors' theatre because the nature of the actors was such that they must take rather than give direction. Literary men like Chapman and Jonson must have had great hopes of it, and at one time or another such dramatists as John Heywood, John Lyly, John Marston, David Barry, and John Mason had a proprietory interest in it, not to mention the original choirmaster directors who were usually dramatists as well as musicians. A share in the profits of the little theatres was thought an appropriate means of relieving even poets like Daniel and Drayton, whose spirit was alien to the type of literature they fostered. In latter days their plays had an understandable faculty for getting into print, so that during the second half of Shakespeare's career, we find available for study, if we exclude the plays of Shakespeare himself, almost as many texts from Blackfriars and Paul's as from the Rose, the Red Bull, the Fortune, and the Globe. The proportion is completely misleading so far as the actual proportion of plays produced by the two types of theatre is concerned, and even more misleading as a gauge of English taste. Unless we are aware of the fact, we are apt to come to peculiar conclusions about the general spirit of the age in Jacobean as compared with Elizabethan times.

III

The Rival Repertories

UNTIL well on in the sixteenth century published plays are so few and their title pages so uninformative that it is hard to determine what is being performed on English stages. It is tempting to treat a play, available through the accident of survival, as typical of its time, with little evidence of the existence of the body of drama it is supposed to typify and little attention to the special conditions of its composition. The very fact of publication should serve as a warning of the unrepresentative character of the play.

Upon the recent recovery of its text, Medwall's *Fulgens and Lucrece* seemed to move the advent of English "romantic" drama back into the fifteenth century; but the work represents less an evolutionary stage in English drama as a whole than an early forerunner of a particular species; certainly, a humanistic experiment in the household of Cardinal Morton should not be identified with the wares concurrently offered by professional strollers. John Heywood's farces and disputations of a generation later are sometimes thought of as primitive gropings; yet Heywood's sphere was the court and the intellectual circle of More and Rastell, his work also quite "advanced" and, so far as we know, quite unrelated to the activity of the professional troupes. *Gammer Gurton's Needle*, far from being the quaint diversion of simple spectators, was a sophisticated genre piece, written by a university fellow for university auditors. The "landmarks" of the early drama rise not from the mainland but from academic archipelagoes; and the various "firsts" often prove to be also practically the "lasts" of their particular kind. *Ralph*

Roister Doister and *Gorboduc*, traditionally designated the first "regular" comedy and tragedy, are as exceptional in respect to the bulk of the plays that followed as of those that preceded them, and may be considered epoch-making only if we exclude from the epoch the drama we value most. Nearly twenty years after its birth *Gorboduc* was cited by Sidney as the swallow that had failed to make a spring, plays generally having remained coarsely irregular.

The famous anthology pieces of early Tudor drama are all humanistic experiments. They are mediators between a native dramatic tradition and a classical-continental tradition, important guides to professional entertainers in the means of weaving together homespun and imported materials; but they themselves are amateur and isolated. They fail to show a regular evolution in form and content from one to another because they are not articulated by a professional theatrical organization catering to voluntary audiences. Their political and moral ideas are, for the most part, such as we shall presently be terming "popular"—not surprisingly in view of the humanistic origin of the popular code. No essential difference marks the political creed of the learned authors of *Gorboduc* and the popular author of *Cambyses*. The plays in which the moral tone seems most exotic, like Heywood's *John John* and Gascoigne's *Supposes*, prove to be close redactions of continental originals. It is not until the pressure of audience tastes is exerted in commercialized theatres that distinct popular and select repertories emerge, with the split in philosophical outlook that is the subject of the present study. We must concentrate our attention upon the known plays of known troupes of actors.

The first fact to be recognized is that we have no specific information about the repertories of the adult troupes catering to the general public for the first century of their existence. The earliest known title of a play assigned to a specific company, or indeed to the popular theatre in general, is *The Market of Mischief* performed by the Queen's Men at Norwich in 1546.[1] Judged by the title alone, the piece could have been of the same type as the unassigned but popular-sounding morality *Mankind*, preserved in a manuscript of the fifteenth century. That *Aesop's Crow*, "wherein the most part of the actors were birds," performed by the King's Men in 1552–1553, and *Self Love*, performed by the same company about the same time,[2] were moral interludes—that is, allegorical and didactic but secular in spirit—seems certain. The name of no particular company is attached to *The Sackful of News* of 1557; but that this "lewd play" belonged to adult professionals is indicated by its performance at the Boar's Head Inn.[3] *Aesop's Crow* was political in its implications, and *The Sackful of News*, at least in the suspicion of the authorities, was both political and subversive. A number of the extant pre-Elizabethan interludes no doubt were acted by the professional troupes, but their title pages do not tell us so. Some of them may be academic in origin or even "closet" pieces. The plays of Bishop Bale, with historical personages and polemical elements grafted upon medieval mystery and morality story material, are just as reliable a clue to the nature of popular repertories at mid-point in the reign of Henry VIII.

Unless there was some body of minstrel drama unknown to us, or unless the folk drama of the villages was appropriated and expanded (and there is little early evidence that it was), the professional actors began by exploiting the more entertaining possibilities of the biblical, hagiological, and moral plays handed down to them from the Middle Ages, and continued to do so until well on in the sixteenth century. Vestiges of this heritage are perceptible in plays until the end of our period, conspicuously in Marlowe's *Doctor Faustus*, and in literally hundreds of details in the plays of Shakespeare. In the eighties Robert Wilson's *Three Ladies of London* and *Three Lords and Three Ladies of London*, and even Greene and Lodge's *Looking Glass for London and England* preserve many conventions of the moral interlude intact. A play on the seven deadly sins, possibly by Richard Tarleton, was a lively item in the repertory of the Queen's Men during Shakespeare's early years in London; and a number of biblical titles appear among the lost plays mentioned in Henslowe's *Diary*. The development of the moral plays through Tudor times, their increasing realism, absorption of new materials, and concern with new issues, need not be reviewed. The persistence of their conventions, and the evolution of their most portentous character, the Vice, are treated excellently in the forthcoming *Allegory of Evil*, by Bernard Spivak. The question for us is, when did the popular troupes begin turning persistently to new subject matter, and what was this subject matter like? The best guess we can make is that the time was shortly before the accession of Elizabeth, and the material was remarkable deeds gleaned from biography and pseudo-biography and from the medieval and chivalresque romances.

If the "Huff-suff-and-ruff" performed by Dudley's (later Leicester's) Men at court in 1560[4] was Thomas Preston's *Cambyses,* the latter is the first extant play that can be assigned to a particular popular troupe. Dudley's Men were at Ipswich in 1563, and the "Berberous Terryne" (Barbarous Tyrant?) performed there in that year[5] may itself be *Cambyses.* We know that the play remained a stock piece for many years, and was available for allusion by Shakespeare and others. John Pikering's *Horestes,* printed in 1567, may be the "Orestes" acted at court in the same year;[6] if so, it probably belonged to the Earl of Bath's Men. Both *Cambyses* and *Horestes* are quite naïve, presenting spectacularly the exploits of active men, their good and bad deeds moralized, along with episodes of boisterous humor. *Cambyses* is a perfect example of popular eclecticism, and *Horestes* of assimilation, as it reveals the way in which such convenient medieval abstractions as Courage and Revenge, along with benign rulers and their armies, could aid an Aeschylean hero in resolving his dilemma. Both plays reflect the public interest in good government.

As might be expected in this frustrating period of dramatic history, our first extensive list of titles belongs to non-extant plays. Between 1571 and 1585 the following plays were performed by various popular companies visiting the court:[7] *Lady Barbara, Cloridon and Radiamanta, Mamillia, Predor and Lucia, Herpetulus the Blue Knight and Perobia, Panecia, Phedrastus, Phignon and Lucia, Philemon and Felecia, Pretastus, History of the Collier, The Painter's Daughter, Tooly, History of Cenocephals, Irish Knight, Mingo, Solitary Knight, Cruelty of a Stepmother, Three Sisters of Mantua, Duke of Milan and the Marquis of Mantua, Pastoral of the Greek Maid, Knight in the Burning Rock, Murderous Michael, Rape of the Second Helen, Four Sons of Fabius, Serpedon, Soldan and the Duke* of . . . , *Beauty and Housewifery*, *History of Ferrar*, *Telemo*, *Pastoral of Phyllida and Corin*, *Five Plays in One*, *Three Plays in One*, *Felix and Philiomena*. London and provincial records preserve a few additional titles:[8] *Story of Sampson*, performed at the Red Lion Inn, London, 1567; *Cutwell*, performed at the Bell Inn, London, 1577; *Red Knight* performed at Bristol, 1576; *The Court of Comfort*, *Queen of Ethiopia*, *Quid pro Quo*, and *What Mischief Worketh in the Mind of Man*, all performed at Bristol in 1577–1578. The titles are surprising in view of the preponderance of moral interludes among published pieces before 1585. Of more than twoscore titles listed, ten at most seem to belong to "traditional" types of plays. For what it is worth, the fact may be noted that a higher percentage of moral interludes were performed before the town officials of Bristol than before the royal court; perhaps only the more modish plays in the repertories were selected by the Master of the Revels. The fact remains that by the 1570's romantic material penetrated the drama in force.

Since no dragons are slain in the plays of Shakespeare, and knightly adventure is not conspicuous in the more widely read plays of his contemporaries, we are apt to lose sight of the fact that dragons, enchanters, armored knights, and damsels in distress peopled the English stage for a considerable period of time. The vogue had passed before play publication became common, and is represented for us chiefly by *Sir Clyomon and Sir Clamydes* and *Common Conditions*, the first certainly and the second probably belonging to the companies and period of the lost plays listed above. Despite their mélange of almost incomprehensible adventure and clownery, either would make a historically more significant item in an anthology than *Ralph Roister Doister*, the doggerel of which is only slightly less harrowing. That by 1580 English drama was generally thought of in terms of such plays is indicated by the composite descriptions that have come down to us. "You shall have Asia of the one side and Africk of the other," said Sidney in his famous condemnation, and he proceeded to mention the lost children, the battlefields, the shipwrecks, and the "hideous monster, with fire and smoke."[9] The English playwright, said George Whetstone in 1578, grounds his work on impossibilities: then in three hours runs he through the world, marries, gets children, makes children men, men to conquer kingdoms, murder monsters, and bringeth gods from heaven and fetcheth devils from hell. . . . Many times (to make mirth) they make a clown companion with a king.[10]

Stephen Gosson in 1582 presents the same picture:

Sometimes you shall see nothing but the adventures of an amorous knight, passing from country to country for the love of his lady, encountering many a terrible monster made of brown paper; and at his return is so wonderfully changed that he cannot be known but by some posy in his tablet, or by a broken ring or a handkercher, or a piece of a cockle-shell.[11]

How deeply the plays of his childhood were etched in the memory of Shakespeare is suggested by his tendency in his last phase to return to many of their features.

Gosson lists "the Golden Ass, the Aethiopian History, Amadis of France, the Round Table" among the works "ransack't to furnish the playhouses in London."[12] Some of these must have been ransacked before the time of our list of plays at court. The "Aethiopian History" is represented, but the dramatists are seeking material outside the familiar tales published by Caxton and his immediate successors. The Spanish romances are represented in *Felix and Philiomena* from Montemayor's *Diana; The Rape of the Second Helen* from de Silva's *Florisel de Niquea;* and *The Irish Knight* probably from the *Historia del Nobile & Valoroso Cavaliero Felice Magno.*[13] That the playwrights were guilty of "feigning countries never heard of, monsters and prodigious creatures that are not, as of the Aris maspie, of the Grips, the Pigmies, the Cranes, and other such notorious lies,"[14] is demonstrated in our list by the *History of Cenocephals,* probably from Mandeville. Greene and Nashe, alluding satirically to the popular repertory, mention besides morality titles such plays, real or imaginary, as *The Twelve Labors of Hercules* and *The King of the Fairies.*[15] The latter suggests that *Huon of Bordeaux* had already been dramatized.

Titles like *Cruelty of a Stepmother* and *Murderous Michael* suggest realistic middle-class tragedies in the category of *Arden of*

Feversham. The kind of subject matter commonly conveyed in the black-letter ballads was being dramatized in the seventies, and, according to Gosson, the plots of continental novellas. That the romances, although the chief, were not the sole quarry of new material is illustrated by this critic of the stage. He describes *The Blacksmith's Daughter* at the Theatre, "containing the treachery of Turks, the honorable bounty of a noble mind, the shining of virtue in distress," and *Ptolemy* (perhaps the *Telemo* of our list) at the Bull Inn, showing "how seditious estates with their own devices, false friends with their own swords, and rebellious commons in their own snares are overthrown."[16] His description of *The Jew,* also shown at the Bull, reminds us of *The Merchant of Venice;* and that of his own play, *Catiline's Conspiracies,* of Lodge's *Wounds of Civil War* and later extant plays in which Roman history provides theatrical entertainment and political exempla.

When Greene tells of his encounter with the actor who beseeches him to write plays because now

The people make no estimation
Of Morals teaching education,[17]

we are led to believe that the repertories were modernized by the "University Wits"—Greene himself, Marlowe, and their group. But the plays of these men did little pioneering in their ingredients, as distinct from their quality; they evidently followed established modes and were written to the specifications of the actors. In the eighties the most novel things—how novel, it is impossible to say—were the revenge plays and the English chronicle plays, both no doubt given impetus by the publication of the collective *Seneca His Ten Tragedies,* 1581, and the *Chronicles,* also collective in a sense, of Stowe and Holinshed. Judged by the titles of lost plays in Henslowe's *Diary,* as well as plays that have survived, Holinshed was ultimately dramatized entire. Tragedies based upon actual episodes of adultery and murder in English homes vied in popularity with the revenge plays; and the exploits of English adventurers, with those of the heroes of exotic romance. The strangely named knights and ladies of the latter yield place to English lovers, often aided by the benign magicians of folk tales. A large part of the plays might well be termed "Biographies." Within a two-year span at the Henslowe theatres, one could relish the careers of Constantine, Machiavelli, Tamar Cham, Pope Joan, and Richard the Confessor, while, among extant plays, the line drawn from *Cambyses* to *Tamburlaine* extends on through the more civilized and English *Captain Thomas Stukeley* and *The Travels of the Three English Brothers*. The audience was ready to contemplate the acts of any remarkable man, approving his virtues, deploring his vices, but always fascinated by his prowess.

Between 1560 and 1613 one hundred and twenty-nine extant plays can be assigned on objective evidence to the popular troupes. Without recourse to the hundreds of lost plays, the titles of which are in many cases known, and the scores of additional extant plays, most of which also probably belonged to the popular troupes, we have enough material to make generalization safe. This is the drama of "scene individable, or poem unlimited" invoked by Polonius. His term "tragical-comical-historical-pastoral" describes most of the plays better than our usual labels. It is a drama of amazing variety in story material and disconcerting flexibility of form. Structure in the main is episodic, in a sense medieval: a "scene" is any piece of continuous action, and an "act" is any group of scenes preceding an interval. If there were four intervals, there were five acts; nicer attempts at structural analysis are usually satisfying only to the critic who makes them. This body of drama shows an infinitely wide range in subtlety and artistry, but a very narrow range in what we may call its view of life. Whereas the subject matter became somewhat more English and realistic as time went on, there is no real break in continuity—so far as emotional and ethical attitudes are concerned—between, let us say, *The Rare Triumphs of Love and Fortune* performed by Derby's Men in 1582, and *The Tempest*, performed by the King's Men in 1611. The average play is romantic, idealistic, positive, and often patriotic and religious. It would be impossible to demonstrate from the plays of the popular theatres that in the seventeenth century Elizabethan optimism yielded to Jacobean pessimism. This generalization can, of course, be combated by dwelling upon particular elements in a particular play, especially if these elements are isolated from the play as a whole; but we are here viewing the drama in the large. The impression of a new era of disillusion is conveyed by the increasing prominence of the rival repertory, to which we must turn before pursuing the subject further.

Before the reign of Elizabeth, we have not so much as the title of a play that can be assigned with certainty to the choristers of Paul's as distinct from the boys of the grammar school, although John Redford's educational interlude, *Wit and Science*, about 1540, may have been written for them. John Heywood seems to have written for the group, but it was after the period of his extant pieces. Of pre-Elizabethan plays by the Chapel children our knowledge is slightly greater. We know that they participated in the court pageantry of the reign of Henry VIII described by the chronicler Hall, that in 1519 they played a "goodly comedy of Plautus,"[18] and in 1553–1554 the moral interlude *Genus Humanum*.[19] Of two remaining pieces, *Troilus and Pander*, 1515, and *Love and Riches*, 1527, brief but suggestive descriptions survive and will be mentioned presently.

To about the year 1565 belongs the isolated text *Damon and Pythias*, written by Richard Edwardes, Master of the Chapel; and to about the year 1567, probably the original version of the extant moral interlude *Liberality and Prodigality*.[20] The records of the Revels Office and a casual allusion by Stephen Gosson preserve the titles of eighteen plays performed by the Paul's boys and the royal chapels between 1572 and 1584: *Narcissus, Iphigenia, Ajax and Ulysses, Alcmaeon, Quintus Fabius, King Xerxes, Error, Mutius Scaevoli, Titus and Gisippus, Alucius, Loyalty and Beauty, Marriage of Mind and Measure, Meleager, Scipio Africanus, Pompey, Cupid and Psyche, Game of Cards*, and *Agamemnon and Ulysses*. Then we have nine extant plays belonging to the boys, all but the last two certainly, and those probably, written in the 1580's: Peele's *Arraignment of Paris*, Lyly's *Campaspe, Sapho and Phao, Gallathea, Endymion, Love's Metamorphosis, Mother Bombie*, and *Midas*, Marlowe and Nashe's *Tragedy of Dido* and the anonymous *Wars of Cyrus*.[21]

The sampling is meager, a few dozen titles of lost works and twelve actual texts representing the whole corpus of drama written for the select audience from the beginning until the blank period 1591–1599; nevertheless we are enabled to make a few generalizations. What strikes one first is the obvious commitment of this repertory to classical subject matter, fictional and historical. *Liberality and Prodigality* is the only true exception among the extant plays, and among the non-extant the exceptions are even fewer than at first appears: Mercury was the Presenter in *Love and Riches*, while Bacchus (probably also Venus) figured in *Loyalty and Beauty*. Almost as obvious is the persistence of certain themes. On the basis of the extant *Campaspe* and *Wars of Cyrus*, we may guess that a number of such plays as *Iphigenia, Ajax and Ulysses, Quintus Fabius, King Xerxes, Mutius Scaevoli, Scipio Africanus, Pompey,* and *Agamemnon and Ulysses* were concerned with heroical sentiments about patrician honor, presented dialectically rather than in action. Again on the basis of extant plays as well as the earlier titles, we can see that the theme of friendship—pervasive in the polite literature of the Renaissance—was a favorite with the chorister companies. One of the few plays departing from classical subject matter treats of the sacrifice of love to friendship in the tale of *Titus and Gisippus*, already borrowed from Boccaccio by Elyot in *The Governor* and by other English writers. A relationship between courtesy literature and the drama of the select audience is perceptible long before the time of Lyly. The *Love and Riches* of 1527 was a contention adjudicated by a sage, who pronounced congenially that a Prince was "by love to be obeyed and served, and with riches to reward his lovers and friends."[22]

The theme by all odds dominant in the plays under survey is love —guilty love, frustrated love, love fantastically fulfilled. On the farcical level we get it in the Plautine comedy, Lyly's *Mother Bombie*, and on the tragic in Marlowe and Nashe's *Tragedy of Dido* and the anonymous *Wars of Cyrus*, as well, probably, as in the lost *Alcmaeon* and *Meleager*. The last two, judged by the indicated subject matter, could have been Senecan in type, perhaps resembling the Gray's Inn tragedy of *Gismond of Salerne*. The lost plays *Narcissus* and *Cupid and Psyche*, as well as Peele's *Arraignment of Paris* and the remaining plays of Lyly, illustrate the approach to the subject through classical myth. The interlude represented by our earliest title, Cornish's Chapel offering of 1515, portrayed "Troilus and Pander richly imparalled, also Calchas and Cressyd imparalled like a widow of honor in black sarcenet and other habiliments for such matter, Diomede and the Greeks imparalled like men of war."[23] Although Edwardes' *Damon and Pythias* sticks austerely to friendship, love seems to have been this dramatist's specialty:

> A sudden change is wrought:
> For lo! our author's muse, that masked in delight
> Hath forc'd his pen against his kind no
> More such sports to write.
> Muse he that list, right worshipful, for
> Chance hath made this change,
> For that to some he seemed too much in
> Young desires to range.[24]

An attack upon the performances of the boys supposedly printed in 1569, *The Children of the Chapel Stript and Whipt*, whether or not it existed only in the imagination of Thomas Warton, is worth quoting: "Even in her Majesty's chapel do these pretty upstart youths profane the Lord's day by the lascivious writhing of their tender limbs, and gorgeous decking of their apparel, in feigning bawdy fables gathered from the idolatrous heathen poets."[25] If this is forgery, it is remarkably well informed. The presiding genius was certainly that "heathen" poet Ovid, or, as Kempe is made to say, "that writer Metamorphoses."[26] Lyly in his prologue to *Midas* tells us that courtiers are for comedy—"their object is love"—and Jonson, speaking for the revived Chapel company, writes, ". . . take any of our playbooks without a Cupid or a Mercury in it, and burn it for a heretic in poetry."[27] Marlowe as well as Lyly brings Cupid on the stage for the select audience.

A taste for the satirical as well as the amatory is in early evidence at the coterie theatres. In Edwardes' *Damon and Pythias* we have, besides the shafts at the "court vulture" Carisophus, the somewhat equivocal portrait of the witty sophisticate Aristippus. The latter may represent an actual person. When the Prologue insists,

> talking of courtly toys, we do protest this flat—
> We talk of Dionysius court, we mean no court but that!

we are reminded of Lyly's prologue to *Endymion*: ". . . we hope in our time none will apply pastimes, because they are fancies; for their liveth none under the sun that know what to make of the Man in the Moon." In effect, probably even in intention, the warnings are an invitation to look for personal and topical satire; similar protestations become habitual in prologues and epilogues to the coterie plays after 1599. Classical comedy, of course, offered the precedent for critical portraiture. In 1563 William Malim of Eton expresses the academic preference for English plays "quae habeant acumen et leporem."[28] Sidney, deploring popular clownery, extolled the corrective value of the roles of boasters and misers in Roman comedy. Thomas Lodge adds his word: "And if we had some satirical poets nowadays to pen our comedies . . . to decipher the abuses of the world in the person of the notorious offenders, I know we should wisely rid our assemblies of many of your brotherhood . . . but yet our men dare not nowadays presume so much as the old poets might, and therefore they apply their writing to the people's vein. . . ."[29] That "the people's vein" was non-satirical was, as we shall see, soon to be offered as evidence of moral superiority by defenders of the popular stage. The satirical elements in the extant plays of Lyly are mild, but the liberty of the "old poets" and the "vetus comoedia" became sufficiently evident at Paul's after 1589 to lead to the suppression of the company, even though on the officially approved side of the Marprelate controversy. It is probably a Paul's play that is alluded to in *Pappe with a Hatchet* and described in Nashe's *Pasquill's Return*:

Methought Vetus Comaedia began to prick him [Martin Marprelate] at London in the right vein when she brought forth Divinity with a scratched face, holding of her heart as if she were sick, because Martin would have forced her. But missing of his purpose, he left the print of his nails upon her cheeks, and poisoned her with a vomit which he ministered unto her to make her cast up her dignities and promotions.[30]

Were it not that a great deal of theatrical history is lost to us for-
ever, we should probably recognize history repeating itself in the
outcries of the "little eyases" mentioned in *Hamlet* after 1600. By
December, 1590, Spenser could ask in his *Tears of the Muses*,

> Where be the sweet delights of learning's treasure,
> That wont with comic sock to beautify
> The painted Theatres, and fill with pleasure
> The list'ners' eyes and ears with melody . . . ?

Now "seasoned wit and goodly pleasance" are fled the stage, and,

> Instead thereof scoffing scurrility,
> And scornful folly with contempt is crept.[31]

Although Spenser's "pleasant Willy" who has ceased to supply audiences with "joy and jolly merriment" makes us think inevitably of
Shakespeare, the early date of the complaint renders the identification highly improbable; however, it should remind us that as early
as 1590 harshly satirical comedy was known, and was contrasted
with more genial modes. The public theatres themselves were involved in the Marprelate controversy; but they were not suppressed,
and we may deduce that they were at least self-preservingly discreet.

The surviving love-honor-friendship plays of the select audience
before 1590, with their basis in classical myth and their relations to
courtesy literature, seem at first glance, despite their satirical cast, a
world removed from the kind of plays produced for the same audience after 1599. Lyly is thought of as a whimsical, indeed innocent,
writer displaying a verbal refinement unknown to the popular stages.
Nevertheless the progression from Lyly to Marston, from the
amatory and satirical to the erotic and cynical, was more predictable
than at first appears. If, as seems probable, *Endymion* actually
adumbrates a recent imbroglio of treachery, adultery, and bloodshed
among the socially eminent,[32] imperturbably whitewashing the principals, we must postulate an oddly indoctrinated audience. When
this audience was prepared to dispense with disguises, it found dramatists ready-made. A group of writers, antagonistic to popular literature and restive in the employ of the actors—self-made scholars like
Chapman and Jonson, and new recruits among inns of court and

university wits like Marston and Middleton—were ready to secede to the élite theatres and supply a new repertory. Jonson's *Cynthia's Revels*, 1600, although unmistakably influenced by the allegorical myth drama of Lyly, witnesses in its induction an impulse to shoulder out the old stock of Chapel plays—"the *umbrae* or ghosts of some three or four plays departed a dozen years since and recently revived . . . : take heed, boy, if your house be haunted with such hobgoblins, 'twill fright away all your spectators quickly." Marston issues the same warning in the same year to the company at Paul's; they will do well if they have

> good plays; but they produce
> Such musty fopperies of antiquity,
> And do not suit the humorous Age's backs
> With clothes in fashion.[33]

Jonson and Marston were seeking a market, and were ready enough to suit the "humorous Age's backs."

Fifty-five extant plays can be assigned with confidence to the coterie theatres between 1599 and 1613, two-thirds of them written by half a dozen playwrights—Jonson, Marston, Chapman, Middleton, Beaumont, and Fletcher. The most striking thing about the list is the overwhelming preponderance of satirical comedies, all but about a dozen of the total being classifiable as such. Most of the rest are tragedies or tragicomedies. Chronicle plays and romances are at a complete discount. Classical stories and settings have, in the main, been abandoned, but the classical allegiances of the authors are in evidence—in the compression and integration of the dramatic structure, at least suggestive of the "unities," and in the simplified and static nature of the characterization. In all but a few of the plays the theme is sexual transgression, coupled in tragedy with treachery and murder, and in comedy with cupidity and fraud. It is a body of drama preoccupied with lust and murder or lust and money, and with the exhibition of the foolish and the foul.

The marked contrast between the public and the private repertories reflects, of course, divergent attitudes toward life, literature, and morality in the general public and the coterie. Popular drama, in turning from biblical and traditionally homiletic themes to history, fiction, and secular biography, did not lose its ethical cast; indeed, the evidence is that the spiritual satisfaction it supplied increased as time went on. The reading vogue of the prose romances themselves represents not only aroused curiosity but a tendency in the general public to appropriate what had formerly been deemed exclusively aristocratic interests and ideals. They appealed to such readers as Cox, the stone mason of Warwickshire, because, in the words of Lee M. Ellison, "they celebrated accomplishment, the dominating personality triumphing over the forces that hemmed him in."[34] In spite of the absurdity of their dream world, and of elements that strike us as ethically obtuse, inducing the same kind of shock as certain episodes in the Old Testament, their general influence was civilizing. Their titles always promised ladies chaste and fair, and men honorable and brave—"the Vertues of the Valiant and the Memorable Attempts of Magnanimous Minds."[35] In their own way they were furthering the presumed ends of the cultural and religious leaders who, as will be remarked in the next chapter, held them in contempt. A man of Sidney's stature was able at least to glimpse the fact, and his tribute to the ballad of *Chevy Chase* is matched by his brief concession to Orlando, "honest King Arthur," and Amadis. "Truly, I have known men that even with the reading of Amadis de Gaul (which God knoweth wanteth much of a perfect poesie) have found their hearts moved to the exercise of courtesy, liberality, and especially courage."[36] The broadside ballads themselves, whatever their limitations as art, were on the average anything but morally debased,[37] and the increasing flow of general reading matter was doggedly edifying.[38] As in the case of Anthony Munday, the popular playwright was often also a purveyor of romances, ballads, and ethical guides.

That the drama of a general public will conform to national ideals in religion, politics, and personal morality is a condition of its survival and growth; and that the plays of the popular troupes were patriotic and Christian in sentiment, indeed in general harmony with the sermons and homiletic literature of the time, should be no occasion for surprise. Humor, as always, supplied an escape vent or area of tolerance, and, to the end, the sock left on the public stages its trackings of earth; but the obscene and scatological remained within well marked boundaries that were not permitted to expand. The "lewd" speeches in Shakespeare's late romances, although indubitably there, are actually fewer and milder than those in the fifteenth century morality play of *Mankind*. It seems possible that the charge of indecency often leveled at the popular stage was more fully justified in the earlier Tudor period, and that considerable reform had taken place before the time of Marlowe.

There seems to have been a period shortly after the building of the Theatre when the companies consciously adopted a moral policy, and debated in several of their plays the issue of their public influence. Gosson speaks of a *Play of Plays* "shown at the Theatre the three and twentieth of February," 1582. Whatever the previous defects of plays, "They shall be now purged, the matter shall be good, . . . simple, sweet, and honest."[39] In 1580 a play of *Delight* had been performed by Leicester's Men at court. It may be the *Play of Plays* synopsized by Gosson. Life denied delight by Zeal is led into a "wilderness of loathsomeness" to the very brink of death, until rescued by Recreation. Given a choice of pastimes, Life chooses comedies because they can be enjoyed safely, at small expense, and in any weather. Zeal, transformed into Moderate Zeal, only stipulates that in the comedies "the matter be purged, deformities blazed, sin rebuked, honest mirth intermingled, and fit time for the hearing of the same appointed."[40] We are reminded of the self-regulatory measures taken in Hollywood through the code of the Breen office. Although the matter has been eliminated from the published text of 1584, *The Three Ladies of London* as performed in 1581 included in its general commentary upon social virtues and vices a vindication of plays: when asked how they like plays, lustful Love "answers that she detesteth them," but Conscience "like a kind-hearted gentlewoman doth allow them."[41] The wide currency of the claim that the drama was morally beneficial is indicated by the angry refutations of the reformers: "Seek to withdraw these fellows from the Theatre unto the sermon, they will say, By the preacher they may be edified, but by the player both edified and delighted."[42] Philip

Stubbes considered it "blasphemy intolerable" that some should hold opinion "that they be as good as sermons, and that many a good example may be learned out of them."[43] The successive letters of condemnation sent by the Lord Mayor of London to the privy council take cognizance of the claim but insist that plays "move wholly to imitation and not to the avoiding of those vices which they represent."[44]

The idea of imitation—but imitation of virtue, not vice—was actually espoused in the creed of the popular entertainers. The few pamphleteers who defended the drama sometimes spoke of its exposure of vice,[45] but those most closely associated with the popular stage stressed the salutary effects of examples of virtue. Whereas comedies once "smelt of Plautus," now

the lewdness of the gods is altered and changed to the love of young men, force to friendship, rapes to marriage, wooing allowed by assurance of wedding, privy meetings of bachelors and maidens on the stage, not as murderers that devour the good name each of other in their minds, but as those that desire to be made one in heart.[46]

What are we taught? "Peradventure you will say that by these kind of plays the authors instruct us how to love with constancy, to sue with modesty, and to loathe whatsoever is contrary unto this."[47] As for the plays of war,

first, for the subject of them (for the most part) it is borrowed out of our English Chronicles, wherein our forefathers valiant acts (that have lain long buried in rusty brass and wormeaten books) are revived, and they themselves raised from the grave of oblivion and brought to plead their ancient honors in open presence, than which what can be sharper reproof to these degenerate, effeminate days of ours?[48]

It is from Thomas Heywood that we get the fullest and most ardent declaration of the creed of the leading London troupes during the generation preceding his *Apology* of 1608–1612. Plays, he states explicitly, disseminate among the populace literary culture and instruction in citizenship. In addition, they appeal to the best in man's nature:

Is thy mind noble? and would'st thou be further stirred up to magnanimity? Behold upon the stage thou may'st see Hercules, Achilles, Alexander, Caesar . . . Our scenes afford thee store of men to shape your lives by, who be frugal, loving, gentle, trusty, without soothing, and in all things temperate. Would'st thou be honorable, just, friendly, moderate, devout, merciful, and loving concord? . . . Women likewise that are chaste are by us extolled and encouraged in their virtues.[49]

The most impressive feature of Heywood's plea is its confident affirmation of preexistent moral sensibilities in the general public such as will surely respond to cultivation:

What English blood seeing the person of any bold Englishman presented and doth not hug his fame and honey at his valor, pursuing him in his enterprise with his best wishes, and, as being wrapt in contemplation, offers to him in his heart all prosperous performance, as if the personator were the man personated, so bewitching a thing is lively and well-spirited action, that it hath power to new-mould the hearts of the spectators and fashion them to the shape of any noble and notable attempt.[50]

No great array of commendatory verse precedes Heywood's pamphlet, but the lines of Arthur Hopton at least prove he had read the work he praises,

Brave men, brave acts, being bravely acted too,
Makes, as men see things done, desire to do.

When the theatrical industry had become stabilized in London, there was too much at stake for the actors to disregard the codes either of the citizens who could end their prosperity by boycott or of the authorities who could end their very existence by administrative fiat. Religious and municipal enemies of the drama were forced to build their case upon patristic references to the Roman mimes, isolated disorders in the playhouses, alleged ill effects of scenes of cozenage or love-making, and such details as oaths and ribald jests. It is remarkable how few are the instances in which serious objection was taken to the plays of the popular theatres, either by the public or by the responsible authorities. The only play by Shakespeare for which there is a record of official action is *Richard II*, and umbrage in this case was taken only to the meanings which could be read into the play at its revival on the eve of the Essex rebellion. Although the Admiral's Men made what capital they could of Shakespeare's slip in retaining from his source the name of a Lollard martyr for his fat rogue in *Henry IV*, the public took the character to its bosom even before he had been redubbed Falstaff. Jonson told Drummond that he was accused of popery and treason in *Sejanus* by Northampton,[51] but all we know is that the Globe audience disliked the play. The *Isle of Dogs* brought governmental wrath upon its authors, Nashe and Jonson, and upon the entire theatrical profession, but it is noteworthy that the play was performed by neither of the regular companies of 1596–1597 but by "inferior players" at the Swan.[52] The companies recognized that it was to their advantage to cooperate with the censor, and until Shakespeare's retirement there is no evidence that any of them ever aimed at a success through notoriety. While the religious and political orthodoxy of the plays may be partly adventitious, since an Edmund Tilney or a George Buc was so potent in the affairs of the players, the same cannot be said of the appeals to magnanimity, and the glorification of courage and chastity. Such matters did not reside in the province of the censor.

When we turn to the literary setting, moral program, and public relations of the select playhouses, we find ourselves in a different world. Romances, ballads, and ethical guides do not give us the literary climate of Blackfriars and Paul's. Among most of the habitués a familiarity with the lighter Latin classics and the Renaissance courtesy works may be assumed; the vogue for the abstruse in serious plays—for "strong lines"—is probably related to the reading of reflective works of the less taxing kind, some of them skeptical and despairing in tone. But the truly smart reading matter in the decade before 1599 was erotic and satirical verse. In a steady stream appeared Lodge's *Glaucus and Scylla*, Marlowe's *Ovid's Elegies* and *Hero and Leander*, Shakespeare's *Venus and Adonis*, Daniel's *Complaint of Rosamund*, Constable's *Shepherd's Song to Venus and Adonis*, Barnfield's *Affectionate Shepherd*, Chapman's *Ovid's Banquet of Sense*, Drayton's *Endymion and Phoebe*, Edwards' *Cephalus and Procris* and *Narcissus*, and Marston's *Metamorphosis of Pygmalion's Image*. The flesh had been discovered. Appearing synchronously with these works, and occasionally appealing to the same interest, was the spate of satires supposedly in imitation of Horace, Juvenal, Persius, and Martial. Partly anticipated in tone by the prose pamphlets of Nashe, Lodge, and Greene, came, beside the early verse of John Donne, Lodge's *Fig for Momus*, Hall's *Virgidemiarum*, Marston's *Certain Satires* and *Scourge of Villainy*, Guilpin's *Skialetheia*, Bastard's *Chrestoleros*, Rankins' *Seven Satires*, Middleton's (?) *Microcynicon*, and the epigrams of Davies, Harington, and Weever. Items from both lists were among the works condemned to be burnt after the restraining order of the Archbishop of Canterbury in 1599.[53]

That the "comicall satyres" of Jonson and others were influenced by the formal characteristics of the nondramatic verse at the turn of the century has been demonstrated by Professor Campbell;[54] the relationship between the satires of the bookstalls and the stages is undeniable. We may guess, however, that if the private theatres had been operating in the nineties, they would have had to cater to the taste for the erotic and satirical long before the time of the Archbishop's restraining order. Certainly after 1599, both the erotic and the satirical strains were channeled into the theatres of the coterie. The resulting repertory is morally ambiguous. One way of catering to a taste for the satirical and erotic is to satirize the erotic. A curious example in the nondramatic verse is Marston's *Metamorphosis of Pygmalion's Image*. Were it not for the author's protest of his moral intention, the reader would never suspect the work of being anything but pornographic. A similar blurring of focus, and the fact that justice is not impartially administered, prove troublesome in most of the coterie comedies. Social distinctions are silently invoked, and the cheat and libertine who is a gentleman is treated differently from the cheat and libertine who is a tradesman, so that inferiority in rank rather than in virtue bears the ultimate onus of attack. Nothing of this kind appears in the plays of Shakespeare and the other popular writers. It does not follow that the playwrights of Blackfriars and Paul's were consciously immoral. Human effort is paralyzed without self-justification, and the writers eagerly sought sanctions. Jonson is almost as fanatical about his moral as about his literary superiority. When Crites of *Cynthia's Revels* fears that the court will feel abused by his "ironical confederacy," he is reassured by Mercury:

> The better race in court
> That have the true nobility call'd virtue,
> Will apprehend it as a grateful right
> Done to their separate merit.[55]

Jonson and, in their strangely incoherent fashion, Chapman and probably even Marston were sincere in their moral aims, or at least in their rationalizations. One feels less confident about the rest. As a group, the coterie playwrights set up as physicians of the commonwealth. The goddess Cynthia herself counsels that sores must be lanced or "all will putrefy."[56] Just as an emetic had been administered in the Marprelate play of 1589, so is one administered to Crispinus in Jonson's *Poetaster* of 1601. Marston's Malevole in *The Malcontent*, says

> Tut, a pitiful surgeon makes a dangerous sore,
> I'll tent thee to the ground.[57]

Boils, sores, infections, poxes are so constantly probed, lanced, and cauterized in this body of drama as to suggest at least to one critic a sadistic impulse.[58] The medical principle is applied in techniques other than verbal surgery. Characters are encouraged in their ill designs by other characters—agents of the dramatist, like Marston's Freevil and Hercules—so that their vice will reach an "impostume" and burst. Each dramatist, while inclined to suspect the others of mere railing, assumes that he himself realizes an ideal of honesty and downrightness:

> what is honest, you may freely think,
> Speak what you think, and write what you do speak,
> Not bound to servile soothings.[59]

In consequence of their kind of honesty, the chorister playwrights sailed close to the wind of libel suits and action by the censor. Individual instances of their daring seem rather admirable, especially when satire was directed at James and his corrupt court; however, somewhat damaging to their standing as reformers is the fact that the same authors who wrote the satirical plays were, as writers of masks, the official eulogizers of the Stuart family. Furthermore, the tendency for the select plays to give offense was of long standing. A Chapel play of 1559 had contained "such matter that they were commanded to leave off";[60] Edwardes had received some kind of check before writing *Damon and Pythias,* and the *Game of Cards* of 1582 was considered as "somewhat too plain."[61] This was considerably before the anti-Marprelate plays at Paul's had created their fatal scandal. The record after 1600 is one of yearly contretemps. In 1601 Jonson's *Poetaster,* although directed primarily against the popular theatres and poetic rivals, contained enough subsidiary satire to incense members of the legal and military professions.[62] About 1602 Chapman's *Sir Giles Goosecap* featured the "drunken humor" of one Lady Furnifall, who was evidently identifiable since the scenes were eliminated before the publication of the play.[63] In 1603 the same author's lost play, *The Old Joiner of Aldgate,* dramatized the notorious episodes preceding the marriage of the Reverend Dr. Milward of Christ Church to the auctioned heiress, Agnes Howe, while the case was still in litigation, so that both Chapman and the Master of Paul's were forced to answer at law.[64] In 1604 Daniel was called before the privy council because his *Philotas* was suspected of being a commentary upon the Essex rebellion. In 1605 *Eastward Ho,*[65] for its hits at the Scots and King James's new-made knights, sent Jonson and Chapman to prison and Marston into hiding. In 1606 Day's *Isle of Gulls* repeated with variations the offense of *Eastward Ho* so that "sundry were committed to Bridewell." In 1608 an unnamed and unpublished play satirized the personal habits of James and his favorites; Marston was summoned before the privy council and detained in prison, whereupon he sought a sphere of wider usefulness in the ministry. It was also in 1608 that the French ambassador complained about Chapman's *Charles Duke of Byron,* with the result that the play was drastically curtailed and the author impelled to seek "shelter." In 1609 "impertinent exception" was taken to Jonson's *Epicoene* (possibly by Lady Arabella Stuart),[66] and the author felt called upon to write a prologue of defense. Marston's *Fawn* and Beaumont's *Woman Hater* also skirted dangerous territory.[67]

In the plays that offended, lines may have been added to the licensed texts, or personal satire pointed up by the costumes and mimicry of the performers. None of them, at least in the published versions, is so objectionable as other coterie plays, like Middleton's *Family of Love* and Sharpham's *The Fleire*, for which there exist no records of reprisal. The most subversive plays were directed at minority religious sects or London citizens as a class. Although legal action followed only when the offense was political or touched persons of consequence, official cognizance was taken of the general tone of the plays when the writ for recruiting choirboys was renewed in 1606. Association with performances at Blackfriars was expressly forbidden, "for that it is not fit or decent that such as should sing the praises of God Almighty should be trained up or employed in such lascivious and profane exercises."[68]

That the Blackfriars company was permitted to continue at all after the offense given James in 1608 suggests that it was more privileged than the public companies. One detail in the regulation of the Blackfriars organization is curious. After 1603 their patent stipulated that their plays receive "the approbation and allowance of Samuel Daniel" at a £10 yearly fee; but Daniel himself considered his post as a sinecure, awarded "not in regard of the pains to be taken" but "in respect of his pains formerly taken in procuring the said patents."[69] What must have occurred is that friends at court had secured for a deserving poet a pension in the form of a claim on Blackfriars earnings, leaving the Master of the Revels still responsible for the actual licensing of plays.[70] Michael Drayton's association with the King's Revels company in 1607–1608 suggests that a similar provision had been made for him at Paul's. The Master of the Revels certainly continued to collect his licensing fees, but the existence of Daniel's post may have enabled the Blackfriars group to slip certain plays into production unread by either censor. When Daniel himself became embroiled in 1604 on the charge of allegorizing about Essex in his *Philotas*,[71] he protested that much of the play had been written before the rebellion, and that it had been given to the stage only with great reluctance. The play is quite different from the usual fare at Blackfriars, and Daniel is telling the truth when he proclaims his affinities with the singers of "Eliza's reign":

> And never had my harmless pen at all
> Distain'd with any loose immodesty,
> Nor ever noted to be toucht with gall,
> To aggravate the worst man's infamy.
>
> . . . .
>
> And therefore, since I have outliv'd the date
> Of former grace, acceptance, and delight;
> I would my lines, late-born beyond the fate
> Of her spent line, had never come to light—
> So had I not been tax'd for wishing well,
> Nor now mistaken by the censuring Stage,
> Nor in my fame and reputation fell,
> Which I esteem more than what all the age
> Or th' earth can give. But years hath done this wrong,
> To make me write too much, and live too long.[72]

It was not longevity but guilt by association that afflicted poor Daniel: Blackfriars was not the setting for "grace, acceptance, and delight."

Of course the managers of the private theatres were not interested in disseminating infection; their only guilt was to be embarked on a commercial enterprise. Profits, not particular kinds of plays, were their concern, and they would have let the boys sing canticles had it proved financially rewarding. Their dilemma is interesting. Prices had to be kept high to preserve the distinctive exclusiveness of the theatres, but those who paid the high prices demanded their money's worth in game of dangerously high flavor. One of the penalties of providing such fare was that the chances of having plays ordered for performance at court were small. At no time in the history of the coterie theatres can their plays properly be called "court" plays although the term was used by Lyly's publisher in 1632. Most of Lyly's plays were *courtly*, but neither they nor the plays of his contemporaries were court plays in the sense that masks were court masks, and Walter Montague's *Shep-*

herd's Paradise of 1633 was a court pastoral;[73] they were not generated in the court or designed exclusively for court consumption. If
plays performed at court be considered as court plays, the vast majority of them will be found in the repertory of the popular troupes.
Only before 1577 was any chorister company the favorite with the
Office of the Revels. Between 1577 and 1582, when both Paul's and
the first Blackfriars were operating, Sussex's Men acted at court
more frequently than either of the boys' companies, the adult
troupes in general performing thirty-one times to the boys' sixteen.[74]
The contrast is even more marked after 1599, when the plays of the
boys ceased even to be *courtly*. Marston's spokesman of 1600 says
of the Paul's company that "the apes in time will do it handsomely"
and "will come one day into the court of requests";[75] and Jonson
certainly had high hopes that *Cynthia's Revels* would bring him to
the Queen's favorable attention, but the boys never did in any conspicuous way come into the "court of requests." Between 1600
and 1613, the select companies were chosen to perform less than
forty times, the popular companies more than two hundred and
forty, with such plays as *The Merchant of Venice, Shoemaker's
Holiday, How to Learn a Woman to Woo*, and *Merry Devil of Edmonton* figuring as "court" plays.[76] If the courtiers of the period
composed any considerable sector of the audience at Blackfriars and
Paul's, they were forced to display a distinction between their official and unofficial tastes in drama, and the proprietors of the little
theatres were forced to accept their patronage in terms of shillings
rather than £10 court fees.

The rapidity with which the plays at Blackfriars and Paul's assumed their distinctive character after 1599 indicates that the tastes
of the coterie were already formed and able to exercise a decisive
influence. The note of exultation over the "good, gentle audience"
was muted as time elapsed. In 1601 one of Marston's characters says,

> This is the strain that chokes the theatres,
> That make them crack with full-stuff't audience,
> This is your humor only in request,
> Forsooth to rail,[77]

and while in this early instance the criticism might have been leveled
at both the general and the select audiences, in consequence of the
war of the theatres, the same type of remark later was aimed frequently and exclusively at the coterie. Day's induction to his *Isle
of Gulls* gives us the neatest summary of the demands of the spectators at Blackfriars—for bitterness, bawdry, and "strong lines":

First Gentleman.
... Is't anything critical? Are lawyers' fees and citizens' wives laid open in
it? I love to hear vice anatomized and abuse let blood in the master vein.
Is there any great man's life charactered in't? ... and there not be wormwood water and copperas in't, I'll not like it.

Second Gentleman.
. . . Is there any good bawdry in't, jests of an ell deep and a fathom
broad, good cuckolding? May a couple of young setters-up learn to do
well in't? Give me a scene of venery that will make a man's spirits stand
on their tiptoes and die his blood in a deep scarlet, like your Ovid's *Ars
Amandi:* there flows the true springhead of poetry and the very crystal
font of Parnassus.

Third Gentleman.
. . . give me a stately-penned history, as this: 'The rugged winds with
rude and ragged ruffs,' &c . . . if it be not high-written, both your poet
and the house, too, lose a friend of me.

Dramatists like Day and Dekker, who wrote for both types of theatre, had to learn the trick of the chameleon. Robert Daborne, who
in 1613 had been writing for Henslowe's heirs to a private playhouse
clientele, the Lady Elizabeth's Men at Whitefriars, took note of the
fact that the Hope was being put in use as a second theatre for the
company: "my other [play] out of your book . . . I will undertake
shall make as good a play for your public house as ever was played,
for which I desire but ten pounds."[78]

That *the drama's laws the drama's patrons give* could be illustrated by many incidental details. The popular audience demanded
the presence of the clown. He was worked into nearly every play,
if only for a few moments to bring "joy o' th' worm" to a Cleopatra.
Often his lines are inadequate to reveal the effect of his role; even
though he spake no more than was set down for him, he could

empty his bag of comical tricks, the grimaces and grotesque gestures. *Tamburlaine* itself, despite the prologue disdaining "such con-
ceits as clownage keeps in pay," contained "fond and frivolous matter" of "some vain conceited fondlings greatly gaped at," which the
publisher sternly omitted from the published text.[79] Whetstone's
complaint of 1578 that, "to make mirth, they make a clown companion with a king" was fiercely repeated by Joseph Hall in 1597;[80]
yet, eight years later, Lear, Shakespeare's kingliest king, was still
thus companioned. About five years later still, in Heywood's *Golden
Age*, a particularly rustic clown is provided as companion to Jupiter! The speeches of the clown were *clownish*, obtuse and fumbling,
less funny in themselves than designed to give the company specialist,
by devices now lost, an opportunity to be funny; it was not left for
neo-classical adapters or modern journalists to discover that these
speeches were not the quintessence of wit. Blackfriars and Paul's
took considerable pride in expunging the clowns from their plays.
The academic author of *The Pilgrimage to Parnassus* had mocked
the popular custom by letting a character enter "drawing a clown
in with a rope."[81] Simple Onion of Jonson's *Case Is Altered* says he
disliked the one play he saw at Blackfriars because "the fool came
out not a jot."[82]

The popular audience was as fond of the old as the select audience
of the new. In *The Downfall of Robert Earl of Huntington*, performed by the Admiral's Men in 1598, choral commentary is provided by the poet Skelton, and an apologetic note is struck because
the play features Robin Hood without the traditional "jests" and
"the merry morrices of Friar Tuck"—these, remarks Skelton rather
plaintively, "have been shown before."[83] In *A Warning for Fair
Women*, performed by Shakespeare's company about the same time,
a concluding speech by Tragedy explains that a revenge motif
could not be worked in because the known facts of the case would
not permit:

> And should I add or else diminish aught,
> Many of these spectators then could say
> I have committed error in my play.

The power of the audience is always acknowledged: one recalls the epilogue to 2 *Henry IV*, almost asking directly if more of Sir John Falstaff is desired, or Lantern Leatherhead in Jonson's *Bartholomew Fair* describing the way classical themes are modified lest they be "too learned and poetical,"[84] or Webster sadly lamenting that at the Red Bull his *White Devil* failed to obtain what chiefly graces a tragedy, "a full and understanding auditory."[85]

The known repertories of all companies until 1613 are presented in Appendix B, with the items so arranged as to permit comparison of the plays in the public and private theatres in various subperiods, the latter determined by the rise and fall of the more important companies. The few moral interludes are marked "M," the remaining plays "C," "T," and "H," in conformity with the rough mode of classification adapted by the publishers of Shakespeare's first folio, where plays ending in a resolution of difficulties (and usually marriage) are Comedies, plays ending in deaths Tragedies, and plays involving English civil and foreign conflicts Histories. In the public theatres, the plays, exclusive of three moral interludes, are in round numbers 49 per cent comedies, 30 per cent tragedies, and 21 per cent histories. (Shakespeare's own plays closely approximate this popular distribution except that he provided more than the average number of history plays.) In the select theatres, the plays, exclusive of one moral interlude, are 85 per cent comedies and 15 per cent tragedies. In view of the prominence of history plays in our conception of the Elizabethan drama, it is notable that, so far as we know, none ever appeared in the coterie theatres. Certain types forming prominent subheads under the classifications Comedy and Tragedy are also missing from the select repertories: there are few romantic or folk comedies, no domestic or middle-class tragedies, and no heroical biographies except where, as in Chapman's *Bussy D'Ambois* and *Charles Duke of Byron*, qualities that would be popularly construed as defects are paradoxically treated as heroical. To avoid circular processes of argument, the many plays unassigned to particular companies are excluded from analysis in the present study; but the point may here be made that an awareness of the distinction in modes at the two types of theatres would prove an aid to conjecture in assigning such plays; thus, to mention plays of different periods, R. B.'s *Appius and Virginia*, about 1564, Robert Wilson's *Cobbler's Prophecy*, about 1590, and Robert Daborne's *Christian Turned Turk*, about 1610, have been assigned by various scholars[86] to private theatres whereas the internal characteristics of each argue for popular presentation. The plays presented by the King's Men between 1609 and 1613 and by Lady Elizabeth's Men toward the end of the same period have been omitted from the above tabulation, since both companies were occupying both types of theatre and presumably selecting new plays suitable for each. However, the plays of Shakespeare in this period, contrary to a common critical assumption, are popular in type.

Apart from a distinct philosophical and emotional emphasis, the two bodies of drama differ in general outline. The terms "public" and "private" are applicable in a number of ways. The one stage is wide as the world, the other narrow as the gardens of Cynthia or the chambers of the *nouveau riche*. The one repertory addresses itself to the interests of a community, the other to the preoccupations of a clique. The public plays emphasize actions, the private ones attitudes; the public plays valiant or villainous deeds, the private ones clever or stupid schemes. Intimations of difference are available even when there are few actual texts to compare: the Office of the Revels provided for the court performance of the Chapel boys' *Loyalty and Beauty* in 1579 "a garland of grapes and leaves for Bacchus and other of roses for [Venus?]" while for the Hunsdon's Men's *Beauty and Housewifery* of 1582 "one battlement of canvas."[87]

To test the difference between the two bodies of drama, one might sample a relatively short list of plays, chosen from the two columns because parallel in time, parallel in theme, or parallel in authorship. The difference between the two repertories is the difference between Preston's *Cambyses* and Edwardes' *Damon and Pythias;* between Greene's *Friar Bacon* and Peele's *Arraignment of Paris;* Lodge's *Wounds of Civil War* and the anonymous *Wars of Cyrus;* Marlowe's *Tamburlaine* and the work sometimes considered an irrelevance in his canon *The Tragedy of Dido.* In later times it is the

difference between Dekker and Webster's *Sir Thomas Wyatt* writ-
ten for the Worcester's-Queen's Men and *Westward Ho* and *North-
ward Ho* written by the same authors for Paul's, between Day's
work in the popular *Blind Beggar of Bednal Green* and *Travels of
Three English Brothers* and his work in the coterie *Isle of Gulls* and
Law-Tricks; between Middleton's work in *The Honest Whore* and
The Roaring Girl for the Fortune and his *Family of Love* for Paul's.
The distinction emerges no matter how one approaches the plays.
It is especially instructive in plays where similarity in theme would
lead us to expect similarity in treatment. Attempts on the virtue of
citizen wives provide a subject for comedy at both types of theatre,
but the difference between Shakespeare's *Merry Wives of Windsor*
at the Globe and Middleton's plays at Paul's is spectacular. The attempt of a prostitute to gain or retain the love of a married man
was the theme of *The Fair Maid of Bristowe* at the Globe, *How a
Man May Choose a Good Wife from a Bad* at the Red Bull, and
I The Honest Whore at the Fortune; but the three plays stand in mutual contrast to the only one in which the prostitute rather than the
wronged wife is central and her power truly formidable—*The
Dutch Courtesan* of Blackfriars. The career of a profligate is the
theme of *The London Prodigal* at the Globe and *Greene's Tu
Quoque* at the Red Bull; but neither play contains a modicum of the
profligacy of *Ram-Alley* at Whitefriars. The Globe's Flowerdale,
although bad enough, exists chiefly as the occasion of good in others,
and the Red Bull's Spendall is a Galahad in comparison with the
Whitefriars' Smallshanks Jr. *The White Devil* at the Red Bull and
The Insatiate Countess at Whitefriars exploit the same story, but
the plays are as different as defiant self-assertion and nymphomania.
Even the revenge tragedies take on a different stamp: even without
the brilliance of its writing Shakespeare's *Hamlet* would be a different kind of play from Marston's *Antonio's Revenge* with its per-
sonified vices and arbitrary criminality. The difference between the
two repertories is the difference, on the lower reaches of artistic
achievement, between Samuel Rowley and Edward Sharpham, on
the middle reaches between Heywood and Marston, and on the upper reaches between Shakespeare and Jonson, although in this last

apposition the genius of the writers complicates the pattern as genius always must.

Only eight of the plays in the "popular" column as it stands
would seem not out of place in the "select" column: Chapman's
Blind Beggar of Alexandria and *An Humorous Day's Mirth*, Jonson's *Every Man Out of His Humor*, *Sejanus*, and *Volpone*, Shakespeare's *Troilus and Cressida* and *Timon of Athens*, and the anonymous *Revenger's Tragedy*. Even this concession, in respect to the
two plays of Shakespeare, can be made only with strong reservations; and we may note that the plays are the only ones of his about
which there is some doubt of their ever having been acted at all.
As regards the others, it is notable that Chapman's were written before a select theatre was available to him, and that both contain
enough farcical intrigue to disguise somewhat their mordant view
of human character. Jonson's *Every Man Out of His Humor* and
Sejanus were hostilely received by the popular audience, and he himself seems to have been dissatisfied with the ending he was compelled
to give *Volpone*. The *Revenger's Tragedy* in the opinion of the
present author is Middleton's *Viper and Her Brood*, originally written for Paul's.[88]

The extant repertories of the individual companies, public and private, are usually too scanty or too much dominated by a single
writer for us to make confident generalizations. However, the indications are that there was little distinction between the bills of the
theatres within the two categories; what would go at Blackfriars
would go equally well at Paul's and Whitefriars. Among the public
theatres the same thing was probably true, at least until 1603. Although the plays other than Shakespeare's surviving from the Chamberlain's repertory are few, yet *Alarum for London*, *Warning for
Fair Women*, *Thomas Lord Cromwell*, and *The Merry Devil of
Edmonton* are precisely of the kind and quality of those presented
by the Admiral's Men. Undoubtedly the missing repertory of the
company was supplied by the same free-lance dramatists whom we
often miscall the "Henslowe" hacks. After 1603 we may detect
some signs of change. The newly built Fortune and Red Bull were

certainly remote from the more fashionable section of London; and a "neighborhood" influence may be perceptible in Heywood's direct appeals to the apprentices. Shakespeare's company was still playing by the Thames, within easy access of gentle as well as common, and this company, in the upshot, proved to be most interested in absorbing the Blackfriars clientele. True, *The Fair Maid of Bristowe*, *The London Prodigal*, *A Yorkshire Tragedy*, and *The Miseries of Enforced Marriage* are as popular in type as any of the earlier plays; but the company also presented *Sejanus*, *Volpone*, and *The Revenger's Tragedy*, and, as early as 1604, appropriated *The Malcontent* from Blackfriars, with an induction actually defending the *vetus comoedia*. We must always remember that the company retained its old pieces as stock, so that a few new plays would make no striking change in the complexion of its repertory; still, the evidence, such as it is, is suggestive of the coming expansion to Blackfriars and the wooing into the fold of such select dramatists as Beaumont, Fletcher, and Chapman. In the "War of the Theatres," as we shall see, Shakespeare's company was a defender of popular ideals from attacks by the coterie. Then came the company policy, tentative after 1603, and positive after 1608, of stealing the thunder of rivals who were not, at the moment at least, a grave economic threat. The upshot demonstrates that it was a good business move, and one that was soon to be imitated by any company that looked to prosper; but the practical adaptability of these King's Men involved some measure of ethical capitulation. There hovers a dubiety about the situation which might occasion a resigned pursing of lips on our part if we were dealing with a mere group of business associates, but which concerns us more vitally in view of the fact that these associates were also artists—and one of them the artist of our idolatry.

IV

The War of the Theatres

THE *Poetomachia* or "war of the theatres" has been viewed as a picturesque spite-combat between Jonson, Marston, Dekker, and a variable number of additional contenders, and sometimes as an amusing little furore cleverly designed to stimulate theatrical attendance.[1] The episode has even been brushed aside, and the "real" war of the theatres pictured as the commercial and political rivalry of the Burbage and Henslowe interests.[2] The commercial rivalry between the latter was real enough, with the popular troupes ready on occasion to copy, cap, and criticize each other's plays; but in their artistic and ethical program they stood together. The conflict is between them, the "common players" with their repertories, and the "little eyases" who cried out on top of question. Rosencrantz is reliable when he speaks of cuffs between the *poet* and the *player*. In addition it was symptomatic of deep-seated tensions, involving class antagonisms, rival moral philosophies, and, in a fashion, even the issue of ancients *versus* moderns.

Elizabethan attacks upon the popular drama are habitually traced to "puritanism"; but some of the most virulent were differently inspired. A tradition of clerical antagonism to the stage extends from early Christian times through the Middle Ages and Renaissance, and the Calvinists became the most militant of the clerics; but the example of Milton and Bacon should remind us that there were puritans who valued the popular drama and nonpuritans who considered it unworthy of notice. In 1585 an Oxford man made a won-

90

derfully simple distinction: "Ludi scenici sunt vel communes et populares, qui ad scurrilitatem potius quam comitatem referuntur, vel academici, quales sunt comoediae et tragoediae recreationis causa institutae."[3] We may assume from their published pronouncements that Bacon would have let this judgment stand, whereas Milton might have reversed it. Apart from the lyrical testimony to his personal joy in the plays, Milton has left a record of his desire to use the drama as an instrument for inculcating right religious and political ideals.[4] Among academic persons of all sects Bacon's attitude was more typical than Milton's; Shakespeare's species of literary activity was heir to a tradition of disdain stemming less from puritanism than from ancient classical invectives against the *profanum vulgus*.

Attacks upon ballads and romances began in England with the campaign of Erasmus and Vives to establish the study of the Roman poets and historians,[5] and continued in the treatises of educators like Ascham who carried out their program. The drama of the people is mentioned with amused condescension in one of the *Hundred Merry Tales* current in the humanistic circles of the early sixteenth century. A simple-minded priest, after reciting the twelve articles of the creed, adjures his flock: "And if you believe not me, then for a more surety and sufficient authority, go your way to Coventry, and there you shall see them all playe[d] in Corpus Christi play."[6] Views that strike us as enlightened, amusing, or excusably militant when uttered by the pioneering humanists lose their attraction as they harden into dogma or begin to reflect class bigotry. Clichés of exclusiveness from classical literature become current among men overinsistent upon their own university status, or disinclined to allow the rank and file any form of literary amusement whatever. Ballads, romances, stage plays, and ethical tracts seemed to be a lamentable travesty of all that true literature should be, and an irritating reminder of self-assertion among the masses. Moreover, mere scriveners' sons could write plays, and "every gross-brained idiot" could produce a pamphlet "of the praise of pudding-pricks" or "write a treatise of Tom Thumb or the Exploits of Untruss."[7] In the satires in the select theatres, sneers are directed not only at popular plays but at such works as the *Gesta Romanorum* and *The Mirror for Magistrates*,[8] the *Sick Man's Salve*[9] and the *Knight of the Sun*. Jonson's Asotus, who considers himself "a little humanitian" because he has read the latter, is of course a citizen's son.[10]

It is perhaps not surprising that the self-made scholars, Jonson and Chapman, became the most vociferous opponents of merely popular literature. "The profane multitude I hate," said Chapman, "and only consecrate my strange poems to those searching spirits whom learning hath made noble and nobility sacred."[11] The approval of the few is more worth than "the passport of a whole city of others,"[12] and so far as readers of his more élite works are concerned, "Away, ungodly vulgars, far away!"[13] Ultimately Chapman tried to erect a philosophy on the principle that anything comprehensible to the vulgar must be false. In the self-portrait in *Sir Giles Goosecap*, Clarence with his paradoxes convinces the admiring Momford that

> illiterate custom grossly errs
> Almost in all traditions she prefers.[14]

The "almost" disappears in the verse epistle to *Andromeda Liberata*:

> As nothing under heaven is more remov'd
> From truth and virtue than opinions prov'd
> By vulgar voices, so is nought more true
> Nor soundly virtuous than things held by few.

Jonson had a clearer head than Chapman and never devised such easy formulas for the discovery of ultimate truth; but his antagonism to the many is often as stridently expressed.

As purely academic literature demonstrated its sterility, in contrast with the fruitfulness of classically fertilized native strains, we should expect a retreat on the part of the critics; but we seldom detect any. Sidney's comments upon English drama, we feel sure, would have been different if written after the appearance of Marlowe and Shakespeare; still, to Joseph Hall, writing in 1597, Marlowe spells only "huff-cap terms and thund'ring threats" and Shakespeare is indistinguishable from the herd of playwrights whom it would be ludicrous to compare with "famous" Seneca. Since Hall gives us

as sustained a piece of "criticism" of the popular drama as any produced during the first decade of Shakespeare's activity, he must be
quoted at length:

> Such soon as some brave-minded hungry youth
> Sees fitly frame to his wide-strained mouth,
> He vaunts his voice upon an hired stage
> With high-set steps and princely carriage;
> Now swooping in side-robes of royalty,
> That erst did scrub in lousy brokery;
> There if he can, with terms Italianate
> Big-sounding sentences and words of state,
> Fair patch me up his pure iambic verse,
> He ravishes the gazing scaffolders:
> Then certes was the famous Corduban,
> Never but half so high tragedian!
> Now, lest such frightful shows of Fortune's fall
> And bloody tyrant's rage should chance appal
> The dead-struck audience, midst the silent rout
> Comes leaping in a self-misformed lout,
> And laughs and grins and frames his mimic face,
> And justles straight into the prince's place;
> Then doth the theatre echo all aloud
> With gladsome noise of that applauding crowd.
> A goodly hotch-potch! when vile russetings
> Are matched with monarchs and with mighty kings;
> A goodly grace to sober tragic muse,
> When each base clown his clumsy fist doth bruise,
> And show his teeth in double rotten row
> For laughter at his self-resembled show.
> Meanwhile our poets in high parliament
> Sit watching every word and gesturement,
> Like curious censors of some doughty gear,
> Whispering their verdict in their fellow's ear:
> Woe to the word whose margent in their scroll
> Is noted with a black, condemning coal.
> But if each period might the synod please,
> Ho! bring the ivy-boughs and bands of bays.
> Now when they part and leave the naked stage,
> 'Gins the bare hearer in a guilty rage
> To curse and ban and blame his likerous eye
> That thus hath lavished his late half-penny:

Shame that the Muses should be bought and sold
For every peasant's brass on each scaffold!

. . . .

Too popular is tragic poesy
Straining his tip-toes for a farthing fee,
And doth beside in rhymeless numbers tread,
Unbid iambics flow from careless head.[15]

A satirist must overstate, and it is interesting to observe one detail of Hall's overstatement: the actual admission fee of a penny
diminishes to the even more contemptible *halfpenny* and *farthing*.
It would be tedious to enumerate all the instances in which the actors were taunted by mention of the penny.

Hall is not quite the typical university man: many such men enjoyed, some even admired, the popular plays; but these were not
the ones for whom a classical education was a hard-won social distinction and a sole hope for worthy employment. Above all, they
were not the ones who had been reduced to competing with non-
university playwrights. The antagonisms involved in the war of the
theatres find expression among the university "predecessors of
Shakespeare" who wrote for the popular stage (and, on occasion,
even defended it) in Marlowe's allusion to "riming mother wits,"
Nashe's attack upon those "taffety fools" the "vainglorious tragedians" and Latinless scriveners who "busy themselves with the en-
deavors of art," Lodge's resolve to write no more "for penny-
knaves delight," and Greene's slur upon "those anticks garnisht in
our colors" including the upstart crow and Shake-scene who supposed himself "as well able to bumbast out a blank verse as the best
of you."[16] These dramatists seemed to resent equally that university men were forced to write for the actors, and that non-univer-
sity men, such as Kyd and Shakespeare, were ready to do so; their
immense service to the art of the theatre was rendered unwillingly
and sometimes even with a sense of shame. Their sentiments were
repeated by others as the actors continued to recruit writers from
all educational levels and from their own ranks. In 1600, Samuel
Rowlands, like Greene, arraigns the poets:

Will you stand spending your invention's treasure,
To teach stage-parrots speak for penny pleasure,
While you yourselves, like music-sounding lutes,
Fretted and strung, gain them their silken suits?[17]

About 1601, the anonymous author of the dramatic exposition of the scholar's hard lot, *The Return from Parnassus*, puts the case in the words of Studioso:

Better it is 'mongst fiddlers to be chief
Than at a player's trencher beg relief.
But is't not strange, these mimic apes should prize
Unhappy scholars at a hireling rate?
Vile world! that lifts them up to high degree,
And treads us down in groveling misery.

.   .   .   .

With mouthing words that better wits have framed
They purchase lands and now esquires are named.[18]

Studioso echoes Nashe in harking back to a time when actors carried their playing gear in knapsacks. It was natural that the university men attributed the prosperity of the actors to the literary quality of the plays written by themselves, without weighing in the enterprise of the companies in establishing themselves in London, or the financial risks of the investors in theatres. It was enough that the actors wore satin suits.

The scholars objected simultaneously to the prostitution of their muses and to the low rates paid for prostitution. The high-minded Chrisogonus of Marston's *Histriomastix* is typical: he is disdainful of Sir Oliver Owlet's Men on general principles, but his immediate grievance is that they refuse his demand of £10 per play. The current rate in 1599 was about £6. From our vantage point it seems shockingly low, whether paid to university men or a poor "dresser of plays about the town" like Thomas Dekker. The latter's *Old Fortunatus* and *The Shoemaker's Holiday*, both written in 1599, still earn their publishers yearly more than the total sum paid their ancient author. Dekker and Chettle's *Patient Grissill* was a run-of-the-mill play; but, if it had contained nothing of worth but the work song and lullaby of old Janiculo, £10 or any other sum we might mention would be as absurd a purchase price as the one actually paid. It is difficult to put a price on poetry. In terms of the market-place, the £6 rate was quite fair. It represented to an acting com-pany one item in expenses that included theatre rental, replenish-ment of wardrobe, wages to hirelings, licensing fees, and the like; and it was paid as a flat rate without reference to the possible failure of the play. If the play was an average success, the £6 in 1599 rep-resented about one-fourteenth of the sum the actors would gross from its performance—a share that the modern writer for the New York, London, or Hollywood stages could scarcely envisage in his dreams. In Jacobean times the purchase price of plays rose much more sharply than wage rates generally, and the initial price was sometimes supplemented when the play showed early promise of unusual earning power. In 1603 Chapman received from Paul's for his *Old Joiner of Aldgate* £13. 6s. 8d.,[19] a sum considerably above Henslowe's current rate, and it may be that writers had been able to make good at the private theatres their demand for higher pay-ments, but Chapman had been paid above average rates by Henslowe himself. We must note, finally, that the prices paid by the actors for plays, however low, were higher than those paid for free-lance writing in general. For a nondramatic work of equal length, an author would receive, in a typical instance, about £2 from the publisher and £2 from the dedicatee,[20] thus preserving his sense of personal dignity at the cost of a £2 deficit. Whatever the rights of the case, the charge that the actors were niggardly passed into gen-eral currency, and poets unassociated with the stage casually affirmed that it was

> a player's vice to be unjust,
> To verse not yielding coin.[21]

The Studiosos of the time would have resented writing for the popular stage, no matter what prices might have prevailed. They had pictured careers of affluence and honor, only to learn that educated youth was in oversupply, and that even posts in country grammar schools were hard to come by. The literature of the time is filled with the plaints of the neglected scholar. That the scholar-gentleman

should be in the employ of the actor-artisan was a humiliating re-
versal of the proper order of things. In the golden age of letters, the
poets had been protégés and companions of Maecenas, the counselor
of an Emperor; and, for the English aspirant to the laurel, self-
identification with Virgil or Horace was not difficult. Although the
universities had known him not, Jonson cast himself as Horace in
his *Poetaster*, and in that play as in *Cynthia's Revels* made clear his
conviction that his place was near the throne. The aristocracy in
England as elsewhere had been the traditional patrons of the arts,
and the poets instinctively sought a noble protector rather than a
public market. The trouble was that patrons had become so few.
There is a current tendency to defend the Elizabethan aristocracy
against the charge of indifference to the welfare of those who were
enriching the age with a national literature,[22] and it is true that many
individual instances of generosity may be found. But it is also true
that the generosity was often indiscriminate and nearly always inter-
mittent, affected as it was by the economic pressures bearing hard
upon the old landowners. Poets and scholars were reckoned among
the more dispensable items when household disbursements needed
curtailing, and the lives of many dependent authors were troubled
by periods of distress when patronage was withdrawn. The most
significant thing about Shakespeare's seeking a patron in the Earl of
Southampton in 1593 and 1594, when plague had closed the theatres,
is that he never repeated the gesture, the inference being that he had
correctly assessed the situation in his day. Francis Meres, although
admiring the "glorified phrase and quaint action" of "our witty
comedians and stately tragedians," laments in 1598 that *by the public
stage*, "for lack of patrons (Oh ingrateful and damned age) our poets
are solely or chiefly maintained, countenanced, and patronized."[23]
Conservatively, the poets, or such of them as stood upon the ancient
dignity of their vocation, identified their interests with those of the
straitened aristocracy and resented dependence upon other segments of society. The character Pyeboord is pathetic as he shows
off the lodgings of his imaginary patron:

 I can tell you, I have great hope to have my chamber here shortly, nay,
 and diet too, for he's the most free-heartedst gentleman where he takes,

you would little think it! And what a fine gallery were here for me to
walk and study and make verses.[24]

To the modern mind, the poet's preference seems sometimes to have
been for sycophancy—for standing literally at a gentleman's trencher
rather than figuratively at an actor's. But these were former times.
Neither the "stinkard" with his penny nor the actor with his £6
resembled Maecenas; and the financial debility of putative patrons
seemed somehow related to the prosperity of all enterprising up-
starts, including the actors.

The unlearned dramatist was deemed no better than an actor; indeed he sometimes was an actor. Jonson lived down his brief
career on the stage, and by sheer force of character won a place
among those predisposed to snub him. It is impossible to overestimate the effect of a university degree upon an individual's social
attitudes in the period under scrutiny. In earlier times the universities had belonged to relatively humble folk destined for religious
orders, and Chaucer's unassuming Clerk of Oxford was their ideal
product; the aristocracy had received their education in the manor
house and in the saddle. But in the mid-sixteenth century the nobility
and landed gentry had begun sending up their sons, creating at Oxford and Cambridge a privileged and glamorous class. Something
like the "gold coast" of our modern universities was created, with its
unsettling effect on the more susceptible of the students from families of lower rank. Confusion in values, and a certain amount of
snobbery, are the inevitable products of such a situation. Elizabethan
biography is rich in illustrations. A Marlowe or a Greene is a young
man uprooted. He is detached from his class but without the means
of becoming fully accredited in any higher class, yet with heightened
aspirations; discontent and disillusion stalk him from the moment he
steps out into the world. The Cambridge *Parnassus* plays are revealing in a way unsuspected by their authors. Our sympathies go
out to the youths who have made the difficult ascent of the Muses'
hill, but their notion of their place in the commonwealth is sadly
defective. Education to them seems to be something automatically
conveying distinction and deserving reward, principally in the form

of leisure to enjoy the arts; all forms of service, except possibly the holding of a rich benefice, seem contemptible.

The English public, while recognizing the wisdom of properly employing scholars, was disinclined to take the scholar *per se* at his own valuation. Laureo, in *Patient Grissill* as performed at the Rose, has spent nine years at the University and returns home unemployed. He laments that from his father he has "pulled more than he could spare"—

> Is't not a shame for me that am a man,
> Nay more, a scholar, to endure such need
> That I must prey on him whom I should feed?[25]

His contrition is most engaging, but when he remarks that he is too proud to do handicraft work, the servant Babulo asks him if he is too proud to eat, and bids him weave baskets with the rest of the family:

> Work apace, apace, apace, apace
> Honest labor bears a lovely face.[26]

In *The Whore of Babylon* at the Fortune, the scholar's discontent is shown transforming itself into treason to the state, when Campeius cries out against his beggary:

> I was not born to this, not school'd to this,
> My parents spent not wealth on me to this.[27]

In *Thomas Lord Cromwell* at the Globe, the scholar's discontent spurs him to the effort that wins high political office and a chance to honor the old peasant his father. The popular pattern of sentiment emerges. The scholar, like the soldier, is a pillar of the state; but he must demonstrate his usefulness and retain his contact with family and fellow citizens. In contrast Chrisogonus in *Histriomastix* at Paul's, and Crites in *Cynthia's Revels* at Blackfriars, seem to consider the state only as their backdrop, and they have no families. They retain the full sympathy of their creators, yet appear to be suffering from a kind of academic hubris. Their virtue, the presumed product of their learning, they hug about themselves as they stalk in proud isolation.

The "university wits" of the type represented by Peele, Marlowe, Greene, Nashe, and Lodge are represented a decade later by Middleton, and, through assimilation, Chapman and Jonson. Their learning is not simply learning, but a gulf between them and their social origins. Jonson's scholarly distinction is admirable, but not his clamorous insistence upon it. Chapman's pretensions are revealed in the self-portrait, Clarence, in *Sir Giles Goosecap*, and in the not unsympathetic caricature, Bellamont, in Dekker and Webster's *Northward Ho*. Bellamont, the playwright and "poor unpreferred scholar," dreams of himself as privy-council member and poet laureate at the French court of which he writes: "Why should not I be an excellent statesman?"[28] Middleton's family were London burghers,[29] involved in those very disputes over money satirized by this clever young man, but he writes as if he belonged to a different species. That Marston was a gentleman by birth rankled with Jonson—"we are a gentleman besides";[30] but Jonson felt socially secure at least in respect to Dekker, who is accused of envy because "better men loved him [Jonson] than loved me."[31] Marks of social rivalry are plain in the controversial plays presently to be reviewed.

Nashe is the chief linking figure between the scholar-playwrights of the eighties and those of the next decade. Our earliest record of Jonson in the role of dramatist associates him with Nashe in the composition of the satirical *Isle of Dogs*. A number of allusions to the "true English Aretine"[32] reveal that he was something of a hero to the authors of the *Parnassus* plays and other academic wits at the turn of the century. All were convinced that he had put down Gabriel Harvey—as, in dexterity of wit, he truly had; but the truth and the liberal spirit were not on the wittier side in this episode any more than in the "battle of the books" at the end of the next century. Nashe's discontent had taken the form not only of bitterness toward an unappreciative world and the citizen class of London, but toward the very type of achievement the Harveys stood for. McKerrow has summed up the controversy thus:

> But above and before all, there was, I think, that ancient opposition between the old and the new, between servility and independence, between prejudice and the right of a man to that consideration which his abilities

and achievements deserved. And it was the Harveys who stood for the future and Nashe for the past.[33]

Nashe's moral and pietistic writings are as troubled as Greene's. He repeats desperately the precepts of a code that has brought him no serenity. Most of the later satirists abandon the precepts, or use them only to fill the interstices in their tirades against the times. Their spirit is truly reactionary. The revolt against the romantic, the glamorous, and the sweet involves a revolt also against most of the liberal ideals of the humanistic tradition, and cannot, as sometimes maintained,[34] be viewed simply as the reassertion of the common sense of the English middle class. The satirists speak against rather than for the middle class, and their destructiveness is attributable, at least in individual instances, to their own social dislocation.

The university wits were not the only "predecessors of Shakespeare"—a term, incidentally, that would have made them shudder. Among others writing in the eighties were Robert Wilson and Richard Tarleton, both actors, Anthony Munday, a former printer, and Thomas Kyd, probably a former scrivener. These were recruits to authorship from what we may call the literate crafts. Of the score of new playwrights who came to the London scene in the nineties, at least by name in Henslowe's *Diary*, only two or three appear to have held university degrees. Chettle, like Munday, was a former printer. Seven or eight were actors. Marston labels the group collectively as scriveners. Heywood speaks of residence at Cambridge; but if he had received a degree he would probably have let us know it. There is no evidence that Dekker was a university man. Drayton and Shakespeare, for all their cultivation, certainly were not. It almost appears as if Greene's exhortation to his fellow graduates of the universities to cease writing for the stage had taken effect, and that a "strike" was in progress. The scholarly dramatist reappears as a conspicuous figure only after the reopening of the private theatres. No more than two-fifths of the popular repertory as a whole was composed by men with pretensions to learning, even if we include Heywood among university writers. On the other hand, four-fifths of the select repertory was composed by men of such pretensions. The unlearned author, the actor or former printer or scrivener, had at least the advantage of feeling unbesmirched by his occupation; in a number of instances his status as a dramatist must have been occasion of surprise and even gratification. We might expect, among these writers as a group, more satisfaction with their world, less all-embracing rancor, than among the learned contingent. Perhaps it is fortunate that Shakespeare stepped into the London scene with moderate expectations—that he qualified as a writer through one of the literate crafts rather than through a pilgrimage to Parnassus.

It would be hard to maintain that there was anything jovial or frivolous about the war of the theatres, despite the characteristic detachment of Shakespeare's allusions to it in *Hamlet*, or the fact that Marston and Jonson, who had been at loggerheads in 1600–1601, were collaborating in 1605. The combat between Marston of Paul's and Jonson of Blackfriars was internecine and personal; both the *Histriomastix* of the former and the *Poetaster* of the latter were full of invective against the "common" stages. If Paul's was willing to perform Dekker and Marston's *Satiromastix*, the rejoinder of Shakespeare's company to Jonson's attack, it was in the cause of Marston and not of the popular drama. Both Paul's and Blackfriars continued to lob missiles at the public theatres after the full barrage had ceased; details in a number of plays, including revisions by Jonson in several written originally for those very theatres, show that the contemptuous attitude of *Histriomastix* and *Poetaster* was no passing phenomenon. Jonson fluctuated as dramatist between the public and private theatres on the principle of repulsion from the company where his latest play had failed; but, except in the prologue to *Epicoene*, he is consistent in his antipopular pronouncements. Beaumont's *Knight of the Burning Pestle* proves that the issues were still alive in 1607.

Histriomastix or The Player Whipt of 1599–1600, in its portrayal of the rise and fall of Sir Oliver Owlet's Men, a ratty company of actor-sharers, and of Posthaste, the hack dramatist, is as abusive of the popular stage as Hall's satires. Witness the words of Chrisogonus, true poet and true scholar, whom the actors fail to appreciate:

> Write on, cry on, yowl to the common sort
> Of thick-skin'd auditors such rotten stuffs,
> More fit to fill the paunch of Esquiline

Than feed the hearings of judicial ears.
Ye shades triumph while foggy Ignorance
Clouds bright Apollo's beauty. Time will clear
The misty dullness of spectators' eyes;
Then woeful hisses to your fopperies.
O age when ever scrivener's boy shall dip
Prophaning quills into Thessalia's spring,
When every artist-'prentice that hath read
The Pleasant Pantry of Conceipts shall dare
To write as confidant as Hercules,
When every ballad-monger boldly writes
And windy froth of bottle-ale doth fill
Their purest organ of invention;
Yet all applauded and puff't up with pride,
Swell in conceipt and load the stage with stuff
Rak't from the rotten embers of stale jests,
Which basest lines best please the vulgar sense,
Make truest rapture lose preeminence.[35]

Responsible for all this are "the dull clods of earth . . . these huge fat lumps of flesh . . . these big-bulk't painted posts"—presumably the actors. In Day's *Law-Tricks*, written for the boys some years after the period ordinarily assigned to the war of the theatres, the charges of Chrisogonus are substantially repeated by one of the characters. Learning held a high place until

empty outsides, shadows daub'd with gold,
Pluck't him down headlong; then 'a lost his wits
And ever since lives Zany to the world.[36]

A speech unequivocally by Author in the scene appended to Jonson's *Poetaster* is just as destructive and unamiably intense as anything said by Chrisogonus:

But that these base and beggarly conceipts
Should carry it, by the multitude of voices,
Against the most abstracted work oppos'd
To the stuff't nostrils of the drunken rout!
O, this would make a learn'd and liberal soul
To rive his stained quill up to the back,
And damn his long-watch't labors to the fire.[37]

The audience—"thick-skin'd auditors," "drunken rout"—as well as actors, authors, and dramatic types came in for a share of abuse.

For Marston, actors continued to serve as an image of falsity—his characters must not "turn player,"[38] must not "swell like a trage-dian"[39] or display "stage-like passion" and "player's eloquence"; but he has left no other commentary so subversive as the caricature of Sir Oliver Owlet's Men in the unacknowledged *Histriomastix*. In Jonson's *Poetaster*, the cringing actor Histrio and his company are submitted to the rending teeth of Tucca:

> Do not bring your Aesop, your politician, unless you can ram up his mouth with cloves; the slave smells ranker than some sixteen dunghills, and is seventeen times more rotten. Marry, you may bring Frisker, my Zany; he's a good skipping swaggerer; and your fat fool there, my Mango, bring him too but let him not beg rapiers, nor scarfs, in his over-familiar playing face, nor roar out his barren bold jests with a tormenting laugh-ter between drunk and dry. Do you hear, stiff-toe? Give him warning, admonition, to forsake his saucy glavering grace and his goggle eye.[40]

The Chamberlain's Men "on the other side of Tiber" are intended in this scene; and that Shakespeare is being talked to or about in the encounter between Histrio and Tucca seems inescapable.[41] The actor called "fat" Mango is perhaps being penalized for his success in the role of Sir John Falstaff. Jonson's appended protestations that he has taxed the players "sparingly" ring hollow: among other things, his Tucca had accused them of pandering for "decayed punks" and selling their boys for "ingles." Suggestions of sexual turpitude were apt to accompany more relevant charges in Renaissance polemics. In Barry's *Ram-Alley*, performed at Whitefriars in 1607–1608, there is an allusion to a popular troupe that shares the wife of one of its members:

> it stands with policy
> That one should be a notorious cuckold,
> If it be but for the better keeping
> The rest of his company together.[42]

Demetrius in *Poetaster* is Thomas Dekker, and his qualities as a "dresser of plays about the town" are presumably those of his type: he is poor ("his doublet's a little decayed"), ignorant (he would reveal the authors whom Horace has plagiarized but that he understands them "not full and whole"), and socially inferior (having access only to "noblemen's butt'ries" and "puisnes' chambers").[43] Anthony Munday seems to have been selected as a butt and represented as Posthaste in *Histriomastix* and Antonio Balladino in Jonson's *Case Is Altered* not because he had given personal offense to anyone, but because his traffic with the public stage had been so long, and because he had written ballads and romances as well as plays. Both men, of course, are represented as pitifully disqualified for the profession of dramatist.

The popular repertory is stigmatized in a succession of plays. It is "brown-paper stuff."[44] The authors steal other men's jests and "waylay all the stale apothegms or old books they can hear of (in print or otherwise) to farce their scenes withal."[45] They produce "beggarly and barren trash" to "tickle base vulgar ears" and "run a broken pace for common hire."[46] These are the strictures not of puritans but of playwrights. One of the most interesting features of the attack is the way it repudiates the informing spirit of the popular drama and nearly every dramatic type except satirical comedy. Only the brainless admire *The Spanish Tragedy*. Doddering Holinshed and plays derived from him are similarly dismissed. In a prologue to *Every Man in His Humor*, written after its public performance, Jonson echoes the criticism of romantic drama formerly uttered by Sidney, Gosson, and Whetstone,

> To make a child now swaddled to proceed
> Man, and then shoot up in one beard and weed
> Past three-score years,

and points directly to Shakespeare's own chronicle plays in allusions to "York and Lancaster's long jars," creaking thrones, and the Chorus that "wafts you o'er the seas." A passage in *Every Man Out of His Humor*, also possibly written after its public performance, excludes from the realm of true comedy the cross-wooings of dukes and countesses "with a clown to their serving man."[47] The description fits romantic comedy generally and might be a synopsis of *Twelfth Night*. In *Histriomastix* there is a brief parody of pathos as exploited by Owlet's Men:

'My son, thou art a lost child,'
(This is a passion, note you the passion.)
'And hath many poor men of their goods beguil'd,
O prodigal child, and child prodigal!'
(Read the rest, sirs; I cannot read for tears.)[48]

And, in *Poetaster,* a parody of popular moralizing in "King Darius'
doleful strain":

'O doleful days! O direful deadly dump!
O wicked world! and worldly wickedness!
How can I hold my fist from crying thump,
In rue of this right rascal wretchedness!'[49]

Amorous and martial strains, and various types of rant, are also illustrated. The athleticism of the popular troupes provokes a mocking allusion in Middleton's *Family of Love,* performed at Paul's after
1602:

. . . 'tis not for youths to play Sampson. Believe it, we saw Sampson bear
the town gates on his neck from the lower to the upper stage, with that
life and admirable accord that it shall never be equalled, unless the whole
new livery of porters set to their shoulders.[50]

A single example will illustrate vividly the contempt of the intellectuals for the popular playwright's stock of philosophy:

Onion.
. . . I am no gentleman-born, I must confess, but *my mind to me a
kingdom is* truly.

Antonio Balladino.
Truly, a very good saying.

Onion.
'Tis somewhat stale, but that's no matter.

Antonio Balladino.
O 'tis the better; such things ever are like bread, which, the staler it is,
the more wholesome.[51]

Francis Beaumont's *Knight of the Burning Pestle,* although lagging
five years behind the attack of 1600–1602, provides the most thorough
as well as the most amusing parody of popular drama and caricature

of citizen auditors. The ridicule of Thomas Heywood, with his glorification of all London from its noble apprentices to its "Fleet privies," is explicit as well as inspired. Just as explicit, although usually unnoticed, is the imitation of the vein of Thomas Dekker in the absurd but engaging scenes of star-crossed love between Jasper and Luce. Old Merrythought, with his invincible singing heart, is a composite of such character types as Dekker's Eyre, Janiculo, and Candido. Finally, it is Shakespeare's *Henry IV* that provides Beaumont's aspiring apprentice with his recitation of a "huffing part." No better dramatists than Heywood, Dekker, and Shakespeare could have been selected to represent the popular school of playwrights. Each was the principal playwright at one of the three public theatres operating at the time, the Red Bull, the Fortune, and the Globe. They are the ones whom Webster in 1612, after his more deferential bow to the more literary dramatists, places in the last but not least category:

I have ever cherished . . . that full and heightened style of Master Chapman, the labor'd and understanding works of Master Jonson, the no less worthy composures of the both worthily excellent Master Beaumont and Master Fletcher, and lastly (without wrong last to be named) the right happy and copious industry of M. Shakespeare, M. Dekker, and M. Heywood.[52]

The little citizen family representing the popular audience, George the grocer, Nell his wife, and Rafe their apprentice, is shrewdly drawn, and except that Nell fails to understand the very type of play designed to please her kind, the behavior of the three tells us many true things about London's humbler playgoers. What distinguishes Beaumont's satire, indeed, is its basis in truth and sympathy. The play was not a success. Hazelton Spencer, in an otherwise scholarly edition of the play, remarks, "Perhaps the satire on their critical attainments was resented by the citizens,"[53] thus revealing how even among literary historians the theatrical world of Shakespeare's time may be imperfectly understood. *The Knight of the Burning Pestle* was performed not before citizens but before the Blackfriars coterie, and probably did not fail so much because it satirized citizens as because it did so without animosity. The grocer is neither a fool nor a niggard, and his wife is not a slut. The self-assertiveness of the pair, and of valiant Rafe, is treated as amusing rather than abhorrent.

The defense of the public theatres against the satires at Black-friars and Paul's consisted chiefly of an attack upon satire itself. When an author of the Cambridge *Parnassus* plays makes Will Kempe say, "O, that Ben Jonson is a pestilent fellow; he brought up Horace giving the poets a pill, but our fellow Shakespeare hath given him a purge that made him beray his credit,"[54] he is probably attributing to Shakespeare Thomas Dekker's *Satiromastix or The Untrussing of the Humorous Poet*, the rejoinder to *Poetaster* performed by Shakespeare's company. Dekker had apparently been working upon a typical popular romance when the occasion for the satire arose, and the scenes attacking Jonson are grafted on to his original design. They are as scurrilous as anything produced by the enemy; and, because the play was also put on by the boys of Paul's, Jonson's charge that Marston had a hand in it may be well founded although the name of Dekker alone appears on the title page. The lampoon is primarily *ad hominem* and contains little generalizing about dramatic ideals. One of the speeches, however, comments significantly upon the invocation to "learned ears" in the prologue to Jonson's *Cynthia's Revels*:

> To other weaker beams his labors close,
> As loth to prostitute their virgin strain
> To every vulgar and adult'rate brain.

The Horace-Jonson of *Satiromastix* is made to say:

> The muses birds, the bees, were hiv'd, and fled
> Us in our cradle, thereby prophecying
> *That we to learned ears should sweetly sing;*
> *But to the vulgar and adulterate brain*
> *Should loath to prostitute our virgin strain.*
> No our sharp pen shall keep the world in awe.
> Horace, thy poesy wormwood wreathes shall wear:
> We hunt not for men's love but for their fear.[55]

The issue was drawn on the point that the popular drama addressed itself to the affections rather than the fears and hatreds of men. The true Horace "loved poets well, and gave coxcombs to none but fools" whereas "thou lov'st none, neither wiseman nor fools."[56] The cause of the public theatres becomes also the cause of the London citizenry: "thou criest ptrooh at worshipful citizens, and call'st them flatcaps, cuckolds, and bankrupts; and modest and virtuous wives, punks and cockatrices."[57] The charge parallels one in a contemporary puritan tract: certain writers "have not been afraid of late days to bring upon the stage the very sober countenances, grave attire, modest and matronlike gestures and speeches of men and women to be laughed at as a scorn and reproach to the world."[58] Jonson's motives in writing of "divine Poesy" are impugned—

> Thy pride and scorn made her turn satirist,
> And not her love to virtue, as thou preachest—

and his malady is diagnosed as arrogance, self-love, detraction, and "stinking insolence."[59]

Histriomastix appears to have had a career on the academic or private stage before Marston honed up its attack on the popular troupes about 1599. Another old play, *Mucedorus*, first published in 1598, was framed in a contest between Comedy and Envy—

> Comedy is mild, gentle, willing for to please,
> And seeks to gain the love of all estates,
> Delighting in mirth, mix'd all with lovely tales—[60]

and Shakespeare's company appears to have seen in these allegorical characters a means of contrasting its own artistic objectives with those of its critics. Although the additions to the Comedy *versus* Envy speeches first appear in print in 1610 (not in a second quarto of 1606), they had probably been made in the Chamberlain's Men's playhouse copy as early as 1601. The mysterious charges of tale-bearing brought against the actor Aesop in the *Poetaster* of that year are reversed in the lines added to *Mucedorus*; and the satirical poet in Envy's employ bears a strong resemblance to Horace-Jonson as pictured by Dekker in *Satiromastix*—"so lean a hollow-cheeked scrag" that he little resembled the true Horace, who was long-bearded and of goodly corpulence[61] (Jonson's own corpulence was a later acquirement):

Envy.

From my foul study will I hoist a wretch,
A lean and hungry meager cannibal,
Whose jaws swell to his eyes with chewing malice,
And him I'll make a poet. . . .
This scrambling raven with his needy beard,
Will I whet on to write a comedy,
Wherein shall be compos'd dark sentences
Pleasing to factious brains,
And every other where place me a jest
Whose high abuse shall more torment than blows.

Comedy laughs when she hears that Envy's motives are to embroil the actors with the authorities:

Ha, ha, ha! I laugh to hear thy folly;
This is a trap for *Boys*, not *Men*, nor such
Especially desertful in their doings,
Whose stay'd discretion rules their purposes:
I and my faction do eschew those vices.[62]

That bland comedy as distinct from bitter envy is the spirit of the popular stage is stated by Heywood in his *Apology for Actors*, published in 1612, but evidently written about four years earlier after one of the indiscretions at Blackfriars had brought official penalties upon the whole theatrical profession:

Now to speak of some abuse lately crept into the quality, as an inveighing against the state, the court, the law, the city, and their governments; with the particularizing of private men's humors (yet alive), noblemen and others. I know it distastes many, neither do I any way excuse it. The liberty which some arrogate to themselves, committing their bitterness and liberal invectives against all estates to the mouths of children, supposing their juniority to be a privilege for any railing be it never so violent, I could advise all such to curb and limit their presumed liberty within the bounds of discretion and government. But wise and judicial censurers before whom such complaints shall at any time hereafter come will not (I hope) impute these abuses to any transgression in us, who have ever been careful and provident to shun the like.[63]

Years later, Heywood expressed his regret that "nothing but Satirica Dictaeria and Comic Scommata are now in request."[64] The practices

at Blackfriars drew from Thomas Dekker a more thoughtful comment than any he had written in *Satiromastix*. The passage appears
in his *Whore of Babylon*, performed at the Fortune about 1607:

I am *Plaindealing*, and must speak truth. Thou hast many physicians,
some of them sound men, but a number of them more sick at heart than
a whole parish full of patients. Let them cure themselves first, and then
they may better know how to heal others. Then have you other fellows
that take upon them to be surgeons and by letting out the corruption of
a state—and they let it out, I'll be sworn—for some of them in places as
big as this and before a thousand people, rip up the bowels of vice in
such a beastly manner that (like women at an execution that can endure
to see men quartered alive) the beholders learn more villainy than they
knew before.[65]

The statement of the popular case is sometimes found in plays de-
riding it. In *Poetaster*, when Tucca accuses Histrio of performing
"humors, revels [*Cynthia's Revels*], and satires that gird and fart
at the time," the player replies: "No, I assure you, Captain, not we.
They are on the other side of Tiber."[66] The most revealing words
are put into the mouth of old Anthony Munday in Jonson's *The
Case Is Altered* as performed at Blackfriars:

Antonio Balladino.
Why look you, sir, I write so plain and keep that old decorum that you
must of necessity like it. Marry, you shall have some now (as, for example, in plays) that will have every day new tricks and write you nothing but humors; indeed, this pleases the gentlemen, but the common sort
they care not for't, they know not what to make on't, they look for good
matter they, and are not edified with such toys.

Onion.
You are in the right; I'll not give a halfpenny to see a thousand on 'hem.
I was at one the last term, but and ever I see a more roguish thing, I am
a piece of cheese. . . .

Antonio Balladino.
True, sir. They would have me make such plays, but as I tell 'hem, and
they'll give me twenty pounds a play, I'll not raise my vein. . . . Tut,
give me the penny, give me the penny, I care not for the gentlemen, I.
Let me have a good ground; no matter for the pen, the plot shall
carry it.[67]

A wealth of historical suggestion is in this passage—in the distinction made between the educated taste for satire and the uneducated taste for story, and in the recognition that in popular drama there is an "old decorum." One fascinating point, reminding us of Heywood's, and even Dekker's and Shakespeare's, affinities with some features of the puritan point of view, is that Jonson puts into the mouth of a popular playwright phrases that would be identified at Blackfriars or Paul's as pious cant—the citizen spectators "look for good matter they, and are not edified with such toys."

Public opinion was opposed to the satirical school. Perkins, perhaps the most popular preacher of the day, was saying that the pure in heart are reluctant even to *name* fornication, avarice, and uncleanness;[68] and distaste for the epidemic of muckraking was not confined to the pious. The motives of the satirists were questioned from the beginning. "You gathered up men's vices as though they had been strawberries, and picked away their virtues as they had been the stalks," said William Ingram as he accused Marston of sin-mongering:

> And lest you should this vilde pretence reveal
> Did hypocrite it with a show of zeal.[69]

Even the authors of the *Parnassus* plays looked askance at Jonson, and accused Marston of lifting his canine leg against the world.[70] That the satirists were themselves guilty of the vices they portrayed was a common charge. It is expressed in Shakespeare before the private playhouses had reopened, but while the verse satires were in full flow. The relatively harmless Jaques is thus addressed:

> Most mischievous foul sin, in chiding sin.
> For thou thyself hast been a libertine,
> As sensual as the brutish sting itself;
> And all th' embossed sores and headed evils
> That thou with license of free foot hast caught
> Wouldst thou disgorge into the general world.[71]

We get from Weever in 1601,

> What beastliness by others you have shown,
> Such by yourselves 'tis thought that you have known,[72]

and from Chettle or Dekker in 1603,

> Alas of such there are too many here,
> All Italy is full of them that snarl,
> And bay and bark at other men's abuse,
> Yet live themselves like beasts in all abuse.[73]

Signs of uneasiness appear among the more conspicuous writers. Marston, the chief object of suspicion, is ferocious in the body of his satirical verse and dramas but oddly obsequious in his prologues and epilogues. He avers that he has always aspired "to be beloved,"[74] that he has "a modest diffidence and self-mistrust,"[75] that his excesses are only "unwilling error" such as proceed from "too rash youthful fervor,"[76] and that his "supposed tartness . . . may modestly pass with the freedom of a satire."[77] The rankest of his plays are accompanied by guarantees that they are exempt from "ribaldry or rage"[78] and from "rude disgraces."[79] Marston was a clever fellow, but his mixed impulses of exhibitionism and self-abasement remind us sometimes of Dostoevsky's buffoons. The notes of deprecation are not confined to him. Chapman says:

> Faith, that same vein of railing
> Becomes now most applausive; your best poet is
> He that rails grossest.[80]

Day affirms that his "ink hath been always simple, without the juice of wormwood" and his "pen smooth without teeth, and so it shall continue."[81] Barry describes his single play as

> Free from the loathsome stage disease,
> So overworn, so tir'd, and stale,
> Not satirizing but to rail.[82]

And Jonson also piously abjures:

> But when it is all excrement they vent,
> Base filth and offal . . .[83]

The plays accompanied by these protests are all typical coterie satires!

Except in *Hamlet* there is nothing by Shakespeare that can be read as an overt allusion to the quarrel just reviewed. Hamlet is interested in theatrical matters, but his attitude is properly Olympian. He has delighted in the tragedians, naturally; he is hospitable when they arrive at Elsinore; he has enlightened views on the art of acting; and, quite apart from the way it may serve his turn, he is not averse to a trial at play writing himself. All is in character. There are hints of his critical limitations, and more than hints of his condescension, verging on mockery—"the lover shall not sigh gratis, the humorous man shall end his part in peace." It is the quintessence of absurdity that he, Hamlet, might one day get him a half-share or whole-share in a "cry of players." As the Prince talks to the Player, our minds can scarcely credit the fact that their lines were written by a player and not a prince. As to the theatrical situation in the city, interesting to be sure, but far away and essentially trifling:

Rosencrantz.
. . . There was, for a while, no money bid for argument unless the poet and the player went to cuffs in the question.

Hamlet.
Is't possible?

Guildenstern.
Oh, there has been much throwing about of brains.

And then, lightly, the actor-author of the chief of the popular companies in London tosses the victory to the enemy:

Hamlet.
Do the boys carry it away?

Rosencrantz.
Ay, that they do, my lord—Hercules and his load too.[84]

And yet, despite the artistic objectivity of it all, we cannot say that Shakespeare gives no clue to his personal attitude. Distributed at random within the speeches of the gossipers are telltale phrases: "the common stages—so they *call* them"; the "writers do them *wrong* to make them exclaim *against their own succession*"; "the nation holds it no *sin* to tarre them to controversy." One detail of the conversation is admonitory. When Rosencrantz explains why the actors are on tour, "I think their inhibition comes by the means of

the late innovation," he is saying, "I think the closing of the theatres
is the result of the recent disturbance of the peace." So far as we
know, no general inhibition of acting resulted from the recriminations of 1600–1601; but satirical vehemence had brought such action
before and was to do so again. Shakespeare, like Heywood, would
have known when his professional welfare was threatened.

He must have felt touched also upon the personal side. When Jonson finally protests,

> Now for the players, it is true I tax'd 'hem,
> And yet but some, and those so sparingly,
> As all the rest might have sat still unquestion'd,
> Had they but had the wit or conscience
> To think well of themselves,

he makes a distinction that he failed to make in his original satires,
where the contempt expressed for the popular drama and its purveyors was all-inclusive; and when he continues,

> Only amongst them, I am sorry for
> Some better natures, by the rest so drawn
> To run in that vile line,[85]

although we feel naturally impelled to list Shakespeare among those
"better natures," there is nothing to indicate that Jonson himself
does so. The prologue to *Cynthia's Revels* repudiates the popular
drama entire, *Poetaster* ridicules Shakespeare's own company, and
the prologue to the revised *Every Man in His Humor* points scorn-
fully to Shakespeare's own plays. We had better admit these facts,
however much we should prefer to believe that the admiration ex
pressed in Jonson's magnificent tribute of 1623 was of early birth.
And we must assume the normal human responses in the circumstances. The Chamberlain's Men had performed two of Jonson's
plays just before his defection to Blackfriars. If they played *Every
Man Out of His Humor* in anything like its published form, they
had shown more confidence in Jonson than in their theatrical experience, or a most charitable inclination to support literary experiment. The failure of the play would have affected them as ad-
versely as its author, and his prologue to *Cynthia's Revels* would

have seemed nothing short of treacherous. Shakespeare as company member and company dramatist was lodged centrally in the public theatre, and he could scarcely have remained indifferent to the invectives aimed at his troupe or the indiscriminate branding of popular plays as "beggarly and barren trash."

Still there was that in Jonson that would have compelled Shakespeare's, or any writer's, respect. It is John Marston that he would have viewed, we should guess, with instinctive antipathy; and, of all the hypothetical identifications of characters in Shakespeare's plays, that of Thersites with Marston has the most to recommend it. Thersites is the strident buffoon hysterically usurping the role of censor. It is tempting to assume that, at the very least, he serves as Shakespeare's commentary upon those admired expositors of human depravity that Marston, Jonson, and Chapman were using pivotally in their plays. But *Troilus and Cressida* remains a mystery. The stuff of the play, we must recognize, supplies Thersites with abundant occasion, even though he is not the accredited satirical spokesman of "comicall satyre" as a type. The assumption that the play was written especially for the inns of court, now widely current, fails to reckon with the fact that there is no recorded instance before or during Shakespeare's career (theories about "courtly" plays like *A Midsummer Night's Dream* and *Merry Wives* notwithstanding) when a regular play was bought, rehearsed, and acted by a professional company exclusively for a special audience. As already noted, "court" plays were public plays acted at court for a fee of £10. To assume that the situation was different at the inns is to ignore the economics of the acting companies as well as Elizabethan habits of frugality. *Twelfth Night* (in no wise resembling *Troilus and Cressida*, by the way) was performed at the Middle Temple in 1602, presumably for the customary fee and certainly to the satisfaction of John Manningham.[86] Why, in the same period, any of the inns should have subsidized a production instead of purchasing a performance, no one has troubled to explain. Equally baffling is the line of reasoning that would make the concluding insults addressed by Pandarus to the audience especially congenial to inns of court ears. Generically, the allusions to panders among the spectators resemble facetious addresses in public theatres, where a "galled goose of Winchester," like a pickpocket or two, could be counted upon as lurking amidst the throng. It is difficult to imagine Shakespeare writing this epilogue on *any* occasion; still, the evidence as it stands places the weight of probability on the side of regular performance at the Globe during or just after the years of *Histrio-mastix*, *Cynthia's Revels*, *Poetaster*, and *Satiromastix*.

Troilus and Cressida does not, of course, traduce ideals of love and honor in the way that the twentieth century reader sometimes fears—or hopes. Its attitudes cannot be measured by comparison with Chaucer's Criseyde and Homer's Greeks, Shakespeare's evaluation of the characters being the one current in his day.[87] His portrait of Joan of Arc in *I Henry VI* would lead us to think him harshly satirical in his youth if we assumed that the Maid had then acquired the venerability we associate with her. *Troilus and Cressida*, like *Measure for Measure*, has proved to be critically ill fated. Ulysses was reputed wise, and Shakespeare placed in his mouth magnificent expression of Elizabethan wisdom, the most widely endorsed commonplaces of the Renaissance; but the situation is such as to give the words a discordant echo. Because the eloquence seems inappropriate to the petty ends to which it is addressed, we are apt to detect irony where none is intended. Finally, our discomfiture in the closing scenes may result from an accident. Here, and here only, in Shakespearean drama are the false and treacherous riding high on Fortune's wheel at the end, while the honorable and true are at its base. But it was long since pointed out[88] that the most remarkable thing about *Troilus and Cressida* is that it would have defeated the expectations of any Elizabethan audience by telling only half a familiar story—in which Fortune's wheel came full circle at last. We must reckon with the possibility that Shakespeare's omission of the retributory sequel was not a calculated effect, and that he had planned a two-part play but given over the project because the first part failed or was dropped in rehearsal. The epilogue in which Pandarus promises that "Some two months hence my will shall here be made," and the publisher's testimony that it was played by the King's Men, and, contradictorily, that it was "never stal'd with the stage, never clapper-claw'd with the palms of the vulgar" may reflect such a history. If the first part only of *Henry IV* had survived, the fall of chivalrous Hotspur and triumph of tavern-haunting Hal might seem just as ironical as the ending of *Troilus and Cressida*.

Yet when all deductions are made, this play retains a quality that distinguishes it from the typically Shakespearean. It is not that great persons are provided with mean motives (the *Henry VI* plays and *King John* are, in this respect, just as unsparing), but that sexual dereliction is treated satirically and with a kind of relish, and knavery and stupidity are harped upon with raucous insistence. We seem to catch the accent of a thesis in the play. *Timon of Athens* is a thesis play, and a mordant one; but in it the treatment is dictated by the theme, and Shakespeare himself seems unreconciled to his project. When *Troilus and Cressida* is read with the satirical dramas of the coterie theatres in mind, it seems filled with odd little probings. "Think, we had mothers," says Troilus, retching at Cressida's weakness; this will give advantage to those "stubborn critics" of all womanhood. When Ulysses replies, "What hath she done, Prince, that can soil our mothers?"[89] our ears have caught fragmentary echoes of an old debate. "Why, sir," says Freevil in Marston's *Dutch Courtesan*, "should we loath all strumpets, some men should hate their own mothers and sisters—a sin against kind, I can tell you."[90]

The voice of Thersites is remarkably like the voice of John Marston. He is at once enraged and exhilarated by the sexual and other abuses against which he inveighs: his railing is uncouth and filled with the imagery of disease. A kind of gleeful morbidity links the pair, and would have made an association inevitable in the minds of contemporaries. We may take our choice—whether another shot in the war of the theatres was being fired, whether Shakespeare was consciously paying the coterie drama the compliment of imitation, or whether, as the most attentive and assimilative of the Elizabethans, he had merely heard midway in his career a new accent which he could use. If the play or any portion of it is a rejoinder to the enemy, it is a strange rejoinder; or if an imitation, a strange imitation. It is quite conceivable that the company which in 1604 appropriated

Marston's *Malcontent* had earlier induced Shakespeare to make a modish gesture, and demonstrate that the Globe could do whatever Blackfriars or Paul's could do. But it would be a disastrous inference that Shakespeare's great tragedies had a similar genesis. And, of course, any theory that *Troilus and Cressida* is a "Blackfriars" type of play is irreconcilable with any theory that *Cymbeline, The Winter's Tale,* and *The Tempest* are also "Blackfriars" types of play. *Troilus and Cressida* had best be recognized as occupying a unique and mysterious place in the canon. When we have examined the rival philosophies of the popular and coterie dramatists, and observed how fundamental were the issues involved, we shall be less likely to assume that Shakespeare would lightheartedly adjust his view of life in conformity with theatrical fashions. The war of the theatres, or rather the clash of ideals of which it was an external symptom, left a deep imprint on Shakespeare's work; but its nature is not illustrated by the tirades of Thersites.

Documentation: Part One

I. THEATRE OF A NATION

1. *Groatsworth of Wit*, ed. Grosart, in Robert Greene, *Works*, XII, 131.
2. Henry Medwall, *Fulgens and Lucrece*, c. 1497, ed. Boas, p. 4.
3. E. K. Chambers, *Mediaeval Stage*, II, 186.
4. *Ibid.*, 185: "rudes agricolae et artifices diversarum misterarum."
5. *Paston Letters*, ed. Gairdner, III, 89. Sir John Paston to John Paston, 16 April, 1473.
6. G. H. Overend, "On the Dispute Between George Maller . . . and Thomas Arthur," *Transactions of the New Shakspere Society*, 1877–1879, p. 426.
7. C. W. Wallace, *First London Theatre*, pp. 141–142.
8. *Histriomastix*, I, i.
9. *Plays Confuted in Five Actions*, ed. Hazlitt, *English Drama and Stage*, p. 215.
10. G. E. Bentley, *Jacobean and Caroline Stage*, II, 643, 646, 648.
11. E. K. Chambers, *Mediaeval Stage*, II, 186.
12. J. P. Collier, *English Dramatic Poetry and Annals of the Stage*, I, 41–55.
13. An Act for the Punishment of Vagabonds . . ., 1572, excerpted in E. K. Chambers, *Elizabethan Stage*, IV, 270.
14. J. T. Murray, *English Dramatic Companies*, II, 287–289.
15. *Ibid.*, 270.
16. *Ibid.*, 335.
17. *Ibid.*, 115–116.
18. A. Clark, "Malden Records and the Drama," *N. & Q.*, 10 Ser., VII (1907), 181.
19. J. P. Collier, *op. cit.*, I, 30–55; E. K. Chambers, *Mediaeval Stage*, II, 186, 188.
20. Oliver Baker, *In Shakespeare's Warwickshire*; E. K. Chambers, *Shakespearean Gleanings*.
21. Henry Algernon Percy, *Regulations and Establishment of the Household*, ed. T. Percy, p. 48.
22. "Two Early Player-Lists," ed. E. K. Chambers, *Malone Society Collections*, Vol. I, Parts I–IV, pp. 348–349.
23. Henry Algernon Percy, *op. cit.*, p. 340.
24. E. K. Chambers, *Mediaeval Stage*, II, 256–257; *Elizabethan Stage*, II, 78.
25. J. P. Collier, *op. cit.*, I, 30; G. H. Overend, *loc. cit.*

26. J. T. Murray, *op. cit.*, II, 396–397.
27. Sheets inserted in end papers, W. W. Greg, *Dramatic Documents from the Elizabethan Playhouses*, Vol. II.
28. E. K. Chambers, *Mediaeval Stage*, II, 255.
29. H. A. Rennert, *Spanish Stage*, p. 17.
30. J. T. Murray, *op. cit.*, II, 361, 363.
31. H. R. Plomer, "New Documents on English Printers and Booksellers of the Sixteenth Century," *Transactions of the Bibliographical Society*, IV, 166–179.
32. E. K. Chambers, *Mediaeval Stage*, II, 347–348.
33. *Groatsworth of Wit*, ed. Grosart, in Greene, *loc cit.*
34. Henslowe, *Diary*, ed. W. W. Greg, I, 188–189.
35. Thomas Dekker, *Satiromastix*, Pearson reprint, p. 229.
36. Ben Jonson, *Poetaster*, III, iv.
37. *Il Return from Parnassus*, V, i.
38. E. K. Chambers, *William Shakespeare*, II, 333.
39. The Derby Household Books, ed. Raines, *Chetham Society Pub.*, XXXI, 32.
40. Thomas Dekker, *Belman of London*, ed. Grosart, *Non-Dramatic Works*, III, 81.
41. J. T. Murray, *op. cit.*, II, 79, 89, 98.
42. *Ibid.*, 105–110, 163–167.
43. Henry Algernon Percy, *op. cit.*, p. 22.
44. A. W. Reed, *Early Tudor Drama*, p. 62.
45. J. T. Murray, *op. cit.*, II, 239–244.
46. Gregory King, *Two Tracts, 1696*, ed. Barnett; A. Harbage, *Shakespeare's Audience*, pp. 33–41.
47. A. Thaler, "Travelling Players in Shakespeare's England," *Mod. Phil.*, XVII (1920), 514.
48. A. Clark, *loc. cit.*, "Et solut. lusoribus domini comitis Essex ludentibus coram burgensibus infra burgam hoc anno. vs."
49. E. K. Chambers, *Mediaeval Stage*, II, 256.
50. B. M. Ward, "The Chamberlain's Men in 1597," *R.E.S.*, IX (1933), 55–58.
51. J. E. T. Rogers, *A History of Agriculture and Prices in England*, Vol. III, pp. 583–663, Vol. V, p. 664.
52. *Mankind*, ed. Adams, l. 459.
53. *Ibid.*, l. 29.
54. *Merry Tales, Witty Questions and Quick Answers*, 1567, ed. Hazlitt, p. 145.
55. Gabriel Harvey, *Letter-Book*, ed. Scott, pp. 67–68.
56. *Thomas Platter's Travels in England 1599*, trans. Williams, p. 167.
57. Henry Algernon Percy, *op. cit.*, p. 340.
58. A. Clark, *op. cit.*, p. 422.
59. J. T. Murray, *op. cit.*, II, 362.
60. *Ibid.*, 298–316.
61. John Marston, *Histriomastix*, III, i.
62. *Merry Conceited Jests*, ed. Bullen, *Works of George Peele*, II, 390.
63. *Ratsey's Ghost*, ed. Harrison, sig. A 4.

64. J. T. Murray, *op. cit.*, II, 233, 336, 343.

65. H. R. Plomer, *loc. cit.*

66. *Documents Relating to the Office of the Revels* . . . *Elizabeth*, ed. A. Feuillerat, p. 409.

67. *Ratsey's Ghost*, sig. A 4 r.

68. G. H. Overend, *op. cit.*, p. 426.

69. Most recently by William Ringler in "The First Phase of the Elizabethan Attack on the Stage, 1558-1579," *Huntington Library Quarterly*, V (1942), 391-418, and in *Stephen Gosson*, p. 56.

70. "Dramatic Records of the City of London," ed. A. J. Mill and E. K. Chambers, *Malone Society Collections*, Vol. II, Part III, p. 291.

71. W. J. Griffin, "Notes on Early Tudor Control of the Stage," *M.L.N.*, LVIII (1943), 51-52.

72. E. K. Chambers, *Elizabethan Stage*, II, 99.

73. "Dramatic Records, etc." ed. Mill and Chambers, p. 296.

74. John Foxe, *Acts and Monuments*, ed. Cattley, Vol. VIII (1839), p. 445.

75. *Acts of the Privy Council*, ed. Dasent, VI, 168.

76. "Dramatic Records from the Lansdowne Manuscripts," ed. E. K. Chambers and W. W. Greg, *Malone Society Collections*, Vol. I, Part II, pp. 148-149.

77. E. K. Chambers, *Elizabethan Stage*, II, 380.

78. "Dramatic Records from the Lansdowne Manuscripts," ed. E. K. Chambers and W. W. Greg, *Malone Society Collections*, Vol. I, Part II, p. 175.

79. E. K. Chambers, *Elizabethan Stage*, IV, 199-200.

80. *Kind-Hartes Dream*, 1592, ed. G. B. Harrison, p. 40.

81. W. J. Lawrence, "The Inn-Yard Playing Places," in his *Pre-Restoration Stage Studies*, pp. 3-27.

82. Except where separately noted the sums for costs and rental receipts may be found in J. Q. Adams, *Shakespearean Playhouses*, and E. K. Chambers, *Elizabethan Stage*, II, 351-474.

83. C. J. Sisson, "Mr. and Mrs. Browne of the Boar's Head," *Life and Letters Today*, Vol. XV, No. 6 (Winter, 1936), p. 102.

84. L. Hotson, *Commonwealth and Restoration Stage*, p. 84.

85. Calculated from the total receipts in Henslowe's *Diary*.

86. C. J. Sisson, "Notes on Early Stuart Stage History," *M.L.R.*, XXXVII (1942), 30-31.

87. Witter *versus* Hemmings and Condell, Court of Requests, ed. C. W. Wallace, *Shakespeare and His London Associates*, p. 51.

88. *Shakespeare's Audience*, 1941. (I wish to correct the statement there on p. 50 that the verses quoted appear in the First Folio. On p. 177 of that book the words "Inhibition re Isle of Gulls" should be deleted.)

89. A. Thaler, "Travelling Players in Shakespeare's England," *Mod. Phil.*, XVII (1920), 497.

II. THEATRE OF A COTERIE

1. *Hamlet*, II, ii, 334–368.
2. See above, p. 14.
3. *Letters and Papers Foreign and Domestic of the Reign of Henry VIII*, ed. Gairdner and Brodie, Vol. XIV, Part 2, pp. 334, 335.
4. E. K. Chambers, *Elizabethan Stage*, IV, 147.
5. A. Feuillerat, *Revels Documents, Edward VI and Mary*, p. 159.
6. T. H. V. Motter, *School Drama in England*, pp. 274–275; Chambers, *op. cit.*, II, 72–73.
7. Sir James Whitelocke, *Liber Famelicus*, ed. Bruce, *Camden Soc. Pubs.*, Vol. LXX, p. 12.
8. Chambers, *op. cit.*, IV, 148–159.
9. C. M. Clode, *Early History of Merchant Taylors*, I, 235.
10. A. Feuillerat, *Revels Documents, Elizabeth*, p. 355.
11. John Bale, *Catalogus*, extract in Chambers, *op. cit.*, II, 197.
12. J. T. Murray, *English Dramatic Companies*, II, 382.
13. Henry Clifton's bill of complaint against the Chapel company at Blackfriars, 1601, ed. F. G. Fleay, *Chronicle History of the London Stage*, pp. 127–132.
14. A. Feuillerat, *Revels Documents, Elizabeth*, p. 219.
15. Henry Algernon Percy, *Regulations and Establishment of the Household*, p. 44.
16. C. W. Wallace, *Evolution of the English Drama*, p. 27, n. 8.
17. Murray, *op. cit.*, II, 215.
18. *Ibid.*, 59–60.
19. *Conversations with William Drummond of Hawthornden*, in Ben Jonson, *Dramatic Works*, ed. Herford and Simpson, I, 137.
20. The best digest of the facts is in A. W. Reed, *Early Tudor Drama*, pp. 55–59.
21. *Ibid.*, p. 60, quoting Machin's Diary.
22. Letter to Leicester, in J Strype, *Life of Grindal*, p. 115.
23. *Acts of the Privy Council*, ed. Dasent, IX, 56.
24. "Dramatic Records of the City of London," *Malone Soc. Collections*, Vol. II, Part III, p. 309.
25. The will, P.C.C. Tirwhite 14, is printed in H. N. Hillebrand, *The Child Actors*, pp. 327–330.
26. Keyser *versus* Burbage *et al.*, Court of Requests, 1610, in C. W. Wallace, *Shakespeare and His London Associates*, p. 95.
27. *Have with You to Saffron Waldon*, in Nashe, *Works*, ed. McKerrow, III, 46.
28. Penshurst Papers, ed. C. L. Kingsford, II (1934), 415.
29. C. J. Sisson, *Lost Plays of Shakespeare's Age*, p. 61.
30. E. K. Chambers, *Elizabethan Stage*, IV, 173.

31. Accounts in Chambers and Hillebrand are supplemented in "Dramatic Records of the City of London," *Malone Soc. Collections,* Vol. II, Pt. III, pp. 318–319; M. J. Dickson, "William Trevell and the Whitefriars Theatre," *R.E.S.,* VI (1930), 309–312; M. Dowling, "Further Notes on William Trevell," *Ibid.,* 443–446; W. J. Lawrence, "The Site of the Whitefriars Theatre," *R.E.S.,* XI (1935), 186.

32. C. W. Wallace, *Evolution of the English Drama,* pp. 38–39.

33. *Ibid.,* pp. 65, 70.

34. For Edwardes and his successors, see A. Feuillerat, *Revels Documents, Elizabeth, passim;* E. K. Chambers, *op. cit.,* IV, 77 f., 142 f.

35. W. J. Lawrence, "The Elizabethan Private Playhouse," *Criterion,* IX (1930), 420–429.

36. See above, p. 20.

37. *Acts of the Privy Council,* ed. Dasent, X, 436.

38. Wallace, *op. cit.,* p. 22.

39. See below, p. 68.

40. *The Elizabethan Home, Discovered in Two Dialogues,* ed. M. St. Clare Byrne, p. 54.

41. E. K. Chambers, *op. cit.,* II, 37.

42. Wallace, *op. cit.,* p. 175.

43. Gosson, *Plays Confuted in Five Actions,* ed. Hazlitt, p. 188.

44. E. K. Chambers, *op. cit.,* II, 39–40.

45. Wallace's account, which assumes that Elizabeth herself backed the venture, is corrected by Chambers, *op. cit.,* II, 42–61.

46. For the Clifton suit, see above, note 13.

47. See especially Marston's *Sophonisba* and its postscript, and the induction to his *Malcontent.*

48. "Blackfriars Records," *Malone Soc. Collections,* Vol. II, Part 1, p. 29.

49. A. Harbage, *Sir William Davenant,* p. 122.

50. Philip Julius, Duke of Stettin-Pomerania, "Diary," ed. von Bülow and Powell, *Transactions of the Royal Historical Society,* New Series, VI, 29.

51. Otto, Prince von Hessen-Cassel, "Itinerarium," ed. Feyerabend, *Englische Studien,* XIV (1890), 440. (". . . um 3 uhr, aber nur von michaelis bis auf ostern.")

52. Evans *versus* Kendal, Suit in King's Bench, ed. Hillebrand, *op. cit.,* 187–189, 332–334.

53. Kirkham *versus* Daniel, Suit in Chancery, 1609, ed. Hillebrand, *op. cit.,* pp. 334–338.

54. C. J. Sisson, *Lost Plays of Shakespeare's Age,* pp. 41–42, 58. Sisson mentions on p. 77 a performance on February 20, a Sunday, but this seems to be a slip.

55. Middleton, *Michaelmas Term,* Induction.

56. This revises upward the estimate in my *Shakespeare's Audience,* pp. 33, 37–39, made before I was aware of the prosperity of Worcester's Men (see above, p. 24).

57. Lyly, *Pappe with a Hatchet,* in *Works,* ed. Bond, III, 408.

58. H. Hall, *Society in the Elizabethan Age*, p. 211.
59. Philip Julius, *op. cit.*, p. 29.
60. Otto, *op. cit.*, p. 440.
61. Dekker and Middleton, *The Roaring Girl*, II, 1.
62. Commendatory verses to Fletcher's *Faithful Shepherdess*, c. 1608.
63. *The Magnetic Lady*, 1632, Induction.
64. C. W. Wallace, *Evolution of the English Drama*, p. 157.
65. Kirkham *versus* Painton *et al.*, 1612, in F. G. Fleay, *Chronicle History of the London Stage*, p. 246.
66. For the theatres of Worcester's Men, see C. J. Sisson, "Mr. and Mrs. Browne of the Boar's Head" and "Notes on Early Stuart Stage History."
67. Jonson, *Poetaster*, III, iv. (Italics mine.)
68. Dekker and Webster, *Northward Ho!* IV, i.
69. Kirkham *versus* Daniel, in Hillebrand, *The Child Actors*, pp. 334–338.
70. Marston, *The Dutch Courtesan*, II, i.
71. C. J. Sisson, *Lost Plays of Shakespeare's Age*, pp. 61, 77–78.
72. Marston, *Jack Drum's Entertainment*, V.
73. Anon., *Wars of Cyrus*, pub. 1594, sig. C3 (ed. Brawner, p. 81).
74. Lyly, *Midas*, Prologue.
75. Marston, *Antonio and Mellida*, Prologue, *Antonio's Revenge*, V, vi, *Jack Drum's Entertainment*, Induction, *What You Will*, Induction.
76. Jonson, *Cynthia's Revels*, Induction.
77. Philip Julius, *op. cit.*, pp. 28–29.
78. Otto, *op. cit.*, p. 440.
79. D. Laing, "Brief Account of the Hawthornden Manuscripts," *Archaeologia Scotica*, Vol. IV (1857), 73–77.
80. Jonson, *loc. cit.*
81. Lyly, *Campaspe*, first Blackfriars, c. 1584. See also the prologue to *Sapho and Phao*, first Blackfriars, c. 1584, and the prologue to *Midas*, Paul's, c. 1589.
82. Jonson, *op. cit.*, Prologue.
83. *Ibid.*, Induction.
84. I. A. Shapiro, "The 'Mermaid Club,'" *M.L.R.*, XLV (1950), 6–17.
85. Marston, *What You Will*, Induction.
86. Guilpin, *Skialetheia*, 1598, sig. A8 *verso*.
87. Sharpham, *Cupid's Whirligig*, II, i.
88. Sharpham, *The Fleire*, I.
89. The will is printed by H. Nobbe in his edition of *The Fleire, Materialien zur Kunde des älteren Englischen Dramas*, 1912, p. 3.
90. Jonson's commendatory verses to Fletcher's *Faithful Shepherdess*.
91. *Certain Elegies, Done by Sundrie Excellent Wits. With Satyres and Epigrams* (1617), 1620, ed. Palmer, 1843.
92. J. T. Murray, *op. cit.*, I, 330, 337, 364.
93. *Calendar of State Papers Domestic, Elizabeth*, ed. Green, V, 227.
94. *Malone Society Collections*, Vol. II, Part II, pp. 147–148 ("Four Letters on Theatrical Affairs").

III. THE RIVAL REPERTORIES

1. J. T. Murray, *English Dramatic Companies*, I, 17.
2. E. K. Chambers, *Elizabethan Stage*, II, 83.
3. See above, p. 21.
4. Chambers, *op. cit.*, IV, 79.
5. Murray, *op. cit.*, II, 288.
6. Chambers, *op. cit.*, III, 466.
7. A. Feuillerat, *Revels Documents, Elizabeth, passim.*
8. Murray, *op. cit.*, I, 141, II, 24, 27, 65; Chambers, *op. cit.*, II, 380, IV, 152.
9. Sidney, *Apology for Poetry*, in G. Gregory Smith, ed., *Elizabethan Critical Essays*, I, 197.
10. Dedication to *The History of Promos and Cassandra*, in Smith, *op. cit.*, I, 59.
11. *Plays Confuted in Five Actions*, in W. C. Hazlitt, ed., *English Drama and Stage*, p. 181.
12. *Ibid.*, p. 189.
13. L. M. Ellison, *Early Romantic Drama at the English Court*, pp. 69 f.
14. *Second and Third Blast of Retreat from Plays and Theatres*, in Hazlitt, *op. cit.*, p. 145.
15. Greene, *Groatsworth of Wit*, in *Life and Works*, ed. Grosart, XII, 131; Nashe, *To the Gentlemen Students of Both Universities*, in *Works*, ed. McKerrow, III, 324.
16. *School of Abuse* (1579), ed. Collier (Shakespeare Society, 1841), p. 30.
17. Greene, *loc. cit.*
18. Edward Hall, *Chronicle*, ed. 1809, p. 597.
19. C. W. Wallace, *Evolution of the English Drama*, pp. 54, 93–95.
20. H. N. Hillebrand, *The Child Actors*, pp. 128–131.
21. Assigned by its editor, J. P. Brawner, pp. 10–20, to Richard Farrant in c. 1575–1576.
22. Hall, *op. cit.*, p. 723.
23. From Richard Gibson's Revels Book, Records of the Exchequer, in Hillebrand, *op. cit.*, p. 324.
24. Edwardes, *Damon and Pythias*, Prologue.
25. Warton, *History of English Poetry*, ed. Hazlitt, IV, 217. (D. Nichol Smith, "Warton's History of English Poetry," *Proceedings of the British Academy*, XV (1929), 96, is of the reluctant opinion that the words are a forgery; but the fact is unproved and perhaps unprovable.)
26. *Il Return from Parnassus*, IV, iii.
27. Jonson, *Cynthia's Revels*, Induction.
28. T. H. V. Motter, *The School Drama in England*, p. 50.
29. Lodge, *Defence of Poetry*, c. 1579, in Smith, *op. cit.*, I, 82–83.
30. Nashe, *Pasquil's Return to England*, in *Works*, ed. McKerrow, I, 92.
31. Spenser, *Poetical Works*, ed. Smith and De Selincourt, p. 482.
32. J. W. Bennett, "Oxford and Endymion," *PMLA*, LVII (1942), 354–369.

33. Marston, *Jack Drum's Entertainment*, V.
34. Ellison, *op. cit.*, p. 60.
35. From the title page of Richard Johnson's *Nine Worthies of London*, 1592.
36. Sidney, *Apology for Poetry*, in Smith, *op. cit.*, I, 173.
37. Rollins, "The Black-Letter Broadside Ballad," *PMLA*, XXXIV (1919), 258–339.
38. L. B. Wright, *Middle-Class Culture in Elizabethan England*.
39. Gosson, *Plays Confuted in Five Actions*, in W. C. Hazlitt, *op. cit.*, p. 189.
40. *Ibid.*, pp. 201–202.
41. *Ibid.*, p. 185.
42. *Second and Third Blast of Retreat from Plays and Theatres*, in W. C. Hazlitt, *op. cit.*, pp. 139–140.
43. Stubbes, *Anatomy of Abuses*, 1583, in W. C. Hazlitt, *op. cit.*, p. 222.
44. "Dramatic Records of the City of London: The Remembrancia," *Malone Society Collections*, Vol. I, Part 1, p. 77.
45. Chettle, *Kind-Hartes Dream*, 1592, ed. Harrison, p. 42.
46. Gosson, *School of Abuse*, ed. Collier, p. 21.
47. Gosson, *Plays Confuted in Five Actions*, ed. Hazlitt, *op. cit.*, p. 181.
48. Nashe, *Pierce Pennilesse*, in *Works*, ed. McKerrow, I, 212.
49. Heywood, *Apology for Actors*, ed. Perkinson, sigs. F4v, G1r&v.
50. *Ibid.*, sig. B4r.
51. "Conversations with Drummond," *Dramatic Works*, ed. Herford and Simpson, I, 141.
52. E. K. Chambers, *Elizabethan Stage*, III, 454, IV, 323.
53. *Transcript of the Stationers Register*, ed. Arber, III, 316.
54. O. J. Campbell, *Comicall Satyre and Shakespeare's Troilus and Cressida*.
55. Jonson, *Cynthia's Revels*, V, i.
56. *Ibid.*, V, xi.
57. Marston, *The Malcontent*, IV, v.
58. M. C. Randolph, "The Medical Concept in English Renaissance Satiric Theory," *S.P.*, XXXVIII (1941).
59. Marston, *The Fawn*, I, ii.
60. A. Feuillerat, *Revels Documents, Elizabeth*, p. 34.
61. Sir John Harington, *Brief Apology for Poetry*, 1591, in G. Gregory Smith, *Elizabethan Critical Essays*, II, 210.
62. Jonson, *Poetaster*, Apologetical Dialogue.
63. Chapman, *Comedies*, ed. Parrott, p. 892.
64. C. J. Sisson, *Lost Plays of Shakespeare's Age*, pp. 12–79.
65. For this and later instances, see E. K. Chambers, *Elizabethan Stage*, III, *passim*.
66. *Ibid.*, III, 370–377.
67. A. W. Upton, "Allusions to James I and His Court in Marston's *Fawn* and Beaumont's *Woman Hater*," *PMLA*, XLIV (1929), 1048–1065.
68. "Commissions for the Chapel," *Malone Society Collections*, Vol. I, Parts 4 and 5, p. 362.
69. Kirkham *versus* Daniel, 1609, in Hillebrand, *The Child Actors*, p. 338.

70. The Master licensed *The Old Joiner of Aldgate* evidently before it reached Paul's in 1603. Cf. C. J. Sisson, *op. cit.*, p. 70.
71. B. Stirling, "Daniel's *Philotas* and the Essex Case," *M.L.Q.*, III (1942), 583–594.
72. Daniel, *Philotas*, Epistle to the Prince.
73. A. Harbage, *Cavalier Drama*, pp. 13–14, 94–95.
74. E. K. Chambers, *Elizabethan Stage*, IV, 93–99.
75. Marston, *Jack Drum's Entertainment*, V.
76. Chambers, *op. cit.*, 112–128.
77. Marston, *What You Will*, III, i.
78. Henslowe, *Papers*, ed. Greg, pp. 72, 79.
79. *Tamburlaine*, To the Gentlemen Readers and Others.
80. See below, p. 93.
81. *Pilgrimage to Parnassus*, V.
82. Jonson, *The Case Is Altered*, I, i.
83. *Downfall of Robert Earl of Huntington*, IV, i.
84. Jonson, *Bartholomew Fair*, V, iii.
85. Webster, *The White Devil*, To the Reader.
86. Chambers, *op. cit.*, IV, 3; III, 516, 271.
87. A. Feuillerat, *Revels Documents, Elizabeth*, pp. 308, 349.
88. On *The Viper and Her Brood*, see H. N. Hillebrand, "Thomas Middleton's 'The Viper's Brood,'" *M.L.N.*, XLII (1927), 35–38.

IV. THE WAR OF THE THEATRES

1. For the discussion of identities, see R. A. Small, *The Stage Quarrel;* J. H. Penniman's Introduction to the Belles Lettres edition (1913) of *Poetaster* and *Satiromastix;* E. K. Chambers, *Elizabethan Stage*, III, *passim*.
2. R. B. Sharpe, *The Real War of the Theatres*.
3. J. Case, *Speculum Moralium Questionum*, p. 183, quoted by Creizenach, *English Drama in the Age of Shakespeare*, p. 428, n. 2.
4. John Milton, "Commonplace Book," *Works*, XVIII, 227; "Outlines for Tragedies," *Ibid.*, XVII, 228–245; *Reason of Church Government, Ibid.*, III, Part 1, p. 240.
5. W. H. Woodward, *Desiderius Erasmus Concerning the Aim and Method of Education*, 1904, p. 114; Vives, *On Education*, pp. 49–50.
6. *Hundred Merry Tales*, 1525, in W. C. Hazlitt, *Shakespeare Jest-Books*, I, 81.
7. Nashe, *Pierce Penniless*, in *Works*, ed. McKerrow, I, 159.
8. Chapman, *May Day*, III, i.
9. Jonson, *Epicoene*, IV, iv.
10. Jonson, *Cynthia's Revels*, III, v.
11. Chapman, *Ovid's Banquet of Sense*, Epistle to Mathew Royden.
12. Chapman, *The Shadow of Night*, Epistle to Mathew Royden.

13. Chapman, *Andromeda Liberata*, line 1.
14. Chapman, *Sir Giles Goosecap*, IV, iii.
15. Hall, *Virgidemiarum* (in *Complete Poems*, ed. Grosart), Book I, Satires III, IV.
16. Marlowe, *Tamburlaine*, Part I, Prologue; Nashe, Epistle to Greene's *Menaphon*, 1589; Lodge, *Scillaes Metamorphosis*, 1589; Greene, *Groatsworth of Wit*, 1592.
17. Rowlands, *The Letting of Humours Blood in the Head-Vaine*, sig. A3.
18. *II Return from Parnassus*, V, i.
19. C. J. Sisson, *Lost Plays of Shakespeare's Age*, p. 69.
20. F. P. Wilson, "Some Notes on Authors and Patrons" in *Joseph Quincy Adams Memorial Studies*, pp. 553–561.
21. Henry Fitzgeffrey, "Notes from Black-Friars," *Certain Elegies*, ed. Palmer, sig. F8.
22. P. Sheavyn's *The Literary Profession in the Elizabethan Age*, and D. Nichol Smith's "Authors and Patrons" will receive valuable supplement in the forthcoming study by Professor Heltzel, and E. Rosenberg's *The Earl of Leicester as Literary Patron*.
23. Meres, "Poetrie" (from *Palladis Tamia*), ed. D. C. Allen, p. 70.
24. *The Puritan*, III, iv.
25. Dekker and Chettle, *Patient Grissill*, I, i.
26. *Ibid.*, V, i.
27. Dekker, *The Whore of Babylon*, Pearson reprint, p. 224.
28. Dekker and Webster, *Northward Ho*, IV, i.
29. M. Eccles, "Middleton's Birth and Education," *R.E.S.*, VII (1931), 531–541.
30. Jonson, *Poetaster*, III, i.
31. *Ibid.*, V, iii.
32. Lodge, *Wit's Misery*, 1596, in *Works*, IV, 57.
33. Nashe, *Works*, ed. McKerrow, V, 67.
34. Baskervill, *English Elements in Jonson's Early Comedy*, pp. 19–21.
35. Marston, *Histriomastix*, III, i.
36. Day, *Law-Tricks*, I, in *Works*, ed. Bullen, p. 10.
37. Jonson, *Poetaster*, Apologetical Dialogue.
38. Marston, *The Malcontent*, IV, iv.
39. Marston, *Antonio's Revenge*, II, iii.
40. Jonson, *Poetaster*, III, iv.
41. H. D. Gray, "The Chamberlain's Men and the 'Poetaster,'" *M.L.R.*, XLII (1947), 173–179. For criticism by P. Simpson and rejoinder by Gray, see *Ibid.*, XLV (1950), 148–152.
42. Barry, *Ram-Alley*, IV, i.
43. Jonson, *Poetaster*, III, iv; V, iii.
44. Marston, *Histriomastix*, IV, i.
45. Jonson, *Cynthia's Revels*, Induction.
46. Jonson, *Poetaster*, V, iii; I, ii.
47. Jonson, *Every Man Out of His Humor*, III, vi.
48. Marston, *Histriomastix*, II, i.

49. Jonson, *Poetaster*, III, iv.
50. Middleton, *Family of Love*, I, iii.
51. Jonson, *The Case Is Altered*, I, i.
52. Webster, *The White Devil*, Epistle.
53. H. Spencer, ed., *Elizabethan Plays*, p. 758.
54. *II Return from Parnassus*, IV, iii.
55. Dekker, *Satiromastix*, Pearson reprint, p. 213.
56. *Ibid.*, p. 260.
57. *Ibid.*, p. 244.
58. *Th'Overthrow of Stage Plays*, quoted by E. K. Chambers, *Elizabethan Stage*, I, 261.
59. Dekker, *Satiromastix*, Pearson reprint, pp. 259–260.
60. *Mucedorus*, Induction.
61. Dekker, *Satiromastix*, Pearson reprint, p. 260.
62. *Mucedorus*, 1610 text, Epilogue.
63. Heywood, *An Apology for Actors*, ed. Perkins, sig. G3.
64. Heywood, *II Iron Age*, edition 1633, Epistle to the Reader.
65. Dekker, *The Whore of Babylon*, Pearson reprint, pp. 214–215.
66. Jonson, *Poetaster*, III, iv.
67. Jonson, *The Case Is Altered*, I, i.
68. W. Perkins, *The Whole Treatise of the Cases of Conscience*, 1608, p. 118.
69. W. Ingram, *The Whipping of the Satire*, 1601, quoted by M. S. Allen, *The Satire of John Marston*, pp. 16–17.
70. *II Return from Parnassus*, I, ii.
71. *As You Like It*, II, vii, 64–69.
72. John Weever, *Faunus and Melliflora*, 1600, quoted by A. Davenport, "The Quarrel of the Satirists," *M.L.R.*, XXXVII (1942), 126.
73. Dekker and Chettle, *Patient Grissill*, V, i.
74. Marston, *The Fawn*, Epilogue.
75. Marston, *The Dutch Courtesan*, Prologue.
76. Marston, *The Malcontent*, Epilogue.
77. *Ibid.*, To the Reader.
78. Marston, *Sophonisba*, Epilogue.
79. Marston, *The Fawn*, Prologue.
80. Chapman, *All Fools*, II, i.
81. Day, *Law-Tricks*, The Book to the Reader.
82. Barry, *Ram-Alley*, Prologue.
83. Jonson, *Poetaster*, Apologetical Dialogue.
84. *Hamlet*, II, ii, 371–377.
85. Jonson, *Poetaster*, Apologetical Dialogue.
86. Sir John Manningham, *Diary*, ed. Bruce, p. 18.
87. W. W. Lawrence, *Shakespeare's Problem Comedies*, pp. 144–169.
88. H. E. Rollins, "The Troilus-Cressida Story from Chaucer to Shakespeare," *PMLA*, XXXII (1917), 428–429.
89. *Troilus and Cressida*, V, iii, 130.
90. Marston, *The Dutch Courtesan*, II, i.

Part Two

TWO VIEWS OF LIFE

I

The Divine Plan

THE poetry of the English Renaissance has been studied in recent years in the light of the thought of the ages, Platonic, Aristotelian, Stoic, Neoplatonic, Patristic, Scholastic, Humanistic, Counterhumanistic, Scientific, with relevance traced through a host of texts, from the *Timaeus* to the treatises of Machiavelli, Copernicus, and Paracelsus, from the *Gospels* to the theorems of Calvin.[1] One does not disparage this learned and enlightening body of discussion by calling attention to its elegiac tone. A product of our age, it is acutely conscious of the stresses to which all bodies of positive doctrine are subject; and the emphasis, at least in a number of the books, is upon the decline and fall of faith. In this respect, the new books contrast remarkably with an old book, Seebohm's *Oxford Reformers*, less erudite than some of its successors but written in more hopeful times. Seebohm obviously felt that in 1867 he was living in an age of enlightenment that had begun in the fifteenth century when Oxford was warmed by the fires of the Platonic Academy at Florence and "the ice of the centuries suddenly was broken."[2] The view was defective, but we should not be too thoroughgoing in its cancellation. At least we should not let the present encircling gloom seem to us so impenetrable that we place the end of the enlightenment at the point where Seebohm placed its beginning.

One reason why the synthesis we know as Christian humanism may seem to have been moving into twilight during the sixteenth century is that, viewed historically, each of the elements that compose it must be allocated to an earlier period. We are apt to identify the synthesis itself with some hypothetical former day of piety, or intellectual clarity, or philosophical grace, and compound a spiritual golden age in which primitive Christians dwelled near the Grove of Academus and listened to discourses by Cicero, Aquinas, and Pico della Mirandola. The current habit of calling Shakespeare's beliefs "medieval"—with a nostalgic tenderness of tone—is symptomatic of this modern mood. We should remember that all the ideas in conflict with the synthesis were older than the synthesis itself, and that the minds awakening to doubts are further evidence of awakening minds. We are even more apt to predate the ending than the beginning of the period of impact of the synthesis. By the beginning of the seventeenth century we catch more often the note of doubt than of belief, of despair than of hope, in the more compelling voices; but it is dangerous to generalize about climates of opinion on the authority of individual spokesmen. Especially in dealing with popular literature, we must allow for a considerable time lag, a long period of seeding between the years when religious, ethical, and political views are first expressed and the years when, if ever, they take general hold. In gauging the attitudes of the English people in the period when Shakespeare was writing, it is more important to know what the school of Erasmus had said than what the school of Montaigne was saying. Not only had the necessary time elapsed, but it had been occupied with unceasing efforts at indoctrination.

One thing that links the sixteenth century more closely to our own than to former times is the importance allotted to persuasion. On the one hand we see a mere development in the techniques of propaganda, manipulated by a Tudor dynasty in order to insure its survival; but on the other, the efforts of true idealists to implement their conviction that men could have life more abundantly only if they understood what was offered them. The two things are not always easily distinguishable, and the uses to which press and pulpit were put may seem admirable or despicable to the observer in proportion to his faith in human nature; however, one cannot contemplate the homilies officially prepared for national consumption without conceding the impulse not simply to tell but to convince, and not some of the people but all the people.

A systematic knowledge of the philosophical basis of belief was not deemed necessary, and no homily was devoted exclusively to natural law and the cosmological order; indeed, as we read early expositions like that in John Rastell's *The Nature of the Four Elements*, about 1517–1526—and this was not so "popular" as one is apt to believe—we realize that modern scholarship might be able to give instruction in the Renaissance world picture to the Renaissance itself. The basic features of the system, however, were known to all literate men and would have been fed into receptive minds by the very habits of speech of schoolmasters, local magistrates, and some of the preachers. A wealth of allusion in the later popular plays argues a general familiarity with the idea that man was the central figure in an orderly, beautiful, and divinely planned universe. The salient fact was that it was a universe of law, not of chance or brute force. "All things that are have some operation not violent or casual," says Hooker in the best of English expositions. "That which doth assign unto each thing the kind, that which doth moderate the force and power, that which doth appoint the form and measure of working, the same we term a law."[3] Himself acting in accordance with Law Eternal, God had decreed for His created universe the Law of Nature, which patterned all being, growing, feeling, reasoning, and prefigured all legal codifications, scientific, moral, civil, international, so that "the obedience of creatures unto the Law of Nature is the stay of the whole world."[4] The law was of God, and all under its sway were the creatures of God and inclined toward perfection—"therefore all things that are, are good."[5] Obedience to the law could be seen in the rhythm of nature, the movement of heavenly bodies, the succession of seasons, the ebb and flow of the sea. Still the appeal was not, as we are apt to believe, of something merely finite, cozy, and well behaved. It was a universe of plenitude, of growth, of cooperation with God in the fulfillment of the plan. There was grandeur in the conception, and there was mystery. Even

in tracts and sermons, "the wond'rous architecture of the world"—
"this majestical roof fretted with golden fire"—could, as in Marlowe and Shakespeare, induce a tone of invocation.

In 1511 Erasmus had let Folly mock philosophers who "frame
countless worlds, and measure the sun, moon, stars, and spheres" as
if "they had access to the secrets of nature . . . , had just come from
a council of the gods," even though they "constantly disagree with
each other" and thus prove that "they do not know the truth."[6]
The sentiment was Erasmus's own, akin to his distaste for theological
contention that obscured essential truths. Belief in a divinely ordered
universe was not dependent upon agreement about its precise mechanical details. As to whether there was a sublunary realm of fire,
or a ninth and crystalline sphere within the primum mobile, or even
a primum mobile, the doctors disagreed. There might or might not
be music of the spheres. For the poet, however, there was music
when wanted, as an item of congruent faith:

> There's not the smallest orb which thou behold'st
> But in his motion like an angel sings,
> Still quiring to the young-ey'd cherubins . . .[7]

Rumors about the Copernican hypothesis, which must have been
current in England at least from the time of Robert Recorde's *Castle
of Knowledge* of 1556, would have struck Elizabethans only as another disagreement among doctors. Creizenach is misleading when
he says, "Shakespeare especially never fails to show himself an adherent of the old theory of the universe."[8] Nowhere in Renaissance
drama to 1613 has the present author come upon an allusion to the
new theory; even the sage Chrisogonus of Marston's *Histriomastix*,
a play for the intellectuals, impresses his listeners with his profundity
by expounding the Ptolemaic system which Recorde, a generation
earlier, had deemed "generally received"[9] rather than true. It is certainly an error to interpret Shakespeare's tragedies in the light of
Donne's pronouncement that the New Philosophy "calls all in
doubt"; and we have been warned against overestimating its early
impact.[10] The word "adherent" is the faulty one in Creizenach's
statement. Shakespeare was no more an adherent to a precisely de-

fined cosmology, old or new, than Erasmus, and his indifference is significant. The sixteenth century was much interested in practical science—in physical phenomena and their uses; but its religion was poetic and ethical, less dependent upon archaic scientific formulations than that of the succeeding age, and, if its interest had been captured, it could have adjusted its metaphor to the Copernican universe, which was, after all, more grand and no less orderly than the Ptolemaic. Bacon's opinion that a multiplicity of atoms would stand in greater need of a "divine marshal" than the four elements suggests the earlier resilience rather than the later brittleness of faith.

The universe was made for man, and man epitomized the universe. As God governed all things, so princes governed states, and fathers families. The family has a greater significance in the system of analogies than is often recognized, especially in political commentary. But most important of all the analogies or correspondences was the subordination of the passions to "Godlike reason" in the microcosm itself, the little world of man. Over the animal nature of men the angelic nature sat enthroned. "The works of nature are all behoveful, beautiful, without superfluity or defect; even so theirs, if they be framed according to that which the Law of Reason teacheth."[11] Nothing in the system received greater stress. The last of the Tudors had ended her long reign when Samuel Rowley's *When You See Me You Know Me* appeared on the stage. In it Cranmer is shown teaching little Prince Edward; and this is the lesson we hear:

> 'Mongst all the creatures in this universe,
> Or on the earth, or flying in the air,
> Man only reason hath, others only sense:
> So what is only sensual is not man but beast,
> For man both sense and reason hath.[12]

In the exercise of his reason, man's will was free. "Man in perfection of nature being made according to the likeness of his Maker resembleth Him also in the manner of working: so that whatsoever we work as men, the same we do wittingly work and freely; neither are we according to the manner of natural agents any way so tied but that it is in our power to leave the things we do undone."[13] For its evocative power a passage from Starkey's *Dialogue* of the 1530's will serve better than pages of exposition. After contrasting the wonders of civilized communities with the rude forest and untilled earth, Starkey turns to his recurrent theme, the divine nature and excellent dignity of man:

> This, if we with ourself reason, and consider the works of man here upon earth, we shall nothing doubt of his excellent dignity, but plainly affirm that he hath in him a sparkle of Divinity, and is surely of a celestial and divine nature, seeing that by memory and wit also he conceiveth the nature of all thing. For there is nothing here in this world, neither in heaven above, nor in earth beneath, but he by his reason comprehendeth it. So that I think we may conclude that man by nature, in excellence and dignity, even so excelleth all other creatures here upon earth, as God exceedeth the nature of man.[14]

We should not mistake for arrogance what is only a resolution to aspire. Man is not equating himself with God, or rivaling God, but engaging in self-exhortation to think well of himself as a creature of God. God's generous spirit descends through creation and sweetens the whole: to know and to love Him remains the ultimate good.

That anyone was good by nature since Adam's fall was a heresy that had presumably been scotched by Augustine. All that can be said is that such early humanists as Colet, More, and Erasmus were heretical by instinct, and, to an amazing degree, their sentiment persisted through the century—a tribute to the efficacy of channeling a message into the schools. Hooker was a professed believer in the fall of man and in salvation by grace alone; still, he has a competing explanation of the presence of evil in the world—"wicked custom, beginning perhaps at the first amongst few, afterwards spreading into greater multitudes"—and now chiefly attributable to defective education![15] Because the confessional that finally defined the doctrine of the English church was designed partly to confound Papists and Anabaptists, and partly to placate the English Genevans, its humanism is not marked; and many of its thirty-nine articles clearly run counter to the attitudes that have thus far been described. It has the ambiguity of most party platforms, but if the articles on Original Sin and on Predestination and Election do not endorse the doctrines of total depravity and a Calvinistic elect, it is difficult to read any meaning into them at all. The nineteenth century apologist has a curious thing to say about Article XVII: he is "strongly disposed to believe" that Cranmer's own views were not Calvinistic, Arminian, nor "even Augustinian," but that he would not have so worded the article "had he intended to declare very decidedly against either explanation of the doctrine of election," whereupon the uneasy commentator softens the rigors of the article so far as his orthodoxy will permit.[16] After 1571, a university degree was obtainable only at the cost of subscription to the Articles; perhaps the melancholy that attacked some notable graduates may be attributed to trauma.

Happily the rank and file, although required to listen to a periodic reading of the Articles, were not required to subscribe or try to understand, but were committed only to the Apostles' Creed. The exposition of Christian faith was supplied by the Book of Homilies. We can understand why this was not a popular work among the more radical reformers. Had More and Erasmus lived to read the Articles, they would have been distressed and bewildered, and probably fortified in their decision to remain with Rome; but they would not have been repelled by the homilies which supposedly explicated them. These were read in rotation year in and year out in the churches of England. The first twelve were published in 1547, the remaining twenty-one in 1563 except for the homily "Against Disobedience and Willful Rebellion," which was added after the insurrection in the North. The last, the most widely known, is the most political. The others have their political elements; but the longer one dwells with them the higher one is apt to assess their spiritual and ethical value and their simplicity and occasional eloquence. They are of unique interest, in bringing us the very words that fell upon the ears of Shakespeare and his contemporaries from childhood to old age.

Alternating between exhortation to moral and civil behavior and explanation of Christian belief, the homilies are in the main conciliatory. Faith is exalted above works; but works, in the sense of moral and charitable behavior, are the evidence of faith. There is

revealed no Erasmian impulse to canonize Socrates, and works before grace are labeled as vain; but they are not, as in Article XIII,
stigmatized as of "the nature of sin," and pagan example in matters of chastity, concord, and domestic probity is sometimes proffered as a shame to Christians.[17] The way that the theological contention about justification by faith or works would be resolved in
the popular mind is suggested by a scene in *A Knack to Know a
Knave*:

> *Priest.*
> . . . good deeds do not justify a man; therefore I count it sin to give
> thee anything.
> *Honesty.*
> See how he can turn and wind the Scripture to his own use, but he re-
> members not where Christ saith, "He that giveth to the poor lendeth unto
> the Lord."[18]

Honesty may have obeyed Homily One, "A Fruitful Exhortation
to the Reading and Knowledge of Holy Scripture," or he may simply have recalled Proverbs 19:17 as the first text quoted in the homily
"Of Alms-Deeds."

In the background is the "misery of all mankind" and "his condemnation to death everlasting by his own sin," but in the foreground is attainable salvation. The doctrine of predestination is by-
passed. The word "election" occurs in contexts like the following
from "Of the Nativity":

> But after he was once come down from heaven, and had taken our frail
> nature upon him, he made all them that would receive him truly, and
> believe his word, good trees, and good ground, fruitful and pleasant
> branches, children of light, citizens of heaven, sheep of his fold, members
> of his body, heirs of his kingdom, his true friends and brethren, sweet and
> lively bread, the elect and chosen people of God.[19]

This was the election of the baptized—not Calvinistic election, or
Arminian election, or national election. Some day error would be
"utterly confounded and put to flight in all parts of the world" so
that, "being at length gathered into one fold, we may in the end
rest all together in the bosom of Abraham, Isaac, and Jacob, then to
be partakers of eternal and everlasting life, through the merits and

death of Jesus Christ our Savior."[20] Whether one's own baptism had been efficacious could be determined by the simple test set forth in the homily of "The Coming Down of the Holy Ghost and Manifold Gifts of the Same":

> The fruits of the Holy Ghost (according to his mind of St. Paul) are these: love, joy, peace, long-suffering, gentleness, goodness, faithfulness, meekness, temperance, &c. Contrariwise, the deeds of the flesh are these: adultery, fornication, uncleanness, wantonness, idolatry, witchcraft, hatred, debate, emulation, wrath, contention, sedition, heresy, envy, murder, drunkenness, gluttony, and suchlike.
> Here is now that glass wherein thou must behold thyself, and discern whether thou have the Holy Ghost within thee, or the spirit of the flesh. If thou see that thy works be virtuous and good, consonant to the prescript rule of God's word, savoring and tasting not of the flesh, but of the spirit, then assure thyself that thou art endued with the Holy Ghost: otherwise, in thinking well of thyself, thou dost nothing else but deceive thyself.[21]

A volume would be required to illustrate fully the extent to which the plays of the public theatres conform to the principles, philosophic and religious, that have been roughly outlined. Combine the message of the Gospels, the conception of "laws and their several kinds" as codified in Hooker, the humane spirit of the circle of Colet, More, and Erasmus, and the moral emphasis of the Homilies, and one has the basic system of the popular drama in the time of Shakespeare. Of primitive delight in action, combat, courage, and trickery there is ample evidence; but the heroes must conform with the system. Henry V must pray before battle, Robin Hood must forgive his enemies, and even Tamburlaine, cruel barbarian though he is, must preserve the chastity of Zenocrate and triumph only over those who merit the scourging of God. Citation must be highly selective, but inferences may be drawn on the extent of the commitment to Christian ethic by the response to its central and most difficult tenet. Freud has described the "all-embracing love of others" as a modification of the sexual instinct, "an impulse with an inhibited aim" (as rational an explanation as any), and has noted that such love is difficult, unreasonable, of questionable utility, and indeed somewhat absurd.[22] In 1562 the official homilist was coping with identical objections in "Information of Certain Places in Scripture." Citing Christ's bidding to turn the other cheek, and Paul's to feed one's enemies, he says, "These sentences, good people, unto a natural man seem mere absurdities, contrary to all reason," and then patiently explains the nature of counsels of perfection.[23] These counsels are presented as exempla in a number of popular plays. In the *Robert Earl of Huntington* plays by Chettle and Munday, the victimized Robert and Matilda return good for evil in almost ceremonial fashion, and in Heywood's *II Edward IV*, Jane Shore forgives her betrayer, Mistress Blage, then is herself forgiven by the Queen she has displaced and the husband she has deserted: "I forgive," says the latter as he completes the cycle in words echoing the *pater noster,*

> as freely from my soul,
> As at God's hands I hope to be forgiven.[24]

In William Rowley's *A Shoemaker a Gentleman* the afflicted Winifred restores the sight of Bassianus her persecutor, and in Heywood's *Fortune by Land and Sea*, Philip Harding refuses to triumph over his crestfallen enemies:

> *Philip.*
> Do you remember with what rude despight,
> What base contempt and slavish contumely,
> You have despis'd me and my dear lov'd wife?

> *Jack.*
> We partly remember it.

> *Philip.*
> So do not I; I have forgot it quite.[25]

In Chettle and Day's *Blind Beggar of Bednal Green*, Momford grieves over the body of Sir Robert Westford, the enemy of his family:

> Glory not in his fall, but rather grieve
> That in his end thou can'st not him relieve:
> Let's bear him in, and, if we can, by art,
> Upon thy foe we'll work a friendly part![26]

Such artless matter is chiefly interesting as it derives in obvious fashion from an accepted ideal, and points to the origin of that ideal. The religious infusion is more impressive when less explicit. In the underplot of *The Honest Whore*, Dekker exploits to the hilt the comic possibilities of reversing the Patient Grissill theme, and his long-suffering husband Candido is an absurd figure; but about the absurdity is an aura wholly lacking in Jonsonian "humors," as we perceive long before we hear Candido's fifth-act *Apologia*:

> Patience, my lord? Why 'tis the soul of peace;
> Of all the virtues 'tis near'st kin to heaven.
> It makes men look like gods: the best of men
> That e'er wore earth about him was a sufferer,
> A soft, meek, patient, humble, tranquil spirit,
> The first true gentleman that ever breath'd.[27]

The old play of *King Leir* is Christian in setting and pietistic in tone, and Shakespeare's *King Lear* is not. To Tolstoy, reading the two plays in a foreign language, this meant a reversion to paganism. But actually, in the effect achieved, Shakespeare's play is the more religious of the two. The impression upon us of the way in which Cordelia, Edgar, and Kent respond to those who despitefully use them is the only fair gauge of the play's Christian orientation. The stress upon lovingkindness, not only in the romances written after his putative "conversion" but in all his plays, is what gives such authority to the term *gentle Shakespeare*, and renders somewhat ridiculous all efforts to "prove" he was no heathen.

The Catholic-Protestant question will be touched upon in a discussion of the politics of the drama, popular and select; we need only note here that the popular drama is antipapal without being militantly anti-Catholic. Even the pope, when presented in opposition to Moors, is respectfully treated,[28] and even a Catholic martyr of the Reformation, when of the stature of Sir Thomas More, is lovingly portrayed—indeed nominated for sainthood.[29] Shakespeare presents his great hero, King Henry the Fifth, as a devout Catholic, and is obviously unperturbed by his benightedness in building

> Two chantries, where the sad and solemn priests
> Sing still for Richard's soul.[30]

The rival play in the popular repertory, *Sir John Oldcastle,* written
to reprove Shakespeare's company for treating disrespectfully the
name of a Lollard martyr, is still uncritical of the great King
Henry, even though he was a persecutor of Lollards. Catholic religious practice, as distinct from Catholic politics, is alluded to only
rarely. In *If You Know Not Me,* the angel who protects the Princess
Elizabeth Tudor from murderous friars "opens the Bible and puts
it in her hand as she sleeps"; in *When You See Me You Know Me,*
Prince Edward Tudor receives a letter recommending "idolatry"
from his sister Mary, and one condemning it from his sister Elizabeth; in *A Shoemaker a Gentleman,* Amphiabel, in giving Albin a
cross, says,

> Wear but this emblem of a Christian,
> Not as a thing material to avail you,
> But for the strengthening of your memory.[31]

Shakespeare's Perdita, who, as a good pagan, should feel no qualms,
apologizes when she kneels before the "image" of Hermione:

> And do not say 'tis superstition that
> I kneel, and then implore her blessing.[32]

Such details are incidental—there is nothing equivalent to the polemics of John Bale, or the debates of the pre-Elizabethan interludists.

Shakespeare often alludes to purgatory, chantries, holy church,
ministers of grace, and the like;[33] and his friars, although more given
to intrigue than to the exercise of their religious duties, are good
and kindly men. Such phenomena are not peculiar to Shakespeare
but appear in the popular plays of even such aggressively Protestant
writers as Dekker. Friar Anselmo of *The Honest Whore* is a more
efficient Friar Lawrence, and Friar Clement of *If It Be Not Good the
Devil Is in It* is the despair of the powers of hell. The mixture of old
and new ways of thinking is amusingly illustrated in Chettle and
Munday's *Death of Robert Earl of Huntington.* Dunmow Abbey
has been portrayed as administered by a bawd, but when the play
ends and the saintly Matilda needs a burial place we get the lines:

Let us go on to Dunmow with this maid:
Among the hallow'd nuns let her be laid.[34]

On the other hand, even when a medieval or continental setting dic-
tates Roman Catholicism as the official religion of a play, it is exceptional for characters to mention absolution when dying or in
danger of death. A priest is called for occasionally in Shakespeare;[35]
but normally, as in the catastrophe of *Romeo and Juliet,* the death of
Catholics is portrayed without mention of the sacrament. The general impression conveyed by the plays is that they are Protestant,
but that their Protestantism is so much like the Catholicism of Colet
and More as to be virtually indistinguishable.

A thousand details could be marshaled to prove that the plays of
Shakespeare and other popular dramatists lack religious consistency.
They were produced in an ingenuous age. Logical consistency is a
scientific virtue, induced by habits of weighing evidence, correlating
causes and effects, exercising the analytical faculty. To a scientific
age like ours, a supernatural age like Shakespeare's is bewildering.
When a dramatist records effects and assumes causes we say that
his play lacks "motivation"; and when his synthetical habits of
thought prove hospitable to disparate ideas we may think of him as
almost schizophrenic. We are constantly confronted by dispropor-
tion, unwariness, a kind of naïveté. In historians like Holinshed we
find the shrewdest observations on human conduct set side by side
with the record of a sheet set out to dry and spotted by an ominous
shower of blood, or the casualty figures of a tragic battle set side by
side with the dimensions of a new chapel. Shakespeare's own mind
was everything but "disciplined," and his plays are full of incon-
gruities. His Protestants use Catholic expressions, and his Catholics
Protestant ones; his Christians, pagan expressions, and his pagans,
Christian ones. In *The Winter's Tale* divine revelation comes from
the oracle of Apollo at Delphi, and yet Polixenes wants his name,
if he prove false, "yok'd with his that did betray the Best."[36] On
the other hand, even the friars and holy nuns invoke the *gods.*

It is not surprising that in the popular drama we should find evidence of Christian faith intermingled with paganism, irreverent

humor, agnosticism, and fatalism. The use of the plural "gods" disregards the basic tenet of Judaic-Christian philosophy, but it was habitual. The gods of the Greeks and Romans were the devils of the Christians, but even Milton was incapable of thinking of them as such. All kinds of spirits found lodging in the woods, streams, oceans, and air of a spiritualized universe, and remained usually benign whether their names were Ceres, Hermes, and Minerva, or Oberon, Ariel, and the like. Sometimes the gods of the ancient pantheon were substituting for the Cardinal Virtues and Deadly Sins, with Diana playing Chastity and Venus playing Lust; but they would often get out of character and express a latent animism more clearly than a taste for symbolized morality. The goddess Fortune could appear as a terrestrial arm of Providence, disciplining the sin of Pride—"an excellent moral," as Fluellen says—but she could also appear as an independent deity of malevolent caprice. We might expect an ancient Briton like Kent to address her in his prayers,[37] but we find that the Christian characters do likewise, although not always so explicitly. Humor failed to observe the religious proprieties, and the malapropisms of clowns like Elbow and Dogberry could include references to villains "void of all profanation in the world that good Christians ought to have"[38] or as "condemn'd to everlasting redemption,"[39] while a respectable housewife like Mistress Ford could speak of going "to hell for an eternal moment or so."[40]

The agnosticism and fatalism have proved greater stumbling blocks to the religious than the superficial features that have been mentioned; however, we should try to distinguish them from their more intellectualized and aggressive relatives, skepticism and stoicism, and to recognize them as the ineradicable token of man's consciousness that he is neither omniscient nor omnipotent, and that the knowledge that has come to him through report is distinct, however superior, from that which has come to him through direct experience. When Marcellus describes the supernatural signs that "some say" mark Christmastide, Horatio replies, "So have I heard and do in part believe it."[41] Antigonus says that he has "heard, but not believ'd, the spirits o' th' dead may walk again."[42] The expression "they say" comes naturally to the lips of characters discussing the unseen world, both in Shakespeare and in other playwrights.[43] Ghosts, omens, and astrological influences may be affirmed in the action of the plays and denied in the words, or denied in the action and affirmed in the words. Hamlet speaks of the "bourne from which no traveller returns" although he has been in close communication with such a traveler; and Theseus, who is one of Shakespeare's most imposing and intelligent characters, argues convincingly against the existence of fairies[44] in a play that teems with them. Edmund, who is a bad man, favors natural explanations of irregular phenomena, and Lafew, who is a good one, denounces such explanations—"ensconcing ourselves into seeming knowledge when we should submit ourselves to an unknown fear";[45] but, in the plays generally, those characters favoring natural and those favoring supernatural explanations are not so easily classifiable as bad and good, and seem simply to illustrate the fact that men are of two minds on the subject;[46] the tendency, however, is to deny only the frivolously miraculous and the compulsive power of evil. Life after death, in Hamlet's most famous soliloquy, is treated as a mere hypothesis; and elsewhere such dubious phrases as "ne'er changing night," "lasting night," "blind cave of eternal night," "being nothing," and "dateless bargain" are used by Shakespeare's Christian characters to describe death.[47] Jeremy Collier was shocked by the joke of the Restoration wit who would not go to heaven readily, i'faith, until he had done more good in his generation.[48] This joke, although without the sexual suggestion, occurs several times in Shakespeare. "God forbid I should be so bold to press to heaven in my young days," says the clown in *Titus Andronicus*;[49] and "God have mercy upon one of our souls!" challenges Sir Andrew in *Twelfth Night*. "He may have mercy upon mine, but my hope is better."[50] There are similar instances, including the unforgettably mixed reflections of Justice Shallow about inevitable death and the price of bullocks at Stamford Fair. Sometimes inadvertently, sometimes with a wry smile, the fact is admitted that mortal man does not put his religion to its ultimate test with alacrity. Nowhere in Shakespeare, however, is there the argumentative quality of the speech by Marston's Isabella:

Were you in health and youth like me, my Lord,
Although you merited the crown of life,
And stood in state of grace assur'd of it;
Yet in this fearful separation,
Old as you are, e'en till your latest gasp,
You'd crave the help of the physician,
And wish your days lengthen'd one summer longer:
Though all be grief, labor, and misery,
Yet none will part with it that I can see.[51]

One further word may be said about the attitude toward death in
the popular drama as exemplified by Shakespeare: the good characters
make better although no more courageous ends than the evil ones;
in about half the instances, their last words are of the afterlife; in the
others, about their reputations and, more frequently, the loved ones
they leave behind.

Corin in *As You Like It* is called a "natural philosopher" because
he knows that a man without money, means, and content is without
three good friends, and that the property of rain is to wet and of
fire to burn, and a great cause of the night is lack of the sun.[52] Hobs
the Tanner in Heywood's *I Edward IV* is praised for minding his
business and making the best of the *status quo*:

> plain men, by observation
> Of things that alter in the change of times
> Do gather knowledge.[53]

The natural philosophy of such characters is usually tinged with
fatalism and, although not pitted against religious formulations,
seems to exist independently of them. The wisdom of experience
and first-hand observation, often expressed proverbially and in the
idiom of the folk, is treated with respect, and the playwrights themselves seem sometimes to be thinking as "natural philosophers."
Shakespeare in the oration of Ulysses and similar oft-quoted passages
can argue with nicety and eloquence the validity of the laws of
order and degree; but he often shows a preference for more homely
reasoning. Kate's speech on the duties of a wife in *The Taming of
the Shrew*, compared with the corresponding speech in the cognate
play, displays a reduction *from* cosmic terms.

Yet in spite of all that has been conceded, the religious and ethical system, the Christian humanism outlined at the beginning of the chapter, remains the system of Shakespeare and the other popular dramatists. Whatever colors are woven into the fabric, the webbing remains the same. The details may raise a doubt, but not the plays as wholes. The total action, the interplay of forces, and the final judgment upon the characters should always be observed. Even the plays of Marlowe, religiously the most daring of the playwrights, will rarely ignore the system and never contravene it, although they may suggest restiveness under its restraints or criticize its presumed subscribers. Marlowe was rebellious by temperament, and probably more adventurous in his thinking than he was permitted to appear in his popular plays. There is none of that Christian tenderness in him illustrated above. But in another fashion, not imposed by the censor or the conditions of their production, his plays are a product of Christian humanism—in their note of aspiration, their spiritual glow, their utter freedom from sordidness. Marlowe's villains are fallen angels. About the other dramatists there can never be any serious question. For them a divine plan existed, and it was knowable and good. Knowledge of it and even belief in the details of that knowledge were variables, but not the conviction that it was good. Faith was, indeed, the substance of things hoped for, and the very lack of precision in the area of belief may have contributed to toughness in the area of faith. Those things that were alien to the system—and we have observed that they were many—were not permitted to collide with it directly. What we never see is a will to disbelieve, or a pride and delight in disbelief.

It is curious that an absence or near-absence of religion in Shakespeare has been conceded by a succession of prominent critics, including Dowden, Raleigh, and Santayana, and that even those who have demonstrated his familiarity with Bible and Prayer Book have hedged on the subject of his true beliefs.[54] Usually they have made insufficient allowance for the extent to which the religion of secular Elizabethans could tolerate impurities, and the facility with which Shakespeare, who was an artist, could "deliberately black out . . . the organic supernaturalism that is yet deeply part of his thinking."[55]

Actually the charge reduces itself to the truism that he was a secular writer. On the basis of the frequency of reference to religious standards, and of paraphrases of specifically Christian texts, there is more religion in Shakespeare than in any other Elizabethan dramatist. Compared with the work of his fellow popular writers, his plays are in this respect simply richer. Compared with the work of the select playwrights, they are different in kind.

Measure for Measure and Chapman's *Bussy D'Ambois* contain a surprising number of passages that invite comparison. For example, the appeal to abandon the cloistered life by Shakespeare's Vincentio:

> Thyself and thy belongings
> Are not thine own so proper as to waste
> Thyself upon thy virtues, they on thee.
> Heaven doth with us as we with torches do,
> Not light them for themselves; for if our virtues
> Did not go forth of us, 'twere all alike
> As if we had them not. Spirits are not finely touch'd
> But to fine issues . . .[56]

Against it may be set that of Chapman's Monsieur:

> If Epaminondas
> (Who liv'd twice twenty years obscur'd in Thebes)
> Had liv'd so still, he had been still unnam'd,
> And paid his country nor himself their right;
> But putting forth his strength, he rescu'd both
> From imminent ruin; and like burnish'd steel,
> After long use he shin'd; for as the light
> Not only serves to show, but render us
> Mutually profitable, so our lives
> In acts exemplary not only win
> Ourselves good names, but do to others give
> Matter for virtuous deeds, by which we live.[57]

In the first passage, the obligation to act is heavenly will, the authority the parables of Christ, and the reward spiritual fulfillment, with the last words (frequently misconstrued) asserting that the tree is known by its fruits. In the second passage, the obligation to act is a combination of self and social interest; the authority, history; and the reward, thrice reiterated, fame. The contrasted nature of the

"light" mentioned in the two passages will alone reveal the way religious suggestion is drained from the second. The contrast is typical.
In the select drama generally, religious reference is rare; and, however Chapman, or Jonson, earned a modern reputation for Christian
humanism, it was not in plays written for Blackfriars and Paul's. All
the playwrights of the coterie, dissimilar in certain other respects—
Lyly, Marston, Middleton, Beaumont, and Fletcher—are alike in
the lack of religious sentiment and inspirational use of Christian
texts. Evidently the dictum that

> illiterate custom grossly errs
> Almost in all traditions she prefers[58]

made no exception of the tradition of Christianity. We are practically told as much in *The Puritan*, performed at Paul's in 1606:
"Almost Religion is come about to fantasy, and discredited by being
too much spoken of—in so many and mean mouths." The subject
was stale. "Nay, did not the learned parson, Master Pigman, tell us
e'en now that all flesh is frail, we are born to die, man has but a
time, with suchlike deep and profound persuasions, as he is a rare
fellow you know."[59]

The only alternatives to the Christian view of life recognized in
the Renaissance were the Epicurean and the Stoic, with the latter
alone possessing anything like respectability. The word "Stoicism"
has been so diversely used in Shakespearean criticism as to have
become almost as meaningless as "Romanticism," and some attempt
must be made to limit its application. Christian ethics, with initial
points of resemblance to Stoic ethics, had absorbed additional Stoic
features in the early centuries of the faith; and the influence was
periodically renewed. The Stoic morality of Cicero was the chief
determinant in making him the favorite classical author of the
Middle Ages and the early Renaissance. Through Plutarch, favorite
biographer, and Seneca,[60] favorite author of plays and precepts,
sixteenth century readers were kept in constant touch with Stoic
ideals; but by this time the ideals were being approved for their
familiarity. Emphasis upon virtue, public and private, upon endurance, and upon reason as controller of the passions had so long

been a feature of Christian thinking that its presence in English
works of Shakespeare's time never argues critical and exclusive Stoic
influence. T. S. Eliot's decision,[61] now possibly amended, that it was
Shakespeare's destiny to express in the greatest poetry an inferior
philosophy seems to have been inspired by monographs on Seneca's
verbal lendings, and on such details as Edgar's speech about man's
enduring his going hence even as his coming hither, or Othello's
valediction upon his past honors and service to the state. Such
speeches do not make the character (or Shakespeare) a *Stoic*. Only
when the ideals in question are presented in isolation from or opposition to Christian ideals do they have critical significance in
Renaissance literature. Sometimes they are so presented, and the
resulting view of life, although with some injustice to ancient thinkers, may be called *Stoicism*. Its mark in the drama is the hero or
commentator who gloomily pits himself against a hostile world, who
has few human relationships or humane impulses, and who is in-
ordinately proud of his virtue, which he is apt to attribute to his
learning. The impartial observer, however, is apt to find this virtue
somewhat lacking in faith, hope, and charity.

The popular drama, although studded with "Stoic" apothegms,
and displays of the "Stoic" virtues, presents no such characters.
Horatio's "blood and judgment are so well commingled" that he is
not "passion's slave" or at the mercy of Fortune's "buffets and rewards";[62] but in this he represents only the ideal human norm. Even
Brutus, the professed Stoic (although recognized by his creator as
something of a backslider),[63] is irrelevantly gentle in heart. In
properly commingling the elements in Brutus,

> Nature might stand up
> And say to all the world, 'This was a man.'[64]

Now Jonson's Crites is of another order. In properly commingling
the elements in him, "Nature went about some fine work, she did
more than make a man when she made him."[65] He has stepped out
of the brotherhood. Almost unendurably self-righteous, Crites per-
sonifies Stoicism rather than Christian humanism—as does Horace in
Poetaster and the other great spirits proffered in the select drama.

Feliche in Marston's *Antonio and Mellida*[66] describes himself as "never surveying any man so unmeasurably happy whom I thought not justly hateful for some true impoverishment" and as far from envying any man because all men are "infinitely distant from accomplished beatitude":

> For when I view with an intentive thought
> That creature fair but proud, him rich but sot,
> Th'other witty but unmeasured arrogant,
> Him great yet boundless in ambition . . .
>
> .   .   .   .
>
> When I discourse all these and see myself,
> Nor fair, nor rich, nor witty, great, nor fear'd,
> Yet amply suited with all full content,
> Lord! how I clap my hands and smooth my brow.[67]

In Chapman, as in Jonson and Marston, the chorusing is Stoic, although in *Bussy D'Ambois* there are interim pleas for Machiavellian *virtu* and the superman of nature, and in *The Revenge of Bussy D'Ambois* for religious fideism. Those who have been brave enough to attempt an analysis of Chapman's thought have worked through to reasonably similar conclusions.[68] In the most recent statement, it is conceded that Chapman considered orthodox Christian morality as that of "the vulgar herd" and adopted "an idiosyncratic scheme of ethics."[69]

Although such philosophical allegiance as the select drama displayed was in the main as described, it was not very strong. The drift was toward a rejection of all codes. "Foh! thou hast read Plutarch's morals," says the smart Clerimont in Jonson's *Epicoene;* "leave this Stoicity alone 'till thou mak'st sermons."[70] Jonson's ridicule of Marston in *Poetaster* includes the detail that he is "a pretty Stoic, too."[71] When Marston wished to portray virtuous men he created Stoics, like Gelosso in *Sophonisba;* but he also delighted in displaying the brittleness of Stoic fortitude. In *Antonio and Mellida*, Andrugio speaks at length upon his freedom and felicity since his loss of power—"I never was a Prince 'till now"; but at the first reminder of his practical situation, he bursts into passionate lamentations.[72] The effect is carefully repeated in *Antonio's Revenge*.

Pandulpho moralizes about his superiority to Fortune's buffets, then suddenly breaks out "despite philosophy" and shrieks that he is "the miserablest soul that breathes."[73] The closest that we come to this kind of thing in Shakespeare is in Act IV, Scene I, of *King Lear*, when Edgar speaks of having seen the worst just before meeting his blinded father; but there is none of the malicious calculation, the obvious delight in pricking bubbles. Shakespeare's characters often cry out against the philosophy that cannot make a Juliet, or let a man endure the toothache patiently; but the focus is upon the force of the pain, not the feebleness of the philosophy. Particular philosophers are not named, and there is no thesis, the artist, as always, refusing to belittle what may be valuable to man or dear to individual men. In the coterie plays, Seneca's wisdom is sometimes alluded to in satirical contexts,[74] and he is attacked in person: "Out upon him! he writ of temperance and fortitude, yet lived like a voluptuous Epicure and died like an effeminate coward."[75]

Even Stoicism then, or the last-ditch philosophy we have been calling Stoicism, held only superficial sway in the coterie drama. Almost as prominent is a leaning toward, or at least intellectual flirtation with, the naturalistic and libertine ideas that had long been anathema to Stoic and Christian alike. We are, of course, dealing with moods and sentiments rather than firm intellectual stands systematically arrived at. Few Elizabethans possessed organized ideas or systematic knowledge about anything; and, although they are not distinguished in this respect from most people of most ages, we are apt to be surprised at the extent to which their "learned men" shared the common trait. Those who have discussed the reading of Nashe, Lodge, Chapman, and Jonson—representative of the belletristic thinkers—have not been impressed with the depth of their studies.[76] Jonson was both the most intelligent and the best read of them, but even his tendency was accretive. Shakespeare had actually assimilated more even of what we call book knowledge than Jonson. Chapman, for all his craving to appear original, was even more anxious to appear erudite. Nashe and Lodge had not penetrated beyond the more obvious classics. The reading of the humble Hey-

wood was, on the evidence of his works, more extensive than that of
Marston, Middleton, Beaumont, or Fletcher. But the coterie writers
were intellectually more self-assertive, and more inclined to seek
sensation in ideas challenging established beliefs. Their taste for the
more licentious Roman satirists proscribed by the early humanists,
and for "debunkers" like Aretine, is indicative. One did not have to
be very learned to be familiar with skeptical thought. It was always
reviewed in refutations by the faithful. The mechanism and the
hedonism of the Epicureans were familiar enough; naturalism, as
distinct from the Law of Nature, could be savored in Lucretius,
Lucian, and others, particularly Pliny, one of the most widely read,
though suspect, classical authors. A passage in Nashe's *Summer's
Last Will and Testament* paraphrases an argument from Sextus
Empiricus on the reasoning powers of dogs, and suggests at least an
interest in skepticism with its accompanying moral relativism. Perhaps there were no first principles! No law but Opinion, no reality
but matter, no reason for not indulging the senses to the utmost.[77]
Such thoughts were fearful but fascinating. The least we can assume
is familiarity with the startling realism of Machiavelli and the
seductively libertine views of Montaigne. The latter's influence on
Shakespeare, although extensively studied, is now recognized as
slight.[78] It is among the select playwrights that we find fellow-travel-
ers.

There is considerable evidence of a tendency to use religion in an
intellectual game—to detect historical flaws in the Bible, and opportunities for jesting in the Creed. "Wit's a disease," writes Field,—

> have we worthy gifts, as judgment, learning,
> Ingenious sharpness . . . ,
> We vent our blessing in profane conceits,
> Or in strong arguments against ourselves,
> Foul bawdry, and stark blindly hold it best
> Rather to lose a soul than lose a jest.[79]

This was a coterie confession of 1609. Over a decade earlier Lodge
had spoken of the "devil derision" whose "nearest profession is
atheism—Nay, such blasphemy uttereth he betwixt the Holy Ghost

and the blessed and immaculate Virgin Mary as my heart trembleth
to think them and my tongue abhorreth to speak them."[80] The
allusion is to the sexual jesting upon articles of religious faith that is
fairly endemic in sophisticated circles, and can be taken less seriously
as sacrilege than as cultural vandalism. Still earlier, by a full generation, the official homilist had felt constrained to issue a warning
against "scorners, jesters, and deriders," and was at particular pains
to supply the true meaning of Psalm 32:17, "I will make David's
horn to flourish."[81] The jokes attributed to Marlowe in the Baines
note[82] are all of a generic type, and the note itself proves only the
existence of a milieu in which they were current. Among young men
of "ingenious sharpness" a revulsion of feeling is evidenced by the
occasional invectives against books and study, from Nashe's

> Nay, I will justify there is no vice
> Which learning and vilde knowledge brought not in,[83]

to Marston's

> The more I learnt the more I learnt to doubt,
> Knowledge and Wit, faith's foe, turn faith about,[84]

lines followed by the epigram, "Delight my spaniel slept," the author's best piece of writing. The penitential moods of Nashe, Greene,
and Lodge, admittedly induced as much by free-thinking as by free-
living, were prophetic of the flights of later wits into religious
fideism, and sometimes the ministry.

We gain some insight into the mood of those who had tasted the
Pierian spring by observing its parallel in our own day. As has been
previously noted, there was little interest in the Copernican theory
even in the smartest literary circles, although Copernicus was the
sixteenth century Einstein; but there was considerable interest in a
more intimate branch of science. The faculty psychology of the late
sixteenth and early seventeenth centuries was far from new, but it
was provoking a new kind of attention. The "humours" as deter-
minants of character and conduct had become a fashionable topic in
speculative circles, in somewhat the same manner as the "unconscious" now, albeit they provided only a faint false dawn instead of
our present blaze of light. Actually there is little distinction, in

philosophical import, between the physiology and psychology of Galen as expounded by Timothy Bright, and the system of Sigmund Freud. The latter will prove better science to the extent that it will account for more clinical data and display more therapeutic utility; but its mystical and ethical vocabulary is misleading, and its disturbing impact, like the ideas about "humours" when they penetrated the Elizabethan nonscientific domain, results from a momentary redirection and narrowing of the focus of attention. The disturbance in the minds of persons like Marston cannot be referred to inadequacies in the inherited cosmological and ethical ideas. That man was a material mechanism, specifically an animal, had not previously been *denied*; it had been clearly recognized that the nonrational elements in his composition were powerful and might at any time gain the upper hand. That the process involved a disturbed adjustment of blood, phlegm, choler, and melancholy (or, as would now be substituted, id, ego, and superego) would have seemed of minor importance to the Christian humanist. The emphasis was upon the reality of a pattern of proper adjustment, its divine origin, its value, and its communicability. In Elizabethan times we seldom encounter professed determinism; but we observe in some quarters the attendant narrowing of the focus of attention to self, and decreased faith in the miracle of human educability.

It is difficult to present the incidental details that suggest skeptical thinking in the coterie plays. Their nature may best be distinguished by comparing them with the nearest equivalent matter in Shakespeare. In Shakespeare the idea is often expressed that things are as they are valued—"There's nothing either good or bad but thinking makes it so"; but the bearing of such passages is usually that of the motto *Honi soit qui mal y pense*, and the effect is to expand the realm of the good. Similarly, when in Shakespeare excessive good is related to evil, the effect is not to blur the distinction between good and evil, but simply to reprove pharisaical righteousness. It would never occur to us to apply to such passages Starkey's words against "the pestilent persuasion of them which say and affirm betwixt vice and virtue no difference to be but only strong opinion and fancy;

they would bring all to confusion and leave no order by nature certain";[85] or Hooker's words against "their brutishness which imagine that religion and virtue are only as men will account them."[86] It is in writers like Marston that such passages as

> Pish, most things that morally adhere to souls
> Wholly exist in drunk opinion,[87]

or

> Philosophy maintains that Nature's wise
> And forms no useless or unperfect thing . . .
> Go to, go to, thou liest Philosophy:
> Nature forms things unperfect, useless, vain,[88]

express a frontal attack upon universal law and the divine plan—the very ultimate in skepticism. Whether such views are advocated is not the point; they receive expression, and not in the mouths of villains. Marston's boldness even extends to the mention of "the genius of quick Machiavel" in one play, and "sound-brain'd Machiavel" in another.[89]

Shakespeare, as has been noted earlier, lets his characters debate the question of natural *versus* supernatural causes, and in a few instances he even lets them voice "scruples" about their Christian faith.[90] Such matter, however, never amounts to damaging argument, and only the evil are vociferous in their doubts. Among the coterie dramatists the equivalent running debate concerns man's obligation, or ability, to assert his reasonable over his sensual nature (as taken for granted by the popular writers), and the matter sometimes amounts to a covert plea for materialistic, deterministic, or libertine ideas. In the late popular play, *The Valiant Welshman*, Voada combats the sensual aggression of Marcus Gallicus in characteristic words:

> Perhaps you'll say that you are flesh and blood.
> Oh, my good lord, were you but only so,
> It were no sin, but natural instinct;
> And then that noble name that we call man,
> Should undistinguisht pass even like a beast.
> But man was made divine, with such a face
> As might behold the beauty of the stars

And all the glorious workmanship of heaven:
Beasts only are the subjects of bare sense,
But man hath reason and intelligence;
Beasts' souls die with them, but man's soul's divine,
And therefore needs must answer for each crime.[91]

In Field's contemporary coterie play, *Amends for Ladies*, Lady Bright, in a similar situation, makes a similar speech, but here the aggressor, Bold, is also given his say:

Your soul? Alas! mistress, are you so fond
To think her general destruction
Can be procur'd by such a natural act,
Which beasts are born to and have privilege in?
Fie, fie! if this could be, far happier
Are sensitive souls in their creation
Than man, the prince of creatures. Think you, Heaven
Regards such mortal deeds, or punisheth
Those acts for which he hath ordained us?[92]

In such encounters the doctrine of restraint is apt to win only the Pyrrhic victory of Niccoli in Valla's *De Voluptate*. That Shakespeare must be placed with the author of *The Valiant Welshman* is illustrated even by *Measure for Measure*, the play that proved most troublesome to nineteenth century critics. Lucio, the libertine, is not supplied with arguments, and Angelo, the apostate, shies away from the religious issue—"I talk not of your soul."[93] He meets Isabella's arguments by distinguishing between voluntary and involuntary sins, not by pleading for sensuality on the authority of animal nature; and yet Angelo is a villain and Bold is not. These distinctions, with the tendency of the popular plays to look for sanctions in upper creation, and of the coterie plays to look for sanctions in lower creation, are symptomatic.

In Marston's *Dutch Courtesan*, Malheureux makes a speech which begins by echoing Ovid's *Amores* and ends by exalting the freedom of animals, thus striking a note as familiar in the coterie plays as in the poems of the young Donne:

O, you happy beasts
In whom an inborn heat is not held sin!

> How far transcend you wretched, wretched man,
> Whom national custom, tyrannous respects
> Of slavish order, fetters, lames his power,
> Calling that sin in us which in all things else
> Is nature's highest virtue.[94]

Malheureux, to be sure, comes to grief; but if the play does not argue the desirability of yielding to "nature" it certainly argues the inevitability of doing so. When Malheureux, before his infatuation with the courtesan, says, "The sight of vice augments the hate of sin," Freevil sarcastically comments: "The sight of vice augments the hate of sin. Very fine, perdy!"[95] Freevil is the author's spokesman, and such mottos as

> No love's without some lust,
> No life without some love,

and

> Of all the fools that would all man out-thrust,
> He that 'gainst Nature would seem wise is worst,[96]

savor somewhat of a new propaganda.

Jonson's Crites in *Cynthia's Revels* inveighs against deterministic and hedonistic notions, lamenting that

> Humor is now the test we try things in,
> All power is just, nought that delights is sin,

and crying,

> O, how despis'd and base a thing is man,
> If he not strive t'erect his groveling thoughts
> Above the strain of flesh![97]

But in *Poetaster* of the following year Jonson lets Ovid plead a case:

> No essence is so dear to moody sense
> As flesh and blood, whose quintessence is sense:
> Beauty compos'd of flesh and blood moves more,
> And is more plausible to blood and flesh,
> Than spiritual beauty can be to the spirit.[98]

Ovid and his associates are punished for their impious charade, but Horace-Jonson seems to exonerate them when he reproves the telltales who preyed

> upon the life of innocent mirth
> And harmless pleasures bred of noble wit.[99]

Our minds are left in some confusion. In view of Jonson's true literary distinction and monumental earnestness, it seems invidious to judge his work by standards that it cannot meet; but the fact remains that his comedies are soulless, and of only the slightest ethical interest. The finely appreciative essay of Professor Levin cannot certainly be considered unsympathetic, yet it seems to concede that the view of life in Jonsonian comedy is "so darkly deterministic that it precludes all possibility of reform."[100] We can at least understand why such a visitor to his dramatic world as Edmund Wilson should have described it as the projection of a mental malaise itemized in one of the more elementary psychoanalytical handbooks.[101] One of the earliest critical judgments upon Jonson was that he was "a mere empirick"[102]—in other words, that he dealt only with surfaces. The writer may only have been repeating, without approving, what others were saying. The charge seems to have been common because Jonson himself took cognizance of it.[103] These present remarks are not intended as an evaluation of Jonson's art, but only as a reminder that it is the last place to look for triumphs of spirit or intimations of a divine plan.

Chapman, when he is not eulogizing pure spirit, displays toleration, indeed admiration, for the passions bred in blood. If they are sufficiently imposing, as in the case of Bussy D'Ambois, they seem in some mystical fashion to render the character too noble for this world. It is a fact worth pondering that there was an audience in Elizabethan times that would accept a Tamburlaine of the boudoir. The power of the libido is a favorite theme in all the coterie plays. Although so alien to the vein of his romantic comedies, the theme is prominent in the plays written by Thomas Dekker in collaboration with Webster for the Paul's boys. In *Westward Ho,* a long soliloquy by the Earl alternates between ecstatic praise of sexual indulgence—"delicious pleasure, earth's supremest good"—and disgust at man's helplessness to resist the "strong magic" of his appetite:

> 'Tis but a minute's pleasure, and the sin
> Scarce acted is repented: shun it then—
> O, he that can abstain is more than man![104]

The sexual preoccupation in the private theatres will be discussed later. At the moment we are interested only in the debate on the conflict between reason and sense, with its substratum of sentiment that sexual indulgence has been too harshly judged:

> Lying, malice, envy, are held but slidings,
> Errors of rage, when custom and the world
> Calls lust a crime spotted with blackest terrors.[105]

Witty Middleton lets his contemptible citizen Harebrain unconsciously become a wit:

> Your only deadly sin's adultery,
> All sins are venial but venereal.[106]

The tendency to brood over the power of nature—specifically to analyze the sexual impulse instead of simply to insist upon its control—led in a few of the later tragedies by Middleton and by John Ford to psychological subtlety and moments of "searching irony";[107] but such artistic fruits are not apparent in the plays of Marston, Chapman, and others during the heyday of the chorister companies. Individual passages are arresting in their insight into human motives, but the characterization as a whole is confused—and the moralizing even more so. Spokesmen are set up in the plays only to be condemned out of their own mouths, and philosophical doctrine is voiced and repudiated in the same breath. Marston's Quadratus has been called "the Author's representative" and "a curious mixture of stoicism and epicureanism"[108]—a curious mixture indeed—while the dramatist's other commentators, Lampatho, Planet, Malvolio, Hercules, and the like, are similarly split down the middle. In Chapman there is the same equivocation. Tharsalio is described in *The Widow's Tears* as one whom debauched companions have

> Turn'd devil like themselves, and stuff'd his soul
> With damn'd opinions and unhallowed thoughts
> Of womanhood, of all humanity
> Nay, deity itself,

until there is no man, woman, or action that his tongue can "glide over, but it leaves a slime upon't."[109] This is so graphic that we seem to see a verminous specimen impaled—but no:

Cynthia.

Brother, I fear me in your travels, you have drunk too much of that Italian air, that hath infected the whole mass of your ingenuous nature, dried up in you all the sap of generous disposition, poisoned the very essence of your soul, and so polluted your senses that whatsoever enters there takes from them contagion and is to your fancy represented as foul and tainted, which in itself, perhaps, is spotless.

Tharsalio.

No, sister, it hath refined my senses, and made me see with clear eyes, and to judge of objects as they truly are, not as they seem, and through their mask to discern the true face of things.[110]

Evidently we are to accept Tharsalio at his own evaluation, because Chapman makes him the triumphant manipulator of the other characters. It is awe-inspiring to observe our own times matching confusion with confusion: Chapman has been praised as having the "cynicism of a philosopher, or at least of a medieval monastic, toward the world and the flesh."[111] But if one will read this play he will discover that Tharsalio—the widow-hunting bravo, quite devoted to the world and the flesh—represents for his creator something quite admirable.

The coterie plays illustrate the difficulty of formulating a philosophy or ethical program out of rejection. It was unfashionable to endorse the Christian humanism in popular currency, and both hard to find and tedious to seek a satisfactory substitute. Canceled, the divine plan left a vacuum; reversed, it left only a diabolical scheme. With nothing to defend, energies must go into attack, with cynicism substituted for idealism, pessimism for optimism, a hymn of hate for a hymn of love:

> Hate honor, virtue, they are baits
> That 'tice men's hopes to sadder fates . . .

All things are error, dirt, and nothing,
Or pant with want, or gorg'd to loathing,
Love only hate.[112]

We may take this as the cry of pain of the disillusioned idealist, and
let the perfection of the symptoms compensate for the imperfections
of the art; or we may plead a more ingenious case and speak of the
homage of desecration: what a beautiful thing is that which this is
not! Probably the best case that could be made out for spiritual
value in this body of drama would relate it to the doctrine of Original Sin, and postulate its creators as gay Augustinians; an idea of the
kind may lie behind the praise of Tharsalio as "a medieval monastic."
The product of the mood expressed was, sometimes, actually fideism
—a turning to God in refuge from the vileness of all His works.
Marston speaks shrewdly on one occasion of

some of our gallant prodigals:
When they have consum'd their patrimonies wrongfully,
They turn Capuchin for devotion.[113]

Marston himself entered the ministry; but we do not know the
nature of his conversion, or even whether conversion was deemed
necessary. Jonson reported that his plays were thought to be such
as might have been written by a clergyman![114]

II

The Dignity of Man

THE conception of human character in Elizabethan drama is so closely integrated with the cosmological and ethical system as to render somewhat artificial a segregate discussion. It is Starkey's "sparkle of divinity" in Faustus, Macbeth, and their like that conveys the sense of tragic waste. We owe such creations to underlying assumptions about universal order and the abnormality of evil. And we owe such creations as Simon Eyre and Falstaff (with our sympathetic laughter) to underlying assumptions that we all share family traits in a brotherhood of man. Characters like these did not appear, and could not have appeared, in the coterie drama. Its philosophical dissidence denied man the dignity for the truly tragic and the complexity for the truly humorous, however horrendous, comic, or theatrically effective its *dramatis personae* might sometimes be.

The doctrine of man's depravity since Adam's fall, with the concordant decay in Nature, carried imposing credentials; but the very essence of Humanism is its break with the *contemptus mundi* tradition. The recrudescence of this tradition in sixteenth century *belles-lettres* owes less to the indignation of the Augustinian monk or the tenacity of the Genevan logician than to "gentleman-like melancholy."[1] The majority of those who cultivated it, other than the poor "unpreferred scholar" whose lot we have discussed,[2] were dilettantes, often withdrawn from the active life of the times. Their writings, whatever protestations accompany them or conversions follow them, convey an impression less of religious austerity than of self-indulgence—an almost sensual enjoyment of gloom. We can only speculate on the inner promptings that would make a Gascoigne produce his *Drum of Doomsday*, or a Donne his *Progress of the Soul*, but such voices often appear to be crying less in than for a wilderness. Not even Montaigne's grave urbanity, of which no English writer was capable, can conceal the relish for destruction in the "Apology for Raymond Sebonde." The contempt for the world and those who infest it, in some of the plays of the select theatres, can be described only as orgiastic.

For John Marston, coterie dramatist unadulterated, there is no such thing as an "uncontaminated springtime." The April rains which in Chaucer had

> bathed every veyne in swich licour
> Of which vertu engendred is the flour,

suggest to Marston an act of sordid copulation:

> The wanton spring lies dallying with the earth,
> And pours fresh blood in her decayed veins.[3]

Anthropomorphic imagery often produces this vision of a man-infected universe. Night is a "snoring world"[4] or one steeped in "sluggish fumes."[5] A marsh squeezes out tears from "spongey cheeks,"[6] and a raging sea suffers from flatulence, "his bowels rumbling with windy passion."[7] Dew is the "cold sweat of night" on "earth's dank breast,"[8] and winter flays the skin from the "nak't shuddering branch."[9] Boaistuau's picture of the earth, "so depraved and broken in all kind of vices and abominations that it seemeth to be a place that hath received all the filthiness and purgings of all other worlds and ages,"[10] and Montaigne's picture of man as "the most miserable and frail" of all creatures, lodged amidst the "filth and mire of the world, fast tied and nailed to the worst, most senseless, and drooping part,"[11] are Marston's:

. . . this earth is the only grave and Golgotha wherein all things that live must rot: 'tis but the draught wherein the heavenly bodies discharge their corruption, the very muckhill in which the sublunary orbs cast their excrement. Man is the slime of this dung-pit, and the princes are the governors of these men.[12]

Comparison with Hamlet's apostrophe to man is inevitable:

I have of late—but wherefore I know not—lost all my mirth, forgone all custom of exercises; and indeed it goes so heavily with my disposition that this goodly frame, the earth, seems to me a sterile promontory; this most excellent canopy, the air, look you, this brave o'erhanging firmament, this majestical roof fretted with golden fire—why, it appeareth no other thing to me than a foul and pestilent congregation of vapours. What a piece of work is a man! how noble in reason! how infinite in faculties! in form and moving how express and admirable! in action how like an angel! in apprehension how like a god! the beauty of the world, the paragon of animals! And yet to me what is this quintessence of dust? Man delights not me—no, nor woman neither, though by your smiling you seem to say so.[13]

Our times are apt to mistake this grand inscription for an epitaph, to assume that Shakespeare is saying what Marston is saying, as if "quintessence of dust" signified the dustiest kind of dust. It signifies actually the precious distillation of the spirit permeating all matter. Man as the "quintessence of dust" is the precise reverse of man, as the "slime of this dung-pit." For Hamlet the earth remains a "goodly frame" with man as its "beauty," and each demurrer is accompanied by "seems *to me*," "appeareth no other thing *to me*," "and yet *to me*"—the sad tappings of a finger upon the speaker's own breast.

Shakespeare always distinguishes thus between the universal and the particular. The single surviving prologue to a Shakespearean tragedy suggests that the dramatist would no more have insisted upon the typicality of the fate of a Lear, Hamlet, Macbeth, or Othello, than upon that of a Romeo or Juliet. But, for Marston, the spectacle of men mired in vice epitomizes life:

> Who winks, and shuts his apprehension up
> From common sense of what men were and are,
> Who would not know what men must be, let such

> Hurry amain from our black-visag'd shows:
> We shall affright their eyes.[14]

Among those who must depart are any who have been duped by a happy childhood. Man is "vermin bred of putrefacted slime."[15] Man is "man's excrement, man breeding man."[16] Hamlet's apostrophe is further parodied in a passage on woman:

in body how delicate, in soul how witty, in discourse how pregnant, in life how wary, in favors how judicious, in day how sociable, and in night how? O, pleasure unutterable![17]

Elsewhere the softness of a woman's breasts is compared with that of "a courtier's tongue, an old lady's gums, or an old man's mentula."[18] Always there is the compulsion to degrade: a "beggar when he is lousing of himself looks like a philosopher, a hardbound philosopher when he is on the stool looks like a tyrant, and a wise man when he is in the belly-act looks like a fool."[19] Twice the illustrious men of the past are enumerated as cuckolds;[20] and twice an abandoned temple is described as "a stinking privy"[21]—a place where the shepherd now "unloads his belly."[22] Marston's stylistic excesses are his own, but his conception of man is that of his milieu.

The select dramatists painted corruption with a gusto unknown outside their circle. Hooker had admitted that "the greatest part of men are such as prefer their own private good before all things, even that good which is sensual before whatever is most divine,"[23] but his mind was incapable of lingering upon the idea; the popular Heywood is never so insipid as when his dramatization of the ages leads him from gold through silver to brass, and he feels obliged to suggest the growth of evil in the world:

> Sometimes even mean fellows
> Abed with noble ladies whom they serve,
> Master with servant, married men with maids,
> And wives with bachelors.[24]

We shall observe that he wrote differently of death in battle or the grandeur of the Thames. It was the rival playwrights that developed expert techniques of generalization about the "strange surquedries" of the world—the universal taint that made legitimacy so speculative that all claims to titles were doubtful, and all acts of cohabitation possibly incestuous.[25] When Dekker and Webster wrote for Paul's, they conformed by composing speeches like Justiniano's:

> Why, even now, at holding up of this finger, and before the turning down of this, some are murd'ring, some lying with their maids, some picking of pockets, some cutting purses, some cheating, some weighing out bribes. In this city some wives are cuckolding some husbands. In yonder village some farmers are now grinding the jawbones of the poor. Therefore, sweet scholar, take summer before you, and lay hold of it.[26]

Middleton's rogues find sanction enough for ill-doing—Goldstone in *Your Five Gallants* because "the world runs on dissimulation,"[27] Pyeboard in *The Puritan* because "every profession makes itself greater by imperfections,"[28] and Witwood in *A Trick to Catch the Old One* because "a multitude of men in the world . . . only sojourn upon their brain, and make their wits their mercers."[29] The way of the world is described by Middleton's mistress-keeping thief:

> Well, what a horrible age do we live in, that a man cannot have a quean to himself! . . . Does my boy pick and I steal to enrich myself, to keep her, to maintain him? Why, this is right the sequence of the world. A lord maintains her, she maintains a knight, he maintains a whore, she maintains a captain. So, in like manner, the pocket keeps my boy, he keeps me, I keep her, she keeps him: it runs like quicksilver from one to another.[30]

Comedy provided intrigue with witticisms, tragedy violence with strong lines: the substance remained the same.

Allusions to excrement, human odors, and physical disease are rife. A curse in Marston, "The sarpego, the strangury, and eternal uneffectual priapism seize thee,"[31] is paralleled in Jonson, "Now the bots, the spavin, and the glanders . . . light on him."[32] Marston's "Here in the city a man shall have his excrements in his teeth again within four and twenty hours"[33] is echoed in Sharpham's "I had rather have my excrement in my nose than in my teeth,"[34] and Middleton's "If ditches were not cast once a year, and drabs once a month, there would be no abiding in the city."[35] There follow descriptions of the aged by four different writers for the private theatres. From Marston's *The Fawn*:

By this light, I'll swear he said his father had the hip-gout, the strangury, the fistula in ano, and a most unabidable breath, no teeth, less eyes, great fingers, little legs, and eternal flux, and an everlasting cough in the lungs.[36]

From Jonson's *Epicoene*:

. . . she spends me forty pounds a year in mercury and hogs-bones. All her teeth were made in Blackfriars, both her eyebrows in the Strand, and her hair in Silver-street. Every part of the town owns a piece of her. . . . She takes herself asunder still when she goes to bed, into some twenty boxes.[37]

From Barry's *Ram-Alley*:

> Would't marry an old crazed man,
> With meager looks, with visage wan,
> With little legs and crinkled thighs,
> With chap-fall'n gums and deep-sunk eyes?
> Why, a dog seiz'd on ten days by death
> Stinks not so loathsome as his breath;
> Nor can a city common jakes,
> Which all men's breeches undertakes,
> Yield fasting stomachs such a savor
> As doth his breath and ugly favor.[38]

From Chapman's *May-Day*:

His breath smells like the butt-end of a shoemaker's horn; a lep'rous scaly hide like an elephant; the son of a sow-gelder that came to town . . . in a tattered russet coat, high shoes, and yet his hose torn above 'em; a long pike-staff on his neck (and a turd in his teeth) and a wallet on his right shoulder.[39]

Such matter makes somewhat incomprehensible the statement that when Chapman transferred his efforts to the private theatres, he learned that "the coarse buffoonery of *The Blind Beggar* which had delighted the gross public of the Rose was not likely to suit the taste of the gentlemen and courtiers who frequented Blackfriars."[40] On the few occasions when the two types of theatre figure in literary criticism, we are apt to get these testaments of faith that the public audience was "gross" and the private audience "refined."

In the popular drama, the tendency is to expose and lecture rogues and then to pardon them, and to give villains swift, clean deaths. In the select drama the tendency is to submit offenders to prolonged physical as well as verbal indignities. This technique in Jonson scarcely needs illustration. Shakespeare at his harshest will lock gulls in dark rooms, but not in privies, and he refuses to have them kicked—as Daw and La Foole are kicked in *Epicoene*, Mendoza in *The Malcontent*, and others. In the coterie plays there is an unhealthy intentness about the way the authors turn upon their characters, even the milder of the authors—in the way, for instance, that Chapman concentrates on the humiliation of Gostanzo in *All Fools*, of Lorenzo in *May-Day*, and Bassiolo in *The Gentleman Usher*. Marston is not one of the milder authors, and the verbal and physical indignities at the conclusion of *Antonio's Revenge* are nothing short of sadistic. After tearing out Piero's tongue, and exhibiting to him his slaughtered child, the avengers stab him in rotation:

> *Antonio.*
> Scum of the mud of hell!
> *Alberto.*
> Slime of all filth!
> *Maria.*
> Thou most detested toad!
> *Balurdo.*
> Thou most retort and obtuse rascal![41]

Thereafter the assassins receive the blessings of the state:

> Blest be you all, and may your honors live
> Religiously held sacred even for ever and ever.[42]

The lines should not mislead us into generalizing about the "primitive" moral notions of the Elizabethans. In Chettle's *Hoffman*, there is different comment upon the vengeance taken by a son for his father's murder:

> Yes, 'tis admirable, 'tis excellent, 'tis well,
> 'Tis meritorious—where? In heaven? no, in hell![43]

In the popular drama, just as any who take up arms against their king become "rebels," no matter what the provocation, so any who take personal vengeance become murderers. Speculation over the reason for Hamlet's hesitation to slay Claudius has been singularly unconcerned with Shakespeare's hesitation to convert his hero into a villain. His audience would have looked askance at any slaying not committed in combat and heat of blood.

Hamlet of the Globe, *Hoffman* of the Fortune, and *Antonio's Revenge* of Paul's are almost adequate in themselves to illustrate the distinct conceptions of the nature of man at the public and the private theatres, even though all are in the Senecan tradition and treat the theme of murdered father and revenging son. In the matter of rottenness, Shakespeare's Denmark seems only slightly spotty when compared with Marston's Venice, while Chettle's Dantzic seems almost idyllic. Chettle supplies torture, madness, multiple murders, and a plethora of skeletons; but the evil is all concentrated in Hoffman himself and his lone assistant. The rulers are just, the victims forgiving, the women chaste. Lucibell seems to have wandered into the play from *A Midsummer Night's Dream* or *Comus*:

> Blush not, chaste moon, to see a virgin lie
> So near a prince, 'tis no immodesty:
> For when the thoughts are pure, no time nor place
> Have power to work fair chastity's disgrace.[44]

In his denouement, Chettle is torn between the impulse to kill off his villain in spectacular fashion by means of his own instrument of torture, and the impulse to keep the torturers decent; he tries to do both, with conspicuous lack of success. The play is as defective as *Antonio's Revenge*, but it is absurd rather than debased. Hamlet escapes the absurdity, and was never in danger of being debased.

The numerical inferiority of the villains in *Hoffman* has its philosophical bearing, ludicrous as the statement may seem. In the nature of his median character, a dramatist reveals whether he thinks with Pelagius or Augustine. A census of the 775 classifiable characters in Shakespeare shows that the good outnumber the evil in the ratio of seven to three, with the proportion varying little in comedy, history, and tragedy, or among representatives of the low, middle, and upper social classes.[45] In the plays of Jonson, Marston, Chapman,

Middleton, and the minor writers for the private theatres the ratio is more than reversed. When a tragedy like *Antonio's Revenge* or a comedy like *The Fawn* comes to an end, Marston can vilify contemptible characters only by enlisting the aid of other contemptible characters—he has left no one else available for the purpose. When Chapman's Monsieur and Bussy D'Ambois vilify each other,[46] they may both be speaking for the author; they are both certainly speaking for the reader. In Jonson and Middleton the servants and other background characters are as defective as the principals, and among the principals the winners are cleverer rather than better than the losers. On the other hand, a count would show that, in the total *dramatis personae* of the popular stage, the Shakespearean ratio of seven to three on the side of the angels holds good.

The morality tradition, with its basis in the psychomachy and conflict between the cardinal virtues and the deadly sins, would insure that in dramatic casts good would at least be represented. The force of the tradition remained strong to the end. In *Cambyses* the vicious king has a virtuous brother, Smirdis, while the upright counselor Praxaspes offsets the corrupt judge Sisamnes. In Heywood's *Woman Killed with Kindness* the frail Anne in the one plot is counterbalanced by the steadfast Susan in the other. In *King Lear* neither the daughters of the one father nor the sons of the other may *all* be vicious. In Dekker's *If It Be Not Good the Devil Is in It*, the infernal powers may prevail over the Lord Prior but not over his coadjutor, the saintly Clement. All readers of Elizabethan drama must be familiar with such juxtapositions. But the representatives of the forces of virtue could never be more than equal to those of vice in the old schematization, and the morality tradition will not account for the preponderance of good characters on the popular stage. As soon as regular plays begin to appear, with their expanded casts, we observe an appeal to optimism, good feeling, and delight in concord. Rusticus and Hodge conclude their fight in *Horestes* with "Nay, let's be friends,"[47] and Hob and Nob theirs in *Cambyses* in compliance with the stage direction, "Shake hands and laugh heartily one at another."[48] The device was never abandoned: in *If You Know Not Me* Dean Nowell weeps with joy at the very thought of ending the enmity between Thomas Gresham and Thomas Ramsey.[49] And, of course, it was sometimes abused: in *The Weakest Goeth to the Wall* the concluding scenes of amity are made limp with Lord Epernon's tears. Usually the authors are successful in avoiding sentimentality through the astringent effects of humor, or the laconic style. It was a knack that the succeeding age quite lost.[50]

Faith in virtue is manifested in the way it was presumed to be communicable. Exposure to it converts erring characters, as in Heywood's *I Fair Maid of the West*, through which the ineffable barmaid Bess steers her unswerving course. Often the promptings are from within. Bourbon, the villain of *The Trial of Chivalry*, must be whetted on to his persecution of Bellamira, and at crucial moments comes dangerously close to turning good.[51] The writers had difficulty in keeping their wicked characters wicked. Evil, on the other hand, is neither contagious nor hereditary. Lustful Cambyses has a chaste queen, and unjust Sisamnes a just son. In *The Blind Beggar of Bednal Green*, a villainous son is opposed by a virtuous father, and in *The Merry Devil of Edmonton* the roles are reversed. Rogues and villains are plentiful, but the sky line is kept steady by the background characters. Even in a story as black and violent as that of *A Yorkshire Tragedy*, the world remains a healthy world, as represented by the blameless wife, the courageous old servant, the conscientious officials, and the "three gentlemen" with their choral comments. The romantic comedies, Shakespearean and non-Shakespearean, amaze us with their power to sustain interest with a pennyworth of evil for a pound of good. In *Mucedorus*, the parents prove as innocent in the end as the stainless lovers. The little knot of villains in Greene's *James the Fourth* are presumably terrific Machiavellians, but they are almost pathetic in their inability to keep afloat in the sea of virtue, created principally by the women. *Fair Em* has among its eighteen characters only two who are seriously flawed. The great tour de force in this kind is Dekker's *Shoemaker's Holiday*. It teems with all kinds of people in all kinds of situations; but with the exception of Dodger the telltale, who speaks only a few lines, every character is sound to the core. Master Hammon, the unsuccessful wooer of Rose and Jane, should by all narrative precedent have been a contemptible creature; but he is the reverse. He lingers in our minds as a plaintive and appealing figure; we hope that he found a heart-free maiden at last.

The popular impulse was always to elevate. We need not linger with the heroes—child heroes like Ned a Barley, centenarian heroes like Old Musgrove, yeoman heroes like George a Greene, royal heroes like Edward of England, women heroes like Lady Jane[52]—although there are examples in every play. More arresting is elevation of character where we should expect the reverse. Mention has been made of the honor paid Sir Thomas More, the Catholic martyr. A parallel instance is offered by the dramatic treatment of Thomas Stukely, the renegade and Catholic adventurer. His politics seem to have been forgotten in his renown as a brave soldier who had companioned with kings. He is treated with respect in Peele's *Battle of Alcazar*, and mentioned with honor in Heywood's *If You Know Not Me*,[53] while the whole of *Captain Thomas Stukeley* is devoted to his exploits—

> It is not one will say unto his men,
> 'Give you assault upon the enemy,'
> [But,] 'Follow me!'[54]

The play helps us solve the riddle of why the first part of *Tamburlaine*, which was the more popular, proved so acceptable in spite of the liberties taken with the principles of order and degree. Unlike Barabas of *The Jew of Malta*, Tamburlaine would not have been viewed as a Machiavellian; he has his standards of probity, and is a lion but no fox. In Rowley's *When You See Me You Know Me*, Henry VIII is most favorably impressed by Black Will, the highwayman. Crime was deplorable, of course; but courage was courage, and in the popular mind highwaymen and pirates received special dispensations. Elevation occurs unexpectedly also in the case of certain women. Jane Shore had committed the almost unpardonable offense of deserting a London husband, but the playwrights commemorated chiefly her charity and penitence; in this case Shakespeare proved the least gentle of the lot.[55] Moll Frith was no more than a notorious trull; but she is charmingly transfigured in Dekker

and Middleton's *The Roaring Girl*. Middleton signed the epistle to
the published text; and it is revealing when the cynic of Paul's becomes the idealist of the Fortune: " 'tis the excellence of a writer
to leave things better than he found them."[56]

The popular stage almost wrested one piece of territory from the
Devil himself. The witches of *Macbeth* certainly carry the scent of
hell, but the wizard who plays a small offstage part in *As You Like
It* is the more characteristic—"most profound in his art and yet not
damnable."[57] Most of the witches and wizards in the plays, from
Bomelia in *The Rare Triumphs of Love and Fortune* to Prospero in
The Tempest, put their dark arts to bright ends, and are saved by
timely abjurations. Even Faustus, though unsaved, is singularly high-
minded, while Greene's Friar Bungay, Munday's John a Kent, and
the interesting Peter Fabel of *The Merry Devil of Edmonton* are
chiefly exercised in helping true lovers to the marriage altar. Fabel
speaks as mournfully as Faustus at the beginning of the play; but
after outwitting the Devil and using his powers in the cause of
virtue, he is permitted to say:

> I used some pretty sleights, but, I protest,
> Such as but sat upon the skirts of art;
> No conjurations, nor such weighty spells
> As tie the soul to their performancy.[58]

Those with supernatural powers in the select plays from Lyly's Dip-
sas to Marston's Erictho are more apt to be damnable, and to have
a vested interest in lechery. Chapman seems to give his blessing to
Friar Conolet in *Bussy D'Ambois*, and perhaps we are not supposed
to be critical when he puts his devil Behemoth at the service of adul-
terers; but we must observe that Bishop Dunstan in the popular *A
Knack to Know a Knave* uses his devil to *prevent* adultery. Doubt-
less both these churchmen might have been better employed than in
invoking devils; but in the play at the public theatre the upshot
would have provoked no laughter under the hills.

Shakespeare's methods of censoring his source materials are observable among other playwrights when they are composing for the
public theatres. Webster's *The White Devil* failed at the Red Bull,

probably because Vittoria proved an unacceptable protagonist, but the dramatist has gone far in reducing the sordidness of the historical events. Vittoria, Brachiano, and Flamineo seem to be motivated by reckless defiance rather than cupidity and lust, while Vittoria's mother and Brachiano's wife are pictured as virtuous rather than as the procuress and adulteress of the actual record. The source of *Greene's Tu Quoque* of the Red Bull was probably *Ram-Alley* of Whitefriars, but the materials have received the customary cleansing. If the indebtedness was the other way around, they have received an equally customary befouling. There was little elevation of source materials at the private theatres. Chapman's *Widow's Tears* actually succeeds in making the original tale of the Ephesian widow in Petronius Arbiter seem somewhat sentimental. *Mucedorus* of the popular repertory and Day's *Isle of Gulls* of the select repertory both derive from Sidney's *Arcadia*. *Mucedorus* is as idyllic as the source, while the *Isle of Gulls* debases the moral tone and the dignity of the characters in a fashion truly spectacular.

It was noted earlier that the coterie plays delight in cruel punishment and scenes of humiliation. In popular plays such is normally not the case. Northumberland, although opposed to the hero of *Sir Thomas Wyatt*, appears noble in adversity. Captain Browne, the murderer in *A Warning for Fair Women*, tries to the end to protect his paramour and goes with dignity to the scaffold. Richard III, in *The True Tragedy* as in Shakespeare, dies bravely on the field of battle. The heathens conquered by Heywood's paragons in *The Four Prentices of London* are never mean or pusillanimous. Even the most ruthless characters show a respect for fallen opponents; Sylla and Marius in Lodge's *Wounds of Civil War*, Danila and Alva in *Alarum for London*, Techelles and Usumcasane in *Tamburlaine*, always provided, of course, that the opponent fell bravely. Agydas is given honorable burial when he takes his life because he can no longer serve Zenocrate—"It was manly done."[59] In Heywood's *Rape of Lucrece*, Tarquin, Sextus, and Tullia are guilty of patricide, usurpation, and rape; but they perish so nobly as almost to obliterate the memory of their crimes. In *Fortune by Land and Sea*, the Purser addresses his piratical fellow:

> Worthy mate,
> We have a flash left of some half hour long;
> *That* let us burn out bravely, not behind us
> Leave a black noisome snuff of cowardice
> I' th' nostrils of our noble countrymen.
> Let's die no base examples.

Then he addresses his home waters:

> Fair Thames,
> Queen of fresh water, famous through the world—
> And not the least through us—whose double tides
> Must o'erflow our bodies; and, being dead,
> May thy clear waves our scandals wash away
> But keep our valors living.[60]

It is in such passages that playwrights like Heywood and Rowley came nearest to achieving poetry.

Human dignity was a quality so prized by Shakespeare that he denied it to no more than a handful of his hundreds of characters. Even the most ridiculous of them are permitted to retain their own self-evaluations, and even the most vile are never made to whimper or crawl. It is curious the extent to which certain "memory pieces" have been exploited as Shakespeare's *philosophy*. The death-sigh of a blasted spirit, like Macbeth's "Tomorrow and tomorrow," and the sabotage of a fantastic, like Jaques's "Seven ages of man," can be taken at face value only by ignoring the plays in which they occur. In *As You Like It* youth is beautiful, and old age wise and warm; yet it is not unusual in modern productions to let a reverential circle form about Jaques and a light descend on his venerable head as he speaks the lines, divesting both youth and age of all meaning and grace. It can scarcely come amiss to point to the devices used throughout the plays to sustain an impression of the dignity of man.

"Coward" and "villain," not "liar" or "bastard," are the epithets most commonly used as the insult direct, intended to provoke combat. But cowardice, so often mentioned, is rarely portrayed. The case of Falstaff has been discussed to the point of supererogation, and we can only conclude either that the dramatist did not intend to make the knight a coward or did not succeed in doing so. Indubitable portrayals of cowardice are confined to a few minor characters. The original Fastolfe in *Henry VI* is more hardly used than in Holinshed, and is made to stand silent while his knighthood is taken from him and his Garter torn away.[61] Thurio's cowardice is not amusing:

> I hold him but a fool that will endanger
> His body for a girl that loves him not.
> I claim her not, and therefore she is thine.[62]

The Duke's answer to this is, "The more degenerate and base art thou," and Thurio disappears from the play. Elsewhere the trait is confined to a few comic characters, Aguecheek, Trinculo, Parolles, and is never displayed in anyone presumably self-respecting. The Roman soldiers in *Coriolanus* are "beat back to their trenches" and reviled, but they make an immediate recovery.[63] Shakespeare's illtreatment of the French does not include delineations of cowardice. They are ineffectual against the English, braggart and treacherous, but not given to cringing. The most hardly used of them all, La Pucelle, proclaims, "Of all base passions fear is most accurs'd,"[64] and is a fighter even in her infamous attempts to avoid the stake. The worst of the villains—Aaron, Richard III, Edmund, Iago—are at least brave men.

Drunkenness shares with cowardice the peculiar distinction of being frequently condemned but rarely displayed in Shakespearean drama. Both vices are too ignoble, evidently, for his pattern of villainy, and too disgusting for his pattern of comic behavior. Hamlet is distressed that the world thinks of the Danes as drunken, "and with swinish phrase Soil our addition."[65] King Claudius is presumably a great drinker, but we never see him in his cups. Of all her suitors Portia most detests the sodden Duke of Saxony: "I will do anything, Nerissa, ere I will be married to a sponge."[66] He does not appear in the play. How Falstaff has achieved his great bulk is a matter of report. He is never shown stuffing himself, like Jonson's Zeal-of-theland Busy, nor is he ever shown reeling-drunk. Christopher Sly, Sir Toby Belch, Stephano, and the Porter in *Macbeth* provide the few instances of amusing drunkenness, and all but the Porter are subjected to reproof. The attitude toward drinking in excess is consistently unfriendly. Amusing demonstration is offered by the experience of Professor Legouis in preparing for the British Academy a lecture, "The Bacchic Element in Shakespeare's Plays."[67] He went through with his project, but found the gleanings so thin that his tone became somewhat rueful. The only estimable character in Shakespeare ever to show the effects of drink is Cassio, and his penitential words[68] have given more aid and comfort to temperance lecturers than any other passage in literature. The usual epithets for drunkenness are "foul," "beastly," and "swinish."[69]

The reluctance to afflict the characters with the meaner vices, and the tendency to mention such vices rather than portray them, is related to the dramatist's general aversion for scenes of humiliation. The aversion explains why acts of penance and speeches of contrition are often almost comically brief, and why certain episodes occur off stage. We hear of Shylock's frenzy over the loss of his ducats and his daughter but do not see it,[70] hear of dust thrown upon the sacred head of Richard II but see him abdicating like a major prophet,[71] hear of plans to hoot Coriolanus out of Rome but see him departing in state.[72] We hear of harsh sentences upon villainous characters but do not see them carried out. When a character is no longer able to resist, he is no longer displayed. No body of literature ever offered fewer opportunities to gloat. The putting out of Gloucester's eyes has been cited as illustration that Shakespeare will spare his spectators nothing. Actually he constantly spares them a great deal. Curiously, he spares them the sight of natural rather than violent deaths—and not simply because of the greater spectacular appeal of the latter. In his chronicles and tragedies, we see scores of characters die by violence; but the old and ill, like John of Gaunt, Edward IV, Henry IV, and Katherine of Aragon are removed from sight just before their dissolution. The few exceptions, Mortimer and Cardinal Beaufort, occur in the early plays. A gush of blood was one thing, the ignominy of the deathbed another. A parallel contrast appears in the treatment of suicide. When the act has about it a touch of splendor, as with Romeo, Juliet, Othello,

Brutus, Titinius, Cassius, Antony, or Cleopatra, it occurs before our eyes. When it is a symptom of psychological collapse, as with Ophelia, Goneril, and Lady Macbeth, it occurs elsewhere. It is never stigmatized as cowardice, and except by Ophelia's "surly priest" religious condemnation is expressed before but *not after* it has been committed.[73]

Characters are portrayed according to their kind, and eagles are given the plumage of eagles. Holinshed comments thus upon the death of the Duke of Gloucester: "This was the end of that noble man, fierce of nature, hasty, willful, and given more to war than to peace."[74] The words might stand as the characterization of many of the nobles in Shakespeare's chronicles. His Gadshill sees them with open eyes as the

> great oneyers, such as can hold in, such as will strike sooner than speak, and speak sooner than drink, and drink sooner than pray; and yet, zounds, I lie; for they pray continually to their saint, the commonwealth, or rather, not pray to her, but prey on her, for they ride up and down on her and make her their boots.[75]

That in his total portrayal of the English nobility Shakespeare has not glozed the facts, has not obscured them in a roseate chivalric glow, is attested by Hazlitt in his composite appraisal:

> The truth is, that there is neither truth nor honour in all these noble persons: they answer words with words, as they do blows with blows, in mere self defence: nor have they any principle whatever but that of courage in maintaining any wrong they dare commit, or any falsehood which they find it useful to assert.[76]

And yet about these "barbarian aristocrats" there is a latent quality that makes the word "nobility" not wholly inapplicable. They are already anachronisms in the historical periods treated, but the time when their qualities were useful to their tribe is made to hover in our consciousness. The quality is epitomized in Hotspur and in his wonderful words:

> O gentlemen, the time of life is short!
> To spend that shortness basely were too long
> If life did ride upon a dial's point.

> Still ending at the arrival of an hour.
> An if we live, we live to tread on kings;
> If die, brave death, when princes die with us![77]

The heroicism of the type could be valued as pure essence in spite of its inutility, as suggested in the widow's epitaph. The honor of her "sweet Harry"

> stuck upon him as the sun
> In the great vault of heaven, and by his light
> Did all the chivalry of England move
> To do brave acts.[78]

We might expect to find opposite qualities in characters at the opposite end of the social hierarchy; but Shakespeare's grooms and peasants are as dauntless in their fashion as his noblemen. They are never servile, and are frequently jaunty and impudent. Of working-men we get only glimpses—the staff in Capulet's kitchen, the carriers at a wayside inn,[79] the sailors who work the ships of Pericles and Alonso; but they are cheerful, sturdy, independent. They seem not to have been told that democracy is non-existent in their world, and the potboys at the Boar's Head Inn are ready to extend the hand of fellowship to the Prince of Wales.[80] The only ones who seem never to have worried about the status of Shakespeare's common people are these people themselves. Puck calls Bottom's company a "crew of patches, rude mechanicals,"[81] and Philostrate describes them as "hard-handed men that work in Athens here," but Theseus says, "If we imagine no worse of them than they of themselves, they may pass for excellent men."[82] Bottom views all humanity with kindly condescension, and his self-assurance is matched only by Dogberry's. The effect is not always comic. Michael Williams comes off well at the end of his tiff with the disguised king: "And what your Highness suffer'd under that shape, I beseech you take it for your own fault, and not mine."[83] The Chief Justice's servant is a match for Falstaff: "I pray you, sir, set your knighthood and your soldiership aside, and give me leave to tell you you lie in your throat if you say I am any other but an honest man."[84] Falstaff receives another kind of rebuke from Feeble, the lady's tailor who stands in his line of conscripts: "A man can die but once; we owe

God a death. I'll ne'er bear a base mind. An't be my destiny so; an't be not so. No man's too good to serve's prince."[85] We should not be hasty in analyzing the nature of the laughter provoked by these strong words in Feeble's weak voice. Shakespeare did not subscribe to the notion that lady's tailors were pusillanimous as a class.[86] No good man's dignity is sacrificed to a joke. While Falstaff is turning every charge of the Chief Justice to ridicule, the accuser remains forthright and austere: his worth becomes as impressive as Falstaff's wit.[87]

Often the way in which characters are permitted to state their case seems purely gratuitous, quite unrelated to the design of the plot. The Prince of Morocco appears in *The Merchant of Venice* only for a moment, but defends his color—"the shadowed livery of the burnish'd sun"[88]—with eloquent fervor. Poins, the impoverished hanger-on of a prince, is once addressed by his companion with withering disdain, but he retains his bravado: "By this light, I am well spoke on; . . . the worst that they can say of me is that I am a second brother."[89] Whether or not any justification for Shylock's actions is implied in *The Merchant of Venice*, he is vindicated in one respect; he faces his enemies squarely and remains formidable to the end, a power to be reckoned with.

The comic butts are always given the last word—a bit of final face-saving bluster. After his shirtlessness has been exposed, Don Armado stamps off with, "I will right myself like a soldier."[90] Malvolio's last words are, "I'll be reveng'd on the whole pack of you!"[91] —a curious way for a flunky to take leave of company which includes a duke and a countess. When Sir Oliver Martext is contemptuously dismissed as a hedge priest, whose offer to perform a marriage ceremony is presumptuous, another comic dramatist would have had him bemoan the loss of his fee; but this sorry figure in Shakespeare says, " 'Tis no matter. Ne'er a fantastical knave of them all shall flout me out of my calling."[92] Parolles and Pistol get the most thorough and deserved come-uppance of any characters in the comedies, but even these are allowed their retorts. "Who cannot be crush'd with a plot?"[93] says Parolles. Only when no one else is by do they vail their tawdry flags. Pistol is alone as he says,

Old do I wax, and from my weary limbs
Honour is cudgell'd.⁹⁴

Falstaff is the gamest of all. The most majestic snub in literature, "I know thee not, old man," is followed by the most magnificent recovery, "Master Shallow, I owe you a thousand pound."⁹⁵ It is a credit to the human species, even though the species is represented by one "so surfeit-swell'd, so old, and so profane."

The victims of tragedy meet the last disgrace with equal resilience. For Shakespearean characters, suffering and death are suffering and death; there is little *book* humility and *book* resignation. The terrors of death have a fearful hold upon the imagination of the characters, as illustrated in the horrified speeches of Juliet and Claudio. But such speeches are never put into the mouths of the actually dying. Even the children meet death with dignity, and one of them with something more. It is doubtful if anywhere in literature treachery and loyalty, hate and love, cruel oppression and courage, lie so compacted as in a few stark lines of *Macbeth*:

> *Enter Murtherers.*
> *Murtherer.*
> Where is your husband?
> *Wife.*
> I hope in no place so unsanctified
> Where such as thou may'st find him.
> *Murtherer.*
>   He's a traitor.
> *Son.*
> Thou liest, thou shag-ear'd villain!
> *Murtherer.*
>   What, you egg!
> Young fry of treachery! [*Stabs him.*]
> *Son.*
> He has kill'd me, mother.
> Run away, I pray you. [*Dies.*] ⁹⁶

This is the death of a true man's son. But even among the villainous there is no groveling. The last we hear from a Goneril or an Iago is a defiant snarl. Macbeth's own

> Blow wind, come wrack,
> At least we'll die with harness on our back![97]

is followed by a moment of weakness, but, like Richard III, he makes a recovery, and his last words, "Lay on, Macduff," are better remembered than those of better men. Lesser offenders, such as Bushy and Green,[98] are denied heroical actions but not their last proud words.

Othello has been described as *"cheering himself up"*—occupying his last moment on earth with a bit of "bovarysme."[99] Unless the critic's intention was to mark out a stylistic defect in the Moor's valediction—and such seems not to have been the case—the complaint covers the whole of popular Elizabethan drama. In what is probably the earliest surviving piece of Shakespeare's writing, Lord Say stands captive before Jack Cade, the Butcher, and their bloody mates. Although old and ill, Say loves his life well enough to plead with base rebels to keep it, but he pleads without sacrifice of manhood:

> *Butcher.*
> Why dost thou quiver, man?
> *Lord Say.*
> It is palsy, and not fear, provokes me.[100]

It is thus these people behave. At last Cade himself, ignorant, ferocious, absurd, is starved out, and slain by Alexander Iden. His last words are:

Iden, farewell, and be proud of thy victory. Tell Kent from me, she hath lost her best man, and exhort all the world to be cowards; for I, that never feared any, am vanquished by famine, not by valour.[101]

For Cade, Othello, or anyone else who wears about him the muddy vesture of decay to speak in this fashion is presumptuous of course, but only in the sense that it is presumptuous to speak at all—or to write critical essays. It may *all* be bovarysme. But as one who, a long time ago, contemplated the human situation with becoming awe was wont to say, "This is a great mystery."

III

Sexual Behavior

CONTRASTING attitudes toward sex, and perhaps an intimation of contrasting patterns of sexual behavior, are discernible in the dramas of the two audiences. The relevance of the material to the practical sex life of the Elizabethans must remain conjectural; all that can be supplied in the way of background is a few general impressions derived from literary and other casual evidence.

Although the word "sex" itself was not in general currency at the time, and the vocabulary of the subject was ethical rather than scientific, the question of continence and incontinence was discussed with uninhibited directness. The type of innocence advertised by ignorance of bodily functions is not portrayed in even the youngest and most virginal of Elizabethan characters. Parents seem to have let their children know at an early age whatever they knew themselves, without evasion or circumlocution. The approach was hortatory, and the parents' ally was neither the euphemist nor the family physician, but the homilist and beadle. In view of the charm and delicacy with which the poets invested its spiritual manifestations, the theory of love worked out by the physiologists was startlingly mechanical,[1] no different in essence from modern lore about glands and hormones. Its chief practical product was misinformation in the dietaries about foods and drinks that would induce or retard heat and the distillation of seminal fluid. The avowed purpose of such discussion was to provide aid to the sterile or ease to the continent. As in many other periods there was a widespread popular notion that sexual indulgence *per se* shortened life.

One of the most striking differences in attitude then as compared to the present was the assumption that intercourse might normally occur as soon as the individual was capable of it. A legally valid marriage could be contracted independently by persons at puberty, and it was assumed that puberty had been attained at least at the age of twelve in girls and of fourteen in boys. The parents who had not provided means for their daughters to wed within five or six years of the legal age were held not wholly blameless for any disgrace they might incur. Although social disapproval attached to the cohabitation of lovers in advance of a regular church wedding, the practice was viewed in a separate light from casual indulgence. For couples regularly betrothed, the sexual act itself completed a legal civil marriage. There was considerable sentiment for delaying marriage until reasonable maturity, and, of course, considerable economic pressure for doing so. The begetting of children before provision had been made for their rearing spelled poverty. A bit of terribly graphic folk-moralizing is uttered by Lear's fool:

> The codpiece that will house
> Before the head has any,
> The head and he shall louse:
> So beggars marry many.[2]

Students and apprentices were expected to remain single. The youth who wished to achieve the livery of one of the better trade companies of London had to reconcile himself to postponing marriage until he was about twenty-four. For him and the woman he would marry, often one of his master's daughters, the prescription was continence. Since few matters relating to sex are wholly untouched by the dramatists, their silence about birth control is significant. Of course the subject was not quite closed to the age, and one of the libels in *Leycester's Commonwealth* was that the earl's physician possessed "the art of destroying children in women's bellies";[3] but in the plays of neither the public nor the private theatres do we find much interest displayed in contraception, abortion, and infanticide. An allusion occurs in Jonson:

Epicoene.
. . . and have you those excellent receipts, madam, to keep from bearing children?

Haughty.
O yes, Morose: how should we maintain our youth and beauty else?[4]

The rarity of such matter is the more remarkable in that "wise women" appear, to supply charms and potions for inducing amorousness or frigidity in women, potency or impotency in men.

The dominant moral philosophy of the time rejected the medieval identification of the sexual impulse with uncleanliness and original sin. The older attitude, linked with contempt for women, appears in the coterie rather than the popular drama, as will be pointed out in the subsequent chapter on marriage. Actually it was reactionary, and the tendency to associate it with bourgeois morality and Puritanism is owing to a misconception. Milton was not idiosyncratic when he hailed wedded love and pictured the sexual fulfillment of Adam and Eve before their fall. The new orthodoxy was concerned with properly channeling the sexual impulse, not anathematizing it, and the answer was marriage. Husbands and wives were not only enjoined to seek no "strange loves" themselves but "virtuously to bring up their children, and provide . . . that they come pure and honest unto holy wedlock, when time requireth."[5] The code was quite simple. Both man and woman should be virginal at marriage, and should cohabit with each other alone until parted by death. It was, of course, repressive, and consequently provocative of that species of rebellion that takes the form of humor; but there was no serious questioning of its validity. Deviations from the pattern were assumed to be personally improvident, socially dangerous, and sinful in the eyes of God. Fornication was weak and contemptible, adultery a crime akin to murder. The moralists preached the code, and artists like Spenser, Shakespeare, and Milton fortified the preaching with the fruits of their imagination.

The Renaissance was little addicted to the type of reasoning which assumes that a code of ethics or a code of law is, or should be, a simple description of prevailing custom, or that an ideal is invalidated by evidence of its distinction from actuality. Although it would have been impolitic to label it so, the sexual code was a mark to shoot at. The task was not to recognize that man possessed qualities in common with animals (which was taken for granted), but that he possessed others which distinguished him as a man. The moral leaders could have drawn small comfort from statistics. Segments of the population were little advanced in culture from the "broods" and "litters" of medieval serfdom, with nothing to lose by sheer promiscuity, while larger segments were more emergent but still bitterly afflicted by poverty and consequent degradation. The indications are that London had more prostitution than any modern English or American city of comparable size, and a corresponding abundance of venereal disease. In the homily "Against Whoredom and Uncleanness" of 1547, we hear that, by

customable use thereof, this vice is grown into such an height, that in a manner among many it is counted no sin at all, but rather a pastime, a dalliance, and but a touch of youth: not rebuked but winked at, not punished but laughed at.[6]

Illegitimacy was common in the realm, as evidenced in every parish register, and in the reiterated rulings in towns like Stratford against giving lodging to pregnant women from the countryside lest their offspring become a burden on the community. A distinction from modern times is the extent to which known illegitimacy reached up through the social scale. Shakespeare's fellow actors were quite substantial, but this did not prevent the bachelor member from having children—an experience shared with several of Queen Elizabeth's "maids" of honor. It would be difficult for modern times to match some of the scandals in Elizabethan and Jacobean high life. It was not a pure age, if such a thing exists, and the principles it evolved were forged in the heat of experience unmitigated by modern insulating techniques. The brothel was just around the corner, and the bawds being carted or the prostitutes beating flax were public spectacles.

The popular drama endorsed the code of sexual rectitude in a way that the coterie drama did not. The illustrations that follow are not intended to prove that public theatres were *against* sin and the private theatres *for* it. Officially, of course, both were against it, and a writer like Marston would have argued that he needed to evoke sin in large quantity to provide himself ample scope for attack. On somewhat mystical principles he had written an erotic poem to prove that erotic poems were erotic. One cannot judge the case by the rationalizations of the authors, the maxims they imbedded in their plays, or the presumed salutary effects of satire. Although both bodies of drama endorse chastity, only the popular plays are chaste. The others are "sexy"—in that they serve appetite and curiosity with erotic stimuli, and reveal inadvertently the latitudes of conduct among leisured people for whom a cultivated sensuality has become an escape from boredom.

In the large number of plays in the select repertories where men and women indulge in premarital or extramarital sexual relations, it is not always easy to determine when the behavior is condemned and when condoned. If the cuckolded husband is a jealous or mercenary old citizen, his wife's ingenuity in deceiving him is viewed with approval. In general, however, the women are granted less latitude than the men, and the first distinction we shall note in these plays is their commitment to a double standard of sexual morality. City gallants are permitted to take their pleasure where they find it, like the rakes of Restoration comedy; and when a whoremaster is satirized it is because of his excesses, failures, awkwardness, or other qualifications as a gull. Sir Walter Whorehound of Middleton's *Chaste Maid of Cheapside* is punished, but not Witgood of *A Trick to Catch the Old One;* and Witgood's is the more typical case. Occasionally the person involved is a romantic figure, or at least not a city type. Little onus seems to attach to Prince Leucippus of Fletcher's *Cupid's Revenge* for having kept Baccha as his mistress. The chief business of the denouement of *Blurt Master Constable*

is to extricate Fontinelle from the difficulties attending his visit to
the courtesan Imperia shortly after his wedding. Freevil's past relations with Franceschina in Marston's *Dutch Courtesan* do not dis-
qualify him as the romantic lover and moralizer of the piece. A number of similar illustrations might be offered.

No corresponding compromise in standards subtends the behavior
of characters in the popular plays. Although more men than women
take liberties in actual fact, it is never assumed that they possess the
right. In *Look About You*, old Faulconbridge says, "Men may be
wanton, women must not range";[7] but his words are turned to ironical use and he himself submitted to ridicule. In *The Death of Robert
Earl of Huntington*, Oxford tries to comfort the Queen about King
John's intended philandering:

> Content, fair queen, and do not think it strange
> That kings do sometimes seek delight in change,
> For now and then, I tell you, poor men range.

He then tells of his own former fondness for the wife of his gamekeeper. The Queen cries,

> Now out upon you, Vere, I would have thought
> The world had not contain'd a chaster man,

whereupon he admits that the affair was platonic:

> Yet had my keeper's wife been of my mind,
> There had been cause some fault with us to find.[8]

In a few inconspicuous instances only is wildness in youth pictured
in terms of sexual license,[9] the playwrights preferring to treat idle-
ness, gaming, or downright dishonesty. Even some of the young husbands who desert their wives, like William Scarborow in *Miseries of
Enforced Marriage* and young Flowerdale in *The London Prodigal*,
are guarded from the sin of adultery. The offense was too grave for
stories of reclamation. It should be realized that Helena's bed trick
upon Bertram in *All's Well* would have been viewed as additionally
praiseworthy since it averted an act of adultery. Lechery is presented
consistently as a failing of clowns. The tradition goes back at least as
far as *Cambyses*, where Huf, Snuf, and Ruf are the ones involved
with Meretrix. In *The Famous Victories of Henry the Fifth*, Prince

Hal likes "a pretty wench that can talk well, for I delight as much in their tongues as any part about them."[10] If his escapades with the Eastcheap girls are ever anything but conversational, the play is silent on the matter; it is the clown Derick that courts "bouncing Bess with the jolly buttocks."[11] (Shakespeare preserves the same distinction between Hal and Falstaff in *Henry IV*.) Among other clowns distinguished by lecherous tendencies are Launce in *The Two Gentlemen of Verona*, Jenkin in *George a Greene*, Dick Coomes in *Two Angry Women of Abington*, Cocke in *The Royal King and the Loyal Subject*, and Much in *The Downfall of Robert Earl of Huntington*:

> *Little John.*
> Thirdly, no yeoman following Robin Hood
> In Sherwood shall use widow, wife, or maid,
> But by true labor lustful thoughts expel.
> *Robin Hood.*
> How like ye this?
> *All.*
> Master, we like it well.
> *Much.*
> But I cry no to it. What shall I do with Jenny then?[12]

Little John's ruling is interesting in itself: the folk heroes were becoming chaste as well as brave.

Nothing is clearer in Shakespeare's own plays than the adherence to a single standard of sexual morality. Falstaff asserts, "A man can no more separate age and covetousness than 'a can part young limbs and lechery";[13] but in Shakespearean drama age is not covetous, and youth is not lecherous. In a fashion that would be ridiculed in contemporary literature, we are informed that the young men have had no guilty relations with women. Romeo is "stainless"[14] as Orsino is "stainless."[15] The very "ice of chastity"[16] is in the kiss of Orlando. Young Malcolm affirms that he is "unknown to women."[17] Florizel compares his love to that of the gods:

> Their transformations
> Were never for a piece of beauty rarer,
> Nor in a way so chaste, since my desires

> Run not before mine honour, nor my lusts
> Burn hotter than my faith.[18]

Ferdinand has "cold virgin snow" upon his heart, and his intentions are as honorable as his hopes "for quiet days, fair issue, and long life."[19] Laertes accepts without demur Ophelia's precept that chastity is as important in him as in herself.[20] In *Measure for Measure*, the Duke in his role as friar chides Julietta thus:

> *Duke.*
> So then it seems your most offenceful act
> Was mutually committed.
> *Julietta.*
> Mutually.
> *Duke.*
> Then was your sin of heavier kind than his.
> *Julietta.*
> I do confess it and repent it, father.[21]

Here a double standard is intimated, but in the action of the play the gravamen is less upon Julietta than upon Claudio. Adam in *As You Like It* attributes his vigorous old age to the fact that in youth he did not imbibe "hot and rebellious liquors" or

> with unbashful forehead woo
> The means of weakness and debility.[22]

Shakespeare is capable of lapses in the sense of humor in this department. In Gower's *Confessio Amantis* the episode of the virgin's converting the patrons of the brothel where she is placed on sale is treated thus:

> Ech after other ten or twelve
> Of yonge men to hire in wente,
> Bot such a grace god hire sente,
> That for the sorwe, which sche made,
> Was none of hem, which pouer hade
> To don hire eny vileinie.[23]

Twine's *Pattern of Painful Adventures* manages to inject a little rudimentary humor into the situation, but in *Pericles* the humor, one

fears, is unconscious. The young men swear off bawdy houses for-
ever, and go out to "hear the Vestals sing."²⁴

There is never any heroic libertinage among Shakespeare's men,
never, as in Fletcher, an anticipation of the Don Juan motif. Those
specified as lecherous—Falstaff, Shallow in his youth, Lucio, Patroclus—are either comic or contemptible. At least in one situation
Falstaff is not the figure in command:

> *Falstaff.*
> I am old, I am old.
> *Doll Tearsheet.*
> I love thee better than I love e'er a scurvy young boy of them all.
> *Falstaff.*
> What stuff wilt have a kirtle of?²⁵

And this does not compare in ignominy with his role in *The Merry
Wives of Windsor*. Those perhaps not lecherous in a comic way but
so infatuated as to become lawlessly involved—Claudio, Cassio,
Troilus, Antony—are all viewed as pitiable.

The married men, like the young lovers, are committed to chastity
in the sense in which the term is used in Shakespeare. Adriana believes she is speaking to a husband who is guilty of adultery:

> How dearly would it touch thee to the quick,
> Shouldst thou but hear I were licentious
> And that this body, consecrate to thee,
> By ruffian lust should be contaminate!
> Wouldst thou not spit at me and spurn at me,
> And hurl the name of husband in my face,
> And tear the stain'd skin off my harlot brow,
> And from my false hand cut the wedding ring
> And break it with a deep-divorcing vow?
> I know thou canst, and therefore see thou do it.
> I am possess'd with an adulterate blot,
> My blood is mingled with the crime of lust;
> For, if we two be one, and thou play false,
> I do digest the poison of thy flesh,
> Being strumpeted by thy contagion.
> Keep then fair league and truce with thy true bed,
> I live unstain'd, thou undishonored.²⁶

But the husband actually has *not* been false to her bed, unlike his prototype in Plautus's *Menaechmi*. The elder Hamlet's

> love was of that dignity
> That it went hand in hand even with the vow[27]

that he had made to his queen in marriage. Coriolanus assures Virgilia that during his absence from her his lip "hath virgin'd it."[28] The terrible bitterness of the husbands who think themselves betrayed— Othello, Posthumus, Leontes—is partly owing to their knowledge that they themselves have been constant.

Dr. Johnson's charge that the dramatist is not "always careful to show in the virtuous a disapprobation of the wicked"[29] does not hold in the case of sexual offenses, and they are viewed with the same seriousness in men as in women. Friar Laurence worries about Romeo's relations to Rosaline,[30] Bassanio feels responsible for Gratiano's good faith to Nerissa,[31] Camillo is more willing to abet his Prince's marriage to a peasant than his seduction of her,[32] Reynaldo does not wish to follow Polonius's instructions to the extent of aspersing Laertes's conduct with women—"My lord, that would dishonour him."[33] The lords speak of Bertram's seduction of "Diana" with horror, and, when asked if he is of Bertram's council, one of them replies: "Let it be forbid, sir! So should I be a great deal of his act."[34] And these are soldiers on campaign! Laertes's double warning to Ophelia against incontinence,[35] and Prospero's double warning to Ferdinand and Miranda are well remembered:

> barren hate,
> Sour eyed disdain, and discord shall bestrew
> The union of your bed with weeds so loathly
> That you shall hate it both.[36]

There is no use adverting to the dramatist's own precipitancy with Anne Hathaway, or to the fact that immediate consummation on the part of Ferdinand and Miranda would merely have meant the substitution of a civil for a church marriage: the play is expressing the loftier ideal of sexual conduct and applying it impartially to men and women.

The natural consequence of the greater freedom granted to men

in the coterie drama was a greater lenience toward the profession
that made possible the exercise of that freedom. The venomous
portrait of a prostitute in Marston's, *Dutch Courtesan* is quite exceptional among plays of the private theatres. Usually prostitution
is treated tolerantly, with the practitioners rather amiable creatures
who aid in the intrigue, and who are fubbed off in marriage as part
of the concluding mirth. Prostitutes are provided with husbands as
a standard device in the comedies of Middleton, as well as in Field's
A Woman Is a Weathercock, Barry's *Ram-Alley*, Beaumont's *The
Woman Hater*, Dekker and Webster's *Northward Ho*, and other
plays. Usually the husbands accept these wives philosophically:
"Tut," says Follywit in Middleton's *A Mad World My Masters*,
"give me gold, it makes amends for vice."[37] In Sharpham's *The
Fleire*, Florida and Felecia, the two daughters of the deposed Duke
of Florence, come to England and calmly resolve to set up as
"whores" since " 'tis hateful to live poor" and "beauty was made
to be enjoyed."[38] Their progress in the profession, varied by attempts
to poison some of their clientele, proves no impediment to a concluding journey to the altar. Middleton's heroes often find their mistresses to be valuable as allies, and Barry's William Smallshanks relies
on his financially. He denies that he "keeps" her—rather she "keeps"
him. Frances, the prostitute in question, is permitted to defend her
profession against those "stricter wits" who "condemn all women
which are prone to love."[39] In a strange medley of speeches, comic
and melodramatic, cynical and sentimental, the courtesan of Middleton's *A Trick to Catch the Old One* also orates in defense of har-
lotry.[40]

Prostitutes do not win husbands or plead their cause in plays of
the public theatres: they are more apt to make their exit like Shakespeare's Doll Tearsheet, cursing the beadles who drag her to Bridewell.[41] The links in authorship make especially revealing the difference between Dekker and Middleton's *The Honest Whore* and *The
Roaring Girl* performed at the Fortune, and Middleton's comedies
and Dekker and Webster's *Northward Ho* and *Westward Ho* performed at Paul's. The same authors who wrote amiably of com-

mercialized vice for Paul's provide exposés and denunciations for the Fortune. *The Honest Whore* is, in large part, a tract against prostitution, and *The Roaring Girl* converts Moll Frith from a jest of the slums into a one-woman vice squad. The scenes of prostitution in the popular plays are homilies. In Cooke's *Greene's Tu Quoque* the lesson is on the cupidity and treacherousness of whores; in Heywood's *The Royal King and The Loyal Subject* on their infectiousness and filth. Captain Bonville, after establishing that the inmates of the brothel are willing to receive him in spite of the diseases he pretends to suffer, cries,

> Say the last lecher that embrac't you here,
> And folded in his arms your rottenness,
> Had been all these, would you not all that filth
> Vomit on me?[42]

We are reminded of the condition of the inmates of the brothel in *Pericles*: the descriptions are humorous, but more grimly so than anything else in Shakespeare.

The Shakespearean antagonism to prostitution is as inflexible as that of the popular drama generally. The courtesans who hover in the half-light in *The Comedy of Errors* and *Othello* are the only ones used with even a modicum of gentleness. A striking feature of Shakespeare's work is that women who have simply shifted lovers assimilate the traits of common prostitutes, even though surrounded by the most aureate literary traditions. He might have treated Dido, Héloïse, and Francesca with the same equivocal sympathy he tendered Troilus; but Guinevere he would have pictured as a "daughter of the game." If Cressida had not already been written down in post-Chaucerian versions of her legend, Shakespeare no doubt would have attended to it. Helen had not been so written down, and her image to Marlowe had suggested only beauty and grandeur; but in Shakespeare she is thus impaled:

> For every false drop in her bawdy veins
> A Grecian's life hath sunk; for every scruple
> Of her contaminated carrion weight
> A Troyan hath been slain.[43]

Granted that these are the words of an angry partisan, yet when Helen herself appears she is made to speak in a way that divests her of any remnant of dignity. Cressida is half coy, half bold, and is greeted with leers wherever she goes. The tributes to Cleopatra's majesty and allure are canceled by epithets matching those on Helen. If she has "delicate cheeks" and "infinite variety," she is also the "ribald-rid nag of Egypt." Antony himself once calls her "a triple-turn'd whore."[44] Prestige cannot survive such terms, as Dryden realized when he expunged them. Shakespeare's Cleopatra is sexually avid, taking "no pleasure in aught an eunuch has,"[45] and when angered, she lets fly with words and fists:

> I'll spurn thine eyes
> Like balls before me. I'll unhair thy head!
> [*She hales him up and down.*]
> Thou shalt be whip'd with wire and stew'd in brine,
> Smarting in ling'ring pickle. [46]

The only other woman who behaves thus in Shakespeare is Doll Tearsheet: "I will have you so soundly swing'd for this! You blue-bottle rogue, you filthy famish'd correctioner . . ."[47] Although Plutarch's Cleopatra is as much degraded as Chaucer's Criseyde, and without intermediary assistance, the dramatist was confronted by the recorded fact that she was faithful at least to Antony, and he makes her increase in stature as evidence of her fidelity grows. At last she wins something of the standing of the wife she craves to be:

> Husband, I come!
> Now to that name my courage prove my title![48]

Shakespeare's Pandarus is even more remote than his Cressida from Chaucer's conception. The sins of his descendants are visited upon him. The most awesome indictment of panders occurs in *Pericles*. Since the speaker is Marina, a tender maid of fourteen who "never kill'd a mouse, nor hurt a fly,"[49] her words are scarcely "in character." The dramatist seems to be bristling through her lips:

> Thou hold'st a place for which the pained'st fiend
> Of hell would not in reputation change.
> Thou art the damned doorkeeper to every

> Custrel that comes enquiring for his Tib.
> To the choleric fisting of every rogue
> Thy ear is liable. Thy food is such
> As hath been belch'd on by infected lungs.

To the pander's excuse that he can find no other work, Mariana replies:

> Do any thing but this thou doest. Empty
> Old receptacles, or common shores, of filth;
> Serve by indenture to the common hangman.
> Any of these ways are yet better than this;
> For what thou professest, a baboon, could he speak,
> Would own a name too dear.[50]

The "common hangman" in *Measure for Measure* balks at a pander as an assistant, and the Duke Vincentio's invective[51] is of precisely the quality of Mariana's. Even Pistol and Nym decline this role,[52] although Pistol succumbs in the end. In no play by Shakespeare could there have appeared the oddly pious pander of Chapman's *Bussy D'Ambois*, the holy Friar Conolet whose versatility was displayed at Paul's; his alignment is with the popular sentiment that accepted as equitable the fact that, of all the erring characters of *The Honest Whore*, only Bots the pander was singled out for punishment.

The glimpses of commercialized vice in Shakespeare are fairly consistent. That complete extirpation is possible, or even politic, is not maintained. Once Mariana is rescued from the brothel, the dramatist displays no further interest in it and, unlike Twine, fails to raid the district. It is assumed, especially in *Measure for Measure*, that brothels are an effect, not a cause, and carry with them their own punishment. The scene in *II Henry IV* where Falstaff sits with Doll on his lap[53] is unique in Shakespeare. One could almost suppose that it sat ill on his conscience, and that he was resolved to make all the participants pay for our reprehensible amusement. In a little episode that follows,[54] the shadow of death falls over Doll's career, and she disappears shrieking her billingsgate. Her associates survive into *Henry V*. There we hear finally that Mistress Quickly is "dead i' th' spital of malady of France,"[55] Bardolph is hanged along with Nym, and Pistol is hounded into oblivion. Shakespeare usually neglects to dispose of minor characters. Granted that these "irregular humorists" were too well remembered to be ignored, he could have pensioned them off; we may guess that, had they not borne the scent of the brothel about them, he would at least have slain them more gently. Mention of prostitution is always accompanied by mention of disease. Falstaff's endearments to Doll have a mixed tone: "We catch of you, Doll, we catch of you. Grant that, my poor virtue, grant that."[56] Timon's snarl is more graphic:

> This fell whore of thine
> Hath in her more destruction than thy sword
> For all her cherubin look[57]

—able to bring "rose-cheeked youth" to the "tub and diet." But even this is mild compared with the allusions in *Pericles,* which are quite horrendous—more salutary, one may suppose, to Elizabethan youth than a course of lectures. Whatever their purpose, and whether casual or emphatic, comic or the reverse, the allusions are ever there.[58]

More impressive actually than the direct preachment is the way the popular plays, in contrast to the select, eschew suggestiveness in speech and action. Granville-Barker attributes the avoidance of sensual display in Shakespeare partly to the fact that the feminine parts were filled by boys, with consequent danger of ludicrousness of effect; but the explanation is largely invalidated by the fact that the companies composed wholly of boys seemed oblivious to such danger. Professor Stoll objects to Granville-Barker's theory on the different and surprising grounds that audiences are shy, and that the Elizabethans shunned the embarrassment of "witnessing or imagining caresses."[59] We shall see in a moment that at least the coterie audiences could trust themselves not to blush. Passing mention may be made of an odd little point concerning aphrodisiacs. While the popular plays will occasionally mention a "posset" taken upon a marriage night, and even a few ingredients, it is the others that linger upon the strange substances calculated to induce "most forcible excited concupiscence."[60] Marston is especially zealous, providing a receipt or two in every play. One of these lists a lion's mustache, distilled ox pith, jelly of cock sparrows, he-monkey's marrow, powder of fox stones, and crabs' guts.[61] In comparison, the specifics of Chapman, "oyster-pies, potatoes, skirret-roots, eringoes,"[62] seem commonplace and those of Markham and Machin, "doves' brains or swans' pizzles,"[63] almost poetic.

The plays of Marlowe demonstrate that there was already a distinction in popular and genteel preferences recognized in the eighties. In *Ovid's Elegies* and *Hero and Leander*, Marlowe was to write the most fleshly verse of the age; but his popular hero Tamburlaine is something of a Victorian: "But tell me, madam, is your grace betroth'd?"[64] the Scythian bandit demurely asks Zenocrate. And after four acts and as many military campaigns, during which she is part of his entourage, he is able to say,

> And for all blot of foul inchastity
> I record heaven her heavenly self is clear.[65]

In the second instalment of his adventures, Tamburlaine, whatever his excesses as a conqueror, is a model husband and a stickler about concubinage among the Turks. In *Doctor Faustus* Helen of Troy presumably responds to the necromancer's request to be made immortal with a kiss; but she appears in and disappears from the play with equal celerity. The reticences in *Edward II* and *The Massacre at Paris* will be mentioned later. There is more suggestiveness in Marlowe's Chapel play of *Dido* than in his others combined. Besides the succession of scenes in which the lovers disappear and then reappear, having consummated their amour in the interval, there are details like the following:

> "Come back, come back," I hear her cry afar,
> "And let me link my body to thy lips,
> That tied together by the striving tongues,
> We may as one sail unto Italy."[66]

Kyd's *Spanish Tragedy* is as nearly risqué as any of the pre-Shakespearean plays of the public theatres, its most sensual lines occurring during the love tryst in Jeronimo's arbor:

Bel-Imperia.
O, let me go, for in my troubled eyes
Now mayst thou read that life in passion dies.
Horatio.
O, stay awhile, and I will die with thee,
So shalt thou yield, and yet have conquered me.[67]

Although Bel-Imperia's former affair with Don Andrea is once mentioned as an "old disgrace," and her meeting with Horatio seems a guilty assignation, her character is almost as ambiguous as Shakespeare's Queen Gertrude's; and the sex-motif is not permitted to obtrude. Lorenzo's excuse for slaying Horatio is simply that his sister was "so meanly accompanied," and Balthazar obviously considers her eligible as a wife. In *Jeronimo*, which could only have been written as a forepiece to *The Spanish Tragedy*, it is assumed that Bel-Imperia's relations with both Don Andrea and Horatio are honorable. Our conclusion must be that, whatever Kyd's sources, he was handling them like Marlowe under external restraints. More erotic interest, despite its chaste preachment, is provided by *The Wars of Cyrus*, performed like *Dido* by the Chapel company. The women are constantly endangered, and we witness Panthea's emorous embraces of the air while sleeping upon a love charm, and Dinon's attempts to seduce the boy Libanio who has assumed his mistress's garb.

After 1599 most plays at the private theatres could be counted upon in one way or another for something "to make a man's spirits stand on their tiptoes and die his blood in a deep scarlet, like your Ovid's *Ars Amandi*."[68] Kissing in the Dido-Aeneas fashion is described in Machin's *The Dumb Knight*—"the true touch with the tongue in the kiss"[69]—and in Marston's *Jack Drum's Entertainment*:

Katherine.
Come, you grow wanton. Oh, you bite my lip.
Pasquil.
In faith, you jest; I did but softly sip
The Roseal juice of your reviving breath.

The exchange is between romantic lovers who must have seemed to their creator to resemble Romeo and Juliet:

Katherine.
Farewell, yet stay, but 'tis no matter too,
My father knows, I think, what must ensue.
Adieu, yet hark, nay faith, adieu, adieu.

Pasquil.
Peace to thy passions 'till next interview.[70]

The scene is embarrassing in more ways than one. Marston's lyrics hover uneasily between the comic and the luscious:

Wrapt in a skin of ivory,
Delicious beauty that doth lie
Lie still, lie still, upon thy back,
And, Fancy, let no sweet dreams lack,
To tickle her, to tickle her, with pleasing thoughts.[71]

The same vein is worked in Barry's *Ram-Alley*:

Before the time that chanticleer
Shall call and tell the day is near,
When wenches lying on their backs
Receive with joy their love-stol'n smacks;
When maids awak'd from their first sleep,
Deceiv'd with dreams begin to weep,
And think, if dreams such pleasure know,
What sport the substance then would show:
When a lady 'gins white limbs to spread,
Her love but new-stol'n to her bed.[72]

In Day's *Isle of Gulls* the "ingenues" exchange views about an erotic dream:

Hippolita.
O, 'twould ha' vex't a saint; my blood would burn
To be so near, and miss so good a turn.

Violetta.
And so did mine too, I warrant you. Nay though
I be but a little pot, I shall be as soon hot as another.[73]

The venerable Chapman was not above supplying small treats. In *May-Day* he describes the twin enticements of a bed and a woman, achieving a curious organic unity between the two:

A bed as soft as her hair, sheets as delicate as her skin, and as sweet as her breath, pillows imitating her breasts, and her breasts to boot, hippocras in her cups and nectar in her lips; oh, the gods have been beasts for less felicity![74]

In the same play but in a different vein is described an attempt upon a woman who proves to be a man: "I played the varlet and took up her coat, and meaning to lay my five fingers upon her ace of hearts, up starts a quite contrary card."[75]

The eroticism is not exclusively verbal. We must guess at the effect in Middleton's *A Mad World My Masters* when the succubus dances "lasciviously" about Penitent Brothel, and in Dekker and Webster's *Northward Ho* when Mistress Greenshield "sleep-walks" into Featherstone's bedroom. In *Westward Ho* and in *Blurt Master Constable* much is made of the banquet and amorous music attending the love trysts. Imperia in the latter play, and Franceschina in Marston's *Dutch Courtesan*, supply a practical demonstration of the caresses and amorous speech of courtesans. In several plays a blank interval is provided while the consummation of an amour is occurring off-stage. In Marston's *Sophonisba* a "treble viol and bass lute play softly within the canopy," and the waiting Syphax says,

> O, you dear founts of pleasure, blood and beauty,
> Raise active Venus with fruition
> Of such provoking sweetness—Hark, she comes!

Then there is a "short song to soft music above," and "enter Erictho in the shape of Sophonisba, her face veiled, and hasteth in the bed of Syphax." After a few ecstatic lines, "Syphax hasteneth within the canopy" and "a bass lute and treble viol play for the act [interval]."[76] The sequel here is bathetic, but in *The Insatiate Countess* there is the same process of sending Isabella, then Gniaca, to bed to the accompaniment of music and amorous speeches, until "after some short song, enter Isabella and Gniaca again, she hanging about his neck lasciviously."[77] In *The Fawn* Tiberio is shown climbing to an upper chamber where he is met by Dulcimel and a Priest. Presumably the marriage ceremony and consummation take place at once since Hercules stands below apostrophizing:

You Genital!
You fruitful well-mixed heats! O, bless the sheets
Of yonder chamber![78]

In Field's *Amends for Ladies* Bold, dressed as a lady's maid, prepares Lady Bright for bed and is invited to share it. Act IV, Scene I, shows the lady "undressed" and Bold "in his shirt." The pair retire to bed, and a speech in the succeeding scene describes the moves in a narrowly averted rape. In the same play one piece of business is prophetic of *Tobacco Road*. It is the type of thing often misattributed to the "robustness" of the age or the requirements of *groundlings*. A marriage is described by Lord Feesimple as he peers through a window:

Look, look! the parson joins the doctor's hand and hers: now the doctor kisses her, by this light! (*Omnes whoop.*) Now goes his gown off. Heyday! he has red breeches on. Zounds! the physician is got o' th' top of her: belike it is the mother she has. Hark! the bed creaks.

After a few more speeches, "a curtain drawn, a bed discovered: Ingen . . ., the Lady [Honour] in a petticoat, the Parson."[79] Evidently the Parson both wedded the pair and witnessed the consummation, although the audience—perhaps because of that modesty mentioned by Professor Stoll—was present only by proxy.

A stage direction in the second act of *A Warning for Fair Women* illustrates the "old decorum" maintained, in contrast, at the public theatres. It portrays the seduction of Mistress Anne Sanders by Captain Browne:

Next comes Lust before Browne, leading Mistress Sanders covered with a black veil, Chastity, all in white, pulling her back softly by the arm. Then Drury, thrusting away Chastity, Roger following. They march about, and then sit to the table. The Furies fill wine. Lust drinks to Browne, he to Mistress Sanders; she pledgeth him. Lust embraceth her; she thrusteth Chastity from her; Chastity wrings her hands and departs.[80]

From this point on, Mistress Sanders is a fallen woman, although the only contact that has been shown us between her and Captain Browne has been strictly allegorical. In *I Edward IV* the seduction

of Jane Shore by the King is as completely lacking in sensual display.
Jane capitulates in the lines,

> If you enforce me, I have naught to say
> But wish I had not lived to see this day.[81]

In Heywood's *A Woman Killed with Kindness* the seduction scene
is so passionless and Anne Frankford's surrender so abrupt that the
modern reader, unfamiliar with the conventions in which the author
was working, and unused to seeing similar opportunities missed in
the literature of today, is either amused or amazed:

> What shall I say?
> My soul is wand'ring and hath lost her way.
> Oh, Master Wendoll, Oh![82]

In the circumstances, however, comment on "lack of motivation" is
somewhat beside the point.

In both comedy and tragedy, the popular school of dramatists not
only failed to cultivate chances for erotic treatment but took considerable pains to avoid it. The exceptions to the rule are few. Several
speeches by Mall Barnes in Porter's *Two Angry Women of Abington* move on from the merry bawdry permitted in popular literature
toward the truly salacious. Heywood himself, in his *Golden Age*,
duplicates the effects of the private theatres when Jupiter is shown
mingling with Diana's nymphs and later winning to the bed of coy
Danaë. The experiment was not repeated in the four later plays of
the Homeric series although opportunities were abundant. It is difficult to illustrate the *absence* of a quality, but mention may be made
of several plays where the nature of the material makes especially
striking the absence of erotic appeal. In Haughton's *Englishmen for
My Money* the six suitors of the three sisters seem to consider reaching a woman's bed tantamount to a wedding; but the action of the
play is athletic rather than amatory. In Heywood's *Wise Woman of
Hogsdon* another bevy of desirable maidens is besieged by another
troop of rival suitors; but the lines and business remain sterile despite
the presence of an unsavory bawd and matchmaker. In *Captain
Thomas Stukeley* the hero is released from prison by his enemy's sus-

ceptible wife, but there is never a suggestion of *quid pro quo*. In
Dekker's *If It Be Not Good the Devil Is in It* the theme is the corruption of a court and a priory by the personal emissaries of Satan,
but the corruption takes no sexual turn. The Prologue abjures "filth"
—"Let those that love Pan's pipes dance still to Pan." The bawdy
songs in Heywood's *Rape of Lucrece* are notorious, but we should
observe that in the serious action of the play Tarquin, when he finds
his victim in her bed, illogically "bears her out" and there follows
no titillating interval.

In Shakespeare the most sensual lines are Troilus's when he is about
to have his assignation with Cressida; they are crudely duplicated by
Falstaff's when he thinks he is about to have an assignation with
Mistress Ford.[83] They are exceptional, as the situation evoking them
is exceptional. In the few plays where an amour is consummated, he
prefers to give a postlude rather than a prelude to the episode or to
treat it by allusion. It is less striking that Mariana and Helena play
the bed trick than that they are permitted to do so with such con-
summate modesty. The nature of the ardor of Romeo and Juliet is
unmistakable, but their speeches, like those of all the young lovers,
are neither luscious nor coy. Cleopatra's seductiveness is a matter of
record rather than of demonstration in the play: when Katharine
Cornell in a recent stage production was charged with lack of "sex
appeal," she might reasonably have asked where Shakespeare had
provided opportunities to display any. The "seduction" of Diana by
Bertram is the most chaste in literature,[84] and the dialogue between
Lysander and Hermia, when resolving to sleep apart in the wood as
a concession to the proprieties,[85] is the most completely delicate.
Composed by a less dextrous artist, either scene would have become
ludicrous.

The best way to assess Shakespeare's deportment in the areas
we are treating is to compare his plays with their sources, and his
emphasis with the opportunities for quite different emphasis offered
by his materials. The subject must be relegated to an appendix,[86] but
we may note here that in thirty-two of his thirty-eight plays no act
of fornication or adultery occurs within the course of the action.

This record of keeping shadows from their shadow-sins is unmatched even among the popular dramatists, not to mention their select rivals. It is the more impressive in view of Shakespeare's favorable, indeed enthusiastic, attitude toward sexual relations which are properly sanctioned. Prudery, greensickness, or neurotic aversions do not appear except as a bane of deranged characters (sometimes naïvely identified in one or other of their moods with their creator). He never pictures a wittol or contented cuckold, never treats a February and May match, never suggests anything in the nature of seignorial sexual rights. Chaucer's assertion that the village beauty was fit

> For any lord to leggen in his bedde,
> Or yet for any good yemen to wedde,[87]

finds no parallel in Shakespeare's works, where a King Cophetua may have his beggar maid only at the price of marriage. Understanding of the code would prevent critical errors. When Shakespeare eliminates from one play scenes of sexual license in the nunneries, or from others the libertinage of a Richard II or an Edward IV, he is not whitewashing Roman Catholic sisters or English kings: he would have exercised the same prerogative if treating of chambermaids and tapsters. He considered, or thought that his audience considered, unchastity a displeasing spectacle. Particularly in the categories of conduct about to be treated, he and the popular school reveal their aversions.

The tastes of the coterie were sufficiently jaded or exploratory (according to the point of view) to require the fillip of the excessive, the devious, the perverse. Consanguinity in lovers, rivals in love, or lovers and go-betweens, is often employed to give sexual intrigue an added piquancy. Incest as a theme appears tentatively in Lyly's *Mother Bombie*, where the lovers Maestius and Serena think they are brother and sister. In Middleton's *Phoenix* Justice Falso proposes incestuous relations with his niece to frighten her into yielding up her fortune; in *The Family of Love* the situation is reversed, and Maria, made pregnant by her lover Gerardine, connives in the blackmailing of her uncle with the charge of incest so as to wrest from him control of her fortune. (The episode, incidentally, provides the "romantic" interest in the play.) The subject of incest was contemplated with increasing intentness, and in plays beyond our purview the theme passed from Middleton, Fletcher, and Ford to John Dryden. Because of our decreasing consciousness of canonical impediments, we no longer recognize the extent to which an incestuous atmosphere hovered about the numerous episodes in which brothers, uncles, and nephews, or fathers and sons shared or contended for the favors of the same woman. In Marston's *The Fawn* Herod cuckolds his elder brother. In Fletcher's *Cupid's Revenge* Duke Leontius weds the mistress of his son. In Middleton's *A Mad World My Masters* Follywit weds the mistress of his grandfather! That such matter was considered disagreeable in the public theatres is illustrated by a comparison of Barry's *Ram-Alley* and Cooke's *Greene's Tu Quoque*.[88] The same widow-hunt is presented in the two plays, but in the second the rivals are no longer father and son. In several plays of the private theatres, mothers and fathers serve, willingly or unwillingly, as bawds or procurers for their own children: Middleton's *A Mad World My Masters* and *Michaelmas Term*, and Sharpham's *The Fleire*. In the last, Duke Antifront is disguised and ostensibly reluctant in acting as pander for his two daughters; but he discharges his duties gaily:

Petoune.
Thou their [the daughters'] leader? Why, do they mean to go to the wars?
Antifront.
I think so, for I am sure here were a couple of gentlemen last night that scour'd their pieces.[89]

One may exercise himself by trying to imagine Shakespeare dealing in such ware.

In the public theatres the one proper attitude toward incest was horror. In *Hamlet* Gertrude's marriage to her brother-in-law strikes her son as incestuous as well as otherwise damnable. Heywood's method of dramatizing sensitive areas in Greek myth was to adopt a disarming matter-of-factness, on the principle that gods will be gods:

'tis the story;
Truth claims excuse, and seeks no further glory.[90]

Jupiter tells Juno that instead of sister he will style her "by a nearer name of wife." She replies, " 'Tis a name I prize 'bove sister," and the episode is invested with almost middle-class propriety.[91] One of the features of Greene's *Pandosto* rejected by Shakespeare when he dramatized the romance in his *Winter's Tale* was the king's courtship of his unrecognized daughter. The sole vestige of the material is revealing. The beauty of Perdita draws from her father a few playful words to Florizel, "I'd beg thy precious mistress." Even this is enough to make Paulina bridle:

> Sir, my liege,
> Your eye hath too much youth in't. Not a month
> Fore your queen died, she was more worth such gazes
> Than what you look on now.

To which comes the perfect reply,

> I thought of her
> Even in those looks I made.[92]

The grace is Shakespeare's, but he is working within restrictions imposed by time and place.

The plays of the private theatres provided a succession of sexual novelties and, in one detail or another, a wide range of perverse suggestion. A few relatively innocuous signs of the tendency appear in Lyly. In *Gallathea* the two girls disguised as boys fall so deeply in love because of their misconception about each other that the only solution is to let them marry, with the sex of one of them (either one) to be miraculously changed at the altar. The play ends with this remarkable marriage pending, the principals still unaware of which is to be the bride and which the groom. In *The Maid's Metamorphosis* the sex of Eurymine fluctuates even more obligingly. But such plays were but "musty fopperies of antiquity." Although supposedly celebrating the chastity of Sophonisba, Marston makes remarkable capital of the unchastity of Syphax, who on one occasion gets into bed with a male Negro who has been substituted for his

victim, and on another is tricked into satisfying the lust of aged
Erictho. He describes various projected rapes, one with accomplices,

> I'll tack thy head
> To the low earth, whilst strength of two black knaves
> Thy limbs all wide shall strain,

and one necrophilic:

> I'll use
> With highest lust of sense thy senseless flesh,
> And even when thy vexed soul shall see,
> Without resistance, thy trunk prostitute
> Unto our appetite.[93]

The zoophilic and gerontophilic are both alluded to in Middleton's
Michaelmas Term—"as an old lady delights in a young page or a
monkey, so there are young courtiers will be hungry upon an old
woman"[94] and the one is dramatized in *Northward Ho*, where Doll
becomes infatuated with aged Bellamont and attempts his seduction.
Modern science has found terms for other phenomena portrayed for
the smart set. In Beaumont's *Woman Hater*, Gondarini is tortured
by being fondled by pretty women. In Fletcher's *Cupid's Revenge*
Princess Hidaspes becomes enamored of a dwarf. In Field's *A
Woman Is a Weathercock* Sir Abraham Ninny is convinced that his
erotic dream has made Wagtail pregnant, while Scudmore proclaims
virtuously,

> I never dreamt of lying with my mother,
> Nor wish't my father's death, nor hated brothers.[95]

In Sharpham's *Cupid's Whirligig* Sir Timothy Troublesome has himself castrated as a means of detecting his wife's infidelity.

Homosexuality engaged the attention of none of the Elizabethans
to the extent that it did their Italian contemporaries, or that it does
the more recherché writers of today; but such tokens of interest
as appear flow in that literary rivulet, previously mapped, from the
erotic and satirical verse of the nineties into the private playhouses.
Donne and Marston share with the Roman satirists a penchant for
the subject. Donne's courtly gossip notes "Who loves whores, who
boys, and who goats,"[96] while Marston, in his portrait of Lais and

others, adverts to the subject with febrile excitement.[97] From Marston's verses we should deduce, probably in error, that sodomy was common in academic and courtly circles in his day. Prominent persons were indeed charged with it during recriminations otherwise instigated including, among men associated with the theatre, Oxford in 1581,[98] Marlowe in 1593,[99] and, possibly, Jonson in 1601 since he is said to have in him "no part of Horace . . . but's damnable vices."[100] As might be expected, there were, among writers, disparate attitudes toward homosexuality in their own society, equated in moral sentiment with bestiality, and punishable at law by hanging, and reflections of it in classical poetry. In Barnfield's *Affectionate Shepherd*, 1594, the love of the shepherd for the boy is expressed in what seem to be sexual terms; but the poet later protested that his work had been interpreted "otherwise than in truth I meant," that Daphnis's love was pure, and the whole thing "nothing else but an imitation of Vergil in the second Eclogue of Alexis."[101] Heywood, in one of his *Pleasant Dialogues and Dramas*, treated the Jupiter-Juno-Ganymede triangle with objective aplomb, after prefixing a caveat:

> Although this fable to the gods extends,
> Base forbid lust in man it reprehends.[102]

The mere hint of sodomy directed at his own times and profession aroused his ire:

> To do as the Sodomites did, use preposterous lusts in preposterous habits, is in that [biblical] text flatly and severely forbidden, nor can I imagine any man that hath in him any taste or relish of Christianity to be guilty of so abhorred a sin. . . . But to see our youths attired in the habit of women, who knows not what their intents be? Who cannot distinguish them by their names, assuredly knowing they are but to represent such a lady at such a time appointed?[103]

His Jove and Ganymede in *The Golden Age*, composed for the Red Bull, appear not as lovers but as fellow warriors. The public theatres rigorously excluded homosexual humor. When a boy disguised as a girl arouses the susceptibility of a man, like Wily in *George a Greene*, and Walgrave in *Englishmen for My Money*, or when a girl disguised as a boy that of a woman, like Viola in *Twelfth Night*, the interest is solely in the ensuing plot complication. If we were to find suggestiveness anywhere, it would be in the jests about Falstaff and his page in *II Henry IV* and *The Merry Wives of Windsor;* but nothing of the kind appears. The fearlessness of misinterpretation, in the use of the language of love for the sentiment of friendship, and in the use of disguise situations, seems to argue that there was nothing like the present-day preoccupation with the subject, outside a very small circle. The only indubitable allusion to homosexuality in Shakespeare is in one of Thersites' diatribes against Achilles and Patroclus (another link between Thersites and Marston), where Heywood's term "preposterous" is anticipated;[104] the only indubitable homosexual joke in a play performed at the public theatres is in the Induction to Marston's *Malcontent* appropriated from Blackfriars; and the only popular play introducing the subject in the plot is Barnes's *Devil's Charter.* The *Storia di Firenze* evidently supplied the author with his material about the career of Roderigo Borgia, Pope Alexander VI, since Francis Guicciardini serves as Chorus in the play; but the English dramatist is less imperturbable than the Italian historian: the stress is upon Borgia's satanic license and the horror of the two youths he victimizes. The matter may have been added to the acting version, which was augmented for publication.

At the private playhouses the restrictions indicated above did not obtain. Marlowe, in plays written for the popular troupes, was not explicit about the relations of Henry III of France to his "minions," or of Edward II of England to Piers Gaveston. The amorous shows planned by Gaveston for his master's delight were necessarily to be performed by boys, but the characters were "nymphs" behaving like the temptresses of Sir Guyon in Spenser's Bower of Bliss.[105] Gaveston is an idolized and corrupting favorite who destroys Edward as a king and a husband; further conclusions about the relations of the two must be deductions of the spectator or reader. But the opening of Marlowe's Chapel play exploits clearly the homosexuality of the Jove-Ganymede myth, and the episode is treated with the same insouciance as the Neptune-Leander episode in *Hero and Leander.* In Jonson's *Poetaster,* Ganymede is again the "catamite":

Ovid (as Jupiter).
Juno, we will cudgel you, Juno: we told thee so yesterday, when thou
wert jealous of us for Thetis.

Pyrgo (as Ganymede).
Nay, today she had me in inquisition too.[106]

This is one of several such allusions in the play. In Marston's *What
You Will* Simplicius Faber is a "Hermaphrodite,"[107] and in his
Malcontent Ferrardo is the Duke's "smooth-chin'd catamite."[108] In
Chapman's *May-Day* Captain Quintiliano's query to Lionello, "Hast
ever practiced, my pretty Ganymede?"[109] is a *double-entendre*. The
theme is treated more expansively in later coterie plays. In John
Mason's *The Turk*, the scenes involving Bordello, Madame Fulsome,
and the page Pantofle are rank, and in *The Honest Man's Fortune*,
Laverdine pursues with overt intentions the page Veramour until the
latter proves to be a woman: "How happy am I! Now we may law-
fully come together without fear of hanging."[110] In levying upon
Piccolomini's *Alessandro* for his *May-Day*, Chapman expunged homosexuality as a component in the plot, and the theme was never
featured centrally even in the coterie plays; however, a suspicious
coloring marks some of the jesting in others than those mentioned
above. The subject was not taboo as comic material, and was introduced with increasing boldness.

In view of its quite genuine strictness, demonstrated as we have
seen in so many ways, it is interesting that the popular drama should
have been constantly charged with "lewdness." It shared this charge
with other forms of popular literature. The ballads were "lewd";[111]
the romances were sometimes "lewd"; and in 1612 the Middlesex justices ordered the suppression of "lewd jigs, songs, and dances" at the
Fortune.[112] Few Elizabethan ballads and romances are lewd in the
usual sense of the word, and the surviving examples of the jigs performed after the plays in the public theatres are not notably so.
Sometimes the word was used simply in the sense of crude or uncouth, but the suggestion of sexual dereliction often adhered to it.
The only justification for its application to the popular drama would
have been supplied by the ribald jests with which some of the plays

were sprinkled—the "sallets in the lines to make the matter savoury."[113] Guilpin speaks of the "old, cold, grey-beard citizen" being stimulated by the "salt la volto jests" at the Curtain.[114] While Matilda in *The Death of Robert Earl of Huntington* stands martyr for her chastity, speaking lines written with obvious sincerity, Brand the villain-clown interjects bawdy remarks directed certainly to the risibility of the audience.[115] The tribute to another martyr to chastity, Heywood's *Rape of Lucrece*, contains comic songs that would pass current in a burlesque show. Such matter resembles the grotesques in the carving of some of the old English churches and strikes one as peculiarly medieval. The instances in the two plays mentioned are extreme examples. A more normal one occurs in *The Travels of Three English Brothers*. The Persian heroine is as pure and "English" as Portia, but the attendant who dresses her for her wedding jests as indecorously as Nerissa.

Shakespeare—Prince Hamlet's objection notwithstanding—is the most fertile of the popular dramatists in producing "sallets" in the lines, and the practice, with its saving features, may best be illustrated through him. In spite of the justice of the oft quoted judgment that Shakespeare's humor is as broad as ten thousand beeves at pasture, we should observe that he does not exercise it at random. Ribaldry does not appear in *Richard II, Julius Caesar*, and *Coriolanus*, where the theme of courtship does not figure; in fact there is little of it in any of the history plays except in the comic portions of *Henry IV;* in the latter, Falstaff's own wit takes a ribald turn less frequently than one would expect. The amount of ribaldry is about in proportion to the prominence of the love interest in the various plays. *Romeo and Juliet* is the great love story among the tragedies, and the jests of Mercutio are as robust as the passion of the lovers, providing a kind of comic ground-bass. The comedies are marriage plays, and the wanton jests anticipate wedding manners. However, the jests diminish in frequency with the decrease in realism. Such romances as *A Midsummer Night's Dream, Cymbeline, The Winter's Tale*, and *The Tempest* contain very few. In *A Midsummer Night's Dream*, we have the following:

Quince.

Yea . . . and he is a very paramour for a sweet voice.

Flute.

You must say "paragon." A paramour is (God bless us!) a thing of naught.[116]

When we observe that these are the "broadest" lines in the play, we realize how restrained Shakespeare could be. In *The Winter's Tale* the characters themselves are the censors; Perdita forbids "scurrilous words," and the clown backs her efforts to keep the country revels on a lofty plane, although not with perfect success. Miranda and Marina, like Perdita, seem to have a restraining effect, but the presence or absence of "scurrilous words" is not a matter of chronology: *The Comedy of Errors* is freer from them than the late romances. It is in those plays which contain ardent or reasonably mature lovers, realistically presented, that the "sallets" are most apt to appear. The notion that they are ubiquitous derives from the great popularity of *The Taming of the Shrew, Romeo and Juliet,* and *Hamlet,* with the vivid impression left by Petruchio, Mercutio, and the Prince of Denmark.

The wanton jests are not distributed indiscriminately among the characters, but are usually uttered by three classes of speaker. The first consists of young gentlemen, bachelors like Mercutio and Hamlet, or married men like Hotspur, but not the young lovers. No lewdness ever issues from the lips of Valentine, Lucentio, Romeo, Bassanio, Lorenzo, Orlando, Fenton, Orsino, Sebastian, Florizel, Ferdinand, or even Troilus. Their reserve is not untrue to life. As Silvius, the minor lover of *As You Like It,* says, their love is

> all made of fantasy,
> All made of passion, and all made of wishes,
> All adoration, duty, and observance,
> All humbleness, all patience, and impatience,
> All purity, all trial, all obedience.[117]

Petruchio scarcely qualifies as a young lover, and in his case the jokes are not left to a bachelor friend. The second class of ribald jesters consists of clowns and servants, although ribaldry is not their chief stock in trade and several prominent ones such as Feste and Launcelot Gobbo scarcely indulge. Lear's Fool is the only one who does so conspicuously and irrelevantly. The third class consists of the women who are courted and their ladies in waiting. That maidens as pure as Portia, Beatrice, and Rosalind should enter this picture may seem surprising; but from first to last the women are more practical and humorous in their attitude toward sex than the men. Their own jests, though unmistakable, are mild, but the reproofs they give their more forward attendants are equally mild. They are not considered as besmirched by listening to the sallies, and Helena even invites them from Parolles.[118] Chaste Hero's joke about reading a letter and finding "Benedick" and "Beatrice" between the sheets is repeated by her old father with delight.[119] It is prudery that is suspect:

> We do not act that often jest and laugh;
> 'Tis old but true: Still swine eats all the draff.[120]

Usually the ladies find it advisable to make risqué exchanges only between themselves. When Maria in *Love's Labour's Lost* engages with men, they go too far for her: "Come, come, you talk greasily; your lips grow foul."[121]

Allusions to cuckoldry—"It is a wise father that knows his own child"—is the only type of ribald jesting, if it may be called so, indulged in by all characters at random. The "horns" joke can scarcely be considered a joke at all; it is a cliché, a symptom perhaps of the Elizabethan preoccupation with family and legitimacy. It seems to come to the lips of characters inadvertently:

> *Miranda.*
> Sir, are not you my father?
> *Prospero.*
> Thy mother was a piece of virtue, and
> She said thou wast my daughter.[122]

Finally, in regard to spokesmen, it should be pointed out that respected characters are protected from the indignity of being unconsciously suggestive. Dame Quickly, and in one instance Malvolio,[123] are among the few characters used in this way:

Falstaff.
Why, she's neither fish nor flesh; a man knows not where to have her.
Hostess.
Thou art an unjust man in saying so. Thou or any man knows where to
have me, thou knave, thou![124]

Dame Quickly is also allowed to be laughably prudish, holding up
her hand in horror at the "genitivo—horum, harum, horum."[125] It is
a trait she shares with Parson Evans, and with no less a person than
Princess Katherine of France.[126]

The final word must be on the nature of the ribaldry itself. Logan
Pearsall Smith declares himself fond of Shakespeare's "ithyphallic
fun": "That is, when I can understand it, which is by no means always easy" because of passages that "even the most earnest and im-
pure-minded thinkers find it difficult to understand."[127] He exag-
gerates the difficulties, which are purely linguistic. Shakespeare's
ribaldry is the least esoteric in the world, and no one familiar with
Elizabethan English can be baffled unless he has lived an extremely
sheltered life. Any failure in understanding is owing to the reluctance of editors to gloss the offending passages. George Steevens in
his variorum edition of 1793 went further in providing commentary
than other scholars, but he cruelly misattributed this particular class
of notes to the Unitarian clergyman, Richard Amner, and seemed
more intent upon his private joke than upon elucidating the text.
Editorial omission has been supplied in large measure by the recent
essay and glossary issued by Eric Partridge, which is useful although sometimes uninformed. Antony's fishing expedition with
Cleopatra was literally a fishing expedition, and any sexual conno-
tations in the passage explicated could have reached the text only
through the three-ply "unconscious" of the Plutarch-North-Shake-
speare mind. Most of what Mr. Partridge sees in the plays, however,
actually is there, besides a remnant that he does not see; and
whatever false impressions he conveys are owing to the nature of
the project—the marshaling into one place of matter scattered in
thirty-seven plays, the bold-face type, and the somewhat evangelical essay. The emphasis is unavoidably wrong. The jokes in their
context are primarily jokes and only incidentally sexual. Their ap-

peal is the appeal of incongruity and impropriety, and although they certainly indicate in Shakespeare a satisfaction with the facts of life, they suggest that he was a man of humor rather than one inveterately lickerish.

The first convention that should be noticed is the invariable use of the pun. A double meaning is wrung from such words as stones, tongue, tale, stand, bauble, and from such phrases as bearing burdens, putting down, turning to men, and the like. In avoiding the literal, Shakespeare and the other dramatists were following intuitively the theory of Castelvetro:

> But it is to be noted that [indecencies] do not make us laugh when they are set openly before the eyes of the body or of the mind in the presence of others; rather they overcome us with shame. . . . Then the aforesaid things make us laugh when they are presented . . . under a veil, by means of which we are able to give the appearance of laughing not at the indecency but at something else.[128]

"Nay, you need not to stop your nose, sir," says Parolles; "I spake but by metaphor."[129] And Shakespeare might have said the same thing, although the metaphor is intended to be easily penetrable:

Speed.
Why then, how stands the matter with them?
Launce.
Marry, thus: when it stands well with him, it stands well with her.
Speed.
What an ass art thou! I understand thee not.
Launce.
What a block art thou that thou canst not![130]

If one fails to reckon with the consistent punning, and reads one of the words in a jest literally, he may find a meaning that would have surprised and disgusted Shakespeare.

Another uniform quality of the ribaldry is its normality and candor. It consists solely of the whisking away of fig leaves, so that the sexual act or organs are unexpectedly imaged—there is no more to it than that. In spite of the puns, the humor is not sly but remarkably frank, and the imagery though concrete is not particularized. The

perverted and bestial are completely barred, and the scatological almost so. The jokes do not necessarily, in fact do not usually, predicate sexual relationships that are illicit. When Margaret is told that
she should be ashamed of herself for telling Hero her heart will
soon be heavier by the weight of a husband, she says: "Of what,
lady? of speaking honourably? Is not marriage honourable? Is there
any harm in 'the heavier for a husband'? None, I think, an it be the
right husband and the right wife."[131] One summarizing illustration
may be given. When Bassanio weds the mistress, Gratiano decides
to wed the maid:

> *Gratiano.*
> We'll play with them the first boy for a thousand ducats.
> *Nerissa.*
> What, and stake down?
> *Gratiano.*
> No, we shall ne'er win at that sport and stake down.[132]

This is completely typical: it occurs in a play with a prominent love
interest; it is spoken not by the romantic lover but by his retainer;
it involves a pun; it is undeniably candid and "ithyphallic." We
should observe also that, although indecent, it is not immoral.

Robert Bridges, in inveighing against Shakespeare's audience,
speaks of the "filthy for the filthy";[133] but the great majority of
readers and critics have recognized that the jokes are an incidental
excrescence, basically healthy. "In comparison of Aristophanes's freedom," wrote the one-time Bishop of Gloucester, "Shakespeare
writes with the purity of a vestal."[134] Dr. Johnson was strict in sexual matters, but although he concurred in the excision of two lines
from *Romeo and Juliet* because "there are higher laws than those of
criticism,"[135] his censorship ended there; and it would be diverting
to know what he would have said of the text of Mr. Bowdler. Coleridge was troubled by the jokes, but finally affirmed, "Shakespeare
may sometimes be gross, but I boldly say that he is always moral
and modest."[136] The term "modest" scarcely applies to the jokes
of the plays in the way that it does to their action; however, those
who have claimed that the jokes have been forgiven Shakespeare

only because he is Shakespeare and can do no wrong have been less than fair to the powers of discrimination of those who love him. There are types of sexual jesting that the lover of Shakespeare would be less willing than anyone else to forgive him.

In the attacks upon the popular drama marking the reopening of the private theatres in 1599–1600, the old charge of lewdness was conspicuous; but the plays at these theatres were soon purveying a quantity and quality of lewdness such as the public theatres never knew. Jonson, Chapman, Marston, and especially Middleton proved of infinite resource, and the vogue tended to grow. Barry's *Ram-Alley* is a compilation of sexual jokes, some of them extremely clever; but other plays, like Sharpham's *Cupid's Whirligig* and *The Fleire*, can be described only as persistently and drearily "dirty." The popularity of the latter plays in published form suggests that they were read as jest books and manuals of sophisticated wit. While the ribaldry in the coterie drama retains the convention of the pun, the simplicity and normality are gone. Most of the jokes have to do with the inordinate sexual appetites of women, the sexual prowess or debility of men, the commercialization of sex especially through the use to which citizens put their wives, and sexual deviation. Two illustrations will suffice. The two merry wives of Marston's *Insatiate Countess* are conversing:

Thais.
But you mean they shall come in at the backdoors?
Abigail.
Who, our husbands? Nay, and they come not in at the fore-doors, there will be no pleasure in't.[137]

In Middleton's *Michaelmas Term*, the prosperity of London citizens is being discussed: "Do you think some merchants could keep their wives so brave but for their whole-sale? You're foully deceived and you think so."[138] In Shakespeare, most "bawdy" of the popular playwrights, there will be found no "bawdy" like this.

IV

Wedded Love

THE conflicting attitudes toward sex extend into conflicting attitudes toward women, marriage, and the family. Of all
the imaginative literature of the age, the popular drama dwells most
persistently upon the charm of courtship, the dignity of wedded
love, and the power of familial affection. When we call it romantic,
we should recognize that its romanticism is in accord with the most
progressive ethical thinking of the English Renaissance. In comparison, the coterie drama is archaic and reactionary.

Analysis will be more meaningful after a glance at the underlying
collision of sentiment about marriage in the sixteenth century. One
of the thousands of sparks struck off was an epigram by Sir John
Harington. Its butt, none too subtly described as "one that had
gotten a benefice and after sought for a belly piece," pleads the
sanctions of marriage

> As, namely, first for honest procreation,
> Next, to avoid dishonest fornication,
> And that late writers, men of passing piety,
> Have found a third cause, mutual society.[1]

The same sanctions in the same order had been listed a generation
earlier in both Edwardian versions of the Book of Common Prayer:
first, "the procreation of children"; second, "a remedy against sin
and to avoid fornication"; and third, "the mutual society, help, and
comfort that the one [spouse] ought to have of the other." The

222

first and second were old in the teachings of the Church—earthly
habitations must be provided for Christian souls, and to marry is
better than to burn; but the third was irrelevant to salvation, mundane, *new*. Harington himself was neither unhappily married nor
inclined to subvert the prayer book, but his sly allusion to the late
writers of "passing piety" who had *found* the third sanction placed
him, momentarily at least, with the cynics and diehards.

The bride's vow in the older ceremonies of Sarum and elsewhere,
"to be bonere and buxum in the bed and at the board," was mundane enough, but little suggestive of mutuality. That marriage should
be a companionship, freely contracted by spiritual peers on the basis of natural affection and moral fitness, was an ideal for which the
Middle Ages had supplied little support in either the practice of
the temporal, or the precept of the spiritual, leaders. The marriage
of convenience, sometimes contracted for infants, was universal
among the fief holders, while the priests ultimately saddled themselves with the paradox that marriage was both a sacrament and a
shame. The message of the medieval pulpit is thus summarized by
Owst:

> Where healthy human nature seems to demand some positive doctrine
> of sexual happiness, they speak only, as in the realm of public affairs, of
> sin and temptation, of forbidden pleasures and lusts, of needful fears
> and repressions, haunted by the same old shadows of Original Sin, the
> same primitive ascetical ideals of their ancestors.[2]

The stridency of the preachers was their own, heightened after the
eleventh century by the final commitment of their estate to a life
of celibacy; but they found no lack of apostolic and patristic authority, and they were disinclined to make the distinctions of an Aquinas.
They could not have invoked the latter in addressing men on the
contaminative touch of women, or in addressing women on the
punitive pangs of childbirth; but their mood was not philosophical,
and the sixteenth century reformers were right in their assessment
of the sentiment if not the precise doctrine of the Church. Even the
less negative preachment of the Lollards, when they adverted to the
subject of matrimony,[3] mentions nothing so visionary as "mutual
society."

Owst follows Coulton in calling the Augustinian injunction to
fly women, whose beauty was but a snare concealing vileness, the
"high ancestry of Puritanism"; but the Puritans themselves would
have contested the lineage. Such a paleo-Puritan as Thomas Becon
anticipated Owst's own eloquence by nearly four hundred years:

> . . . the most holy state of godly matrimony hath he [the Pope] most
> vilely and most wickedly enbased, cast down, and made almost of no
> reputation. No Turk, no Jew, no Saracen, no Infidel, no Ethnic, no
> Heathen, no Miscreant—no, no Devil hath at any time so vilely and
> wickedly taught and written of this blessed state of honourable wedlock
> as this wicked Bishop of Rome and his adherents have done.[4]

The "Puritan art of love" described by the Hallers[5] was not ascetical.
It assumed, to be sure, a superlative degree of godliness in the properly mated pair, but it also assumed the normality of concupiscence,
the practical equality of the sexes, and the need for "lovability" as
well as high character in the spouse. Even comeliness was conceded
its merits. The women of Abraham, Isaac, and Jacob replaced those
of Adam, Samson, David, and Potiphar in the foreground of the picture.

In formulating a new official definition of the nature of marriage
and, as an essential preamble, one of the nature of women, the Puritans were collaborating with the rest of the nation. The way had
been paved by the circle of Christian humanists in the early decades
of the century. Colet, More, Erasmus, Vives, Elyot, and others were
concerned with the status of women and marriage; and, although
there is a medieval quality in some of their witticisms about women,
it is clear that monkish aversions were alien to their enlightened
minds. They found a dignity accorded the husband-and-wife relationship in much of the classical literature they loved, and, perhaps
more important, modern instances of that dignity in the kind of
homes from which most of them had sprung. Their concern with
confusion in canon law, child marriages, and fraudulent annulments
is less important than their ready assumption of the rationality and
spiritual endowment of human beings regardless of sex. Their faith,
as regards women, is most clearly expressed in More's *Utopia* and

several of the Colloquies of Erasmus; and its practical turn, by their own human relationships and the treatises on the education of women which they composed or sponsored. The treatises indicate that the possibilities implied by the term "mutual society" were already past the speculative stage.

The antifeminist satires that form a distinct genre in the secular literature of the Middle Ages increased rather than decreased in number during the sixteenth century,[6] but they tended to direct their attack less and less upon the irremediable; moreover, they were answered, and the answerers were of all religious persuasions. The Protestant program for a married clergy helped to erode former prejudices;[7] a state considered suitable for the moralists themselves could scarcely be depicted as wholly void of positive merit. The new way of life often proved mollifying, and Luther's own successful marriage must have inspired his pronouncement that a wife should be as a friend and neighbor. It is interesting to observe the hints of new sentiment in the prayer book carrying over into the first book of homilies: adultery, of course, was forbidden of God; but there might be more immediate restraints upon the conduct of husbands and wives—"They must so delight one in another's company, that none of them covet any other."[8] We can only speculate on the effect of the uxoriousness of King Henry VIII. The cause of women was in a measure abetted by the widespread sympathy for Queen Catherine; and the cause of love marriages, curiously enough, by Henry's own penchant for marriages of inconvenience. An amusing scene in Rowley's *When You See Me You Know Me* shows the King pacing the floor during Jane Seymour's labor pains, for all the world like the young husband outside a modern maternity ward. Not only does he direct that the mother be saved before the child, thus striking a blow at inhumane theology, but he makes a remarkable secular pronouncement:

> Mother o' God, this is a woman's glory,
> Like good September vines, loaden with fruit.
> How ill did they define the name of woman,
> Adding so foul a preposition
> To call it woe to man. 'Tis woe from man

If woe it be; and, then, who does not know
That women still from men receive their woe?[9]

Venus Genetrix may be hovering somewhere in the offing, but the
mind boggles at the thought that Rowley's sentiment owes something to cults of Venus and cults of Mary or the medieval literary
movements they are presumed to have inspired. The spokesmen of
the Middle Ages had a pedestal for woman as well as a pit, an Ovid
for an Augustine, and it is customary to set off against priestly ful-
minations the gracious love lyrics of the Provençal poets and the
elaborate courtesy code of *l'amour courtois* as fostered by Eleanor
of Aquitaine and Marie de Champagne, codified by Andreas Capellanus, and reflected in romances from Chrétien's to Chaucer's. The
lady, far from being depreciated, was to her lover as a lord to a vas-
sal. For those who could not accept the underlying iniquity of
courtly love, there was the alternate religion of beauty in women,
platonic in inspiration, and fervidly expressed in Dante, Petrarch,
and the rapt discourse of Castiglione's Pietro Bembo. The cultural
influence of these aristocratic and poetic fashions was undeniably
great, but we are apt to overestimate it. The materials of the literary historian are the partial records preserved in writing, and we
may sometimes think we are explicating human nature and human
institutions when we are only briefing the disputes of articulate
minorities. The Church and the aristocracy produced obverse images of the same thing, competing types of formalism, competing
types of asceticism, equal and opposite rejections of reality as known
to human beings outside the cloister or the tiny courtly milieu.

It is a delightful experience to read Mr. Lewis's *Allegory of Love*,
and to observe the talented author plucking the flower "monogamic
idealism" out of the nettle "courtly adultery"; but we may question
if the work does really demonstrate that wedded love was "the peculiar flower of a peculiar civilization"[10] (sixteenth to nineteenth
century English), or that the dignification of women and, ultimately,
marriage in the poems surveyed signalizes one of the three or four
recorded "real changes in human sentiment." Our memories of details from the records of many cultures in many ages seem to people

with protesting ghosts the shrine erected to *l'amour courtois* and its Renaissance transfiguration in *The Faerie Queene*. Some of the ghosts whisper from the pages of Chrétien and Chaucer themselves. It is true that, in the love story which became dominant in secular· literature after the mid-twelfth century, the heroines are usually married women or mistresses; but, if poetic orthodoxy identified romantic love with the clandestine and adulterous, there was much heresy abroad in the land. Even if we focus our attention on the proper works, and admit that the moods of the celebrants of the medieval cults reappear in the moods of the later celebrants of wedded love, with a borrowing of tropes and picturesque patterns of conduct, we can only conclude that there is an affinity among poets. Within an exclusively literary frame we can discuss only literary phenomena. We cannot assume that human experience is non-renewable, indeed non-existent, apart from literary expression.

The ideal of love that became vocal in the sixteenth century is distinguished by its *utility*. The courtly cult, at least as expounded by the doctrinaire Andreas, countenanced rape,[11] the single sexual practice condemned in all cultures. In assuming that each love affair was a special case, or that lovers and husbands belonged to mutually exclusive categories, or that institutional theory could survive universally contrary practice and parenthood could remain satisfactorily speculative, the cult was amazingly unrealistic. It served neither the emotional nor the practical needs of any imaginable society. To the Elizabethan Englishman, platonic love would have been more comprehensible, but only slightly more. Continency was recognized as a "gift" in the prayer book, but its incidence was regarded as so low as to be practically negligible. We hear often the half-hearted concession that

> wedlock is an ordinance from Heaven,
> Though junior to the single purity,[12]

but even the forty-five-year reign of a virgin queen that raised the prestige of women could not preserve the prestige of virgins. The transvaluation of values, by which Chastity ceased to be a virtue *per se* and became no more than an aspect of fidelity, has been lamented. But the loss seems less great when we recognize that Chastity did remain a virtue *per se* in theory, but in practice transferred much of her former prestige to Constancy, a humbler but more serviceable sister. Certainly, for Shakespeare and his age, "chastity" and "constancy" became almost synonymous. Some delightful lines occur in an obituary tribute to Elizabeth herself written by Lady Diana Primrose, who was sturdier than her name. Chastity, said the lady, hangs in the Queen's *Chain of Pearl;* but,

> whether it be termed virginal
> In virgins, or in wives styl'd conjugal,
> Or vidual in widows, God respects
> All equally, and all alike affects.[13]

The doctrine expounded in the last chapter of *Il Libro del Cortegiano* that "sensual love is evil at every age," although most excusable in youth, and womanly beauty should be regarded as the ladder of the soul to heavenly beauty, is called by Lord Morello a dream. His judgment, "To engender beauty in beauty, forsooth, would be to beget a beautiful child in a beautiful woman,"[14] appears to be that of Shakespeare, even in his Sonnets and the most courtly and artificial of those. It was not until after 1633 that a cult of platonic love had a brief vogue among *précieuses* at the court of Queen Henrietta Maria, and William Davenant (another Morello) "had command t'interpret what he scarce" understood.[15] John Milton's ideals of love, as he himself avers, were nourished by the reading of Plato, Xenophon, the Latin elegiac poets including Ovid, Dante, Petrarch, and the Arthurian romances presumably from Chrétien to Spenser.[16] If it had been pointed out to him that, of these, only Spenser had unmistakably celebrated *wedded* love, he would have repeated the ancient apothegm that the bee sucks honey where the spider sucks poison. That Spenser, Shakespeare, and Milton all sprang from the same broad sector of society in the same age suggests that the ideal we are treating was not essentially a literary product.

The social revolution, bringing increasing importance and assertiveness to the middle classes, accounts in large measure for the religious and poetic endorsement of wedded love. Eileen Power, in her survey of woman's position in the Middle Ages, presents facts rarely expressed in the didactic and imaginative literature of the time to show that women in the towns had achieved equality with men in moral estimation and practical affairs. The bourgeoisie "showed a greater sense of the normal personality of women than did either the Aristocracy or the Church," allowing them something like a resting place in the "oscillation between the pit and the pedestal."[17] At the same time it evolved the strictest notions of feminine decorum: "Then, as now," says Coulton, "Mrs. Grundy was a bourgeoise."[18] What we are allowed to contemplate is the conjugal partnership in an environment sufficiently free to admit of social rewards and punishments. In a modern fable by C. S. Forester,[19] an African king is about to dine on one of his elder wives, but is diverted by a raid which isolates the two of them in the wilderness. Their interdependence in this unenclosed existence ignites a spark of affection in the savage breast, the wife ceases to be only a potential meal, and the pair enjoy at least a modicum of that "mutual society" specified in the Book of Common Prayer. True, Mr. Forester is an Englishman, writing in the tradition of Spenser, Shakespeare, and Milton—not yet quite dead even in the gloomy view of C. S. Lewis—but his tale is plausible; one may wildly surmise that a few of the lesser cannibals had discovered the third advantage of marriage earlier than their king. It is doubtful if men and women have been capable of purely material relationships since the birth of imagination and superstition. Such psychological constants as sheer egotism, which transfers to desired objects some of the quality of one's own cherishable self, sheer force of habit, which can endear even an old coat, sheer pride of possession, in a poor thing but one's own, may be mentioned without too much sentimentality as starting points in the spiritual amelioration of physical and economic relationships between the sexes. First steps can lead to far journeys, perhaps even without much in the way of institutional aids. We have no statistical check on whether Chaucer's *Franklin's Tale* affords a glimpse into more, or fewer, medieval homes than his fabliaux and his *Troilus and Criseyde,* but we can be certain that the conception of a certain type of woman and a certain type of marriage was not newborn in the sixteenth century. We can be equally certain that the conception had never before been so widely disseminated or so articulate. In addition to the religious, literary, and social factors that have been roughly sketched, we must reckon with the ever widening circle of those who read the Bible—with its twin impact as the word of God and a domestic chronicle.

The "monogamic idealism" of the popular drama is truly phenomenal. That the young lovers permit no interference in their choices, parental or otherwise, that they court for marriage and marry for love, that the women are at least the moral equals of the men, and that the mutual faith of husband and wife is regarded as tremendously important, are all so evident as to pass frequently unremarked.

> *Vernon.*
> I doubt not but by the marriage of your child
> You seek such comfort as the sacred state
> Yields you as parents, us as children?
> *Curtis.*
> What else, son Vernon?
> *Vernon.*
> And those high blessings no way are attained
> But by the mutual sympathizing love,
> That, as combining hands, so should the hearts
> Of either party, else it cannot be?
> *Curtis.*
> All this is true, son Vernon.[20]

This exchange appears at the beginning of *Captain Thomas Stukeley,* the main business of which is to glorify an English adventurer (who proves to be not much of a husband), and its casualness is typical of many plays. In others the issue of love and marriage is consciously debated. Wilkins's *Miseries of Enforced Marriage* is a tract against matches of convenience and wayward husbands; and, although the treatment is awkward and insensitive, its preachment parallels that of the ministers and pamphleteers. The young couple lecture each other like lovers in the *proviso* scenes of later comedy of manners,

but in a marvelously different frame of reference: "To be a wife is
to be dedicate," begins Scarborrow; and "As women owe a duty, so
do men," replies Clare, and each proceeds to expound what the
dedication and duty consist of.[21] In play after play, the good wife
is defined by representation, like Mistress Arthur in *How a Man
May Choose a Good Wife from a Bad*:

> Is she not loyal, constant, loving, chaste,
> Obedient, apt to please, loath to displease,
> And jealous of your reputation?
> Is she not virtuous, wise, religious?[22]

At all levels of society, the suitors seek goodness, beauty, lovability,
and they themselves are truly in love. In *A Warning for Fair Women*
the old yeoman reproves the suitor of his serving girl Joan, "Why,
John Beane, canst part with thy love without a kiss?" And the dis-
traught youth makes amends: "Ye say true, father John; my business puts kissing out of my mind. Farewell, sweet Joan."[23] Such lines
bring our fingers directly to the popular pulse. It is the business of
the children to select their own, not their parents' candidates, and it
is the business of the parents to accept defeat. Says Philip Harding
in *Fortune by Land and Sea*,

> Do men use
> By other hearts and eyes their wives to choose?[24]

and Lady Mary in *The Royal King and the Loyal Subject*:

> My father is my father, but my husband,
> He is myself. My resolution is
> To profess constancy and keep mine honor,
> And rather than to queen it where I hate,
> Beg where I love—I wish no better fate.[25]

Shakespeare's lovers defy parental interference as a matter of
course, with the girls particularly obdurate—Juliet, Silvia, Bianca,
Hermia, Jessica, Anne Page, Imogen, and others. A few, like Perdita
and Miranda, find scarcely opposition enough to allow their powers
full scope. Helena seems inclined to resurrect her father in order to
resist him. "What was he like?" says she. Her imagination "carries

no favour in't but Bertram's."[26] We are reminded of Rosalind's "But what talk we of fathers when there is such a man as Orlando?"[27] Ophelia is the pathetic exception, lacking the wisdom to revolt against a father even when the father is a Polonius. Of those who treated the Romeo and Juliet story, Shakespeare went farthest in shifting the onus of guilt from the lovers to their parents. Old Capulet knows what is due a daughter—"My will to her consent is but a part," he tells his own candidate for her hand; but he has tragically limited her "scope of choice."[28] The tune is the same in every key. I "obey you, love you, and most honour you," says Cordelia to Lear, but

> Why have my sisters husbands, if they say
> They love you all?[29]

Desdemona's speech to Brabantio is identical in substance:

> My life and education both do learn me
> How to respect you: you are the lord of duty;
> I am hitherto your daughter. But here's my husband;
> And so much duty as my mother show'd
> To you, preferring you before her father,
> So much I challenge that I may profess
> Due to the Moor my lord.[30]

It was assumed that sexual desire in woman was normal, not repugnant, and that the "right reason" that controlled the passions of men was also possessed by women. The popular playwrights displayed no interest whatever in virginity. Delia, a minor character in *The London Prodigal*, has no wish to wed, and Matilda in *The Death of Robert Earl of Huntington* buries such wishes with her love; but characters of this nature are hard to find. Matilda's resolution is a matter of wonder to the other characters—"For, being mortal, sure thou hast desire!" (Her maidenhood is called "a martyr's pain."[31]) When Millicent in *The Merry Devil of Edmonton* overhears that her father plans to take her to Cheston, "there to become a most religious nun," she exclaims, "I'll first be buried quick!"[32] Averting such a danger could crown a comedy. When Margaret, the fair maid of Fressingfield in Greene's *Friar Bacon*, thinks she has lost Lord

Lacy, she says, "All love is lust but love of heaven," and resolves to remain in the nunnery of Fremingham. Then arrives a post from her love:

> *Ermsby.*
> Choose you, fair damsel, yet the choice is yours,
> Either a solemn nunnery or the court,
> God or Lord Lacy. Which contents you best,
>
> *Margaret.*
> The flesh is frail. My lord doth know it well,
> That when he comes with his enchanting face,
> Whatsoe'er betide, I cannot say him nay.
> Off goes the habit of a maiden's heart,
> And, seeing Fortune will, fair Fremingham
> And all the show of holy nuns, farewell!
> Lacy for me, if he will be my lord.[33]

The cheers of the audience seem to echo down the years.

For sexual abstinence as an ideal in itself, for votresses of Diana or brides of the Church, we find no advocacy in Shakespeare. Chastity, in this sense, is viewed only as respectable eccentricity. The tribute to the aspirations of Isabella as a novice of St. Clare, "a thing ensky'd and sainted,"[34] and to England's virgin Queen, walking "in maiden meditation, fancy-free,"[35] will occupy a line or two, while Theseus's warning to Hermia will be an oration:

> question your desires,
> Know of your youth, examine well your blood,
> Whether, if you yield not to your father's choice,
> You can endure the livery of a nun,
> For aye to be in shady cloister mew'd,
> To live a barren sister all your life,
> Chaunting faint hymns to the cold fruitless moon.
> Thrice blessed they that master so their blood
> To undergo such maiden pilgrimage;
> But earthlier happy is the rose distill'd
> Than that which, withering on the virgin thorn,
> Grows, lives, and dies in single blessedness.[36]

The "blessedness" in these lines appears like a fate worse than death, and Hermia is spared for "earthlier" happiness. All the others are likewise, even Isabella, although her escape is narrower than the rule. The stage was cleared at the end of the old comedies by letting the couples walk off hand in hand. It is difficult to imagine Isabella making off singly toward the nunnery of St. Clare, without so much as replying to the Duke's proposal.

A recent critic has argued for Shakespeare's devotion to the "old Catholic virtue of chastity as a virtue *per se*."[37] He is of the whimsical school, but on this point at least seems in earnest. He should explain why the dramatist did not attest to his reverence for virginity by letting a few of his heroines retain it, or at least retain it a little longer than they do. The function of earthy Mercutio and the Nurse in *Romeo and Juliet*, says Professor Wilson, is to remind us "that the marvellous blossom of love which forms the main theme of the story is not a mere poet's dream, a pleasing fancy, but a piece of real life rooted deep in the crude common soil of human nature."[38] But we should be aware of the fact even if the lovers were the only characters in the play. Juliet's speech of impatience at the delay—the most brief delay—of her bridal night ends:

> O, I have bought the mansion of a love,
> But not possess'd it; and though I am sold,
> Not yet enjoy'd. So tedious is this day
> As is the night before some festival
> To an impatient child that hath new robes
> And may not wear them.[39]

This needs no supplement from Mercutio or the Nurse. As Julia in *The Two Gentlemen of Verona* folds the letter containing her name and Proteus's, she says:

> Thus will I fold them one upon another.
> Now kiss, embrace, contend, do what you will.[40]

It is Rosalind's belief that Time "trots hard with a young maid between the contract of her marriage and the day it is solemniz'd. If the interim be but a se'nnight, Time's pace is so hard that it seems the length of seven year." No doubt it is for this reason that she thinks Oliver and Celia should marry incontinent lest they be incontinent before marriage.[41] Part of the taming of Katherina consists of Petruchio's "making a sermon of continence to her" on their bridal night.[42] The kind of ballads[43] sung by Ophelia in her distraction seems to reflect the frustration of her desire for Hamlet. Prospero's worried speeches to Ferdinand and Miranda and Friar Laurence's to Romeo and Juliet recognize the realities:

> you shall not stay alone
> Till Holy Church incorporate two in one.[44]

Failure to make her lover wait is the only offense of the one erring woman in Shakespeare treated gently.[45]

It is clear that the cognate assumptions of the popular drama were that women possessed sexual impulses, and that they were not promiscuous; confidence in the latter explains the easy acceptance of the former. That constancy in women was a credible and pleasing spectacle is illustrated by nearly every play. Unchaste women appear only in the underworld or in tragedies. The "homiletic tragedies" in which adultery leads to disaster are overwhelmed in number by what might be called, with equal justice, the "homiletic comedies" where a woman's constancy saves the day. The constant maids range from princesses like Fidelia in *The Rare Triumphs of Love and Fortune*, Amadine in *Mucedorus*, and Angelica in *Orlando Furioso*, to the invulnerable barmaid Bess in Heywood's *Fair Maid of the West*. In *Fair Em* the girls are all exemplary, princesses and artisans' daughters alike, and the maid of the mill is such as to allay in King William the Conqueror some incipient twinges of misogyny. Her reproof to her fickle lover echoes the marriage vow:

> I tell thee, Manville, hadst thou been blind,
> Or deaf, or dumb, or else what impediments might
> Befall to man, Em would have loved, and kept,
> And honored thee—yea, beg'd, if wealth had failed,
> For thy relief.[46]

Surprisingly, in view of the usual stress of romantic fiction, the constant maids are no more plentiful than the constant wives. These retain their love and defend their honor in the face of adversity, abuse, temptation, and dire threats. Again, only a sampling need be mentioned: Dorothea in Greene's *James the Fourth*, Lady Faulconbridge in *Look About You*, Luce in *The London Prodigal*, Bellafront in *II The Honest Whore*, and "sweet, lovely, loving Jane" in *The Shoemaker's Holiday*. An old legend is infused with a new spirit of domesticity in Dekker and Chettle's *Patient Grissill*; and in *How a Man May Choose a Good Wife from a Bad*, Mistress Arthur becomes a Grissill of contemporary London:

> if, as I well think, you cannot love me,
> Love where you list, only but say you love me:
> I'll feed on shadows, let the substance go.[47]

Meekness, however, is not the desideratum. In defense of their honor the wives are heroical, their heroism ranging from the willingness of a duchess to sew for a living—

> We have not fall'n, though want did wrestle hard,
> Our fingers' ends our honors have sustained[48]—

to the martyrdom of a Lucrece. In Marlowe's *Tamburlaine*, Olympia, the wife of the captain slain at Balsera, extorts death from the conqueror to avert dishonor.[49] The last measure of sacrifice, the death of a loved one, is usually averted. In *George a Greene* occurs the following episode:

> *James.*
> Well, Jane, since thou disdain'st King James's love,
> I'll draw thee on with sharp and deep extremes;
> For, by my father's soul, this brat of thine
> Shall perish here before thine eyes,
> Unless thou open the gate and let me in.
> *Jane.*
> O deep extremes! My heart begins to break!
> My little Ned looks pale for fear—
> Cheer thee, my boy; I will do much for thee.
> *Ned.*
> But not so much as to dishonor me.
> *Jane.*
> And if thou diest, I cannot live, sweet Ned.

Ned.
Then die with honor, mother, dying chaste.
Jane.
I am armed.
My husband's love, his honor, and his fame
Joins victory by virtue. Now, King James,
If mother's tears cannot allay thine ire,
Then butcher him, for I will never yield.
The son shall die before I wrong the father.
James.
Why then he dies.
                    (*Alarum within. Enter a Messenger.*)
                                           Messenger.
My Lord, Musgrove is at hand.
                                           James.
Who? Musgrove! The devil he is! Come,
My horse!
                                 (*Exeunt omnes.*)[50]

This is dramatized balladry, but it is part of the Shakespearean setting: *Measure for Measure* must be read in the perspective it provides. Not always is the treatment high-pitched and extravagant.
There are constant sweethearts and loving wives who appear in
workaday surroundings. The quiet devotion of Sir John and Lady
Cobham in *Sir John Oldcastle* is as authentic in its way as the
camaraderie of Hotspur and his sweet Kate, or the mutual regard of
Brutus and Portia. Most impressive is the way in which these good
women compare with the bad as artistic creations: it was they that
kindled the imagination of the creators, with the phenomenal result
that virtue seems more interesting than vice.

Shakespeare's archetypal woman is instinctively monandrous.
Some word for constancy—"virtuous," "chaste," "honest," "true," or
the like—appears invariably in the inventories of womanly qualities
scattered through the plays,[51] no matter how short the inventory or
how diverse the personality and social station of the woman or
women involved. Hector's challenge to the Greeks is that

> He hath a lady wiser, fairer, truer,
> Than ever Greek did compass in his arms.[52]

Jessica is "wise, fair, and true,"[53] Silvia, "virtuous," "mild and beautiful";[54] Rosalind, "the fair, the chaste, the unexpressive she";[55] and little Anne Page, in words befitting her homelier surroundings, "pretty, and honest, and gentle."[56] Benedick's specifications are very exacting; but it is the moral qualities he mentions twice,[57] and finally settles for in Beatrice. Even the relatively few offending women, with the possible exception of Cressida, are not portrayed as promiscuous. In conceding that Jonson's good women are "all without dramatic color," C. H. Herford remarks that Shakespeare "makes us forget to ask whether his are 'good' because they are above all delightful and human."[58] He does this by giving them humor, intelligence, a capacity for friendship, and a few endearing faults, rather than by mitigating their essential virtue. In their love affairs the question of their "goodness" can scarcely arise, because their lovers have no rivals even in their memories or imaginations. No figure to correspond to Romeo's Rosaline has appeared in Juliet's past. The force of the dramatist's predilections is revealed by his last heroine: Miranda has not even *seen* another young man.

It was still the consensus of opinion that women were less stable than men, even though the moralists were advocating tolerance instead of indulging in invective:

For the woman is a weak creature, not endued with like strength and constancy of mind; therefore they be the sooner disquieted, and they be the more prone to all weak affections and dispositions of mind, more than men be; and lighter they be, and more vain in their phantasies and opinions.[59]

And yet in Shakespeare, despite the occasional allusions to their "waxen" hearts, women are the constant sex. Juliet is not quite eighteen in Bandello, is eighteen in Painter, sixteen in Broke, and not quite fourteen in Shakespeare. Perdita is sixteen, Miranda fifteen, and Mariana fourteen. Whenever the age of the heroine is optional in his sources, Shakespeare makes it extremely young. To Frank Harris this seemed evidence of his "fierce sensuality."[60] Rather it is evidence of his impulse, reasonable or unreasonable, to portray in woman complete absorption in the lover, complete isolation from all other men. Romeo may say that the lips of Juliet,

> even in pure and vestal modesty,
> Still blush, as thinking their own kisses sin.[61]

In the eyes of Hero appears "a fire to burn the errors" of her false
accusers.[62] The virginal quality, in his special sense, persists in marriage. "Am I that name, Iago?" asks Desdemona, bewildered at being
called a whore. When the image of the adultress is forced into her
mind, she says, "I do not think there is any such woman."[63] When
Imogen is similarly accused, there is a similar absence of degrading
denial:

> False to his bed! What is it to be false?
> To lie in watch there and to think on him?[64]

The charges against Hermione are greeted by the indignant incredulity of an entire court. Shakespeare makes the quality of constancy incandescent by polarization—between the actual Desdemona,
Imogen, and Hermione, and the women their mind-sick husbands
imagine them to be.

Again the reader must be asked to look upon this picture, and
on this. Among the coterie dramatists, the ideal of wedded love,
on the few occasions when it is expressed at all, serves to high-light
the squalor of marriage as it is assumed normally to be. In Middleton's *The Phoenix* occurs a passage that, with certain reservations,
might be called Miltonic:

> Reverend and honorable Matrimony,
> Mother of lawful sweets, unshamed mornings,
> Dangerless pleasures! thou that mak'st the bed
> Both pleasant and legitimately fruitful!
> Without thee
> All the whole world were soiled bastardy.
> Thou art the only and the greatest form
> That put'st a difference between our desires
> And the disorder'd appetites of beasts,
> Making their mates those that stand next their lusts.[65]

In Marston's *What You Will* there is a similar invocation serving a
similar purpose:

But O! 'tis grown a figment, love a jest,
A comic poesy! The soul of man is rotten
Even to the core.[66]

In Chapman's *The Gentleman Usher* are actually portrayed a good marriage and a wife who "both sense and soul delights";[67] but the atmosphere is that of the miraculous.

The aura of evil surrounding women and sexual union, in marriage or out, clung on in the private theatres. In the eighties, when *The Rare Triumphs of Love and Fortune* and *Mucedorus* were the typical courtship plays of the popular troupes, with the Fidelias and the Amadines surmounting practical obstacles to marriage and recognizing no others, the lovers at Blackfriars and Paul's suffered elegant torments as they gazed at forbidden fruit. In Lyly, Alexander must resist the attraction of Campaspe, and Hephestion that of Timoclea, leaving love to commoners like Apelles; the nymphs of Diana must be *cured* of their passion for the youths of Lincolnshire; Sapho must be *cured* of her passion for Phao; Endymion must expect from Cynthia, at the most, a kiss. The hero of the anonymous *Wars of Cyrus* must, like Alexander, rise superior to the promptings of the flesh. There is a vast amount of sexual frustration in these plays, or would be if they would come alive. In Peele's *Arraignment of Paris*, Colin dies for the love of Thestylis, and Oenone is forsaken by Paris. In Marlowe and Nashe's *Dido* Anna pines for Iarbas, Iarbas pines for Dido, and Dido pines and dies for Aeneas, who is called away by his higher destiny. The themes, transmitted mainly through Italian courtesy literature and pastoral, derive from the aristocratic cults in which the love of women was a threat to honor, friendship, and all higher good.

After 1599 the treatment of love and marriage in the private theatres is less archaic than reactionary, less aristocratic than antibourgeois; and the failure to endorse the current popular ideals of feminine normality is marked by few vestiges of rival ideals. In comedy the young men make their own marriages; but they are marriages of convenience, and the personal qualities of the brides, while presumably good in most cases, receive nothing like the stress given their more material assets. The chaste women are like those of Jonson, mere wraiths, while the unchaste ones are limned with gusto. Chapman's women are mostly prurient and irrational, but he alone in the group displays nostalgia for the creeds of courtly and platonic love. His good women, like Cynanche in *The Gentleman Usher*, Eugenia in *Sir Giles Goosecap*, and Cornelia in *Caesar and Pompey*, are presented as exceptions to a rule; they are women cured of their womanhood, evidently by means of a classical education. Broken fossils of notions from *l'amour courtois* are queerly imbedded in *Monsieur D'Olive*, *Sir Giles Goosecap*, and *I Bussy D'Ambois*: in the first, Marcellina's heavy husband is forced to recognize that no harm attends her status as Vandome's mistress "by rights of court-ship";[68] in the second, Chaucer's Pandarus, Troilus, and Criseyde are attenuated into Momford, Clarence, and Eugenia; in the third, Friar Conolet who arranges the liaison of Bussy and Montsurry's wife is a sort of practicing Andreas Capellanus. Platonic love re-ceives tribute in the first two of these plays and in several others by Chapman. In *The Gentleman Usher* the loss of beauty and even life recommends itself to Margaret as the means by which her love and Vincentio's "must needs be all in soul."[69] In *The Revenge of Bussy D'Ambois*, Clermont, the complete "Senecal" man, presents his views:

> So when humanity rules men and women,
> 'Tis for society confin'd in reason.
> But what excites the bed's desire in blood,
> By no means justly can be constru'd love;
> For when love kindles any knowing spirit,
> It ends in virtue and effects divine,
> And is in friendship chaste and masculine.[70]

The love of Clarence for Eugenia in *Sir Giles Goosecap* is "without passion, and therefore free from alteration," and "being mental, needs no bodily requital."[71] He does not wish to be diverted from contemplating "eterness" by her body (his own is a sufficient en-cumbrance), and their marriage is to resemble music and the opera-tion of pure reason. For children of this marriage, except possibly an occasional syllogism or snatch of music from the spheres, the prognosis is not good.

Chapman's mind was essentially unoriginal; he is not very difficult to understand if one does not expect too much. Ideas collected in magpie fashion lie helter-skelter in his plays, without any synthesizing principle. His profundities are all commonplaces reversed, so that he achieves nothing new and vitalizes nothing old. His dissidence in respect to the current popular ideals of wedded love takes us backward rather than forward, and we find men again choosing between carnality and spirituality, women again oscillating between the pit and the pedestal. The allusions in his plays to the insatiability and coyness of women, the "certain itch in female blood," are general in their application. "Did she not suck it (as others of her sex do) from her mother's breast? And will you condemn that as her fault which is her nature?"[72] Eudora in *The Widow's Tears* is won to take Tharsalio as her husband when she hears that "he's the most incontinent and insatiate man of woman that ever Venus blessed with ability to please them. . . . I have known nine in a night made mad with his love."[73]

Chapman is only one of the select dramatists to work variations on the theme resuscitated by the formal satirists and epitomized in some lines of Donne:

> Foxes and goats; all beasts change when they please,
> Shall women, more hot, wily, wild than these,
> Be bound to one man, and did Nature then
> Idly make them apter t' endure than men?[74]

Jonson's Truewit is of the opinion that women find rape an "acceptable violence" and none since the days of Edward the Confessor have been "contented with one man."[75] Marston's Malevole says, "Their blood is their only God; bad clothes and old age are only the devils they tremble at."[76] Middleton's Sir Penitent cries,

> To doat on weakness, slime, corruption, woman!
> What is she, took asunder from her clothes?[77]

Fletcher's Mercury, followed from the bed by Maria, says,

> The Devil cannot keep these women off
> When they are fletched once.[78]

And Field's Scudmore, jilted by Bellafront:

> women, women!
> He's mad, by heaven, that thinks you anything
> But sensual monsters.[79]

When characters in Shakespeare speak thus, it is a symptom of madness; those quoted above are unlucky or malcontent, but presumably sane, and a number of the women in the plays substantiate their charges. The ambition of Philautia in Jonson's *Cynthia's Revels* is to send for any man she desires, and to have him beheaded or castrated if he denies her;[80] Haughty, Centaure, and Mavis in *Epicoene* are organized nymphomaniacs; Camelia in *Jack Drum's Entertainment* seeks a stupid husband as cover for a career of adultery; Taffata in Barry's *Ram-Alley*, like Chapman's Eudora, is won by the suitor of superior sexual competence. The chaste women introduced into plays as foils to the unchaste are scarcely audible. Lady Lentulus in Marston's *Insatiate Countess* speaks a total of thirty-six lines in one scene and four in another; Phronesis, Thauma, and Time in Jonson's *Cynthia's Revels* are actually mutes; chaste Clorin is shaded by lustful Cloe in Fletcher's *Faithful Shepherdess* in spite of the title.

The case of Marston is especially curious. Instead of taking for granted that sexual desire is normal in women, in the fashion of the popular writers, he *espoused* the cause—with results that are indescribable. Sophonisba is his paragon of chastity, and her frankness about womanly decorum—"We must still seem to flee what we most seek"[81]—is, at best, untimely. The ingénues, Dulcimer, Rossaline, Crispinella, instead of being engagingly natural, as intended, are overwhelmingly meaty. Dulcimer is self-described as "healthy, lusty, vigorous,"[82] and she is indeed. Rossaline wants a husband with a "bouncing thigh," and a typical specimen of her repartee is, "I'll spit in thy mouth, and thou wilt, to grace thee."[83] Crispinella defends her freedom of speech by saying, "You shall have an hypocritical vestal virgin speak that with close teeth publicly, which she will receive with open mouth privately." Her own fastidiousness, like her honesty, is demonstrated in a startling way:

Marry, if a nobleman or a knight with one lock visit us, though his unclean, goose-turd-green teeth ha' the palsy, his nostrils smell worse than a putrified maribone, and his loose beard drop into our bosom, yet we must kiss him with a curtsy—a curse, for my part. I had as leave they would break wind in my lips.[84]

Marston's plays are not without their tributes to the transports of wedded love. Zuccone of *The Fawn* is taken back by his good wife Zoya after promising practically to subsist on aphrodisiacs.[85] Albano, the grass widower of *What You Will*, knows that sorrow's crown of sorrow is remembering happier days:

> O, Celia, how oft
> (When thou hast laid thy cheek upon my breast
> And with lascivious petulancy sued
> For hymeneal dalliance, marriage rites)
> O, then how oft with passionate protests
> And jealous vows hast thou oblig'd thy love
> In dateless bonds unto Albano's breast![86]

But nothing can compare with the Marstonian tribute to "monogamic idealism" in the single line, "He that is wise pants on a private breast."[87]

Since any of Marston's plays may be defined as a five-act lapse in taste, it would be pointless to dwell thus on the grossness of his women were it not indicative of a general deficiency among the coterie writers. Chapman is as delicate as any of them, yet is unable to protect even the most ethereal of his women from indelicate suggestion. In *Monsieur D'Olive* Dicque says: "But I pray thee, Licette, what makes the virgin lady, my lady's sister, break wind so continually and sigh so tempestuously? I believe she's in love."[88] One of the entrances of the *spirituelle* Eugenia in *Sir Giles Goosecap* is thus heralded:

> *Momford.*
> Witty Mistress Winifred, where is your Countess, I pray?
> *Winifred.*
> Faith, your lordship is bold enough to seek her out, if she were at her urinal.

Momford.
Then sh'as done, it seems, for here she comes to save me that labour.
[*Enter Eugenia.*][89]

Again a warning must be posted against attributing this sort of thing to Elizabethan ruggedness of manners—the brawny spirit of the age. It does not occur in Shakespeare or, for that matter, even in the plays of such humble hacks as Samuel Rowley, while among the coterie writers only Lyly avoids offense, and he at the cost of extreme artificiality. Every feminine character in Elizabethan drama who conveys an impression of both reality and charm was created for the multitude. It is quite confusing—as if the plebeians knew something of refinement and were unaware that Blackfriars, not the Globe, was the haunt of the cultivated. Perhaps we are witnessing the effects of the early labors of the bourgeois Mrs. Grundy.

Enough has been said of the underlying attitudes toward the sex about which, then as now, the family unit revolved. There remains the subject of regard and disregard for sanctions. The nature of wedding ceremonies in Elizabethan times, civil and religious, and the highly synoptic fashion in which such ceremonies are represented by the playwrights, need not concern us. There is no time for banns in the theatre, and preliminaries are often disposed of in breathtaking haste, with the actual ceremony consisting of a few words, a brief report, or even a symbolic mask. A song by Hymen could serve as well as an officiating bishop with a special license from the diocesan consistory. We should not puzzle ourselves over technicalities; when a dramatist says a couple are married, they are married. Modern sensibility is apt to be shocked when a legally valid spousal, however manipulated, is treated as a sufficient sanction for sexual intercourse, when mutual love is not. In the case of Shakespeare's Helena and Bertram, or Mariana and Angelo, the modern tendency is to call the play satirical, or to blame Helena, or Mariana's accomplice Isabella, rather than Shakespeare himself. The fault, however, if fault it is, lies with the dramatist and his ethical outlook. He might have defended himself by remarking that marriage is a social institution, and that mutual love, however desirable, cannot serve in lieu of legal processes as the ultimate sanction because it is publicly less discriminable and more subject to abuse. In a few decades Ford's Giovanni and Annabella would be pleading mutual love as sanction for their incest. Shakespeare might have added that *All's Well* and *Measure for Measure* dealt with very special cases, that Bertram and Angelo were his own creations, and he would see to it that their first conjugal transports in misapprehension would be succeeded by others in mutual love. The important point is that Helena and Mariana go to the hymeneal bed with both love and certificate. In this they are completely typical. Even Shakespeare's most infatuated heroines are unwilling to fling their caps over the windmill. Romeo soon hears Juliet's reservation,

> If that thy bent of love be honourable,
> Thy purpose marriage,[90]

just as "Cesario" hears Olivia's,

> What shall you ask me that I'll deny
> That, honour sav'd, may upon asking give?[91]

For those ethical thinkers whose favorite pleonasm is the phrase "conventional morality," Chapman is the man, not Shakespeare. In *The Gentleman Usher* Margaret chooses Vincentio in preference to his father, and is willing to dispense with legal marriage:

> Are outward rites
> More virtuous than the very substance is
> Of holy nuptials solemnized within?
> Or should laws made to curb the common world,
> That would not be contained in form without them,
> Hurt them that are a law unto themselves?

Vincentio concurs that he and Margaret are

> As far remov'd from popular sects,
> And as unstain'd with her abhorr'd respects.[92]

The only comment that could be extracted from Shakespeare's plays is that none can claim exemption from the laws that contain the world in form, and "breach of custom is almost breach of all." Recently, the availability of "current morality" (Elizabethan cum Victorian) for purposes of art has been dismissed in a casual allusion to Heywood's Mistress Frankford and "Little Em'lys."[93] Uneasy critics have felt called upon to defend Shakespeare from holding to the "Pamela-concept of chastity."[94] Even Quiller-Couch has unguardedly deplored Isabella's respect for "marriage lines"[95] in his discussion of *Measure for Measure.* But it is less important that the code should be sometimes misliked than that it should often be misunderstood.

Respect for legal sanctions is both expressed and implied in the plays of the popular repertories. In those of the select repertories, disrespect is rarely expressed, even by Chapman, but often implied. Adultery was in high favor at Blackfriars and Paul's as a theme of laughter. Lazarillo de Tormes in *Blurt Master Constable* and Justiniano in *Westward Ho* conducted schools for wives, discussing at length the methods of cuckolding husbands. The methods were shown in practical fashion in a number of comedies. The practitioners were rarely punished, and were sometimes approved, with the approval not always tacit. In Middleton's plays alone may be instanced the successful ventures of Mistress Purge in *The Family of Love*, Mistress Newcut in *Your Five Gallants*, Lady Kix in *A Chaste Maid in Cheapside*, besides the earnest efforts of Madame Harebrain in *A Mad World My Masters.* Mistress Brabant in Marston's *Jack Drum's Entertainment*, Mistress Greenshield in Dekker and Webster's *Northward Ho*, and Mistress Winifred in Chapman, Jonson, and Marston's *Eastward Ho* all equip their husbands with deserved horns. In Dekker and Webster's *Westward Ho* we are given a climactic surprise in the discovery that the wives are chaste. In Markham and Machin's *The Dumb Knight*, after Mistress Lollia with the aid of the bawd Colloquintida has achieved adultery, her husband is ordered to forgive and cherish her by no less a person than the King of Cyprus. The contented cuckold appears not only in the notorious instance of Middleton's Allwit, but in Chapman's Quintiliano in *May-Day* and other figures. The Captain in Middleton's *The Phoenix* tries to sell his wife, and Antonio in Fletcher's *The Coxcomb* tries to share his—in order to win "everlasting glory"[96] as a loving friend.

Of course Antonio is a *coxcomb;* but here as in most of the plays
a spirit of amusement rather than *saeva indignatio* infuses the treatment of cuckoldry, voluntary or involuntary. Duke Basilius in Day's
Isle of Gulls is singularly light-hearted:

> *Lisander.*
> But, madam, now I am known to you, what further request you?
> *Duchess.*
> Exchange of looks and freedom of thy bed,
> Thy presence, thy embracements, thy kind of love,
> For which my amorous thoughts have long line sick.
> *Duke* [*overhearing*].
> Thank you, good wife. And a duchess long to give her husband the
> horning, let it never grieve butchers to do homage at Cuckold's Haven.[97]

There is a little more ethical *entrain* in most of the serious plays, for
instance Marston's *Malcontent*:

> *Mendoza.*
> Took him to favor, nay, even clasp'd with him?
> *Aurelia.*
> Alas, I did.
> *Mendoza.*
> This night?
> *Aurelia.*
> This night.
> *Mendoza.*
> And in your lustful twines the Duke took you?
> *Aurelia.*
> A most sad truth.[98]

Aurelia "clasps" with several, but she and the Duke (himself, of
course, a lecher) are reconciled in the end. Husbands take back
their errant wives as a rule. Although Tamyra is dismissed from
Montsurry's house at the end of *Bussy D'Ambois*, she is still on the
premises in its sequel and talking like the injured party. In the same
author's *Widow's Tears*, Lysander convinces himself against the evidence that Cynthia is as chaste as she claims.

In plays of the public theatres, the betrayed husband is usually unavailable for comment upon his wife's infidelity, having been murdered as its consequence. The concatenation of adultery and death gave rise to a distinctive tragic genre.[99] In the tragedies where the husband survives, the wife is sometimes forgiven but is never taken back to bed and board. The kindness of Heywood's Master Frankford and Master Shore is strictly circumscribed, and the kisses they give the departing sinners must be recognized as an immense concession.[100] Heywood is not extenuating guilt but speaking in his own way of the pity of it. Grotesque as the comparison may seem, the sentiments of the ghost in *Hamlet* are those of Frankford and Shore —with the same horror at the sin but solicitude for the beloved sinner: "Leave her to Heaven." With the single exception of Chapman's *Blind Beggar of Alexandria*, which might be so called, the popular troupes never played a comedy of adultery. Even Jonson had to toe the line when he wrote for them: Mistress Kitely in *Every Man in His Humor* errs only in the suspicion of her husband, like Mistress Ford in *The Merry Wives of Windsor*. A number of wives are a trial to their husbands, like Mistresses Barnes and Goursey in Porter's *Two Angry Women of Abington*, Mistress Eyre in *The Shoemaker's Holiday*, and the successive wives of Candido in *The Honest Whore*; but they are not unfaithful. When it occurs to Viola that the miraculous patience of Candido might be vanquished if she took a lover, what she actually does is have her stranger-brother *pose* as a lover. There was no other alternative at the Fortune if the comedy was to remain a comedy. When a wife's virtue is assailed, as in *A Knack to Know a Knave* or *Satiromastix*, friends and relatives rally about to protect what seems to need no protection in the first place.

Adultery in Shakespeare is never treated with humor, tolerance, or "understanding." It is never linked to the inadequacy or prior dereliction of the spouse, or with natural ennui, but with moral debility, as in the case of Antony, unbridled appetite, as in the theory of Iago, or sheer mystery—an arbitrary proneness to "prey on garbage"—as postulated by Hamlet. The characters who contemplate individual instances of it speak with scathing contempt, and those who are haunted by the fear that it may be universal cry for

civet to sweeten imaginations "foul as Vulcan's stithy." When
Diomede is asked by Paris whether Menelaus or himself deserves
Helen the more, he answers that they deserve her both alike:

> He, like a puling cuckold, would drink up
> The lees and dregs of a flat tamed piece;
> You, like a lecher, out of whorish loins
> Are pleas'd to breed out your inheritors.[101]

This is the consensus of opinion of Greeks and Trojans alike in their
Shakespearean guise. In *The Winter's Tale* Prince Mamillius is something of a child-Hamlet. One explanation of his sickening to death
is his shame at the supposed sin of his mother and consequent taint
upon himself[102]—a detail not found in Greene's *Pandosto*. That the
thought of an adulterous mother might prove lethal seems beyond
the ken of those who think Hamlet's mood inadequately motived:

> *Queen.*
> Have you forgot me?
> *Hamlet.*
> No, by the rood, not so!
> You are the Queen, your husband's brother's wife,
> And (would it were not so!) you are my mother.[103]

The importance of the theme in the play can scarcely be overesti-
mated; one of the advantages that Laertes has over the Prince is his
faith in the "chaste unsmirched brows" of *his* mother.

The supposed transgression of a particular woman could cast a
universal pall. "We are all bastards,"[104] cries Posthumus in his
moment of anguish. Othello's own words are more often plaintive or
frantic than gross, but Iago's describe the malady with which he is
infected.[105] The same malady in Leontes is self-expressed.[106] Lear
describes one of the dreadful figures in his own phantasmagoria:

> Behold yon simp'ring dame,
> Whose face between her forks presageth snow,
> That minces virtue, and does shake the head
> To hear of pleasure's name.
> The fitchew nor the soiled horse goes to't
> With a more riotous appetite.
> Down from the waist they are Centaurs,
> Though women all above.[107]

This is matched by raving Timon's

> Strike me the counterfeit matron,
> It is her habit only that is honest,
> Herself's a bawd.[108]

Lear's outburst seems amazingly irrelevant until we recall that the unnatural conduct of his daughters has made him doubt their legitimacy. A keystone has been eroded. A world of unkindness must of necessity be a world of cuckoldry, or, in more universal terms, a world of animal cruelty must be a world of animal lusts. Coleridge's view that the blinding of Gloucester was intended as consonant with his record of adultery may need some modification; but in the words of Edgar it finds authority in the text:

> The gods are just, and of our pleasant vices
> Make instruments to scourge us.
> The dark and vicious place where thee he got
> Cost him his eyes.[109]

Edmund is presumably the typical issue of violated wedlock. With the single exception of Faulconbridge in *King John*, who values his illegitimacy on eugenic grounds and jocularly condones his mother's sin,[110] the bastards in Shakespeare are stigmatics. Margarelon, the baseborn son of Priam, appears only for a moment in *Troilus and Cressida*, but long enough to cast a grotesque shadow as manipulated by Thersites.[111] Caliban among his other shortcomings is a bastard.[112] So also is villainous Don John in *Much Ado About Nothing*, and his cruelty, unlike that of Girondo in the source tale by Bandello, issues from pure malice. The bastardy of the evil Cardinal Beaufort in *I Henry VI* is noted,[113] as is that of evil Orleans. The latter is thus addressed by Lord Talbot:

> Contaminated, base,
> And misbegotten blood I spill of thine,
> Mean and right poor, for that pure blood of mine
> Which thou didst force from Talbot, my brave boy.[114]

The heroic death of John Talbot and his father's grief are so nobly dramatized that a reader of Holinshed is apt to be disturbed to discover that Orleans was not the only baseborn warrior in the melee, and that Lord Talbot's pure-blooded John was not his only son to die a hero's death: "There died also the Earl's bastard son, Henry Talbot."[115] Shakespeare has coolly expunged *this* bastard.

What has been called the "sex-nausea" in Shakespeare's later plays might with much greater accuracy be called "adultery-nausea"— and it seems to have been shared by the nation. The veneration for legitimacy may seem almost superstitious, the hatred of adultery almost fanatical; but in observing the lees, we should not forget the good wine in the cask—the ideal of basic human loyalties, the tranquil home, the nurture of beloved children. Milton's invocation to wedded love incorporates a social theory:

> By thee adulterous lust was driven from men
> Among the bestial herds to range; by thee,
> Founded in reason, loyal, just, and pure,
> Relations dear, and all the charities
> Of father, son, and brother first were known.[116]

The popular drama is filled with images of family solidarity. An appeal to the love of small children, already in evidence in such medieval plays as the Brome *Sacrifice of Isaac*, is conspicuous in the earliest of the plays of the professional troupes. *Cambyses* dwells alike on the painful parting of the evil Sisamnes and his son and the good Praxaspes and his "young child":

> *Praxaspes.*
> Farewell, my dear and loving babe! Come kiss thy father dear!
> A grievous sight to me it is to see thee slain even here . . .
> *Young Child.*
> O father, father, wipe your face,
> I see the tears run from your eye . . .

The child pleads for his life as a boon to his mother, and when the plea fails, we hear the mother's lament:

> What grief in womb did I retain before I did thee see!
> Yet at the last, when smart was gone, what joy wert thou to me!
> How tender was I of thy food, for to preserve thy state!
> How stilled I thy tender heart at times early and late!

With velvet paps I gave thee suck with issue from my breast,
And danced thee upon my knee to bring thee unto rest.[117]

It is such elementary pathos that is parodied in Marston's *Histrio-mastix*;[118] but the vein continues in the grief of Lady Bruce in *The Death of Robert Earl of Huntington*, of the parents of little Martin and Lenchy in *Alarum for London*, and others, and is no different in kind from the famous lines of Constance:

> Grief fills the room up of my absent child,
> Lies in his bed, walks up and down with me,
> Puts on his pretty looks, repeats his words,
> Remembers me of all his gracious parts,
> Stuffs out his vacant garments with his form.[119]

Plays like *The Travels of the Three English Brothers*, *A Shoemaker a Gentleman*, and *The Royal King and the Loyal Subject* reach their climax in the joyful exhibition of a baby:

> Had'st thou sought earth or sea, and from them both
> Extracted that which was most precious held,
> Thou nothing could'st have found to equal this—
> This the mixt image of my queen and me.[120]

In Wilkins's dramatic tract we hear that children make a marriage:

> Some husbands are respectless of their wives
> During the time that they are issueless,
> But none with infants bless'd can nourish hate,
> But love the mother for the children's sake.[121]

In Dekker and Chettle's *Patient Grissill* much is made of the deprived mother's yearning to look at her babes—"*Enter Grissill stealingly*"—but, characteristically, the noble father is just as affectionate:

> Give me this blessed burthen, pretty fool!
> With what an amiable look it sleeps,
> And in that slumber how it sweetly smiles,
> And in that smile how my heart leaps for joy.
> Furio, I'll turn this circle to a cradle
> To rock my dear babe.[122]

The sentiments of Rowley's King Henry VIII are equally suburban,[123] and those of the two kings in Shakespeare's *Winter's Tale*:

Polixenes.
He's all my exercise, my mirth, my matter;
Now my sworn friend, and then mine enemy;
My parasite, my soldier, stateman—all.
He makes a July day short as December,
And with his varying childness cures in me
Thoughts that would thick my blood.
Leontes.
                              So stands this squire
Offic'd with me.[124]

The meaning of the death of children is assumed to be beyond the understanding of the childless: "You have no children, butchers!" cries Margaret;[125] "He has no children," says Macduff;[126] and Constance, in rejecting comfort, says, "He talks to me that never had a son."[127]

There had been many Prosperos in the plays of the public theatres before the time of *The Tempest*, solicitous fathers ranging in type from the gamekeeper of Fressingfield in Greene's *Friar Bacon*, Sir Rees ap Vaughan in *Satiromastix*, Lord Fitzwater in the *Death of Robert Earl of Huntington* to the King of Aragon in *Mucedorus*. In *II Honest Whore* old Friscabaldo disguises himself to serve as guardian angel to his daughter; in *The London Prodigal*, old Flowerdale does likewise for his son. There are as many instances of loyal children. Cordilla in the older play of *King Leir* is not the only prototype of Shakespeare's kind daughter. Matilda ministers to ancient Fitzwater in *The Downfall of Robert Earl of Huntington*, Bess to old Momford in *The Blind Beggar of Bednal Green*, while Diana offers to beg for Lodowick in *The Weakest Goeth to the Wall*. In Heywood's *Four Prentices of London*, the father, the daughter, and four sons are constantly rescuing one another and having joyful reunions. "A Sion, a Jerusalem, a Father!" is the battle cry of the brothers, and at one point, "Everyone by turn takes up their father and carries him."[128] In *The Travels of the Three English Brothers* we find the same fusion of martial glory and domestic solidarity:

We in all are three
Sons of one father, branches of one tree:
Should a rough hand but violently tear

> One scion from a tree, the rest must bear
> Share in the hurt; the smallest wound that drains
> Blood from our breasts empties our father's veins.[129]

In one of the two concluding dumb shows the father and sons, widely separated in space, view each other through a perspective glass and "offer to embrace."

In *Fortune by Land and Sea*, Young Forest is the perfect pattern of "a most loving son"; but even Frank, the black sheep of the family, dies rather than let his father be called "an old dotard":

> you know he is my father,
> And what he doth is but paternal love;
> Though I be wild, I am not so past reason
> His person to despise.[130]

The Blind Beggar of Bednal Green contains one of those last-minute rescues so dear to popular literature. Young Stroud, a would-be gallant, has said, "I shall have mine, too, one day when the old man's dead," and his yeoman father now stands on the scaffold:

> Heaven's will be done,
> But I would fain have seen mine unkind son.[131]

Whereupon the youth arrives breathlessly to effect his rescue. In *Thomas Lord Cromwell*, the hero stands in the robes of high office surrounded by the nobility of England, when the old peasant his father appears humbly before him:

> nay, be covered, father.
> Although that duty to these noble men
> Doth challenge it, yet I'll make bold with them.
> Your head doth bear the calendar of care:
> What Cromwell covered and his father bare!
> It must not be.[132]

King Lear is but one of the plays in which a fissure within families, unkindness in blood kin, is equated with universal chaos.[133] The very mundane *Miseries of Enforced Marriage* shows a character trying to avert bloodshed between two of his brothers:

> O, do but hearken!
> When do the sun and moon, born in one frame,

Contend but they breed earthquakes in men's hearts?
When any star prodigiously appears,
Tells it not fall of kings in fatal years?
And then if brothers fight, what may men think—
Sin grows so high, 'tis time the world should sink.[134]

The common soldiers of *If You Know Not Me* place Queen Mary's treatment of Princess Elizabeth within the frame of their humble experience: "Well, sirs, I have two sisters, and the one loves the other, and would not send her to prison for a million."[135] Susan Mountfort's concern for her brother in Heywood's tragic *Woman Killed with Kindness* has its realistic complement in Phil Barnes's concern for his sister in Porter's comic *Two Angry Women of Abington*. The theme is ubiquitous. Love of his sister seems to be the only selfless emotion of which Shakespeare's Octavius is capable.[136] Familial responsibility involved body and soul; and, however we assess the moral value of the ideal, we must recognize that in this popular drama man was, at least in the literal sense, his brother's keeper. The normality of the mutual devotion of husbands and wives, parents and children, brothers and sisters, was taken for granted, with exceptions to the rule no matter for jest.

Presumably the members of the coterie had experienced the usual amenities of home life; but one would scarcely suspect it while reading the plays designed to please them. For a few painful moments in *Antonio's Revenge* Marston tries to portray a pathetic child, evidently under the impression that he was duplicating the effects of the Hubert scenes in *King John*. Julio says to his murderer,

> Buss me. Good
> Truth, I love you better than my father, deed![137]

Such attempts are rare—if for no other reason than that small children, excepting the pert waifs who serve as pages, rarely appear in the *dramatis personae*. Their absence is characteristic of smart literature, past and present. There is great emphasis upon sex, occasional mention of pregnancy, but then a hiatus until the children are grown, and the natural enemies of their parents and one another. A baby figures in Middleton's *Chaste Maid in Cheapside* in a christening at the Allwit household; the scene is hilarious but suggestive of a Walpurgisnacht. Another baby, borne by Lady Kix but sired by Master Touchwood, effects the happy denouement of the comedy. Between the matter cited from the popular plays, and this from Middleton, no greater distance is conceivable. Dekker's *Shoemaker's Holiday* compared with Middleton's *Michaelmas Term* gives the measure of the difference between the treatment of domestic relationships at the public and the private theatres. The Eyre family, brash as its members may be, is cohesive, while Quomodo's wife, son, and servants are all treacherous, and he is worse than they. Middleton features a faithful son in *The Phoenix*, and, of course, the ideal of familial love is not unknown to him and his school; but they do not portray it frequently and cannot portray it vividly. When Sir Edward Fortune in *Jack Drum's Entertainment* loses his daughter, he proves scarcely inconsolable:

> Broach me a fresh butt of canary sack,
> Let's sing, drink, sleep, for that's the best relief
> To drown all care and overwhelm all grief.[138]

In *Antonio's Revenge*, Andrugio's widow remains constant to his memory, but only because of some very alert haunting on the part of his ghost. Tharsalio, in Chapman's *Widow's Tears*, seems anxious that his brother make proper disposal of his estate, yet is delighted to win a bet by proving him a cuckold. Domestic turpitude, on the other hand, is painted large, and seems to have been credible, or at least enjoyable, in any degree. A year or so after Shakespeare's heartbroken Leonato had defended his daughter against false charges of unchastity, a father in a Paul's play found it to his advantage to concoct such a libel himself. Marston's Piero calls his daughter the putrid ulcer of his royal blood, and alleges that he has seen

> an incestuous slave
> Clipping the strumpet with luxurious twines.[139]

Day after day at Blackfriars, Paul's, and Whitefriars, the audiences contemplated the erosion of the closest bonds known to man —in the lusts of the flesh in tragedy, and the love of money in comedy. "Are your fathers dead, gentlemen, you're so merry?" asks Fitsgrave in Middleton's *Your Five Gallants.*[140] In *The Puritan,* Edmond, Idle, and Pennydub all rejoice in bereavement. Pennydub tells how he has ridden post "day and night, to bring you the merry news of my father's death."[141] In Day's *Law-Tricks* Polymetes gets the joyful tidings:

> News, news, my hearts, will make your jocund souls
> Dance in your bosoms![142]

In Jonson's *Epicoene,* Sir Dauphine parts with his victim (only an uncle in this case) in what we are supposed to accept as manly bluntness: "I'll not trouble you till you trouble me with your funeral, which I care not how soon it come."[143] Some of the characters who speak in this fashion are recognized as contemptible, but others are not so conceived. The line of satire grows blurred, jest becomes earnest, and the ugly mask leaves its imprint on the living face. A century later Aimwell of *The Beaux' Stratagem* will be able to respond to news of his brother's death with "Thanks to the pregnant stars that framed this accident!"[144] his amiable creator being quite unaware that he is recording a perversion and defeat of the human spirit. Of course neither the popular nor the coterie plays held a steel mirror up to Elizabethan women, marriage, and the family. The coterie image was not wholly false: "Few matrimonies there be," said the homilist, "without chidings, brawlings, tauntings, repentings, bitter cursings, and fightings."[145] But the popular image, romantic though we may call it, was much more true. The race survived, and we may make the minimum assumption that most Elizabethans were really the progeny of their presumed parents, that mothers and fathers reared their children, and children let their mothers and fathers die a natural death and disposed decently of their bodies. That we may assume more than this, we guess from reading Shakespeare and observing the shape he gave to the people's dreams. We have no statistics with which to test the popular and coterie images, and we should learn nothing of value if we had. We might as well discuss the relative truth and falsity of pasture land and the jungle.

V

The Commonweal

THE Elizabethan drama is no place to look for discussion of the prerogatives of Parliament, the limits of Privy Council authority, and the claims of nonmonarchial forms of government. Such topics fell under the ban of the censor. Political economy was deemed to be as much a specialty as theology, and the playwrights were not ordained; furthermore the Tudor dynasty felt never so self-assured that it could relinquish its power to restrain particularized public criticism. It was possible, however, to dramatize English history, and thus to express the new national consciousness as well as interest in basic ideals. One could not treat the claim of the Stuarts to the English throne, or the ambitions of the Earl of Essex, but one could display the disastrous effects of a disputed succession. The political ideas in Shakespeare's own "histories" have lately been studied in relation to the *De Casibus* tradition, the "myth" of manifest Tudor destiny and divine right, and the accounts of English reigns in Hall, Holinshed, and other orthodox chroniclers. The persistence of these ideas in the Greek and Roman plays, despite the intervention of North's *Plutarch* with its antique republicanism, has also been carefully reanalyzed. It is not the purpose of the present brief survey to sum up or evaluate this admirably learned discussion,[1] but to attempt to gain perspective by dispersing the attention over a wider field, observing Shakespeare among his fellow dramatists, the "histories" among the other types of plays. We meet kings and subjects, lords and commons, signs of political health and symptoms of political illness even in farces and romances.

It is, of course, in the history plays that the political interest is most central; and it is significant that Shakespeare wrote more such plays than any other Elizabethan except possibly Thomas Heywood. The type was exclusively popular. The total absence of history plays in the select repertory cannot be attributed to accident. It is true that Paul's and Blackfriars were closed in the nineties when most of Shakespeare's histories were written; but the type was already popular during the earlier career of the chorister troupes and was by no means dead at the time of their revival. The whole era of Tudor history was opened to dramatic treatment at the death of Elizabeth in 1603, but the select writers failed to join Dekker, Heywood, Rowley, and others in its exploitation. Not until after 1610 was fresh material so hard to find that the author of *The Valiant Welshman* was forced, as he said, to "search the chronicles of elder ages."[2] The techniques of the day would have permitted the staging of battles at Blackfriars, Paul's, and Whitefriars, even if battles be considered, mistakenly, as the desiderata of history plays. And the youth of the actors would have been no bar. The managers showed no hesitation in casting boys as Alexander, Aeneas, and Bussy D'Ambois, and certainly a boy could have impersonated an English king as convincingly as an "insatiate countess." We can only conclude that the history plays, like the chronicles upon which they were based, were *de trop* in the coterie. The fact could be deduced from the tone of the comedies and tragedies. Whereas those of the public theatres usually appeal to a sense of community, those of the private theatres do not. Instead of drawing together in fellowship, the characters stand in isolation and view one another with mutual hostility. There may be love between two of them, or working agreements among three or four, but there is little evidence of faith in unifying ideals.

Some attempt, however inadequate, must be made to describe the idea of a commonwealth prevalent in the sixteenth century. Hooker, as always, provides a rational perspective:

. . . forasmuch as we are not by ourselves sufficient to furnish ourselves with a competent store of things needful for such a life as our nature doth desire, a life fit for the dignity of man; therefore to supply these
defects and imperfections which are in us living single and solely by
ourselves, we are naturally induced to seek communion and fellowship
with others. This was the cause of men's uniting themselves at the first
in politic societies, which societies could not be without government, nor
government without a distinct kind of Law. . . . Two foundations there
are which bear up public societies; the one, a natural inclination whereby
all men desire sociable life and fellowship; the other, an order expressly
or secretly agreed upon touching the manner of their union in living
together.[3]

Starkey puts the idea in glowing terms:

. . . we should have a multitude of people convenient to the place,
flourishing with all good abundance of exterior things required to the
bodily wealth of man, the which living together in civil life, governed
by politic order and rule, should conspire together in amity and love,
everyone glad to help another to his power, to the intent that the whole
might attain to that perfection which is determined to the dignity of man's
nature by the goodness of God, the which is the end of all laws and
order, for which purpose they be writ and ordained.[4]

The voices are often less ingratiating than these, but the message
remains the same. "The subjects," says Gosson, "must sweat in obedience to their Prince; the Prince must have a care over his poor
vassals . . .: it be the duty of every man in a commonwealth one way
or other to bestir his stumps."[5]

Hooker and Starkey were not cloistered dreamers, but were ac-
tively in touch with the problems of civil and ecclesiastical government. At the beginning of the century the circle of Erasmus and
More were coolly discussing the dubious value of an aristocratic
class, and the desirability of elected rather than hereditary rulers;
the ultimate reliance upon that evasive entity, the "Christian Prince,"
was not strictly voluntary. Egalitarian sentiment among the humanists is evident in the very earliest of the extant interludes, Medwall's
Fulgens and Lucrece of c.1497. In *Gentleness and Nobility*, printed
by John Rastell about 1523, the Plowman is permitted to outargue
the Merchant and the Knight. The concluding words are spoken by

the Philosopher, who wishes that civil authorities might be appointed and removed on utilitarian principles:

> Yet I think now, under your corrections,
> The thing that maketh a gentleman to be,
> Is but virtue and gentle conditions,
> Which as well in poor men oftimes we see
> As in men of great birth or high degree.[6]

Such views were less freely expressed after the Peasants' Revolt had
spread fears of anarchy over Europe; but some very familiar slogans—
on all men being created equal, on the greatest good of the greatest
number, on receiving from each according to his abilities and giving
to each according to his needs—are only an extension of a social
philosophy not only tolerated by the Tudor monarchs but recognized by them as quite valid. Whatever the monarch's "divine right"
or absolute administrative authority, his function was to serve the
nation, and to obey as well as enforce its laws. Class distinction was
sanctioned on the principle of division of labor rather than as a system of rewards and punishments. All classes were to serve all other
classes, none to exist merely for the convenience of the one above
it. Such was the ideal; and it was not empty, however far it tran-
scended reality. "The animating and persistent force of the humanists who formulated English policy in the sixteenth century," says
a recent analyst, "was their fundamental liberalism."[7]

In economic thinking, there was no sick suspicion of wealth as
an evil in itself. Degradation was not the route to salvation, and it
was recognized that the least member of the commonwealth had a
body to be maintained as well as a soul to be saved. Starkey wants
prosperity so that no man's mind shall "be covered and cloaked and
never come to light, but stopped and let by penury and poverty";[8]
and Hooker seems to be echoing his words when he advocates a
journey to the kingdom of God without "impediment and let"—
penury must be removed "inasmuch as righteous life presupposeth
life."[9] We should not judge such sentences by what, with greater or
less justice, are sometimes considered to be their dire modern consequences. Man was not "economic man," and wealth was not

viewed as an end in itself. The modern social historian thus describes the Elizabethan attitude:

A religious theory of society necessarily regards with suspicion all doctrines which claim a large space for the unfettered play of economic self-interest. To the latter the end of activity is the satisfaction of desires, to the former the felicity of man consists in the discharge of obligations imposed by God. Viewing the social order as the imperfect reflection of a divine plan, it naturally attaches a high value to the arts by which nature is harnessed to the service of mankind. But, more concerned with ends than with means, it regards temporal goods as at best instrumental to a spiritual purpose, and its standpoint is that of Bacon, when he spoke of the progress of knowledge as being sought for "the glory of the creator and the relief of man's estate."[10]

The reign of Elizabeth spanned a period when Europe was still quaking after one of the greatest economic, political, and religious upheavals in history. England was still threatened by domestic disruption and foreign invasion. The agricultural revolution, the alienation of the church lands, the price inflation, the expansion and momentary collapse of the cloth industry, and the two brief and almost catastrophic reigns of the lesser Tudors must be seen in the background. The continuing laments over enclosures, usury, profiteering, rack-renting, and the like were justified; but the worst abuses were all legacies of what are sometimes assumed to have been more idyllic times. The need was for a strong and solicitous central government that would provide time for healing, and Elizabeth and her Privy Council supplied the need to an extent that the most sanguine observer of 1558 could never have anticipated. Within five years Cecil was able to enumerate truly remarkable gains. The debased currency had been reformed, and working conditions stabilized. Foreign friends had been enlisted against foreign foes, and religion had been "settled" in a fashion that, however offensive to modern taste, was tolerant as compared with contemporary procedures elsewhere. With restrictions and palliations, such as price controls and a humane poor law, the administration continued to combat disorder, unrest, and too rapid an encroachment of newly powerful sectors of society. It practiced power politics abroad and paternal despotism at home; but, unscrupulous as its tactics may sometimes have been, it never made the error of elevating expediency into a principle. By neither the central government, nor the host of justices who enforced its edicts, nor the spokesmen of the Church, was a distinction drawn between public and private morality; ancient sanctions were sought for modern ends, and old personal virtues marshaled against new social vices. There is nothing inconsistent in the disgust of the English, even the officeholding English, with Machiavelli's "lack of idealism." They certainly did not imitate his "psychological error in ignoring it."[11]

To the modern mind the distinction between Elizabethan despotism and outright tyranny is scarcely perceptible. The reason is that, in our political thinking, we have come to believe in contract and force rather than religion and morality as the decisive political curbs. To the Elizabethans it would have seemed terrible to call the autocrat who ruled them a tyrant, even if her claim to the throne had been much less legal than it was. Shakespeare's Leontes is an absolute monarch:

> Why, what need we
> Commune with you of this, but rather follow
> Our forceful instigation? Our prerogative
> Calls not your counsels . . .

Yet even the enraged Paulina only skirts the charge of tyranny:

> *Paulina.*
> I'll not call you tyrant,
> But this most cruel usage of your queen,
> Not able to produce more accusation
> Than your own weak-hing'd fancy something savours
> Of tyranny, and will ignoble make you,
> Yea, scandalous to the world.
>
> *Leontes.*
> On your allegiance
> Out of the chamber with her! Were I a tyrant,
> Where were her life? She durst not call me so
> If she did know me one.[12]

Any apology for a modern police state based upon the Tudor precedent (defined as a necessarily despotic receivership during the liquidation of feudalism) entirely misses the point. It is the denial of religion and any universally valid moral system that differentiates the modern despotism; its head can be absolute in a fashion beyond the uttermost reach of an Elizabeth: he can deny participation in universal error, and arrogate to himself a frightful righteousness. Elizabethan drama itself, in a way strangely unremarked, exonerates the regime: it could never have come into being under a tyranny. The plays—whether histories, comedies, or tragedies—usually predicate in their action the type of political organization in operation in England in their time, yet they freely depict the evil as well as good in royal and aristocratic leadership. The drama of no modern police state would dare depict so many defective dictators, commissars, or gauleiters, however fictitiously named.

Elizabeth's reign was, of course, marked by inequities, compromises, and individual instances of corruption. Bad harvests, like those of the nineties, brought seasons of pinching famine, and the poor laws were often small comfort to workmen in the losing race of wages against prices. The system of monopolies designed to aid government financing operated at the cost of enriching favored individuals. The picture is by no means Utopian. Nevertheless, the half-century as a whole was one of steady improvement, with more people enjoying more things than ever before, and with an even greater number able to give a shape to their hopes. Trevelyan portrays it as an oasis, and speaks of class divisions that "were not rigid and even not strictly hereditary" and of "a greater harmony and freer intercourse of classes than in earlier or in later times."[13] The lesser landed gentry and the commercial classes were the chief beneficiaries of the reign, and the relation between them may be considered, according to the point of view, as a war or as a new *entente cordiale*. There is probably more social as well as psychological truth in Shakespeare's picture of the marriage of gentle Master Fenton and bourgeois Anne Page than in Jonson's and Middleton's pictures of predatory courtships, even though we habitually think of the former as "romantic" and the latter as "realistic."

Like all administrations, Elizabeth's was penalized for its success, and many who previously owned nothing gained enough by the end of the reign to make felt their desire for more,[14] while others whose gains had not been proportionate were convinced that they had been stripped of all. Literary satirists, emotionally allied with the latter, added their shrill note to the clamor. We should not leap to the conclusion that the Renaissance dream had been shattered by an Elizabethan awakening. Men could still believe in "the manner of their union in living together" without being servile or blind. Neither the political thinkers, nor the practical politicians, nor the dramatists such as Shakespeare, had discovered the means by which good leadership could be insured, or economic forces prevented from becoming dehumanized or destructive; but they were conscious enough of the desired ends. To place one's trust in the throne was not to be "feudal," and to share the official distaste for rebellion was not to be "undemocratic." We need not be frivolously nostalgic for monarchic government and social stratification, or carry our devotion to Shakespeare so far as to endorse the system that he endorsed; but we should judge the system on the basis of its own national precedents.

Literary critics who have lately painted the gathering clouds in the sixteenth century as a background for an agonized Donne and a mordant Jonson have told something less than the truth. The line of distinction between the aristocratic and mercantile classes was blurring then, just as the line of distinction between the mercantile and working classes may be blurring now—with parallel sensations, among those in the invaded areas, of an Earth torn from its axis. It is interesting to observe present dejection or elation manifesting itself in discussions of Tudor society—approached, of course, with a post-Lockean, Jeffersonian, Marxist frame of reference. There are often postulated a "bourgeois" hero and a "feudal" villain, or, more frequently, a "feudal" hero and a "bourgeois" villain. Literary critics are quite severe upon the "rising bourgeoisie," unmindful of the contribution to culture of such "bourgeois" educational foundations as St. Paul's and the Merchant Taylors', and of the fact that Spenser, Marlowe, Donne, Shakespeare, Herrick, Milton—indeed, every considerable poet except Sidney—was recruited from the emergent middle class. The quite common assumption that Shakespeare was distressed by the new social fluidity disregards the fact that his family was one of its beneficiaries, and he personally one of the "new men." No better illustration of the trend could be offered than John Shakespeare's removal from the tenant acres of Snitterfield to become a principal burgess of Stratford, and his son William's removal from the house on Henley Street to become a London entrepreneur, and then a landed gentleman of his native Warwickshire. It is possible that his sympathies were aligned with those who complained about his own upstart success at the Heralds' College; but we should not assume that they were, or select evidence from his plays to prove it. Social change is usually regarded as social decay by those whose prerogatives seem to be threatened, and by their academic and literary dependents.

Creizenach finds that Shakespeare, and the Elizabethan dramatists generally, fought for the old (feudal) ideas against the new,[15] and Tucker Brooke concurs.[16] But Smirnov, in a Marxist interpretation, remarks that Shakespeare was the "ideologist of the bourgeoisie, the exponent of the program advanced by them when, in the name of humanity, they first challenged the feudal order, but which they later disavowed,"[17] and Donald Morrow concurs.[18] When an article on Elizabethan pessimism in a philological journal tells us that "the 'freedom and courtoisie' of chivalry, the more lovely ideals of a more stable society, had given way before the parsimony and assertiveness of a rising bourgeoisie,"[19] we seem to be in safe anti-Marxist, pro-feudal territory—until we recall that the Communist Manifesto also pictured feudalism as rather lovely: "The bourgeoisie, whenever it got the upper hand, put an end to all feudal, patriarchal, idyllic relations . . ."[20] Keynes, as a nonfeudalist, spoke of Shakespeare's coming just at the moment when England was "in a financial situation to afford" him, and flourishing "in the atmosphere of buoyancy, exhilaration, and the freedom of economic cares felt by the governing class . . . [and] engendered by profit inflation."[21] L. C. Knights, who perhaps may best be described as a crypto-feudalist, surveys "drama and society," and although he recognizes that it is such writers as Heywood that have a "sense of community" he is more concerned with "the better-class dramatists." Those popular writers who show an interest in society, particularly Dekker, are a bore, whereas Jonson, who shows little such interest (but is anti-bourgeois) is both magnificent and "popular." One hesitates to discount findings so earnestly presented, but one can scarcely ignore their sectarian coloration, or the tendency to identify the philosophically true with the artistically preferred. Donne's lyrics, says this analyst, are "important," whereas the main body of Elizabethan poetry is "an accomplishment . . . a superior pastime"—as a matter of fact, *musical.*[22]

The debate over the Shakespearean attitude to the common people has not always been held more firmly in historical focus, and has certainly been no more conclusive. It is impossible to review the discussion. Most prominent commentators since the time of Goethe have contributed to it, including such diverse personalities as Hazlitt, Charles Knight, Whitman, Browning, Swinburne, Sidney Lee, Stopford Brooke, Bradley, Shaw, and Tolstoy, and their forces are about equally divided. The most judicious analyses have come from scholars.[23] On such a question as the political character of the rank and file viewed as an abstraction, we could hardly expect that Shakespeare's *dramatis personae* or Shakespeare himself would be wholly consistent. His offstage "multitude" is wavering, fickle, giddy, in dozens of places; but in as many more his "people" or "commons" are stable enough to exert a restraining moral influence upon the great. His attitude toward the "common man" has often been deduced from his portrayal of rebellious mobs—in *Julius Caesar, Coriolanus, II Henry VI,*[24] and the "ill May-Day" scenes of *Sir Thomas More*—and from the tendency of his characters to express disgust at the stench of crowds. Cleopatra is the most eloquent:

> Mechanic slaves
> With greasy aprons, rules, and hammers, shall
> Uplift us to the view. In their thick breaths,
> Rank of gross diet, shall we be enclouded
> And forc'd to drink their vapour.[25]

It would be rash to conclude that Shakespeare thought English workmen "mechanic slaves," however critical he may have been of their
collective aroma. The Elizabethan conception of the nature of rebellion will be described presently; the only point that need be
made here is that Shakespeare, in depicting rebels as ludicrously ignorant, credulous, and irresponsible, was using the kindest means of
condemnation available. His method was precisely that of the other
popular dramatists. Henry Chettle introduces rebels in the following
stage direction: "Enter Stilt and a rabble of beggarly-looking soldiers, old Stilt, his father, with his scarf like a captain, and Fibs.
A scurvy march is played." Prussia, presented as a far more sympathetic character than Cleopatra, speaks thus:

> Upon these traitors, valiant gentlemen!
> Let not that beast, the multitude, confront
> The majesty of me, their awful duke,
> With garlic breath and their confused cries.
> Strike their Typhoean body down to fire
> That dare 'gainst us, their sovereign, conspire.[26]

Murley's rebels in *Sir John Oldcastle*, Brett's rebels in *Sir Thomas
Wyatt*, and Spicing's rebels in *I Edward IV* are no more respectfully treated than Cade's rebels in Shakespeare's *II Henry VI* although their comic quality is less fully and skillfully limned. These
plays, written by such unaristocratic collaborators as Chettle, Heywood, Munday, Dekker, and Wilson, were performed in the Henslowe theatres. The audience was composed mainly of common
people, but it would not have occurred to them to equate themselves
with a mob.

Shakespeare's characters call one another "peasant" and "groom"
even when the social difference is only that between one degree of
nobility and another; but the villains and fools are most fond of
these epithets, and the peasants and grooms we actually meet are
usually quite worthy. Noble qualities are often attributed to noble
birth, but just as often they are not. Shakespeare never juxtaposes in
his scene the courageous death of a patrician and the craven death
of a plebeian, as Webster does on several occasions. Humble characters are often given ludicrous names and traits, but there is some-

thing endearing and even ennobling about them. We get a far different impression if we attend to the whole conception of the character of Bottom, instead of to his name alone and the fact that he is a weaver. Truly undemocratic literature assumes that lower-class persons (except criminals) have no individuality at all, and virtually no existence. Such a stain mars Spenser's otherwise bright escutcheon.

In general we may say that the popular drama displays more democratic tendencies than might be expected and more than are commonly recognized. It is only the popular drama that shows a consciousness of the claims of the humblest members of the commonwealth, frequently classified as "poor men." These, of course, are not to be misused. One of the charges against the corrupt judge of *Cambyses* is that he violated "the simple man."[27] In *The Famous Victories* Prince Hal, even in his unregenerate days, upbraids a henchman: "Now, base-minded rascal, to rob a poor carrier!"[28] But the absolute worth of the humble is also insisted upon. In *I If You Know Not Me* a point is made of the loyalty shown to Princess Elizabeth Tudor by her cooks, the common soldiers, a clown, a small boy, and "three poor men."[29] In *The True Tragedy of Richard III* and *II Edward IV*, it is the poor serving men that are willing to take the risks in relieving Jane Shore. In *The Royal King and the Loyal Subject* Captain Bonville finds that the clown is the only one who does not judge him by his rags: "Why, may not a poor man have as good eyes as another?"[30] In *I Edward IV* the peasants, Hobs and Grudgeon, are more generous in contributing to the English war chest than the fashionable Goodfellow and Hadland. Like the proud pinner in *George a Greene*, Old Strowd in *The Blind Beggar of Bednal Green* recognizes no worthier class than his own:

> I am as proud
> And think myself as gallant in this gray . . .
> As he that goeth in rattling taffety.
> Let gentlemen go gallant, what care I,
> I was a yeoman born, and so I'll die.[31]

It is part of Old Strowd's code always to take part with the weaker side. Many such characters appear in the plays. Stump, the poor one-legged soldier, is the hero of the Globe's *Alarum for London*. In *The Weakest Goeth to the Wall*, distressed nobility find a good friend in a mender of old clothes:

> I am Barnaby Bunch, the botcher, that ne'er spent any man's goods but my own. I'll labor for my meat, work hard, fare hard, lie hard for a living. I'll not charge ye a penny; I'll keep your counsel, and ye shall command me to serve you, your wife, and your daughter, in the way of honesty.[32]

Shakespeare's old Corin is much the same sort.

Scattered through the plays are such dicta as "Why, shepherds are men and kings are no more";[33] "A poor man that is true is better than an earl if he be false";[34] "I am a man though subject";[35] "If gentleness make gentility, we are gentle."[36] When the Marquess of *Patient Grissill* is warned that it will disgrace him to wed a peasant girl, he replies,

> No more, Mario, than it doth disgrace the sun
> To shine on me.[37]

The same kind of occasion calls forth the same kind of remark from Perdita in *The Winter's Tale*:

> The selfsame sun that shines upon his court
> Hides not his visage from our cottage, but
> Looks on alike.[38]

A few casual words of leave-taking in *Cymbeline* state the orthodox view of temporal inequality and eternal equality:

> *Arviragus.*
> Brother, stay here.
> Are we not brothers?
>
> *Imogen.*
> So man and man should be,
> But clay and clay differ in dignity,
> Whose dust is both alike.[39]

True, the shepherdess Perdita is really of royal birth, the fine old miller in *Fair Em* really a knight, and Heywood's four glorious apprentices really the sons of an earl. High birth augured well. However, one might himself become an ancestor. The followers of Sir

Thomas Shirley, like the followers of Henry V, are invited to gentle their condition by acts of valor.⁴⁰ In *I Edward IV*, the knighted Lord Mayor of London proudly affirms that he began life as a nameless foundling.⁴¹ We must not look for impeccable logic. It was proper to remain in one's present station, in conformity with the principle of order and degree; but it was also proper to rise in the world. The blacksmith's son who became lord chamberlain is the hero of *Thomas Lord Cromwell*. His resolution to make a name for himself suggests, in its strange wording, the conflict between old ways of verbalizing, new ways of feeling:

> Why should my birth keep down my mounting spirit?
> Are not all creatures subject unto Time:
> To Time who doth abuse the world,
> And fills it full of hodge-podge bastardy?
> There's legions now of beggars on the earth,
> That their original did spring from kings,
> And many monarchs now whose fathers were
> The riffraff of their age.⁴²

No stigma attached to marrying outside one's own class. When such marriages are treated, the stress is not upon the luck or material gain of the one who makes the socially or economically advantageous match, but upon the triumph of true love, true worth, or true English blood. The marriage of King Edward IV to an English commoner is treated with approval,⁴³ and that of Princess Mary to Brandon is blessed by Henry VIII himself:

> I hold thee happier in this English choice
> Than to be Queen of France.⁴⁴

The ladies seek assurance that their wooers are cultivated, but show no further interest in rank. Princess Amadine in *Mucedorus* and Princess Odellia in *The Weakest Goeth to the Wall* are equally indifferent to the birth of their wooers:

> I'll marry none but thee.
> I know thy bringing up, though not thy birth;
> Thou art deriv'd from Adam, form'd of earth:
> From that first parent all descended are,
> Then who begat or bare thee, that's not my care.⁴⁵

The attitude is duplicated in the village maid, Bettris, of *George a Greene*:

> I care not for earl, nor yet for knight,
> Nor baron that is so bold,
> For George a Greene, the merry pinner,
> He hath my heart in hold.[46]

Shakespeare provides just as large a proportion of interclass marriages as the others; and, as with them, the expression of hesitation, if it occurs, is more likely to come from the person of lower rank. When the reverse is true, the reluctant one, like Bertram in *All's Well*, is branded a snob. Bertram is lectured by his King:

> 'Tis only title thou disdain'st in her, the which
> I can build up. Strange is it that our bloods,
> Of colour, weight, and heat, pour'd all together,
> Would quite confound distinction, yet stand off
> In differences so mighty. If she be
> All that is virtuous, save what thou dislik'st,
> A poor physician's daughter, thou dislik'st
> Of virtue for the name.[47]

The speech continues in the same vein for twenty-one more lines. It is absurd to say that either it or the play in which it occurs is uncharacteristic of Shakespeare.

In Samuel Rowlands' *The Letting of Humours Blood in the Head-Vaine*, 1600, there is a reference to Singer and Pope, rival comic actors of the Admiral's and the Chamberlain's Men:

> Are plowmen simple fellows nowadays?
> Not so, my masters; what means Singer then,
> And Pope, the clown, to speak so boorish when
> They counterfeit the clowns upon the stage?
> Since country fellows grow in this same age
> To be so quaint in their new-printed speech
> That cloth will now compare with velvet breech.[48]

The type of clowning alluded to is familiar enough in the plays of Shakespeare. We might say that the citizens in the public theatres were laughing at the expense of the peasantry just as the gentlemen in the private theatres were laughing at the expense of the citizens.

Such is actually the case, but there was a vast difference in the nature of the laughter. The popular plays never impugn the moral worth of the peasants, and never picture the members of lower and middle classes as preying upon each other. There is no class war. The select plays, in contrast, constantly impugn the moral worth of the citizens, and assume a constant state of class hostility. In Field's *A Woman Is a Weathercock*, 1609–1610, the practice of the preceding decade in the coterie theatres is freely admitted:

> I'll think
> As abjectly of thee as any mongrel
> Bred in the city; such a citizen
> As the plays flout still, and is made the subject
> Of all the stages.[49]

The war is described by the merchant Quomodo in Middleton's *Michaelmas Term*:

> There are means and ways enow to hook in gentry,
> Besides our deadly enmity, which thus stands,
> They're busy 'bout our wives, we 'bout their lands.[50]

The war had been declared as soon as the chorister companies were revived. In *Every Man Out of His Humor*, performed by the Chamberlain's Men in 1599, Jonson excused his satirical treatment of a citizen and his wife: "No more, assure you, will any grave, wise citizen, or modest matron, take the object of this folly in Deliro and his wife, but rather apply it as the foil to their own virtues."[51] But in the following year, after Jonson had transferred his activity to Blackfriars, the more contemptible pair of citizens, Albius and Chloe of *Poetaster*, were presented without apology. Thereafter practically every comedy at the select theatres featured a stupid or usurious citizen and his climbing or adulterous wife. Master and Mistress Mulligrub of Marston's *Dutch Courtesan* are relatively likable examples of the type. Less overt hostility to citizens appears in Chapman's extant comedies than in those of Jonson and Middleton; but the recovered account of his lost comedy, *The Old Joiner of Aldgate*, proves that he also produced plays of the standard sort.[52] In a typical plot, a London citizen (a Lucre or a Hoard) is tricked out of the estate he has wrested by fraud or usury from a landed gentleman, while his wife is seduced, his daughter is won by a fortune hunter, and his son displays his idiocy. If the citizen is single, he is usually married off to a whore. In Middleton the triumphant gentry is represented by such characters as Fitsgrave in *Your Five Gallants*, Easy in *Michaelmas Term*, and Gerardine in *The Family of Love*. Oddly, as in the popular drama, the social classes seem both fluid and fixed. The usurer-victim and the gentleman-victor may stand in the relationship of uncle and nephew, while a marriage with a rich girl of the city is the conventional genteel objective; still, gentlemen remain gentlemen (and admirable) while citizens remain citizens (and contemptible). Marston, Jonson, and Chapman indicate their resolution to depart from the type in *Eastward Ho*, but their representation of citizen virtue can scarcely be described as whole-hearted. The bourgeois family is split in equal parts: for the wise Master Touchstone there is the silly Mistress Touchstone; for the chaste daughter Mildred, the sluttish daughter Gertrude; for the good apprentice Golding, the bad apprentice Quicksilver. The chief merit of the virtuous half of the family is that they *know their place*. The ugliest feature of the city comedies is the sexual depravity attributed to the merchant class: many a shopkeeper stands ready to prostitute his wife.

It is interesting to observe the response in the public theatres to the attack upon the citizens. In a play celebrating the career of Thomas Gresham, a city hero, we hear that in his New Exchange there will be "such a girdle of chaste eyes" that courtiers will swear "they lied when they did scoff."[53] An exemplum appears in *The London Prodigal* when a shabby gentleman receives charity from a London wife and then offers to become her pander or paramour:

Young Flowerdale.
Now God thank you, sweet lady. If you have any friend, or garden-house where you may employ a poor gentleman as your friend, I am yours to command in all secret service.

Citizen's Wife.
I thank you, good friend. I prithee let me see that again I gave thee; there is one of them a brass shilling: give me them, and here is half-a-crown in

gold. (*He gives it her.*) Now out upon thee, rascal! Secret service!
What doest thou make of me? It were a good deed to have thee whip't.
Now I have my money again, I'll see thee hanged before I give thee a
penny. Secret service![54]

When Mistress Page receives Falstaff's letter and exclaims, "What
unweighed behaviour hath this Flemish drunkard pick'd (with the
devil's name!) out of my conversation that he dares in this manner
assay me!"[55] it would not have been lost upon the spectators at the
Globe that a housewife was speaking of a knight, and that middle-
class virtue was being vindicated.

Of course the popular playwrights did not defend usury. Chettle
attacked those who thought "there is no felicity but in excessive possession of wealth,"[56] and Dekker attacked the "true city doctrine—
to care for *one*."[57] But distinctions were made. London's debt to the
wealthy burghers is stated in *II If You Know Not Me*:

> Behold their charity in every street,
> Churches for prayer, almshouses for the poor,
> Conduits which bring us water . . .[58]

The play portrays the proper mercantile code as followed by
Gresham, the great merchant, Hobson, the wholesaler, and John
Tawnycoat, the simple chapman. Banister and Friskiball in *Thomas
Lord Cromwell* are likewise exemplary businessmen. An interesting
parenthetical clause appears in a speech in *Captain Thomas Stukeley*:
Vernon, we hear,

> Was never owner of a ship in's life,
> Nor merchant venturer, *though both trades be good*,
> But well-deriv'd, of rich and gentle blood.[59]

Commerce, though middle-class, was honorable. Antonio, not Shylock, is the *merchant* of Venice. The *usurer* in Haughton's city
comedy for the Rose Theatre, *Englishmen for My Money*, is not a
native Londoner but an immigrant Portuguese. The dramatists preferred to think of the increasing wealth of the middle-classes as
coming from foreign trade, as in the case of Dekker's Simon Eyre;
and again the point must be made that their attitude, although
romantic, resulted in less distortion of the truth than did that of the

coterie realists. There was nothing new about usury and the worship of gold, or satirical condemnation of them; Jonson's treatment of avarice, to which so much social significance has been attached, belongs to a literary tradition dating back to Aristophanes.

It is quite fair to say that the difference between the popular and the select drama is the difference between social consciousness and class animosity. Old-fashioned plays like *A Knack to Know a Knave* and *Nobody and Somebody* are explicit in their preachment, as is the occasional "problem play" like Wilkins's *Miseries of Enforced Marriage*; but the majority bring their message indirectly. Charlatanry is exposed in Heywood's *Wise Woman of Hogsdon*, and an ideally charitable will is briefed in his *I Fair Maid of the West*, with provisions for maimed soldiers, for setting up "young beginners in their trade,"[60] and the like. Casual dialogues, even in such unexpected places as *Pericles* and *A Christian Turned Turk*, treat of the relationship between ignorance, poverty, and crime. Clifford Leech in a stimulating essay has said of the playwrights: "They never succeed in speaking for a social group as something which they delight to belong to. Even Dekker, with his surface realism, writes of the London citizens with a playful condescension."[61] Granted that such is the case, it can scarcely be reckoned a defect. The attack upon the citizens by the writers of Blackfriars and Paul's inspired a defense by the writers of the Globe, the Fortune, and the Red Bull, rather than a counterattack upon the gentry. The playwrights were speaking not for a class but for the whole community, and they persisted in portraying gentleness in the gentry, and nobleness in the nobility, where such qualities ought to be found and sometimes were.

The whole body of romantic and historical literature to which the popular drama relates was concerned with the actions of persons of high rank, and it is natural that most of the characters in most of the plays, including Shakespeare's, should be kings, peers, knights, and other "right honorables." It has proved to be matter of offense to some modern readers that characters of lower rank usually appear in the capacity of servants, and that their worth is estimated almost exclusively according to the fidelity with which they serve.[62] What is apt to escape notice is that the lords and gentlemen also appear in the capacity of servants to those above them, and that service, even menial service, had not then acquired its present tarnish. Lord Burghley was a good servant from the Queen's point of view; the Queen, a good servant from God's point of view—or so it was her lonely destiny to hope. There was no absolute distinction between tending to a royal mistress's treasury and tending to a yeoman master's horse. In the human community the obligations of master and man were personal, moral, and reciprocal. When Adam in *As You Like It* is called an "old dog" by Oliver, he says, "God be with my old master! he would not have spoke such a word."[63] Orlando proves to be the right kind of master—as willing to carry the old man on his back as to accept the loan of his life's savings. Adam's fidelity is called "the constant service of the antique world."[64] The Butler in *The Miseries of Enforced Marriage* is called "the old time's ancient conscience."[65] It was common to point back to the past as a golden age of service, but not in admiration of serfdom or servility. The good servant is legally and spiritually free. He counsels his master, upbraids him, and, when necessary, resists him. Bad orders are obeyed only by bad servants—servants bad for the master:

> Every good servant does not all commands!
> No bond but to do just ones.[66]

All actions, including disobedience, are in the master's interest. The reward is to be regarded as kindred rather than as employee. To find servants who are not good from the master's point of view or any other, one need turn only to the coterie plays. Nothing is more illustrative of their atmosphere of disintegration. At their best, the servants are witty pages who provide mirth by mocking their masters. At their more common worst, they infect, like Eros in Chapman's *Widow's Tears;* are infected, like Gumwater in Middleton's *Mad World My Masters;* or betray, like Zanthea in Marston's *Sophonisba.* Bussy's ingratitude to Monsieur, his master and patron, in Chapman's tragedy would have struck a popular audience as being far from admirable; and Cutbeard's betrayal of Morose in Jonson's comedy would have provoked only very uneasy laughter.

All the plays of Shakespeare, indeed nearly all the plays of the popular repertory, contain good servants. Sometimes they are the most interesting and admirable persons represented—like Harpool in *Sir John Oldcastle*, or the Steward in *Timon of Athens*. Apprentices are regarded as the servants of the craftsmen to whom they are indentured, and in plays like *The Shoemaker's Holiday* and *The Honest Whore* that picture workshops they always prove faithful when the stakes are down. In return—"master, journeymen, and 'prentices, one table serves for all."[67] It is interesting to observe that, as the old Vice of the moral interludes bifurcates into the semi-realistic villain and the semirealistic clown, the clown becomes the comic servant with his "viciousness" quite evaporated—like Mouse in *Mucedorus*, Babulo in *Patient Grissill*, and Launcelot in *The Merchant of Venice*. Launcelot may shift masters, but not betray one while in his service, even though that master be a Shylock. The master-betrayer Warman in *The Downfall of Robert Earl of Huntington* becomes a pariah and attempts to hang himself. Homes in *Sir Thomas Wyatt* actually does hang himself, to everyone's satisfaction, even though Suffolk, the master he has betrayed with his "Judas kiss," is something of a villain in the piece.

The master-servant relationship as presented in the popular repertory conveys a sense of community, and harmonizes with the political sentiment of the plays. Just as the defects of a master do not justify betrayal, so the defects of a king do not justify revolt. When King John dies and Faulconbridge says,

> my soul shall wait on thee to heaven
> As it on earth has been thy servant still,[68]

the words seem fulsome because so little in accord with either Faulconbridge's character or John's deserts. But it is really not John and Faulconbridge that now occupy the stage but royal king and loyal subject; and in the relationship a number of others are analogically and emotionally implied—that of master and man, captain and soldier, even father and son. Shakespeare is usually able to make the thing psychologically more convincing, but when Horatio speaks in the same fashion at the death of Prince Hamlet, and Kent at the death of King Lear, or when Enobarbus dies of shame after his desertion of Antony, we must not seek a basis for their behavior either in modern psychology or in chivalric convention. Thomas Wyatt, though a stout Protestant, resists the plot to seat Lady Jane Grey upon the English throne instead of Mary Tudor, his rightful Queen:

> I loved the father well, I loved the son,
> And for the daughter I through death will run.[69]

Sir Thomas Wyatt and *I If You Know Not Me* are among the most Protestant of Elizabethan plays, yet in both the Queen presented is not a "bloody" Mary, but a deferentially treated English Queen. Truly, as Mr. Hart has pointed out, the duty of loyalty to the throne was dinned into the subjects' ears; but, in Shakespeare at least, "divine right" and other terms of the homily of rebellion are echoed by some very dubious characters, including Don Armado, Dame Quickly, Richard III, and Claudius. Perhaps already existing convictions made the efforts of the propagandist seem superfluous to most people, possibly even somewhat amusing. We can agree that Shakespeare "was trying to do the state some service";[70] but the direction his efforts took must have been instinctive. The whole of the popular drama is infused with the emotion of loyalty to the throne—as naïvely expressed in *George a Greene*:

> We are English born, and therefore Edward's friends,
> Vowed unto him even in our mother's womb,
> Our minds to God, our hearts unto our king.
> Our wealth, our homage, and our carcasses
> Be all King Edward's.[71]

The John whom Faulconbridge mourns was not a good king; nor is he represented as one by Shakespeare. John is an even worse king in Chettle and Munday's *Death of Robert Earl of Huntington*. Lady Bruce and her child, starved to death by his tyranny, are shown in tableau, and heroic Matilda is hounded by his lust. When Lord Leicester speaks rousingly against him, the words are obviously approved. But when he proposes a revolt to "our elected king, Louis of France," he is rejected by the bereaved Bruce and all the other sufferers:

> For though kings fault in many a foul offence,
> Subjects must sue, not mend with violence.[72]

It is difficult for modern minds to understand, much less approve, an attitude so supine; but the age has left us its explanations. John Stockwood's domestic manual, *A Bartholomew Fairing for Parents*, 1589, contains the following characteristic observation:

> . . . there are many children found sometimes far to exceed their fathers in wit and wisdom, yea and in all other gifts both of mind and body, yet is this no good reason that they should take upon them their father's authority.[73]

With these words in mind we are better able to appreciate what the popular playwright is doing when he puts a speech like the following into the mouth of a villain:

> For say a father do forget to shew
> The love by nature he doth owe his son,
> In my opinion 'tis no sin at all
> If such a son cast off the awful duty
> Which to his father otherwise were due.
> In all things just proportion must be kept:
> If the king care not for the commonwealth,
> Why should the commonwealth respect the king?[74]

Why indeed? we are apt to ask. But by the Elizabethans the refutation would have been readily perceived as imbedded in the argument. How is it possible to cast off an "awful duty" without sin and with "just proportion"? Are not evil fathers bad enough, without advocating that evil fathers be matched by evil sons? But the threat of reprisal will discourage the abuse of power. Then must fathers deal justly with sons only through fear of reprisal? It is thus the debate would go. To understand Shakespeare's politics, we must recognize the basic distinction between his concept of a nation and ours. Our nation is an organization; his, an organism, specifically a family. The signatories of our "social contract" are all human beings; those of his are human beings of the one part and God of the other.

In Marlowe's *Edward II*, Shakespeare's *Richard II* and *King John*, and other plays of the public theatres, not all histories, we discern a recurrent pattern. Subjects are the victims, and a monarch the vic-

timizer, until the moment of revolt; then the same subjects become
the victimizers, and the same monarch the victim. The shift of
sympathy is puzzling only if we suppose that the old playwrights
shared our own *quid pro quo* assumptions about social relationships
—not if we recognize that both subjects and monarchs are being
weighed in an absolute scale of ethical values and admonished alike.
The evil of rebellion is more frequently displayed as an effect than as
a cause of a weak or tyrannous reign; but this is no sign of political
dissidence. The import, rather, is that rebellion, unjustified even
against a Richard, Edward, or John, would be heinous indeed
against a relatively blameless Elizabeth. In attributing the condemnation of rebellion merely to Tudor "thought control," ignoring its
ethical and religious basis, we attribute to dramatists and audiences
more dwarfish minds and spirits than we have any right to do. This
is not to say that the histories were exclusively, or even always
primarily, political in interest, or that their intention was always
didactic. There was the appeal of stirring action, the pageantry, the
clashing wills, the display of valorous deeds. Shakespeare's interest
in famous people for their own sake is always evident. When did
Bolingbroke's will to get his own swell into a will to get more than
his own? Was Henry V provoked or seduced into invading France?
Was Wolsey sometimes sincere? Over individual persons and events
the imagination plays freely; but the spectators are invited to pass
final judgment—according to a code that, whatever its defects, was
neither irrational nor incoherent.

   That a king should "rule with laws, eke justice"[75] (or answer to
God), is assumed in all popular plays from *Cambyses* on. Shakespeare makes clear his idea of the royal role in hundreds of places.
The subject's soul is his own, but his duty is the king's. The king's
power is an inalienable legacy; but whether a usurper's sin is transmitted with his crown to descendants is a moot point. Might it not
depend upon the descendants, and the cleansing operations of the
jus naturale? Here there was room for the same kind of heterodoxy
as in the issue of original sin and total depravity. A ruler, to use his
power rightly, should have

the king-becoming graces,
As justice, verity, temp'rance, stableness,
Devotion, patience, courage, fortitude.[76]

The ideal combination of qualities, strength and virtue, is not always
—perhaps not usually—present in actual kings, but there is no remedy
for its absence except endurance. Apart from its violation of universal ordinances, revolt involves the risk of civil war, anarchy, and
foreign invasion, all more woeful to "poor men"—indeed, especially
to them—than the rule of an evil king. Of course Shakespeare be-
lieved in order, degree, and justice—as who does not? It is strange
how often the speech of Ulysses in *Troilus and Cressida* is quoted to
illustrate the conservatism of the past, as if the newer ideal were
chaos. Such passages illustrate Shakespeare's literary facility and the
intensity of his social feeling—although the latter is better illustrated
in other ways—but certainly no reactionary temperament. The instrumentality by which chaos might be avoided was endorsed in the
absence of a competing instrumentality. There was no program of
popular government to advocate, no party to join.

Perhaps it is regrettable that Shakespeare was so practical, so much
the political realist, and could not, like Sir Thomas More, conceive
of more than one kind of religious society. He failed to detach himself from his own times when he treated of Roman republican history, and he gave scant attention to political speculation and perennial social dreams. We may wish that he had felt inclined or free to
set one of his tales in Utopia, or even that the vision of a society that
needs no government had inspired him to write more than the few
whimsical words of the futile old man in *The Tempest*. On the other
hand, his ideas are more vital, and no more "antiquated," than those
of the intellectuals. Among the coterie dramatists, only Jonson and
Chapman give evidence of any political thinking at all. Jonson's ideas
are Ciceronian, and orthodox enough, although expressed without the
conviction that might give them the breath of life. Chapman's also
are in the main respectable generalizations about justice and virtue,
in spite of the Machiavellian coloration of certain passages. In *The
Revenge of Bussy D'Ambois* and in the *Charles Duke of Byron* plays,
Chapman is obviously musing at times over the doubtful right of a

king to rule stoic saints and great-hearted men of *virtu*, and sympathy
is extended to subjects who fall off in their allegiance. In this we
have, at best, a negative criticism of the available political system.
Nothing very clear emerges, and certainly nothing useful; one
painstaking analyst of Chapman's political thought concludes by
quoting Swinburne on his "tangled and ravelled lines of thought."[77]
In the works of both Jonson and Chapman appears evidence of
personal sycophancy toward the hereditary great such as cannot
be found in the works of Shakespeare.

The distinction between popular and select attitudes toward the
existent political institutions is signaled most subtly in the nonhis-
torical plays. In Jonson's *Every Man in His Humor*, Justice Clement
sets things right in the end. In his *Bartholomew Fair*, Justice Overdo
is the most deranged creature in a deranged world. It would be a
mistake to attribute the contrast to the lapse of time and the substitution of Jacobean pessimism for Elizabethan optimism.[78] Clement is
typical of the popular, and Overdo of the select repertory. The plays
of the latter rarely end with pacifications effected by a representative of the community as a whole; indeed the person of highest authority is as likely as not to be pictured as an ass. Piero in Marston's
Antonio and Mellida is unable in moments of crisis even to sustain
his role as a villain:

 Keep you the court, the rest stand still, or run, or go, or shout, or
search, or send, or call, or hang, or do do do su su su something. I know
not who who who what I do do do, nor who who who where I am.[79]

Lorenzo in *What You Will* responds to his subjects' plea for redress
in a fashion described with peculiar care:

 Enter the Duke, coupled with a lady, two couples more with them, the
men having tobacco pipes in their hands. The women sit. They dance a
round. The petition is delivered up by Randolfo. The Duke lights his
tobacco pipe with it and goes out dancing.[80]

Both plays were on the stage several years before the accession of
James. In Chapman's *The Widow's Tears* an idiotic governor, and

in Fletcher's *The Coxcomb* an idiotic justice, mangle affairs at the end instead of setting them right. In none of these plays were the satirical touches really germane to the plots. They seem to be examples of unfocused cynicism, or else parody of popular dramatic devices.

Most of the comedies of the public theatres end with a ruler or local magistrate settling differences among the characters or blessing the settlement they have found for themselves. He may be an unspecified English king, as in Dekker's *The Shoemaker's Holiday*; or a national hero, such as William the Conqueror in *Fair Em* or Richard the Lion-Hearted in *The Fair Maid of Bristowe*; or simply the local squire, like Sir Ralph Smith in Porter's *Two Angry Women of Abington*. When the setting is foreign he is usually a duke, as in the two parts of *The Honest Whore*. One need look no further than Shakespeare for a number of examples of this role, in characters as different as Theseus in *A Midsummer Night's Dream* and Vincentio in *Measure for Measure*. When the person in highest place is not such as may be looked to for justice and amity, the play is most likely to be a tragedy; even then a good successor is usually supplied at the end as a symbol of a surviving community and of hope for better days.

It must be confessed that sometimes the human community seems to have extended only to the national boundaries. The devotion to things English is expressed in curious ways. One of the dumb shows in Kyd's *Spanish Tragedy* treats of John of Gaunt's conquest of Castile, a subject that its presumed Spanish audience would scarcely have considered pleasing. Although necromancy was admittedly deplorable, English necromancy in Greene's *Friar Bacon* must be shown as more potent than German necromancy. *The Trial of Chivalry* is a romance about the French, but Pembroke, the English earl, and Dick Bowyer, the English captain, stand out as eminences. Barnaby Bunch of *The Weakest Goeth to the Wall* is another displaced Englishman in Europe—he is convinced that his countrymen have even a superior smell.[81] Generalizations like the following from *Thomas Lord Cromwell* are quite common:

Lust dwells in France, in Italy, and Spain,
From the poor peasant to the prince's train;
In Germany and Holland riot serves,
And he that most can drink, most he deserves.[82]

Haughton's *Englishmen for My Money* leans heavily upon prejudice for its effects, as in a speech by one of the heroines to a French follower:

Though I am Portingale by the father's side,
And therefore should be lustful, wanton, light;
Yet, Goodman Goosecap, I will let you know
That I have so much English by the mother
That no base slavering French shall make me stoop.[83]

Shakespeare is not free from this taint, although normally he reserves his strictures for the particular foreigners with whom England is making war. In the parade of nationalities provided by Portia's suitors in *The Merchant of Venice*, the French lord gets off lightly, as do the Neapolitan, the Dutchman, and the Moor; but the German is a drunkard, and the Scotsman a coward. No one is accused of lechery. The English baron is a poor linguist and an extravagant dresser—not a very weighty indictment. Elsewhere in Shakespeare, foreigners repeat these charges about the English, and, in addition, that they are foolhardily brave, eccentric, or "mad," sexually frigid, and, once, that they are uncharitable.[84] In *Henry V* Shakespeare makes at least a gesture toward drawing Ireland and Scotland into the native fraternity. Wales, of course, already "belonged"—however comical all individual Welshmen might be. In a sense, the select drama was more international in spirit. Unfortunately, however, the tendency was to let Englishmen share foreign vice rather than foreigners English virtues.

One interesting aspect of the contrasting social spirit of the two bodies of drama appears in the realm of religious tolerance. The popular dramatists were severe on Catholicism, evidently associated in the public mind with foreign enemies, but surprisingly easy on Puritans. Shakespeare's plays contain no caricatures of Puritans. There is nothing about his comic clergymen to distinguish them as such, except possibly the name and outcast lot of Sir Oliver Martext. On the principle that Puritans are prigs and hypocrites, it has been maintained that Malvolio, who is a prig, and Angelo, who is a hypocrite, are intended as Puritans; but the logic leaves something to be desired. Neither character has the trick of speech characteristic of stage Puritans at the time, and manipulated with such comic effect by Falstaff. The cleverest person in *Twelfth Night* says of Malvolio that "sometimes he is a kind of Puritan," then immediately retracts the statement;[85] we should take her word for it. There are incidental gibes at Puritans in Shakespeare's plays, but they are quite few and quite mild. So is it with the other popular playwrights. Clergymen such as Sir Aminadab in *How a Man May Choose a Good Wife from a Bad* and Sir Nicholas in *The Weakest Goeth to the Wall* offered opportunities for caricature that were not seized. Timothy Thinbeard in *II If You Know Not Me* is a venal Puritan, but he receives very slight attention. Even in the plays of Dekker, where we should most expect it, there is no satire to speak of[86] until we come to *If It Be Not Good*, in which Puritans prove to be troublemakers even in hell. The conspicuous attacks upon the sect appear in the plays of Jonson, Chapman, Middleton, Barry, and other writers for the coterie; its trenchant character scarcely needs illustration.

It has been pointed out that the religious sentiment of the popular plays is not essentially un-Catholic;[87] however, for Catholicism in its official aspects there is no sign of toleration. Shakespeare's own friendly feeling for friars does not extend to cardinals and popes, and he leaves no doubt of his partisanship wherever, in the history plays, England and the Roman church appear in conflict. Antipapal feeling seems to have been strongest at the time of Marlowe's *Doctor Faustus* and *The Massacre at Paris*, but it is expressed in dozens of later plays intended for the public theatres up to and past the time of Dekker's *Whore of Babylon*. It is one of the things that can make even Heywood forsake his customary good humor. The signs of tolerance all appear in the coterie plays. There are no caricatures of Catholics to match its caricatures of Puritans. Chapman's allusions to the faith are apt to be favorable,[88] and in his *Revenge of Bussy*

D'Ambois, he goes to the truly amazing length of letting his hero Clermont excuse Guise for Bartholomew's Eve:

> Had faith and true religion been preferr'd
> Religious Guise had never massacred.[89]

Jonson, a professed Catholic between 1599 and 1613, was naturally compelled to be more discreet. The absence of religious interest of any kind in the typical coterie play suggests that the tendency to attack Puritanism rather than Catholicism was owing only to the antipopular bias. Observe the group selected for ridicule in Barry's *Ram-Alley* when a performing monkey is imitated on the stage:

> *Smallshanks.*
> What can you do for the great Turk?
> What can you do for the Pope of Rome?
> Hark, he stirreth not, he moveth not, he waggeth not.
> What can you do for the town of Geneva, sirrah?
> (*He holds up his hands in sign of praying.*)
>
> *Constantia.*
> Sure this baboon is a great Puritan.[90]

In a play at the public theatres, the hit would have been at the "Pope of Rome"—on the principle that he was the greater danger to England.

The statement that Elizabethan drama is filled with patriotic sentiment that appears regularly in literary histories should be amended to read that *popular* Elizabethan drama is filled with such sentiment. Except for Lyly's allegorical compliments to the great figures of Whitehall, and three or four scattered tributes to Elizabeth,[91] there is nothing in the sixty-seven plays of the select repertory to suggest pride in England or concern for national solidarity. The absence of history plays in this repertory is a cognate phenomenon, not an explanation. In the popular plays, the patriotic sentiment is not confined to the histories. The lines from Shakespeare's *King John* that served Churchill so well before the Battle of Britain—

> This England never did, nor never shall,
> Lie at the proud foot of a conqueror—[92]

are of a type that appears even in romantic comedies. King William
defies the Danes in *Fair Em*:

> I nill regard him nor his Danish power,
> For if he comes to fetch her forth my realm,
> I will provide him such a banquet here,
> That he shall have small cause to give me thanks.[93]

In *The Blind Beggar of Bednall Green* the nation stiffens against the
French:

> Thus, our disjointed kingdom being made strong,
> Each member seated in his proper seat,
> Let's in to praise his Name whose powerful hand
> Protects the safety of our peaceful land.[94]

Even when writing of the mythical reigns of Cymbeline and Lear,
Shakespeare could not quite dismiss the thought of Albion as an in-
violable fortress. But it is the histories, of course, that chiefly reveal
him as one of that almost extinct species—the artist and thinker who
is also a patriot. In the last of the great sequence the choruses are
anthems, and the poet comes as near as ever he did to speaking in his
own person:

> O England! model to thy inward greatness,
> Like little body with a mighty heart,
> What mightst thou do that honor would thee do,
> Were all thy children kind and natural![95]

The *Englishness* of Shakespeare is not his greatest strength. To many
it has seemed to be his greatest weakness. And yet in these the most
hortatory of his lines, in this the most chauvinistic of his plays, there
is a note in concord with his conception of the divine plan, the
dignity of man, and the whole system of human relationships and
obligations. In the word "natural" a philosophy lies compact. It reveals a way of thinking and feeling before which national boundaries
might one day melt away.

VI

Shakespeare's Tradition: Conclusion

AS Shakespeare has expanded as a myth, he has dwindled as a man. In the eyes of innocence he has dwindled to the vanishing point: no mere man could have so jogged the world, although the feat might have been managed by an earl. The commoner failing is to concede him a sort of negligible identity, as when we gravely affirm, despite our own possibly moderate intellectual powers, that he was a great artist but, of course, no *thinker*. The most insidious form of the nullifying impulse lurks in the doctrine, misderived from Keats, that he was a person of "great negative capability." Divested of pious embellishment, this doctrine maintains that he was preternaturally supple—an arch-contortionist—thus offering only a new metaphor to add to the mirror, the echo, the warbler of woodnotes, the inspired savage, the windharp through which vagrant notions suspired with a musical hum. It is doubtful that such a poet has ever existed. The act of creation is an act of selection. And just as a random inclusiveness could produce only the monstrous, so an "impartial" selection of symbols conveying antithetical ideas could produce only nullity or worse. In Whitehead's dictum, "To acquiesce in discrepancy is destructive of candour, and of moral cleanliness."[1]

Shakespeare did not acquiesce in discrepancy. That we are now forced to *prove* what we instinctively *know* (and what was once taken for granted) is the strange fruit of the art-for-art theorizing that has muddied critical thinking since the mid-nineteenth century.

This movement has drawn all its strength from skepticism. As one loses faith in the power of his own age to discriminate between right and wrong, one loses faith in such power in any former age. The evidence of an artist's illusory belief that he shared in this power in his age may be charitably ignored in view of the distinction of his technique. If one finds it impossible to respond to dramatic art purely as design, one may at least credit the superior dramatists with a faculty for suspending ethical judgment to an extent far in advance of their time. If the symbols used—the characters, the actions, the speeches—persist in obtruding ethical ideas, let these symbols be paired in such a way as to cancel each other out, or let them be attributed, like the bawdy jokes, to the demands of the groundlings.

If the aesthete and the skeptic have tended to drain Shakespearean drama of its content, the modern moralist has sometimes perpetrated an equal act of violence. He has displayed a small sample of this content as if it were the whole, and has pronounced judgments upon its value without sufficient preliminary effort in understanding. Recurrent statements about Shakespeare's political illiberalism, or "filth," or snobbery, or "stoicism" are cases in point. It would seem obvious that the further an age recedes from us in time, or the greater the obscurity surrounding the conditions of its creative life, the longer we should pause before generalizing. Yet many have spoken confidently of the tastes of the "groundlings" without the vaguest notion of what a groundling was like, and have dogmatized upon the "Elizabethan" attitude toward this thing or that without considering the chance that there may have been more "Elizabethan" attitudes than one. Possibly the most mistaken single utterance ever made about Shakespearean drama came from Robert Bridges, competent in almost every literary subject except the one he had elected to discuss, when he traced all the defects and none of the merits in the plays he loved to those "wretched beings"[2] who composed their original audience. If there is any virtue whatever in the attempt made in the present study to distinguish between audiences and their influences, it is a pity that the attempt was not made long ago.

Our final endeavor will be to enforce the idea of Shakespeare as a participant, to speculate upon the effects on him of the theatrical competition and philosophical tensions in his day, to sum up that view of life for which he stood as opposed to something else for which he never stood. The attempt to supply answers to putative questions from the reader, with the awareness that these answers will themselves suggest questions, may give the discussion the appearance of a series of digressions; perhaps it may best be described as a unilateral debate.

Whether or not one has read Bridges's strictures upon the Elizabethan audience, he has certainly read Prince Hamlet's; and it is not impossible that he has failed to distinguish between the views of the Prince and those of his creator. We may well begin with the odd little fact that one of Hamlet's phrases has passed into general currency in a sense quite contrary to the speaker's apparent intention. The words "caviar to the general" are nearly always used ironically, with purveyors of "caviar" receiving the cuff rather than "the general" who fail to relish it. Folk suspicions of the exotic would have stamped the term with its present impress whatever Shakespeare's purpose when he coined it (or whatever the merits of caviar); but we must not assume that such tampering has occurred. *Hamlet* was written when the plays of the popular repertory were being dismissed categorically as shapeless, noisy, barren, and lewd. *Hamlet* itself was a play of that repertory. In its course another kind of play is mentioned—one with *form* ("well digested in the scenes"), *classical restraint* ("more handsome than fine"), and *genteel refinement* ("no sallets in the lines"). But alas! it pleased not the million, it was caviar to the general.

A speech from the play is delivered upon request.[3] From time to time it is interrupted:

> *First Player.*
> "But who, O who, had seen the mobled queen—"
> *Hamlet.*
> "The mobled queen"?
> *Polonius.*
> That's good! "Mobled queen" is good.

When Polonius's attention wavers, he is accused of being capable only of "a jig or a tale of bawdry"—a play, that is, such as might pass at the Globe. The quoted speech runs parallel to Aeneas's tale of the slaughter of Priam by Pyrrhus in *The Tragedy of Dido* by Marlowe and Nashe—as "played by the Children of her Majesty's Chapel":

> At which the frantic Queen leapt on his face,
> And in his eyelids hanging by the nails,
> A little while prolong'd her husband's life:
> At last the soldiers pull'd her by the heels,
> And swung her howling in the empty air,
> Which sent an echo to the wounded King:
> Whereat he lifted up his bed-rid limbs,
> And would have grappled with Achilles' son,
> Forgetting both his want of strength and hands,
> Which he, disdaining, *whiskt his sword about,*
> *And with the wind thereof the king fell down.*[4]

In *Hamlet* we get:

> "roasted in wrath and fire,
> And thus o'ersized with coagulate gore,
> With eyes like carbuncles, the hellish Pyrrhus
> Old grandsire Priam seeks. . . .
> Pyrrhus at Priam drives, in rage strikes wide;
> *But with the whiff and wind of his fell sword*
> *Th' unnerved father falls.*"

Unless we are ready to believe that Shakespeare was submitting this sample of the unaffected style—"as wholesome as sweet"—quite without guile, we must yield to the suggestion of parody. That he should choose as target the one coterie play by Marlowe, whom he admired, need not seem surprising. Marlowe was dead and would feel no resentment in Elysium. Shakespeare had previously parodied Lyly, and he could have parodied nimbly the styles of Jonson, Chapman, Marston, or any of the others who were proclaiming their disdain for the drama of the vulgar; but elsewhere in *Hamlet* he signals his wish that the War of the Theatres would die down. We may guess that, at the moment, he was amusing himself. The word "wind" in the Marlowe passage reads "wound" in the only substantive text; and, although the misprint seems obvious and has been assumed by all editors, we must recognize that our evidence of Shakespeare's awareness of the pretentiousness of a particular coterie play relies partly upon a textual emendation. No weighty structure should be erected upon such a foundation; still, it might be well if we sometimes permitted a smile to touch the lips of that remote and impassive countenance bequeathed us by the Droeshout engraving and the mode of our veneration—if we sometimes imagined a Shakespeare amused, or a Shakespeare indignant.

Amusement and indignation are very human responses, and we need not rely upon a doubtful explication of an episode in *Hamlet* to assume that Shakespeare responded to the pressures of experience in a human way. Every surviving record of his life contributes to a pattern of normality, or, if the word has lost its clarity, of recognizability. In the practical world, his aspirations, ways, and cares seem to have been those of most other men. Every surviving specimen of his writing demonstrates, if nothing else, his intelligence. The least we know is that he was a real actor-author in a real public theatre; and the least we may infer is that he was capable of evaluating himself and his situation. Does it not follow that he neither accepted nor viewed with indifference the judgment that the popular plays were inferior as a class? To have written as he did, he must have cared about writing and taken pride in his own ability. That he showed little interest in seeing his plays in print suggests absorption in his medium rather than indifference to it. Plays were not books, and books were not plays. Ultimately he may have taken more interest in the preservation of his work than the records indicate. It was the property of his company, and was guarded from the press as company policy. It was printed wholesale in 1623 when the company had built up a Fletcherian repertory and was entering the one period in theatrical history when Shakespeare's appeal was declining. We do not know what requests Hemmings and Condell may have received before receiving their mourning rings. Still, the point need not be pressed. Many things have been fashioned with love, without thought of their being preserved as memorials by posterity.

All of which heralds the suggestion that from the time he was called the "only Shake-scene of a country," and especially while his school was being challenged by those who shunned "the vulgar sort," Shakespeare was aware of the basic nature of the antagonisms splitting authors and audiences, that he accepted a role in the conflict, and that one of the operative forces in his creative life was the impulse to meet aggression by expressing his tradition in works unanswerably good. Certainly others seem to have recognized his role. About the time of *Hamlet* itself, a fictitious Kempe is made to say, "Our fellow Shakespeare puts them all down,"[5] with the "all" representing the coterie challengers. Ten years later John Davies of Hereford puts it more suggestively,

> Some others rail, but rail as they think fit,
> Thou hast no railing but a reigning wit.[6]

Here is implied not only conflict, but something of its nature. Shakespeare's tragedies and "dark" comedies are themselves now sometimes conceived of as a form of railing, but Davies evidently considered them the reverse. The reason should be apparent to anyone who has read extensively in the drama of the decade or has attended the analysis according to repertories attempted in the present book. Shakespeare was aware that his strength resided as much in certain shared values as in his own superior technique. He did not make the error of trying to match cynicism with cynicism, gloom with gloom, gay destructiveness with gay destructiveness. He did not make the error, either, of ignoring cynicism, gloom, and destructiveness, or their breeding place in the dank reaches of the human spirit. The intention of this book has not been to level down and simplify him to the likeness of a poetic Rowley, to endorse the notion of a medieval, rustic, insular, and conformist Shakespeare, a bland, *gemütlich* Shakespeare—one who "boosted" but did not "knock" or, in the words of a current lyric, was as corny as Kansas in August, as wholesome as blueberry pie. He was an optimist and idealist; but, in defiance of the system of labeling currently in vogue, he was not therefore stupid and blind. There is no mood or idea in the select drama that is unexpressed in his. This is not to say that he combines and balances. Rather he reduces to proportion, places in perspective. He assimilates and transforms the thought of his antagonists at the same time that he excels their art. He has a *reigning* wit. He *subdues*.

To recognize this sign of *entraînement* in Shakespeare's plays is neither to convert them into sermons nor to trace their quality to pique generated in a situation of petty literary rivalry. Shakespeare's values were those of many people, including groundlings who, in Hamlet's not unimpeachable judgment, were capable only of inexplicable dumb shows and noise. The voice that we listen to is the voice of more than one man; it is the voice of a culture in growth. The notion sometimes advanced, that Shakespeare was skeptical at heart about the worth of the values he expressed, but willing to sing for a price to anybody's tune, should tax the patience of all who have read his plays. No imaginable degree of genius would have enabled him to effect so superlative a deception. That he was concerned with their effective manipulation more than with the values themselves *at the moment of manipulation* is true but irrelevant. He was an artist and therefore a manipulator. But for his success to be what it was, there had to be the antecedent sincerity. Shakespeare wanted to say what his audience wanted him to say.

If anyone can ask how an artist of the intelligence postulated above could have accepted the values described in this book—so cribbed and "Victorian," so bourgeois and grubby—the fault lies in its author's limited powers of exposition and failure to stimulate the reader's own powers of abstraction and imaginative extension. The values have been treated, with inevitable crudity, only as reflected in areas of human relationship so broad and elementary as to be *always* prominent in *every* play. The defects in the method should not be construed as defects in the plays—or in the values. A great poet could accept the values because they were great values. They represented a synthesis of such products of Judaic and Hellenistic philosophy as had shown the highest power of survival—literally, the best that had been known and thought in the world. Nothing since Shakespeare's time has impeached the evidence of an ordered universe, however more diffidently it must now be defined, or of the superiority of an ethic of love. If such evidence is ever forthcoming, Shakespeare's plays will cease to give pleasure. Pleasure of a kind is conceivable in an amoral chaos, but not such as derives from the contemplation of things to be won or lost, accepted or rejected, rejoiced over or mourned. The preciousness of the moral order is most exalted in a play like *King Lear*, where it appears to be in such dreadful jeopardy; but Shakespeare's universe is always one where there is something to be happy or sad *about*—which is to say that it is the universe of the great philosophers.

One is tempted in a summing up to follow the analogic patterns of thought of the Elizabethans themselves. Shakespeare's man, like his universe, is no accident, but something worthy of a Creator. Sometimes he is the beauty of the world, sometimes harsh, jangled, out of tune, sometimes the tool of falsehood and malice, but never, even at his worst, the generation of slime. Shakespeare's family is also a microcosm, and presumed to be the school of those sentiments of loyalty and kindness which must extend into other human relationships if organized society is to exist. However inadequately they may sometimes fill the role, the parents in the plays view themselves as creators, not "breeders." His norm of marriage is the precise reverse of the loveless, faithless, sterile arrangement of Mr. Eliot's Edward and Lavinia Chamberlayne,[7] which is now proffered to us as reasonably satisfactory provided the principals can be reconciled to its meanness. Shakespeare's political assumptions appeal less than do any of his others to what is best in modern idealism. He wrote for a theatre of a nation, not a theatre of the world, and for a society that was far from classless; yet he faced in the direction of what was in his day (and is in ours) the future, and in his conception of the community there is a breadth of sympathy unequaled among the writers for the theatre of the urban clique.

We should hesitate to patronize the values expressed in Shakespeare's plays even when the mode of their application seems no longer relevant. His sexual code threatens to succeed his political code as chief barrier to the sympathy or understanding of modern readers. It must be pointed out that the first, like the second, was of enormous utility in his day, when science was not yet competing with self-control to reduce the incidence of venereal disease and bastardy. Happily a less limited defense is available. Nothing seems rarer in human experience than sustained Paphian joy, as signaled by the curious fact that our missioners of continence are exceeded in grimness only by our missioners of incontinence. Defective sexual codes seem to be less threatening to human composure than the absence of codes, or doubts about their nature and validity. To the sociological observer, contemporary literature seems schizoid, revealing a tortured oscillation between the attraction and repulsion of sexual license.[8] This is precisely the quality evident in the plays of those dramatists, notably Marston, who three and a half centuries ago stood in contrast to Shakespeare, with the result, then as now, an impaired artistry.

However sincere the intentions of the artist, the overtly erotic is resistant to discipline, providing a kind of stimulus so certain of response that the part played by art becomes indiscriminable and consequently unimportant. In those novels now edging competitively forward into formerly unoccupied terrain, the authors seem aware that the non-exploratory portions are likely to seem tedious, and, acting unconsciously upon a Blackfriars precedent, they fill such interstices with the grotesque and brutal; or they convert betrayal into a comic theme and portray the petty adulteries of petty people with a quiet equanimity that passes for irony. It is difficult to assess the quality of these works abstracted from the element of the sensational, more difficult still to analyze their artistic impact. The erotic and non-erotic are far less easy to distinguish than for legislative purposes we assume; and in tranquil reflections upon certain works ideas of approval are oddly interrupted by moments of doubt, and even sensations of hypocrisy. The restrictive code with which Shakespeare's art conformed—or perhaps we should say the code which it confirmed—never acted as a blight upon his plays. They neither lack joy nor suppress essential truths about human sexuality; rather they gain in authenticity by the manner in which, in them, the sexuality is diffused. At the same time the code militated against the production of erotica, to which our ultimate objections may be more intellectual than moral. Art may be no more than a substitute for something else, but great art must be at least a substitute for something reasonably complex.

That Shakespeare drew strength from sharing with his audience a high estimation of values great in their implication and not indefensible even in the contemporary mode of their application will probably be conceded. The objection may be raised that the drama of his rivals has been misrepresented, with an appeal to prejudice lurking in the very use of the weighted word "coterie." The use of the word will presently be defended, but there will be no claim to a spirit of detachment. Such claims are illusory. Especially in walking over old battlefields, one has no alternative to taking himself along. As one reads the Prologue to *Cynthia's Revels* and reflects that *Old Fortunatus*, *The Shoemaker's Holiday*, *Sir John Oldcastle*, *The Two Angry Women of Abington*, *Henry V*, *Julius Caesar*, and *As You Like It* were among the plays composed for the "vulgar and adult'rate brain" in the public theatres just before Jonson withdrew from them, one may feel his hackles rise even though it amuses him that they should. This voice of the past seems to merge with voices of the present, passing similarly obtuse, pretentious, indeed heinous judgments upon *The Pickwick Papers* because it is not *Hard Times*, upon *Vanity Fair* because it is not *Daniel Deronda*, upon Housman because he is not Hopkins, or other things loved well, however unwisely. The voice sounds harsh, ungenial, indeed somehow terrifying, because it offers always other things rather than more things, and questions the right of choice. For each poet celebrated, some other poet must needs be slain. No doubt there is hazard in carrying back into the past claustrophobic irritations induced by the constricting present; but this study has proceeded by demonstration, and it is with the facts of this demonstration that students of literature are invited to reckon. The issues may be indicated by an attempt to answer certain inevitable questions.

Does not human nature and human experience present us with a mixed landscape, swamps and jungles as well as lovely woods and uplands, deserts as well as fertile valleys, depths as well as heights, and is not all of it worthy of expression in art? Granted that a few rare artists may be able to keep the whole landscape in view, does it follow that there must be no other kind—the ones, let us say, who can memorialize permanently a single aspect, even though it be a desert or a swamp? The answer is that of course there must be such artists. This question sounds nothing hostile because it admits a hierarchy in the realm of art not determined exclusively by the qualities required of works for mere admission into that realm. The only objection that could be raised to it is that it is not always asked ingenuously. The plea that certain things should also be expressed often comes from those who consider them as the only things worth expressing, and who claim, distractingly, for particular works a symbolic wholeness which these works actually do not have. If Donne had written plays, he would have written for Blackfriars and Paul's, and in the denigrating fashion of their school. The existence of such plays, provided they displayed the genius of Donne's verse satires, would tend, in the school of literary criticism now dominant, to reduce Shakespeare to the rank of a mere Spenserian, assuming, of course, that Shakespeare's "limitations" were conceded. This would be unfortunate. Donne, in later life, would have wished to see the plays destroyed—a contingency also that can be contemplated only with distress. To make distinctions is not to advocate exclusions. That which is desert art and no more is, generically, neither better nor worse than that which is garden art and no more. No degree of authenticity, fervor, or technical excellence can lift it to the highest level. This is only to affirm that art is a part of life. The critic as specialist is prone to rank works of art exclusively according to those qualities which he is peculiarly equipped to evaluate, or, in defense of his presumed prerogative, to overestimate his ability to detect philosophical as well as aesthetic values. He forgets, to his peril, that he is less strategically placed to evaluate works of art as a part of life than are those for whom life is more than art. Returning to that microcosm of life and art with which the present book has been concerned, I maintain that the popular drama came nearer than the coterie drama to being literature of the full landscape, and that the public theatres were the only possible nursery in his time for the kind—the greater kind—of artist that Shakespeare was.

But, one may ask, does not the very method of using one school of artists as foil for another, especially when the other includes such an imposing person as Shakespeare, tend to reduce it not to a lower place but to no place at all? Are not these somewhat bullying tactics? And was not the achievement of the coterie dramatists such as to elevate them at least above popular hacks, and had they not something more to offer Shakespeare than mere stimulus to persevere in a different way of writing? There is justice in these objections. It may be pointed out, however, that much of the body of this study that reads like judgment contains only description. The ethical bias of everyone is so strong that the mere demonstration that one thing adheres to a certain principle while another does not will sound like a summary condemnation of the second. It may also be pointed out that ample grounds have been provided for anyone predisposed to condemn the popular drama as consisting of "musty moral types" or, in more modish terms, afflicted with "dissociation of sensibility." No one is obliged to subscribe to the particular hierarchy in the realm of art implied in the present study, or to admire in Shakespeare anything but his skill. The statement that perhaps it was part of Shakespeare's "special eminence to have expressed an inferior philosophy in the greatest poetry"[9] displays at least the virtue of a moment of candor. Provided one recognizes what Shakespeare's philosophy is, he has the right to express his own value judgment upon it. More debatable is the right to assume that poetry can be better than its content. It can, of course, be worse.

Concerning the literary achievement of the coterie writers and its influence upon Shakespeare, a great deal could be said. The scope of the study has prevented the pursuit of ramifications and the preservation of nice distinctions. Jonson has been placed with the coterie writers even though he wrote nearly as often for the popular troupes, and that is not unjust, because his inclinations and influence linked him with their group; but it is unjust to associate writers so disparate in sincerity and literary gift as Jonson and Sharpham merely because they had qualities in common. Jonson has many of Sharpham's defects, but Sharpham has none of Jonson's qualities. This is the fault of the historical approach and can scarcely be atoned for by apologies. There is also distortion in grouping writers so disparate in personality and period as Edwardes, Lyly, and Marston. If we should visualize a simon-pure popular dramatist and a simon-pure coterie dramatist, we should see that the difference between them varies within the Elizabethan age itself. In Edwardes's time they would have looked upon each other's work with mutual interest; in Lyly's, with mutual condescension; and not until Marston's, with mutual antipathy. From the beginning the popular drama was both the more indigenous and the more broadly affirmative; but only as time passed did the difference assume the nature of issues, with the dichotomy so clear as to justify the sort of schematization presented in the present book. The widening fissure is symptomatic of a widening fissure in the English social structure itself.

The writers of the private theatres performed an important service in carrying on the earlier academic tendency to import and experiment, and in enriching the language of drama with the substance of literary allusion. Like the university writers generally, they helped to provide Shakespeare with his education, and he may have owed something to Marston as he certainly owed something to Lyly. The fact remains that he did more with what he received than could those direct beneficiaries of university training from whom he received it. This is one of the times when the fairest flowers grew from seeds that blew over the garden wall—a concession we may surely make without seeming to join the forces of anti-intellectualism. Every human achievement begins with a heritage, but no institution or segregate group of men can establish exclusive claims as custodians or heirs. In no era may education be identified with particular institutions, or cultivation with particular classes. There has been an effort ever since Shakespeare's eminence has been recognized, no less determined because usually unconscious, to free him from the odium of being what he actually was, a man of the people and a common actor—or rather to appropriate him, to dub him with a little elegance, to steer him into the orbit of that noble lord or this member of the cognoscenti. It is a saddening phenomenon, exposing the gap between those things to which all pay lip service and those others by which many are more truly impressed—a little like trying to add to the beauty of the Gettysburg Address by wistfully surmising that Lincoln was acquainted with, or even related (by marriage on his mother's side) to the friend of an eastern banker. No one has ever demonstrated how it would have aided Shakespeare as artist to possess a noble patron; and, because he did less dedicating than almost any other writer of his time, there seems to be little reason why anyone should try.

So far as Shakespeare's affiliations are concerned, no one who has read the coterie plays extensively will regret the distinction *in kind* of Shakespeare's. The coterie plays are more *literary* on the average than the popular plays, but they are not on the average superior as dramatic art or poetry. Most of them are overwritten and under-imagined. Few penetrate modern anthologies, and none would have a chance on the modern stage, except *Eastward ·Ho, Epicoene,* and *The Knight of the Burning Pestle*—all distinguished by the infiltration of materials standard in the rival repertory. There were things the coterie writers could do superbly well, but they were small things. Even a minor writer like Barry displayed genius in devising what may be called the socio-sexual joke. When one of his harlots is described as possessing "a little thing her friends [parents] have left her, which with putting to best use and often turning, yields her a poor living,"[10] the delightfully smug phrases link usury and prostitution so that they become virtually the same thing. Shakespeare's joke, linking war and prostitution—"to serve bravely is to come limping off, you know; to come off the breach with his pike bent bravely, and to surgery bravely"[11]—seems boisterous and countrified by comparison. But Barry, like the rest, was cripplingly limited in imaginative range. Neither he nor any of his fellows, including the greatly endowed Ben Jonson, could write anything like Imogen's response to the news that her absent husband thinks her false to his bed.[12] Neither could Shakespeare have written it, except for something not devised by himself, an established ideal and the class of sentiment it had attached to itself. The popular writers tried to do many more things than the coterie writers. Shakespeare did these many things well. Ultimately there was nothing proffered by the rival group that he could profitably learn.

There remains the possibility that he was forced to learn, even against his inclinations, for he was sharer in a commercial enterprise as well as a creative artist. His company was, after all, the one which appropriated Marston's *The Malcontent,* bought *The*

Revenger's Tragedy, and finally acquired both Blackfriars and most of its writers. No problem could be more fascinating than Shakespeare's situation during the few years preceding his retirement, and it should be discussed some time with the refinement it deserves. Two other large public theatres were bidding for the custom of that diminishing portion of the London citizenry still impervious to the rising tide of sectarian opposition to the stage. The "select" audience, increasing in size, was clearly the one with which the destiny of the drama would presently reside. What was Shakespeare to do? It would be unfortunate if the old autobiographical fallacy (that we owe the greatest plays ever written to their author's being "in the depths") should merely yield place to another; but it must be pointed out that the years 1599–1608 were those in which the theatrical situation in London would have placed Shakespeare most *upon his mettle*. It is the period preeminently in which, in the view presented a few pages back, we see in his plays when compared with those of the rival repertory a commentary upon the negations of that repertory, and a species of conquest by assimilation and transformation. After 1608 Shakespeare's company was consolidating a different kind of conquest. Shakespeare may have recognized that his role had changed, that the tactical victory of his company was prophetic of the end of his kind of drama. The decreased strenuosity of his last plays, the valedictory quality that marks them, may reflect this new situation. There is no change in their fiber, no true similarity to the romances of Fletcher, which are distinguished by the substitution of ornament for fiber and of sophistic rhetoric for moral feeling. Florizel and Perdita, Ferdinand and Miranda, are not the bric-a-brac that Fletcher was fashioning for connoisseurs. Fletcher's Euphrasia stands in about the same relationship to Shakespeare's Perdita or Miranda as Dryden's Almanzor to Marlowe's Tamburlaine. It would be less easy to demonstrate that Shakespeare abandoned the popular archetype than that he killed it by perfecting it. At any rate his last plays are its perfect monument. Twenty-five years were yet to pass before the always hopeful Heywood would be saying,

And what's now out of fashion, who is't can tell,
But it may come in fashion and suit well?[13]

or Tatham, that Fletcher might still look fair on a dark night,

But Shakespeare, the plebeian driller, was
Founder'd in's *Pericles*, and must not pass.[14]

But even by 1611 there must have been quite a few of the King's
Company patrons who were saying that Shakespeare was well
enough—for a *country author*.

A most pertinent question remains. Has not the present book
confused literary genres? Were not those stigmatized as "coterie"
writers simply satirists, whose values were the same as Shakespeare's,
but who defended them in a different way? One hesitates to respond with a categorical no, lest he seem deficient in the spirit of
charity. That their values were the same as Shakespeare's is, in a
sense, true, because, in last analysis, there are no others. If put to
the question, each writer would have endorsed the whole schedule
and argued that his plays did likewise. What they failed to do was
to display any faith that the values did or could prevail in the lives
of men, or any real concern that they should. Such writers can
scarcely be described as decadents. They neither ignored nor repudiated the modes of thinking and acting that insure the survival of
the race. They may perhaps be described as predecadents. The concession that a cause is lost is an invitation to relax. The logical
sequel is to join in the final indulgences, to savor the faint fine odors
of decay.

We become aware, as we read, of a number of impulses more
operative than reforming zeal. One was to take the line of least re-
sistance: it *was* difficult not to write satire. Another was to pro-
claim, with the perennial glee of the immature, the discovery that
mankind does not always practice what it preaches, that there are
differences between appearance and reality, as if previously none
had been perceived. A third was to abrogate the force of certain
principles, with their tiresome restrictions, by showing them canceled in the world at large. This last is the gravest of charges as well
as the most difficult to substantiate; but when we find that all the

vines are eaten we suspect that the little foxes have been about. We must be thinking, of course, of *impulses,* of currents in the air set in motion by a complex of forces, not of the individuals who yielded to them. As men, the coterie writers presumably were neither better nor worse than the popular writers, indeed were sometimes the same. Jonson was a person of somewhat dissolute habits, but there was integrity at his core. Chapman's devotion to literature was almost saintly. Marston made a very fine parson for all we know to the contrary. And Middleton seems to have been just a writer trying to get along.

These impulses, these ghosts moving about in the drama of Blackfriars and Paul's, cannot be exorcised by the incantational powers of the word "satire," as the authors themselves so desperately assumed. Satire of a kind is abundant also in the popular plays, but, as in Shakespeare, it is directed at such things as the pomposity of a Malvolio, not the brutality of a Cornwall. Criminal lusts, greed, cruelty, and treachery are no laughing matters, and a strange insensitivity afflicts writers who assume that they are. The best defense of the coterie plays is the assumption that they are purposely dehumanized, that the playwrights were dramatizing the psychomachy with the virtues expunged, a dance of the deadly sins for those who fancied comic ballet. The trouble is that, as comic ballet, the plays do not come off. The artists are not sufficiently in control, there are too many inadvertences. One of the most remarkable things about the plays is the indication of compulsive factors in their creation. The authors attack more than they set out to attack, and expose the automatic nature of their responses: the brawniness of the vice we can attribute to conscious design, but not the puniness of the virtue.

The theatre of the nation was a good place, and the drama it fostered was good. We can cite titles and quote passages to prove that the popular plays were bombastic, bigoted, sentimental, banal, formless, shoddy, or the like; but to this body of drama as a whole, even with Shakespeare's contribution removed, the epithets cannot be made to stick. The marvel is that anything so casually and plentifully produced could have achieved the artistic and spiritual level that it did. The poor plays—and there were plenty of them—were not poor by popular demand. It is not easy to be a popular artist, and even in those gifted times not every aspirant was able to come up to the mark. Often the dramatists did not write as well as they could. When one was doing part of a play for part of a fee, and dealing with a landlord who was serving as factor for a company of actors, the ultimate consumer might well be cheated: the evil of absenteeism takes manifold forms. But when the maker must face the user of the thing he has made, only reluctantly will he use bad materials or scant his work. Shakespeare escaped one kind of temptation—he stood in plain view while his wares were delivered to the people of England; but another kind of temptation was always there: he could, without immediate sacrifice of prosperity or prestige, have relied upon sheer cleverness. The opportunities of an amoral commercialism were as available then as now—the temptation to supply the minimum quality at the maximum price, with one's fellow men viewed simply as customers. That Shakespeare never succumbed must be referred to his manhood—his sense of identity with and responsibility to those thousands of other men who honored him with their trust.

The place which the Elizabethan coterie reserved for itself was not so good as the place from which it withdrew, and we have something to learn from that fact. What follows, relating so indirectly to the quality of Shakespearean drama, may seem impertinent; but the examples of history cannot be relied upon to operate by chance, and in the cultural conflicts of our day there has been too great a tendency to let games go by default.

Withdrawal is an error in every age, and no age has been more confidently addicted to it than our own. It has become a commonplace that the best art is the art of the few. Such may possibly be the case; but we are nagged by the misgiving that the art of the few, although perhaps the best now available, may still not be very good. We want from our times more than a choice between the insipid and the indigestible. The problem of distinguishing coterie literature has been complicated by the prodigious increase in the population. A novel can now sell several hundred thousand copies, and still be coterie literature. Sixty-two million Americans each week were purchasing screen tickets in 1949,[15] while another group, probably as large as the total population of Shakespeare's England, felt qualified to view their lowly pleasures with condescension or contempt. Our coteries form a pattern of concentric circles, with the innermost circle occupied by a mere handful of men. Neither the superiority nor the inferiority of the art which pleases the sixty-two million may be assumed, or the art of the six thousand, the six hundred, or the six. The test of crude numbers is invalid, whether the number serving as criterion be large or small.

Shakespeare was far from being the greatest writer of his day if we apply the test of crude numbers. Arthur Dent's *The Plain Man's Path-Way to Heaven* appeared in the same year as *Hamlet,* and won a score of readers for every reader and spectator of Shakespeare's play. Why then, we may ask, has such significance been attached in the present study to the size of Shakespeare's audience? Has the entire discussion been irrelevant? Or should we lay aside *Hamlet* and devote our days to *The Plain Man's Path-Way to Heaven?* The answer would seem to be obvious enough. The size of Shakespeare's audience has been discussed in relation to that of other dramatists writing for other London theatres. "Popular" and "coterie" are relative terms, deriving their meaning from each other as used in appropriate contexts. "Literature," if taken to signify both plays and devotional tracts, is too indiscriminate a word to supply an appropriate context. So also may be "drama," since works in the same large category may still be incommensurable; but in using the words "popular" and "coterie" we commit no injustice if we listen carefully for our cue. Although the plays at Blackfriars and Paul's may not, in a strict sense, have been commensurable with the plays at the Fortune and Globe, their authors, in assuming superiority, implied that they were. In the same fashion the modern writer for the élite takes the initiative and defines the field of conflict with his first contemptuous allusion to the art of the "mass audience." To issue the challenge is always tempting, because, on the basis of the qualities offered for comparison, superiority can usually be demonstrated and victories easily won. But it is also dangerous, because a wider range of qualities is bound ultimately to be invoked.

Shakespeare is still occasionally claimed as a coterie poet, but only among the badly informed, who have heard rumors of his being a "King's man" or having something to do with the "private theatre" at Blackfriars. The error is more prevalent in respect to Chaucer and Milton. Each had a small audience, and the test of crude numbers is confidently applied, with an *a priori* assumption brought forth in the guise of a conclusion based upon facts, that the audience was small because the quality of the writing was high. But both were recognized as the greatest narrative poets of their centuries by those who had access to their work, including literary rivals and political enemies. The circulation of literary works must always be interpreted in the light of contemporary levels of literacy, opportunities for leisure, and the like. Bunyan's *Pilgrim's Progress* was accessible to much larger numbers than *Paradise Lost*, and attracted those numbers; but the significant thing is not that it outsold the greater work, but that it was not itself outsold by anything artistically inferior within its class. The general public, or at least that sector of it with any susceptibility to art at all, chooses the best art that is placed within its reach, as the Shakespearean instance indicates.

Chroniclers of English literature have found it convenient to recognize a royal line of authors, and chapter headings such as "The Age of Chaucer" or "The Period of Pope" are familiar to us all. There are mostly interregna before the late sixteenth century and disputed successions after the early nineteenth, but at least from Spenser to Wordsworth the line appears to be both continuous and fixed. If we inquire how these regnal figures came to be chosen, we discover a process of nomination and election, with the first function performed by some sector of contemporary society and the second by posterity. None was unappreciated in his own day, or appreciated only by what may properly be called a coterie. Each was recognized as the best of those doing the kind of thing that he was doing. Naturally the recognition was accorded by those who had access to and interest in that kind of thing. It remained for posterity to decide if that kind of thing was the best and most characteristic of its age.

In the literary world of our own day, we witness a more than usually determined effort by a critical élite to usurp the role of posterity—to tell us not only which authors do certain things best, but also what those best things are, to pronounce on both degree of quality and value of kind, to nominate and elect. The claims of the critics have been put in explicit terms when, in answer to the question of who are the arbiters of literary greatness, the answer is given that the arbiters are those who say that they are, the critics of conviction, the ones who give the most sustained and serious attention to literary matters. The answer is enticingly simple, but it draws no authority from history. Among Elizabethan dramatists Jonson won the suffrage of the kind of men described. Actually these men were right about the quality of Jonson's work, but wrong, in the opinion of posterity, about the value of its kind as compared with Shakespeare's kind. Critics, and especially those in vociferous coteries, have not always been right even on matters of quality, and the annals of nomination are strewn with names like Cartwright, Waller, "Ossian," and Erasmus Darwin, once hailed as incomparable and immortal. The record of the British government in selecting poets laureate has been somewhat spotty, but scarcely more so than the record of the virtuosos. Certain modern works, indubitably distinguished, are accusingly cited as examples of neglect by the general public. They are called "unpopular" with the word given the accent of an accolade. But most of these works are not really unpopular; rather they are non-existent in the popular domain. To pass upon their quality is the prerogative of those interested in their kind. The intention here is not to indulge in the cheap irony of saying they are good books for those who like books of that kind, but to define the agencies of significant judgment. To pass upon the value of their kind is the prerogative of neither those who attend to them nor those who do not, but the prerogative of posterity.

Literary historiography is a fairly new thing, and its processes have had a confusing, sometimes corrupting, influence upon literary criticism. Critics have been induced to treat the literature of their own generation as if it were the literature of the ages, with themselves its appointed historians, commissioned to distinguish between "major" and "minor" writers and to designate the immortals. The works most favored are those presenting at once the problems usually associated with a "classic." If the work requires collation of texts, identification of allusions, and interpretation of symbols, the presumption that it itself is a "classic" appears to be very strong, and its author is accorded symposia of criticism and books of homage while still in the prime of life. Major trends and major countertrends in literature are traced to separate works by the same genius, and full-scale revivals are conducted for others unjustly neglected for perhaps a decade. The rites of birth, confirmation, death, and exhumation are practically synchronous. The bulk of the large body of criticism inspired by the favored works consists of explication. We are apt to be misled by something that, in the art of prestidigitation, is known as "misdirection" and assume that the ore of meaning extracted by such painful processes can be nothing less than gold.

The situation is not one at which we can afford to be amused. The imposing reputations do not result primarily from the foibles of critics professionally eager to cope with "difficulty." The favored works have in common a much more portentous quality. It is easy to visualize a composite figure formed of those authors nominated and incontinently elected as the monumental artists of the past half-century. We can even supply a title for his composite masterpiece—*The Epic of the Waif.* It expresses both a yearning for communion and a conviction of the illusory character of such signs of communion as appear among men. It wrestles with disunity; yet to unifying ideals it displays indifference, and of appearances of their efficacy it is often derisive. It formalizes more crudely than masterpieces should. Human destiny is sometimes viewed as an epic conflict between *Künstler* and *Bürger*, with the first of these fell opposites about to perish before overwhelming odds although the second appears not to have received notification that the battle has been joined. It is at once the most plaintive of works and the most arrogant. The entire population of some capital city of the world will be summarily dismissed as paralyzed, lost, or dead. The work is assumed to have achieved spiritual stature when mankind is not dismissed, but is pitied or patronized. The work may appear in the form of memoirs, thinly disguised autobiography, symbolic parody in verse or prose, tales or lyrics linked by motif, verse drama, or even realistic—sometimes proletarian—novel. If the last, there hovers about the hero an aura of vagrancy. Sympathy is extended to the disinherited masses, except for the particular members who happen to be the hero's kinsmen; and ideas of salvation are linked to sexual activity, provided it is athletic, rebellious, or at least unrelated to procreation.

The defect of *The Epic of the Waif* is less the theme than the spiritual poverty of the treatment. Loneliness is an ancient theme in literature, and its treatment, usually muted, has often been very beautiful. We remember Ruth amidst the alien corn, precious friends lost in death's dateless night, haunting images from a hundred poets. Loneliness is the most exclusively human of the forms of suffering, the most closely related to the capacity for love; but it loses its beauty and great promise if treated frivolously or petulantly, if reduced to frustration, if expressed as the plaint of the persecuted or the whine of the rejected. Instead of a universal emotion shared, we get an individual *malaise* communicated. The twentieth century master fails to effect the proper transmutation: he seems to be too obsessed, or to have too much personally at stake. He is more literary than the masters of the past, in the sense that he is more exclusively literary. The masters of the past we picture in various roles, sometimes associating them with their works—Chaucer riding to Canterbury, Shakespeare musing over the skull of Yorick, Milton lecturing Adam and Eve; or else with their contemporaries—Pope scheming against his foes, Johnson dogmatizing at the Cheshire Cheese. But this twentieth century master we can picture only writing. Literature is his refuge, and by literature he seems possessed. He is faced not toward his listeners but toward his own pages, and the rigidity with which he holds this posture is construed as integrity, as devotion to Art. That he should be either an exile or a recluse is, of course, *de rigueur*.

If this composite work by this composite master truly expresses the essence of human experience in the twentieth century, then the critics are truly speaking for posterity, and a hiatus such as has never existed before now exists between the best art and society. But the affirmation that such is the case does not make it so. Twentieth century man may not be having precisely the experience the critics think that he should, and may be finding his mood more honestly expressed in quite different products of his time. Such a demurrer entered on behalf of ordinary people is apt to be dismissed as irrelevant, because it is only the élite that count, or because ordinary men are too paralyzed, lost or dead to recognize despair when they have it. It is difficult to pin belletristic prophets down. If we complain of the "message" of *The Epic of the Waif*, our attention is directed to its technique, its virtuosity often truly remarkable; but, if any feature of this technique evokes from us a word of dissatisfaction, we are soon made aware of our callow imperviousness to the "message." The literature of despair has been exalted in the realms both of social dynamics and of religion, and only brazenness can maintain that it has not. Nothing conceived of as a moral force can claim immunity from moral judgment, or refuse to abide our question.

On those occasions when the twentieth century master has pronounced directly upon social and philosophical matters—as he has done on a remarkable number, from the nature of the New Deal to the nature of worship—he has revealed an almost childish impudence or naïveté. He might still, as an artist, be intuitively wise, but we dare not take the fact for granted. Our problems are so complex that we need light from every quarter, and must not rely solely upon sects of poets, novelists, and their interpreters in the reviews. Impulses of negation are perennial, and the current crop was too early in evidence to be traced to the impact of depressions, inflations, and world wars. It makes an enormous difference to us whether particular works of art are a diagnosis of a diseased society or a symptom of a diseased sector. When we ask if certain forms of contemporary literature are not dangerously devaluating us, inviting us to lower our heads for the ax, we are told to remember Dachau and Buchenwald. It is because we remember them that we ask the question. Too often we have heard someone, with the heroic thoroughness of the sedentary, affirm that it is time for the holocaust, accepting *The Epic of the Waif* as his evidence, and its creator as a new scourge of God. A nontheoretical holocaust would, as likely as not, take the form of a world-wide distribution of gas chambers.

It is the scent of bigotry about the idols of the modern coterie that is most disturbing. It is a scent wholly missing from such artists as Shakespeare. Universal, many-sided, protean as he may be, there is still one role in which Shakespeare cannot be conceived—the role of the Grand Inquisitor. It is not only because he is compassionate, humorous, intellectually unassuming, but because in his treatment of human beings he declines to categorize. Even his mobs, supposed evidence of his limited tolerance, break up into this man, that man, the other man; this one cruel, that one stupid, the other merely comic. Such mobs are more encouraging to contemplate than a sentimentally conceived but undifferentiated "common people." The most ominous feature of our coterie literature is its unabashed categorizing—its burghers with stunted souls, its masses disinherited or otherwise, its classes educable or uneducable, its whole populations of cities paralyzed, lost, or dead. Centuries of heroic moral endeavor were required to advance the idea that abstractions are only abstractions, freemen and slaves, conquerors and conquered, masses, classes, populations—and that only the individual is real. Whether the underlying impulse is to annihilate or to save, there is something sinister about the literary emergence of this new abstraction—this Everyman named Futility.

Recent claims for the centrality of Art derive from the notion that it fills the supposed vacuum left by the supposed recession of religious faith. Foolhardy though it is to combat a cliché, we may question whether there is really less religious faith now than formerly, or a decrease in its quality. No generalization so vast is susceptible to proof. The quality of spiritual states is difficult to assess. It is easy to confuse the comforts of torpor with the consolations of faith, as when we brood over the supposed state of grace of the peasant of old; but this peasant's descendant is more likely to be literate, and although literacy may be evaluated (now or in the sixteenth century) only as an implement of economic or political control, still control by the word is not inferior to control by starvation or the whip. It is also less predictable in effect. When Caliban says,

> You taught me language, and my profit on't
> Is, I know how to curse,[16]

his words may be given a dreadful modern significance; but language brings Caliban more than ability to curse. He uses it to describe the wonders of his island, and, at the end, to announce his discovery that a drunkard is not a god. This is no place for generalizations about what modern man is, or what properly expresses him. We need only recognize the *possibility* that his indifference to the literary qualities of *The Epic of the Waif* may be related to his wisdom in rejecting its kind. More germane to the present discussion, we must recognize that the critics have been exercising judgment in an area where literary criticism of the past has failed to demonstrate its competence, and have been evaluating kind as well as quality. In the last analysis, their pronouncements are not literary criticism but sectarian doctrine.

The robes of priesthood are always imposing, especially to the bewildered young, and we should be ever on the alert to scrutinize those who assume them. Doctrine must be examined as doctrine, and estimates made of its efficacy by observation of its fruits. What if the fruits are only withdrawal—and further withdrawal—and still further withdrawal? Compared with the men of letters who have withdrawn into the inner sanctum of our culture, the tiniest of the concentric circles, such old coterie playwrights as Jonson, Marston, and Chapman were virtually street singers. The intellectual and spiritual superiority of these men is far from self-evident. Some have archaic notions of leadership and assume that contact with the ones to be led is unnecessary, that all will be accomplished through an exchange of communiqués among the high command; some are sick within, with literature as their private therapy or private vengeance; some are deficient in creative strength and move toward a hypothetical center where there is only self and therefore no competition; most are categorizers, convinced that attempts to reach any but the few mean a debasement of art because all but the few are debased.

We might question whether, with such an assumption, anyone would have the right to address his energies toward art at all, or to anything but practical measures for eradicating so hideous a disease. The least we must demand is a precise statement of the nature of the evidence.

It is our duty to ask what there was, in such various times and under such various conditions, to make predictable the emergence of the Judaic and Homeric poets, or a Chaucer, a Shakespeare, a Cervantes, a Molière, a Wordsworth, or a Dickens. Their artistic accomplishment still beggars our attempts to praise it, and yet all were speaking to an expanding, not a contracting, circle of men. One thing their times and places had in common was not being our time and place; but to accept this as the great advantage is to embrace the mustiest of all fallacies. The only common denominator was the existence of a human race to which to speak, and on such a basis even the most doleful can scarcely claim that our times are excluded. If Shakespeare had begun with assumptions about the incapacity of the audience available to him, we should not have his plays. It is puerile to say that he lived in "happier times." Counsels of despair, as this study has tried to demonstrate, fell upon his ears as insistently as upon any poet's today. The great artist who appears among us will not begin with the assumption that the values subtending great art are dead, or that the ability to apprehend them, although once dispersed among men, has recently flickered out. Great art must be now, as it has always been, primarily an act of faith.

Optimistic words in literary circles are fashionably regarded as a solecism, but our situation is not truly so hopeless. Great art may be germinating in unsuspected places. Only a decade before Shakespeare's plays began to appear, Philip Sidney was speaking eloquently of the bankruptcy of English drama, dwelling especially upon the defects of those very themes and techniques that Shakespeare was destined to glorify. Sidney was guilty of errors in analysis —he traced true weaknesses to false causes—but his was a magnanimous spirit; and he was incapable of the ultimate error, of attributing the poverty of art to the degradation of his people. His strictures were positive: all would be well if the dramatists would observe the unities and imitate the proper features of *Gorboduc*.

There is a wonderful difference in tone between his essay and the *obiter dicta* of critics similarly placed in our own day when they mention the screen. This newest, most characteristic, complex, and universal art of the twentieth century is still held by all *serious* critics in a kind of quarantine. If Sidney were living to write of the screen, he might follow the usual procedure of judging by the average instead of the best products; but he would not display pride in ignoring the form or withhold prescriptions for its improvement. Elizabethan drama did not need Sidney's prescription, but there was good augury in his solicitude. Some Elizabethan critics, ultimately Ben Jonson among them, modified their conception of the proper nature of dramatic art as a result of Shakespeare's accomplishment. Perhaps they should have been willing to act upon evidence less overwhelming.

In defending the art of the general public, we find much in the world about us to moderate our evangelical zeal. In attacking the art of the coterie, we find some things that give us pause. Our obligation is to "find out the soul of goodness" in all things, but our interim reports must place the emphasis where, according to our lights, the effect will be most beneficial. I am ruefully aware that I myself should have no forum, were there no books for minorities. There must, of course, be art for minorities also—art of experiment, art of dissent. The fact is so obvious that we are apt to view experiment and dissent as ends in themselves. It would be senseless to attack our "little" magazines and our "little" theatres, with their truly essential effort; but it is not senseless to attack the spirit that can render the effort nugatory or destructive. Those engaged in this effort must always remember that they are workers in an arboretum and that the forests and orchards lie elsewhere—must remember also that, in their arboretum, the acorns are not all oaks, the acorns are not all fertile, and the acorns are not all acorns so that infertility is the best we can hope for. Art is great when it establishes contact with significant numbers and kinds of people, and artists are great when deeply aware of their identity with those people and responsibility to them. About conscious exclusiveness there is something niggardly—deadly to the very spirit of creation. When art itself is spiritually arid, indifference to it signals no spiritual aridity. The defense of art must always rest upon the particular merits of particular works, never upon an indictment of mankind. One may say these things without laying claim to a great humanistic spirit, but only to a sense of propriety.

Shakespeare was great because he was worthy of his tradition. It was the tradition of the theatre of the nation, with its impulse to go to the people, and the tradition of Christian humanism, which was lighting up the minds of those people. Shakespeare's tradition was also the age-old tradition of the artist, the creator, the magnanimous and confident giver. In a sense he did bring "caviar to the general"—he withheld nothing from the banquet he spread before them. In the present book a suspicious odor has hung about caviar, but only because of the dubious means by which the piquancy is sometimes achieved, not because of any contempt for the novel, the rich, the rare.

By way of redress, and to make the purpose clear, let me conclude with a tribute to an artist who brings *only* caviar. He is a painter quite unknown to fame. Some years ago he was fascinated by the art of the advanced schools, and ever since has been walking simultaneously in several new directions. Persons whose judgment in such matters cries in the top of mine see no promise in his work. To me it looks only peculiar. Yet each time he shows me a painting, his eyes are aglow with the certainty that I shall recognize a lovely thing. When mine fail to kindle, he turns to his work to puzzle out just what small detail must be wrong. Thus far the only exhibitions open to him have been those on the sidewalks of Washington Square. In season he sits by his paintings in the day, and bundles them up in the evening. So far as I know, he has not made a sale. Still I have never heard him inveigh against the multitude or what it admires. Washington Square is full of paintings and people on June afternoons. He looks at all the former with charity and at all the latter with hope. The man is an eccentric. If he had been born with a little talent, he would be a genius. As it is, I am beginning to think of him, in one sense at least, as an artist in Shakespeare's tradition, and even to detect in his canvases a kind of splendor.

Documentation: Part Two

I. THE DIVINE PLAN

1. A. O. Lovejoy, *The Great Chain of Being*, 1936; H. Craig, *The Enchanted Glass*, 1936; D. Bush, *The Renaissance and English Humanism*, 1939; T. Spencer, *Shakespeare and the Nature of Man*, 1942; E. M. W. Tillyard, *The Elizabethan World Picture*, 1944; F. P. Wilson, *Elizabethan and Jacobean*, 1945; H. Haydn, *The Counter-Renaissance*, 1950.
2. F. Seebohm, *The Oxford Reformers*, p. 3.
3. Hooker, *Ecclesiastical Polity*, in *Works*, ed. Keble, I, 200.
4. *Ibid.*, I, 208.
5. *Ibid.*, I, 215.
6. Erasmus, *The Praise of Folly*, p. 95.
7. *The Merchant of Venice*, V, i, 60–62.
8. W. Creizenach, *English Drama in the Age of Shakespeare*, p. 112.
9. F. R. Johnson, *Astronomical Thought in Renaissance England*, p. 117.
10. M. H. Nicolson, *The Breaking of the Circle*, p. 98.
11. Hooker, *op. cit.*, I, 233.
12. S. Rowley, *When You See Me You Know Me*, sig. G4v.
13. Hooker, *op. cit.*, I, 220.
14. Thomas Starkey, *Dialogue Between Cardinal Pole and Thomas Lupset*, pp. 12–13.
15. Hooker, *op. cit.*, I, 235.
16. E. H. Browne, *An Exposition of the Thirty-nine Articles*, p. 425.
17. *Certain Sermons or Homilies*, pp. 42, 121, 131, 456.
18. *Knack to Know a Knave*, ed. Collier, *Five Old Plays*, p. 411.
19. *Certain Sermons or Homilies*, pp. 363–364.
20. *Ibid.*, p. 418 ("The Coming Down of the Holy Ghost").
21. *Ibid.*, pp. 410–411.
22. S. Freud, *Civilization and Its Discontents*, pp. 70, 81 f.
23. *Certain Sermons and Homilies*, p. 334.
24. Heywood, *II Edward IV*, V, ii.
25. Heywood, *Fortune by Land and Sea*, IV, i.
26. Chettle and Day, *Blind Beggar of Bednal Green* (in Day, *Complete Works*, p. 47).
27. Dekker and Middleton, *I Honest Whore*, Scene xiii, Pearson reprint, p. 90.

28. Day and Wilkins, *The Travels of the Three English Brothers*.
29. Munday *et al.*, *The Book of Sir Thomas More*, V, ii.
30. *Henry V*, IV, i, 317–319.
31. W. Rowley, *A Shoemaker a Gentleman*, II, ii.
32. *The Winter's Tale*, V, iii, 43–44.
33. C. F. T. Brooke, *Shakespeare of Stratford*, pp. 152 ff.
34. Chettle and Munday, *Death of Robert Earl of Huntington*, V, ii.
35. *Richard III*, III, iv, 89; *Hamlet*, V, ii, 47; *Measure for Measure*, II, i, 35.
36. *The Winter's Tale*, I, ii, 419.
37. *King Lear*, II, ii, 180.
38. *Measure for Measure*, II, i, 55–56.
39. *Much Ado About Nothing*, IV, ii, 58–59.
40. *Merry Wives*, II, i, 49–50.
41. *Hamlet*, I, i, 158, 165.
42. *The Winter's Tale*, III, iii, 16–17, 39–41.
43. *Macbeth*, II, iii, 60; *Romeo and Juliet*, IV, iii, 44; Heywood and Webster, *Appius and Virginia*, V, iii; Day, *Humor Out of Breath*, I, i.
44. *A Midsummer Night's Dream*, V, i, 2–22.
45. *All's Well That Ends Well*, II, iii, 1–6.
46. For this debate see, among others, *Macbeth*, I, iii, 83–85, III, iv, 60–68; *King Lear*, I, ii, 132–145, 164; *Othello*, I, iii, 322–337; *All's Well*, I, i, 231–234; *Julius Caesar*, I, ii, 140–151, iii, 28–30; *I Henry IV*, III, i, 154–155; *II Henry IV*, III, i, 80–92; *Henry V*, I, i, 67–69; *Antony and Cleopatra*, II, iii, 32–33.
47. *Richard III*, II, ii, 46; *King John*, III, iv, 27; *Richard III*, V, iii, 62; *Richard II*, V, v, 41; *Romeo and Juliet*, V, iii, 115.
48. Jeremy Collier, *A Short View*, p. 62.
49. *Titus Andronicus*, IV, iii, 90–91.
50. *Twelfth Night*, III, iv, 182; *All's Well*, IV, iii, 270–272.
51. Marston, *The Insatiate Countess*, V, i.
52. *As You Like It*, III, i, 24–33.
53. Heywood, *I Edward IV*, Pearson reprint, p. 47.
54. H. C. Beeching, "On the Religion of Shakespeare," in Shakespeare, *Works*, ed. A. H. Bullen, Vol. X, 349; R. Noble, *Shakespeare's Biblical Knowledge and Use of the Book of Common Prayer*, pp. 48–51.
55. W. J. Grace, "The Cosmic Sense in Shakespearean Tragedy," *Sewanee Rev.*, L (1942), 434.
56. *Measure for Measure*, I, i, 30–36.
57. Chapman, *Bussy D'Ambois*, I, i.
58. See above, p. 92.
59. *The Puritan*, I, i, and ii.
60. N. T. Pratt, Jr., "The Stoic Base of Senecan Drama," *Transactions American Philosophical Assn.*, LXXIX (1948), 1–11.
61. T. S. Eliot, *Selected Essays*, p. 80 ("Seneca in Elizabethan Translation," 1927).

62. *Hamlet*, III, ii, 72–75.
63. *Julius Caesar*, V, i, 100–116.
64. *Ibid.*, V, v, 74–75.
65. Jonson, *Cynthia's Revels*, II, iii.
66. M. Higgins, "The Convention of the Stoic Hero As Handled by Marston," *M.L.R.*, XXXIX (1944), 338–346.
67. Marston, *Antonio and Mellida*, Induction.
68. H. Craig, "Ethics in the Jacobean Drama," *Essays in Dramatic Literature*, ed. Craig, pp. 25–46; R. H. Perkinson, "Nature and the Tragic Hero in Chapman's Bussy Plays," *M.L.Q.*, III (1942), 263–285; R. W. Battenhouse, "Chapman and the Nature of Man," *ELH*, XII (1945), 87–107.
69. W. Farnham, *Shakespeare's Tragic Frontier*, pp. 24–25.
70. Jonson, *Epicoene*, I, i.
71. Jonson, *Poetaster*, III, i.
72. Marston, *Antonio and Mellida*, IV, i.
73. Marston, *Antonio's Revenge*, IV, v.
74. Jonson, *Epicoene*, IV, iv.
75. Marston, *The Malcontent*, III, i. See also *Antonio's Revenge*, II, iii.
76. R. B. McKerrow, in Nashe, *Works*, V, 129–136; A. Walker (writing about Lodge), "The Reading of an Elizabethan," *R.E.S.*, VIII (1932), 264–281; F. L. Schoell, "George Chapman and the Italian Neo-Latinists of the Quattrocento," *M.P.*, XIII (1916), 215–238; E. W. Talbert, "Current Scholarly Works and the 'Erudition' of Jonson's *Masque of Augurs*," *S.P.*, XLIV (1947), 605–624.
77. G. T. Buckley, *Atheism in the English Renaissance*; L. I. Bredvold, "The Naturalism of Donne in Relation to Some Renaissance Traditions," *J.E.G.P.*, XXII (1923), 471–502; E. A. Strathmann, *Sir Walter Raleigh*.
78. A. Harmon, "How Great Was Shakespeare's Debt to Montaigne?" *PMLA*, LVII (1942), 988–1008.
79. Field, *A Woman Is a Weathercock*, IV, i.
80. Lodge, *Wit's Misery*, in *Works*, IV, 16.
81. *Certain Sermons and Homilies*, pp. 330, 337.
82. Printed in C. F. Tucker Brooke, *Life of Marlowe*, pp. 107 f.
83. Nashe, *Summer's Last Will and Testament*, in *Works*, ed. McKerrow, III, 277–278.
84. Marston, *What You Will*, II. See also *Antonio's Revenge*, IV, i.
85. Thomas Starkey, *op. cit.*, p. 17.
86. Hooker, *op. cit.*, p. 239.
87. Marston, *Antonio's Revenge*, IV, i. See also *The Fawn*, I i.
88. Marston, *Antonio and Mellida*, III.
89. Marston, *Jack Drum's Entertainment*, I, i; *Antonio's Revenge*, IV, i.
90. *Richard II*, V, i, 11–17; *King John*, III, i, 211–216.
91. *The Valiant Welshman*, V, i.
92. Field, *Amends for Ladies*, IV, i.
93. *Measure for Measure*, II, iv, 57.

94. Marston, *The Dutch Courtesan*, I, i.
95. *Ibid.*
96. *Ibid.*, I, ii.
97. Jonson, *Cynthia's Revels*, I, v; V, iv.
98. Jonson, *Poetaster*, IV, ix.
99. *Ibid.*, IV, vii.
100. H. Levin, Introduction to Ben Jonson, *Selected Works*, p. 6.
101. E. Wilson, "Morose Ben Jonson," *The Triple Thinkers*.
102. *Il Return from Parnassus*, I, ii.
103. Jonson, *Poetaster*, IV, iii.
104. Dekker and Webster, *Westward Ho*, IV, ii.
105. Marston, *The Dutch Courtesan*, II, i.
106. Middleton, *A Mad World My Masters*, I, ii.
107. F. P. Wilson, *Elizabethan and Jacobean*, pp. 107–108. See also U. M. Ellis-Fermor, *The Jacobean Drama*.
108. M. S. Allen, *The Satire of John Marston*, p. 138.
109. Chapman, *Widow's Tears*, II, i.
110. *Ibid.*, I, i.
111. "George Chapman," *Times Literary Supplement*, May 10, 1934, p. 329.
112. Marston, *What You Will*, I, i.
113. Marston, *The Insatiate Countess*, II, i.
114. Jonson, *Conversations with Drummond*, in *Dramatic Works*, ed. Herford and Simpson, I, 138.

II. THE DIGNITY OF MAN

1. For diverse views of Elizabethan melancholy, see D. C. Allen, "The Degeneration of Man and Renaissance Pessimism," *S.P.*, XXXV (1938), 202–227; L. Babb, "Melancholy and the Elizabethan Man of Letters," *H.L.Q.*, IV (1941), 247–261; T. Spencer, "The Elizabethan Malcontent," *Joseph Quincy Adams Memorial Studies*, pp. 523–536.
2. See above, pp. 94–101.
3. Marston, *What You Will*, I, i.
4. Marston, *Jack Drum's Entertainment*, II.
5. Marston, *The Malcontent*, III, ii.
6. Marston, *Antonio and Mellida*, IV.
7. *Ibid.*, I.
8. Marston, *The Malcontent*, III, iii.
9. Marston, *Antonio's Revenge*, Prologue.
10. Boaistuau, *Théâtre du Monde*, trans. John Alday, Address to the Reader.
11. Montaigne, "Apology for Raymond Sebonde," *Essayes*, trans. Florio, ed. Stewart, pp. 398–399.

12. Marston, *The Malcontent*, IV, v.
13. *Hamlet*, II, ii, 306–324.
14. Marston, *Antonio's Revenge*, Prologue.
15. *Ibid.*, IV, iv.
16. Marston, *The Dutch Courtesan*, II, i.
17. Marston, *The Malcontent*, I, v.
18. Marston, *The Dutch Courtesan*, IV, i.
19. *Ibid.*, I, ii.
20. Marston, *The Malcontent*, IV, v; *The Fawn*, IV.
21. Marston, *The Malcontent*, II, v.
22. Marston, *Sophonisba*, IV, i.
23. Hooker, *Ecclesiastical Polity*, in *Works*, ed. Keble, I, 244.
24. Heywood, *The Brazen Age*, Pearson reprint, p. 234.
25. Marston, *The Malcontent*, I, iii, III, iii.
26. Dekker and Webster, *Westward Ho*, II, i.
27. Middleton, *Your Five Gallants*, II, i.
28. Middleton, *The Puritan*, I, ii.
29. Middleton, *A Trick to Catch the Old One*, I, i.
30. Middleton, *Your Five Gallants*, III, ii.
31. Marston, *The Malcontent*, II, iii.
32. Jonson, *Poetaster*, I, ii.
33. Marston, *The Fawn*, II, i.
34. Sharpham, *Cupid's Whirligig*, II, i.
35. Middleton, *Michaelmas Term*, III, i.
36. Marston, *The Fawn*, I, ii.
37. Jonson, *Epicoene*, IV, i.
38. Barry, *Ram-Alley*, IV, i.
39. Chapman, *May-Day*, II, i.
40. T. M. Parrott, ed., in George Chapman, *The Comedies*, p. 893.
41. Marston, *Antonio's Revenge*, V, v.
42. *Ibid.*, V, v.
43. Chettle, *Hoffman*, II, iii.
44. *Ibid.*, III, i.
45. A. Harbage, *As They Liked It*, pp. 163–173.
46. Chapman, *Bussy D'Ambois*, III, ii.
47. Pikering, *Horestes*, line 165.
48. Preston, *Cambyses*, line 821.
49. Heywood, *If You Know Not Me*, Pearson reprint, p. 263.
50. For a comparison see A. Sherbo, *English Sentimental Drama.*
51. *The Trial of Chivalry*, II, iii.
52. All in *George a Greene.*
53. Heywood, *II If You Know Not Me*, Pearson reprint, p. 293.
54. *Captain Thomas Stukeley*, lines 664–665.
55. See Appendix C.
56. Dekker and Middleton, *The Roaring Girl*, To the Comic Play-Reader.

57. *As You Like It*, V, ii, 65.
58. *The Merry Devil of Edmonton*, V, ii.
59. Marlowe, *I Tamburlaine*, III, ii.
60. Heywood and W. Rowley, *Fortune by Land and Sea*, V, i.
61. *I Henry VI*, IV, i, 9–47.
62. *The Two Gentlemen of Verona*, V, iv, 133–136.
63. *Coriolanus*, I, iv, 30–62.
64. *I Henry VI*, V, ii, 18.
65. *Hamlet*, I, iv, 19–20.
66. *Merchant of Venice*, I, ii, 92–108.
67. In *Aspects of Shakespeare* (British Academy Shakespeare Lectures).
68. *Othello*, II, iii, 291–294.
69. *The Taming of the Shrew.* Induction, i, 34; *Macbeth*, I, vii, 67; *Timon of Athens*, III, v, 68–74; *Antony and Cleopatra*, II, vii, 104–105; *As You Like It*, II, iii, 48–49, IV, i, vii; *Twelfth Night*, I, v, 138–139; *The Tempest*, V, i, 295–296.
70. *The Merchant of Venice*, II, viii, 12–24, III, i.
71. *Richard II*, V, ii, 30, IV, i, 162–318.
72. *Coriolanus*, III, iii, 139–141, IV, i, 1–57.
73. *Romeo and Juliet*, III, iii, 119–120; *Hamlet*, I, ii, 131–132, III, i, 55–85; *King Lear*, IV, vi, 37–38, IV, vi, 221–223; *Cymbeline*, III, iv, 77–79.
74. Holinshed, *Chronicles*, II, 837.
75. *I Henry IV*, II, i, 80–91.
76. William Hazlitt, *Characters of Shakespeare's Plays*, in *Collected Works*, ed. Waller and Glover, I, 274.
77. *I Henry IV*, V, ii, 82–87.
78. *II Henry IV*, II, iii, 18–21.
79. *I Henry IV*, II, i.
80. *Ibid.*, II, iv.
81. *A Midsummer Night's Dream*, III, ii, 9.
82. *Ibid.*, V, i, 72, 219–221.
83. *Henry V*, IV, viii, 58–60.
84. *II Henry IV*, I, ii, 95–98.
85. *II Henry IV*, III, ii, 250–254.
86. *The Taming of the Shrew*, IV, iii, 86–170.
87. *II Henry IV*, I, ii.
88. *The Merchant of Venice*, II, i, 1–12.
89. *II Henry IV*, II, ii, 69–70.
90. *Love's Labour's Lost*, V, ii, 734.
91. *Twelfth Night*, V, i, 386.
92. *As You Like It*, III, iii, 108–109.
93. *All's Well That Ends Well*, IV, iii, 310.
94. *Henry V*, V, i, 89–90.
95. *II Henry IV*, V, v, 51, 76.
96. *Macbeth*, IV, ii, 80–85.

97. *Macbeth*, V, v, 51–52.
98. *Richard II*, III, i, 31–34.
99. T. S. Eliot, "Shakespeare and the Stoicism of Seneca," *Selected Essays, 1917–1932*, p. 111.
100. *II Henry VI*, IV, vii, 97–98.
101. *Ibid.*, x, 69, 77–81.

III. SEXUAL BEHAVIOR

1. L. Babb, "The Physiological Conception of Love in the Elizabethan and Early Stuart Drama," *PMLA*, LVI (1941), 1020–1035.
2. *King Lear*, III, ii, 27–30.
3. *Leycester's Commonwealth*, ed. 1641, pp. 23, 71.
4. Jonson, *Epicoene*, IV, iii.
5. *Certain Sermons and Homilies*, p. 122.
6. *Ibid.*, p. 108.
7. *Look About You*, line 2317.
8. *Death of Robert Earl of Huntington*, IV, iii.
9. Young John Gresham in Heywood's *II If You Know Not Me;* Spendall in Cooke's *Greene's Tu Quoque.*
10. *Famous Victories of Henry the Fifth*, line 120.
11. *Ibid.*, line 420.
12. *Downfall of Robert Earl of Huntington*, III, ii.
13. *II Henry IV*, I, ii, 256–257.
14. *Romeo and Juliet*, III, ii, 13.
15. *Twelfth Night*, I, v, 277–278.
16. *As You Like It*, III, iv, 19.
17. *Macbeth*, IV, iii, 126.
18. *The Winter's Tale*, IV, iv, 31–35, 151–153.
19. *The Tempest*, IV, i, 24, 55.
20. *Hamlet*, I, iii, 46–51.
21. *Measure for Measure*, II, iii, 26–29.
22. *As You Like It*, II, iii, 50–51.
23. John Gower, *Confessio Amantis*, lines 1426–1431.
24. *Pericles*, IV, v, 5, 7.
25. *II Henry IV*, II, iv, 293–296.
26. *The Comedy of Errors*, II, ii, 132–148.
27. *Hamlet*, I, v, 48–59.
28. *Coriolanus*, V, iii, 48.
29. Samuel Johnson, "Preface," in *Plays of Shakespeare*, ed. I. Reed, I, 262.
30. *Romeo and Juliet*, II, iii, 44.
31. *The Merchant of Venice*, III, ii, 210.
32. *The Winter's Tale*, IV, iv, 540–541.

33. *Hamlet*, II, i, 27.
34. *All's Well That Ends Well*, IV, iii, 52–55.
35. *Hamlet*, I, iii, 24–44, 84–85.
36. *The Tempest*, IV, i, 15–22, 51–54.
37. Middleton, *A Mad World My Masters*, V, ii.
38. Sharpham, *The Fleire*, I.
39. Barry, *Ram-Alley*, I, i, V, i.
40. Middleton, *A Trick to Catch the Old One*, V, ii.
41. *II Henry IV*, V, iv.
42. Heywood, *The Royal King and the Loyal Subject*, Pearson reprint, p. 50.
43. *Troilus and Cressida*, IV, i, 69–72.
44. *Antony and Cleopatra*, III, x, 10, IV, xii, 13.
45. *Ibid.*, I, v, 9–10. See also II, v, 55–56.
46. *Ibid.*, II, v, 63–66.
47. *II Henry IV*, V, iv, 21–24.
48. *Antony and Cleopatra*, V, ii, 290–291.
49. *Pericles*, IV, i, 78.
50. *Ibid.*, IV, vi, 173–179, 185–190.
51. *Measure for Measure*, III, ii, 20–28.
52. *Merry Wives of Windsor*, I, iii, 83–87; *Henry V*, V, i, 90.
53. *II Henry IV*, II, iv.
54. *Ibid.*, V, iv.
55. *Henry V*, V, i, 86–87.
56. *II Henry IV*, II, iv, 49–50.
57. *Timon of Athens*, IV, iii, 61–63, 86–87.
58. *Comedy of Errors*, IV, iii, 55–58; *Henry V*, II, i, 79–81; *Troilus and Cres-
    sida*, V, i, 15–28, V, ix, 35–57; *Measure for Measure*, I, ii, 44–47; *Cym-
    beline*, I, vi, 120–126; *Pericles*, IV, ii, 6–27; etc.
59. E. E. Stoll, "Modesty in the Audience," *M.L.N.*, LV (1940), 570–576.
60. Marston, *The Fawn*, II, i.
61. Marston, *The Malcontent*, II, ii.
62. Chapman, *May-Day*, II, i.
63. Markham and Machin, *The Dumb Knight*, I, i.
64. *I Tamburlaine*, I, ii, V, ii.
65. *II Tamburlaine*, IV, i and iii.
66. Marlowe and Nashe, *Tragedy of Dido*, IV, iii.
67. Kyd, *The Spanish Tragedy*, II, iv.
68. See above, p. 83.
69. Markham and Machin, *The Dumb Knight*, I, i.
70. Marston, *Jack Drum's Entertainment*, II.
71. *Ibid.*
72. Barry, *Ram-Alley*, IV, i.
73. Day, *Isle of Gulls*, II, iv.
74. Chapman, *May-Day*, II, i.
75. *Ibid.*, V, i.

76. Marston, *Sophonisba*, IV.
77. Marston, *The Insatiate Countess*, III.
78. Marston, *The Fawn*, I.
79. Field, *Amends for Ladies*, V, ii.
80. *A Warning for Fair Women*, Act II, lines 24–28.
81. Heywood, *I Edward IV*, Pearson reprint, p. 76.
82. Heywood, *A Woman Killed with Kindness*, Pearson reprint, p. 112.
83. *Troilus and Cressida*, III, ii, 9–30; *The Merry Wives of Windsor*, V, v, 1–25.
84. *All's Well That Ends Well*, IV, ii, 1–49.
85. *A Midsummer Night's Dream*, II, ii, 35–65.
86. See Appendix C.
87. Chaucer, *The Miller's Tale*, lines 3269–3270.
88. See above, p. 000.
89. Sharpham, *The Fleire*, II.
90. Heywood, *II Iron Age*, Pearson reprint, pp. 430–431.
91. Heywood, *The Golden Age*, Pearson reprint, pp. 51–52.
92. *The Winter's Tale*, V, i, 223–228.
93. Marston, *Sophonisba*, III, i, IV, i.
94. Middleton, *Michaelmas Term*, I, i.
95. Field, *A Woman Is a Weathercock*, II, i.
96. John Donne, "Satire IV," *Works*, ed. Hayward, p. 134.
97. Marston, *Certain Satires*, II and III.
98. *Calendar of State Papers, Domestic Series, of the Reign of Elizabeth*, II (1581–1590), 38–40.
99. In the Baines note, printed in C. F. Tucker Brooke, *Life of Marlowe*.
100. Dekker, *Satiromastix*, Pearson reprint, p. 260.
101. Richard Barnfield, *Cynthia*, 1595, Prefatory Epistle, and Sonnet XIX.
102. Heywood, *Jupiter and Juno*, Pearson reprint, p. 203.
103. Heywood, *An Apology for Actors*, ed. Perkinson, sig. C3.
104. E. Partridge, *Shakespeare's Bawdy*, p. 16, suggests three other "possibilities," only one of which, *II Henry IV*, II, i, 14–17, is possible.
105. Marlowe, *Edward II*, lines 50–72.
106. Jonson, *Poetaster*, IV, v.
107. Marston, *What You Will*, II, i.
108. Marston, *The Malcontent*, I, ii.
109. Chapman, *May-Day*, III, iii, 228–234.
110. Fletcher, *The Honest Man's Fortune*, IV, i.
111. H. E. Rollins, "The Black-Letter Ballads," *PMLA*, XXXIV (1919), 258–339.
112. C. J. Sisson, *Lost Plays of Shakespeare's Age*, p. 126.
113. *Hamlet*, II, ii, 460.
114. Guilpin, *Skialetheia*, sig. B8v.
115. *Death of Robert Earl of Huntington*, V, i.
116. *A Midsummer Night's Dream*, IV, ii, 11–14.
117. *As You Like It*, V, ii, 100–104.

118. *All's Well That Ends Well*, I, i, 122–123.
119. *Much Ado About Nothing*, II, iii, 144.
120. *The Merry Wives of Windsor*, IV, ii, 108–109.
121. *Love's Labour's Lost*, IV, i, 139.
122. *The Tempest*, I, ii, 55–57. See also *The Taming of the Shrew*, V, i, 35; *Much Ado About Nothing*, I, i, 104–195; *The Winter's Tale*, V, i, 124; etc.
123. *Twelfth Night*, II, v, 95–97.
124. *I Henry IV*, III, iii, 144–147; see also *II Henry IV*, II, i, 12–19.
125. *The Merry Wives of Windsor*, IV, i, 64–70.
126. *Henry V*, III, iv, 54–58.
127. *On Reading Shakespeare*, pp. 9, 17.
128. Lodovico Castelvetro, *Poetics of Aristotle*, 1571, trans. Gilbert (in *Literary Criticism Plato to Dryden*, p. 314).
129. *All's Well That Ends Well*, V, ii, 11–12.
130. *The Two Gentlemen of Verona*, II, v, 22–27.
131. *Much Ado About Nothing*, III, iv, 24–30.
132. *The Merchant of Venice*, III, ii, 213–217.
133. Bridges, "On the Influence of the Audience," in *Works of Shakespeare*, ed. A. H. Bullen, X, 334.
134. William Warburton, Preface to Shakespeare, *Plays*, ed. I. Reed, I, 240.
135. Shakespeare, *Plays*, ed. I. Reed, XX, 80.
136. Samuel T. Coleridge, *Coleridge's Shakespearean Criticism*, ed. Raysor, I, 135.
137. Marston, *The Insatiate Countess*, I, i.
138. Middleton, *Michaelmas Term*, IV, ii.

IV. WEDDED LOVE

1. Sir John Harington, *The Epigrams*, ed. McClure, p. 200.
2. G. R. Owst, *Literature and Pulpit in Medieval England*, p. 377.
3. "Of Wedded Men and Wives," in John Wyclif, *Selected English Writings*, ed. Winn, pp. 105–106.
4. Thomas Becon, *The Boke of Matrimony*, in *Works*, Tome I, f. ccccclxxv.
5. W. and M. Haller, "The Puritan Art of Love," *H.L.Q.*, V (1941–1942), 235–272.
6. L. B. Wright, *Middle-Class Culture in Elizabethan England*, pp. 465–507; F. L. Utley, *The Crooked Rib*.
7. C. L. Powell, *English Domestic Relations*, pp. 171 f.
8. *Certain Sermons or Homilies*, p. 122.
9. S. Rowley, *When You See Me You Know Me*, sig. A4.
10. C. S. Lewis, *The Allegory of Love*, p. 360.
11. Andreas Capellanus, *The Art of Courtly Love*, ed. Parry, p. 150.

12. W. Rowley, *A Shoemaker a Gentleman*, I, iii.
13. Lady Diana Primrose, *A Chain of Pearl*, in John Nichols, *Progresses Elizabeth*, III, 644.
14. Castiglione, *The Book of the Courtier*, trans. Opdycke, pp. 288, 296.
15. Davenant, *The Platonic Lovers*, Prologue; cf. A. Harbage, *Cavalier Drama*, pp. 36, 167.
16. W. Haller, "Hail Wedded Love," *ELH*, XIII (1946), 86–87.
17. E. Power, "The Position of Women," in *The Legacy of the Middle Ages*, ed. Crump and Jacob, pp. 401–433.
18. G. G. Coulton, *Medieval Panorama*, p. 625.
19. Forester, *The Sky and the Forest*, 1948.
20. *Captain Thomas Stukeley*, ed. Simpson, lines 30–39.
21. Wilkins, *The Miseries of Enforced Marriage*, I.
22. *How a Man May Choose a Good Wife from a Bad*, I, i.
23. *A Warning for Fair Women*, Act II, lines 231–233.
24. Heywood and W. Rowley, *Fortune by Land and Sea*, Pearson reprint, p. 233.
25. Heywood, *The Royal King and the Loyal Subject*, II, ii.
26. *All's Well That Ends Well*, I, i, 92–94.
27. *As You Like It*, III, iv, 41–42.
28. *Romeo and Juliet*, I, ii, 17–18.
29. *King Lear*, I, i, 100–103.
30. *Othello*, I, iii, 183–189.
31. Chettle and Munday, *Death of Robert Earl of Huntington*, IV, ii.
32. *The Merry Devil of Edmonton*, I, i.
33. Greene, *Friar Bacon and Friar Bungay*, V, i.
34. *Measure for Measure*, I, iv, 35.
35. *A Midsummer Night's Dream*, II, i, 164.
36. *Ibid.*, I, i, 67–68.
37. W. Bliss, *The Real Shakespeare*, p. 288.
38. J. D. Wilson, "The Elizabethan Shakespeare," in *Aspects of Shakespeare* (Brit. Acad. Lectures), p. 225.
39. *Romeo and Juliet*, III, ii, 26–31.
40. *The Two Gentlemen of Verona*, I, ii, 128–129.
41. *As You Like It*, III, ii, 42–43, 331–335.
42. *The Taming of the Shrew*, IV, i, 186.
43. *Hamlet*, IV, v, 48–66.
44. *Romeo and Juliet*, II, vi, 36–37.
45. Julietta in *Measure for Measure*.
46. *Fair Em*, V, i.
47. *How a Man May Choose a Good Wife from a Bad*, I, ii.
48. *The Weakest Goeth to the Wall*, Malone Soc. reprint, lines 1139–1140.
49. Marlowe, *II Tamburlaine*, IV, ii.
50. *George a Greene*, ed. Adams, ll. 336–355.

51. *King John*, II, i, 432; *The Taming of the Shrew*, II, i, 292–300, III, ii, 197, V, ii, 136–175; *The Merchant of Venice*, III, ii, 163–165; *As You Like It*, I, ii, 39–42, III, iii, 18–45; *Twelfth Night*, III, i, 161–164; *Othello*, II, i, 149–159, III, iii, 183–187, IV, i, 188–203; *Antony and Cleopatra*, II, ii, 246–248; *Cymbeline*, I, iv, 63–64; *The Winter's Tale*, V, iii, 26–27, V, v, 85–88, etc.

52. *Troilus and Cressida*, I, iii, 274–275.

53. *The Merchant of Venice*, II, vi, 56.

54. *The Two Gentlemen of Verona*, IV, iv, 185.

55. *As You Like It*, III, ii, 10.

56. *The Merry Wives of Windsor*, I, iv, 148–149.

57. *Much Ado About Nothing*, II, iii, 28–37.

58. C. H. Herford, "Life of Jonson," in Ben Jonson, *Dramatic Works*, ed. Herford and Simpson, I, 125.

59. *Certain Sermons or Homilies*, p. 448.

60. Harris, *The Man Shakespeare*.

61. *Romeo and Juliet*, III, iii, 38–39.

62. *Much Ado About Nothing*, IV, i, 163–164.

63. *Othello*, IV, ii, 118, iii, 86.

64. *Cymbeline*, III, iv, 42–43.

65. Middleton, *The Phoenix*, II, ii.

66. Marston, *What You Will*, III, i.

67. Chapman, *The Gentleman Usher*, IV, iii.

68. Chapman, *Monsieur D'Olive*, I, i.

69. Chapman, *The Gentleman Usher*, V, iv.

70. Chapman, *The Revenge of Bussy D'Ambois*, V, i.

71. Chapman, *Sir Giles Goosecap*, III, ii.

72. Chapman, *All Fools but the Fool*, III, i.

73. Chapman, *The Widow's Tears*, II, ii.

74. Donne, *Complete Poetry and Selected Prose*, ed. Hayward, p. 68.

75. Jonson, *Epicoene*, II, ii, IV, i.

76. Marston, *The Malcontent*, I, vi.

77. Middleton, *A Mad World My Masters*, IV, i.

78. Fletcher, *The Coxcomb*, IV, i.

79. Field, *A Woman Is a Weathercock*, II, i.

80. Jonson, *Cynthia's Revels*, IV, i.

81. Marston, *Sophonisba*, I, ii.

82. Marston, *The Fawn*, III.

83. Marston, *Antonio and Mellida*, I, i, II, i.

84. Marston, *The Dutch Courtesan*, III, i.

85. Marston, *The Fawn*, V.

86. Marston, *What You Will*, III, i.

87. Marston, *The Dutch Courtesan*, II, i.

88. Chapman, *Monsieur D'Olive*, II, i.

89. Chapman, *Sir Giles Goosecap*, II, i.

90. *Romeo and Juliet*, II, ii, 143–144.
91. *Twelfth Night*, III, iv, 231–232.
92. Chapman, *The Gentleman Usher*, IV, ii.
93. T. S. Eliot, "Thomas Heywood," *Selected Essays, 1917–1932*, p. 157.
94. W. Bliss, *The Real Shakespeare*, p. 288.
95. In Introduction to Shakespeare, *Measure for Measure*, ed. Quiller-Couch and Wilson, p. xxxi.
96. Fletcher, *The Coxcomb*, II, i.
97. Day, *The Isle of Gulls*, II, iii.
98. Marston, *The Malcontent*, II, v.
99. H. H. Adams, *English Domestic or Homiletic Tragedy*.
100. Heywood, *A Woman Killed with Kindness*, Pearson reprint, p. 156; *II Edward IV*, Pearson reprint, p. 183.
101. *Troilus and Cressida*, IV, i, 60–63.
102. *The Winter's Tale*, I, ii, 330, II, iii, 13–17.
103. *Hamlet*, III, iv, 14–16.
104. *Cymbeline*, II, v, 2.
105. *Othello*, I, i, 86–91, 109–117, II, iii, 13–22, III, iii, 395–396, IV, i, 71–73, 188–207, IV, ii, 47–81.
106. *The Winter's Tale*, I, ii, 179–207, 285–291.
107. *King Lear*, IV, vi, 120–127.
108. *Timon of Athens*, IV, iii, 112–114.
109. *King Lear*, V, iii, 170–173.
110. *King John*, I, i.
111. *Troilus and Cressida*, V, vii, 16–23.
112. *The Tempest*, V, i, 273.
113. *I Henry VI*, III, i, 42.
114. *Ibid.*, IV, vi, 21–24.
115. Holinshed, *Chronicles*, III, 236.
116. Milton, *Paradise Lost*, IV, 753–758.
117. Preston, *Cambyses*, lines 541–542, 546–548, 586–592.
118. See above, pp. 105–106.
119. *King John*, III, iv, 93–97.
120. Heywood, *The Royal King and the Loyal Subject*, IV.
121. Wilkins, *The Miseries of Enforced Marriage*, III.
122. Dekker and Chettle, *Patient Grissill*, IV, i.
123. S. Rowley, *When You See Me You Know Me*, sigs. G3–G4.
124. *The Winter's Tale*, I, ii, 166–172.
125. *III Henry VI*, V, v, 63.
126. *Macbeth*, IV, iii, 216.
127. *King John*, III, iv, 91.
128. Heywood, *Four Prentices of London*, Pearson reprint, p. 246.
129. Day, W. Rowley, Wilkins, *The Travels of the Three English Brothers*, ed. Bullen, p. 71.
130. *Fortune by Land and Sea*, I, i.

131. Day and Chettle, *The Blind Beggar of Bednal Green*, ed. Bullen, pp. 46, 60.
132. *Thomas Lord Cromwell*, IV, iv.
133. *King Lear*, I, ii, 117–120, II, i, 47–52, IV, ii, 46–49, etc.
134. Wilkins, *The Miseries of Enforced Marriage*, V.
135. Heywood, *I If You Know Not Me*, Pearson reprint, p. 209.
136. *Antony and Cleopatra*, III, ii, 50–61.
137. Marston, *Antonio's Revenge*, III, iii.
138. Marston, *Jack Drum's Entertainment*, II.
139. Marston, *Antonio's Revenge*, I, iv.
140. Middleton, *Your Five Gallants*, IV, viii.
141. Middleton, *The Puritan*, IV, i.
142. Day, *Law-Tricks*, IV, ii.
143. Jonson, *Epicoene*, V, iv.
144. Farquhar, *The Beaux' Stratagem*, V, iv.
145. *Certain Sermons or Homilies*, p. 447.

V. THE COMMONWEAL

1. H. B. Charlton, *Shakespeare, Politics and Politicians;* J. L. Palmer, *Political Characters of Shakespeare;* E. M. W. Tillyard, *Shakespeare's History Plays;* L. B. Campbell, *Shakespeare's "Histories";* M. W. MacCallum, *Shakespeare's Roman Plays and Their Background;* J. E. Phillips, *The State in Shakespeare's Greek and Roman Plays.*
2. *The Valiant Welshman*, To the Ingenuous Reader.
3. Hooker, *Ecclesiastical Polity*, in *Works*, I, 239.
4. Starkey, *A Dialogue Between Pole and Lupset*, ed. Cowper, p. 206.
5. Gosson, *School of Abuse*, ed. Collier, p. 41.
6. *Gentleness and Nobility*, ed. Cameron, p. 34.
7. W. G. Zeeveld, *Foundations of Tudor Policy*, p. 269.
8. Starkey, *op. cit.*, p. 36.
9. Hooker, *op. cit.*, p. 240.
10. R. H. Tawney, *Religion and the Rise of Capitalism*, pp. 126–127.
11. E. M. W. Tillyard, *Shakespeare's History Plays*, p. 22.
12. *The Winter's Tale*, II, i, 161–164, iii, 116–124.
13. G. M. Trevelyan, *Illustrated English Social History*, II, 23–24.
14. L. Stone, "State Control in Sixteenth-Century England," *Economic History Review*, XVII (1947), 120.
15. Creizenach, *The English Drama in the Age of Shakespeare*, p. 106.
16. C. F. Tucker Brooke, *Shakespeare of Stratford*, pp. 144 ff.
17. A. A. Smirnov, *Shakespeare*, p. 93.
18. D. Morrow, *Where Shakespeare Stood.*

19. A. L. Williams, "A Note on Pessimism in the Renaissance," *S.P.*, XXXVI (1939), 243–246.
20. Marx and Engels, *Manifesto of the Communist Party*, p. 11.
21. J. M. Keynes, *A Treatise on Money*, II, 154.
22. L. C. Knights, *Drama and Society in the Age of Jonson*, pp. 127, 171, 175, 228, 246, 269.
23. F. Tupper, "The Shakespearean Mob," *PMLA*, XXVII (1912), 486–523; A. H. Tolman, "Is Shakespeare Aristocratic?" *PMLA*, XXIX (1914), 277–298; A. Thaler, *Shakespeare and Democracy*, pp. 3–44.
24. B. Stirling, *The Populace in Shakespeare*.
25. *Antony and Cleopatra*, V, ii, 209–213.
26. Chettle, *The Tragedy of Hoffman*, III, ii.
27. Preston, *Cambyses*, ed. Adams, line 333.
28. *Famous Victories of Henry the Fifth*, ed. Adams, lines 34–35.
29. Heywood, *I If You Know Not Me*, Pearson reprint, p. 221.
30. Heywood, *The Royal King and the Loyal Subject*, II, i.
31. Day and Chettle, *The Blind Beggar of Bednal Green*, ed. Bullen, p. 39.
32. *The Weakest Goeth to the Wall*, lines 495–500.
33. *Mucedorus*, III, i.
34. *George a Greene*, ed. Adams, lines 542–543.
35. Heywood, *The Royal King and the Loyal Subject*, V.
36. W. Rowley, *A Shoemaker a Gentleman*, I, ii.
37. Dekker and Chettle, *Patient Grissill*, I, i.
38. *The Winter's Tale*, IV, iv, 455–457.
39. *Cymbeline*, IV, ii, 2–5.
40. In Day and Wilkins, *The Travels of the Three English Brothers*.
41. Heywood, *I Edward IV*, Pearson reprint, p. 57.
42. *Thomas Lord Cromwell*, I, ii.
43. Heywood, *I Edward IV*, Pearson reprint, pp. 6–7.
44. S. Rowley, *When You See Me You Know Me*, sig. G4v.
45. *The Weakest Goeth to the Wall*, lines 1207–1210.
46. *George a Greene*, ed. Adams, lines 251–254.
47. *All's Well That Ends Well*, II, iii, 125–131.
48. Rowlands, *The Letting of Humours Blood in the Head-Vaine*, 1600, sig. D8.
49. Field, *A Woman Is a Weathercock*, II, i.
50. Middleton, *Michaelmas Term*, I, i.
51. Jonson, *Every Man Out of His Humor*, II, vi.
52. C. J. Sisson, *Lost Plays of Shakespeare's Age*, pp. 12–79.
53. Heywood, *II If You Know Not Me*, Pearson reprint, p. 291.
54. *The London Prodigal*, V, i.
55. *The Merry Wives of Windsor*, II, i, 23–25.
56. Chettle, *Kind-Hartes Dream*, 1592, p. 44.
57. Dekker, *If It Be Not Good the Devil Is in It*, Pearson reprint, p. 324.
58. Heywood, *II If You Know Not Me*, Pearson reprint, p. 277.

59. *Captain Thomas Stukeley,* lines 1952–1954.
60. Heywood, *I Fair Maid of the West,* IV, i.
61. Leech, "Catholic and Protestant Drama," *Shakespeare's Tragedies,* pp. 223–224.
62. Tolstoy, *Tolstoy on Shakespeare* (addendum by E. Crosby, "Shakespeare's Attitude to the Working Classes"), pp. 138–139.
63. *As You Like It,* I, i, 85–88.
64. *Ibid.,* II, iii, 57.
65. Wilkins, *The Miseries of Enforced Marriage,* V.
66. *Cymbeline,* V, i, 5–7.
67. W. Rowley, *A Shoemaker a Gentleman,* I, ii.
68. *King John,* V, vii, 72–73.
69. Dekker and Webster, *Sir Thomas Wyatt,* Pearson reprint, p. 89.
70. A. Hart, *Shakespeare and the Homilies,* p. 76.
71. *George a Greene,* ed. Adams, lines 105–109.
72. Chettle and Munday, *Death of Robert Earl of Huntington,* IV, ii.
73. Quoted by C. L. Powell, *English Domestic Relations,* p. 131.
74. *The Weakest Goeth to the Wall,* lines 1333–1340.
75. Preston, *Cambyses,* Prologue.
76. *Macbeth,* IV, iii, 91–95.
77. C. W. Kennedy, "Political Thought in the Plays of George Chapman," in *Essays in Dramatic Literature,* ed. Hardin Craig, pp. 73–76.
78. R. W. Chambers, *The Jacobean Shakespeare and Measure for Measure.*
79. Marston, *Antonio and Mellida,* III.
80. Marston, *What You Will,* I, i.
81. *The Weakest Goeth to the Wall,* lines 249–251.
82. *Thomas Lord Cromwell,* III, iii.
83. Haughton, *Englishmen for My Money,* IV, iii.
84. *The Tempest,* II, ii, 17–40.
85. *Twelfth Night,* II, iii, 151–166.
86. M. G. M. Adkins, "Puritanism in the Plays and Pamphlets of Thomas Dekker," *Univ. of Texas Studies in English,* XIX (1940), 86–113. See also *ibid.,* XXII, 86–104.
87. See above, pp. 143–145.
88. Chapman, *Monsieur D'Olive,* II, ii; *The Gentleman Usher,* V, ii, 33–44.
89. Chapman, *Revenge of Bussy D'Ambois,* II, i.
90. Barry, *Ram-Alley,* IV, i. ("In sign" emends "instead.")
91. Peele, *Arraignment of Paris,* V, i; Chapman, *I Charles Duke of Byron,* IV, i; Jonson, *Cynthia's Revels, passim;* Marston, *Antonio and Mellida,* I, i.
92. *King John,* V, vii, 112–113.
93. *Fair Em,* IV, ii.
94. Chettle and Day, *The Blind Beggar of Bednal Green,* ed. Bullen, p. 116.
95. *Henry V,* Prologue to Act II, lines 16–19.

VI. SHAKESPEARE'S TRADITION: CONCLUSION

1. A. N. Whitehead, *Science and the Modern World*, p. 265.
2. R. Bridges, "On the Influence of the Audience," *Works of Shakespeare*, ed. A. H. Bullen, X, 334.
3. *Hamlet*, II, ii, 524–526, 483–496 (Italics mine). For a review of the debate over the satirical or nonsatirical intention of this speech, see S. L. Bethell, *Shakespeare and the Popular Dramatic Tradition*, pp. 180–189.
4. Marlowe and Nashe, *The Tragedy of Dido*, II, i (italics mine).
5. *Il Return from Parnassus*, IV, iii.
6. Davies, *The Scourge of Folly*, S.R., 1610, Epigram 159, in E. K. Chambers, *William Shakespeare*, II, 214.
7. T. S. Eliot, *The Cocktail Party*.
8. A. Ellis, "Sex—the Schizoid Best Seller," *Saturday Review of Literature*, Vol. XXXIV, No. 11 (Mar. 17, 1951), pp. 19, 42–44.
9. T. S. Eliot, "Seneca in Elizabethan Translation," *Selected Essays*, p. 80.
10. Barry, *Ram-Alley*, V, i.
11. *Il Henry IV*, II, iv, 53–56.
12. *Cymbeline*, III, iv, 42–43. See above, p. 239.
13. Heywood, *The Royal King and the Loyal Subject*, printed 1637, "To the Reader."
14. Tatham, Commendatory verses to Richard Brome, *A Jovial Crew*, 1641.
15. *Variety*, Vol. CLXXVII, No. 8 (Feb. 1, 1950), p. 1.
16. *The Tempest*, I, ii, 362–363.

APPENDICES

[APPENDIX A]

Size and Earnings of Coterie Theatres

Only such matters as may illustrate and amplify the discussion of the number of spectators (see above, pp. 42–47) are touched upon here. At the first Blackfriars a separate suite of two rooms was included in the lease; but if these were used as the theatre, as J. Q. Adams believes (*Shakespearean Playhouses*, p. 101 n.), a space twenty-six by forty-six feet would have had to serve for tiring house, stage, and auditorium, so that no more than two hundred spectators could have been accommodated. The estimate by W. J. Lawrence (*The Elizabethan Playhouse and Other Studies*, p. 234) places the first Blackfriars capacity at two hundred and forty: no one is apt to quarrel with my estimate that the maximum was four hundred. As regards Paul's, we have nothing to go upon but analogy with the first Blackfriars. The assumption that the same premises were used after 1599 as before 1591 itself involves risk; however, although Pierce may have occupied different quarters from Westcote, the probability remains that he housed his theatre in his residence and song school. The absence of data on Paul's after 1599 (except for an allusion to its small stage) suggests that its size was inconspicuous. The assumption of a maximum capacity of four hundred seems justified.

In commendatory verses to Fletcher's *Faithful Shepherdess*, a second Blackfriars play, the audience is placed at a thousand; but that this is a round number is demonstrable. In *The Whore of Babylon*, a Fortune play of c. 1607, Dekker speaks of "places as big as this, and before a thousand people," in a context that makes it clear he is referring to the second Blackfriars; but we know that this theatre was *not* as big as the Fortune, and we must scale down Dekker's "thousand people" just as we must qualify his "as big as this." The second Blackfriars was evidently designed for adult actors on the

339

model of the public theatres, and an idea of the limits of its capacity may be obtained by a comparison with the Fortune. The building contract of the latter (Henslowe, *Papers*, ed. Greg, pp. 4–7) gives over-all dimensions of eighty by eighty feet, with sufficient height for three galleries, as the space available for tiring house, stage, and spectators. The largest space available for tiring house, stage, and spectators in James Burbage's segment of the Blackfriars Priory (Adams, *Shakespearean Playhouses*, p. 196) was forty-six by sixty-six feet, with a height sufficient for two and possibly three galleries. We have, then, a ground space of 6,400 square feet at the Fortune to compare with a ground space of 3,036 square feet at the second Blackfriars, with the number of galleries in the latter in doubt. The capacity of the Fortune has been estimated by John Corbin (*Atlantic Monthly*, XCVII [1906], 372) at 2,138 or more, and by myself (*Shakespeare's Audience*, pp. 22–23) at about 2,344. If the yard at the Fortune had been allotted to seated instead of standing spectators, my mode of calculation would have resulted in an estimate of 2,015 for the capacity of the house. Assuming that the Blackfriars hall was adapted with the economy of space effected at the Fortune (an initial improbability), and that three galleries were provided, we may use the equation made available by our knowledge of the ground dimensions of the two theatres: 6,400 (ground space of Fortune) is to 3,036 (ground space of Blackfriars) as 2,015 (adjusted estimate of Fortune capacity) is to x (estimate of Blackfriars capacity). This works out to 955 as the maximum estimate of the capacity of the second Blackfriars. Reducing the number of galleries to the more probable two gives us, by the same method of reckoning, a capacity of 696. C. W. Wallace (*The Children of the Chapel at Blackfriars*, pp. 42, 50–51) believes that the overhead room permitted three galleries, but he is lavish in the space he allots each spectator and so estimates a capacity of only 558 to 608. J. Q. Adams (*Shakespearean Playhouses*, p. 197) believes there were two galleries; E. K. Chambers (*Elizabethan Stage*, II, 514), only one, with the documentary allusion to "galleryes" indicating a single tier in two sections, one on each side of the hall. If, as Chambers believes (*ibid.*, pp. 554–555), the upper floor or Parliament chamber of the frater house of the Priory was used, instead of the high-ceilinged hall beneath it as postulated in the above calculations, the tiring house may have stood outside the forty-six-by-sixty-six-foot space specified as the total ground dimensions of the theatre; but the seating space thus gained at the ground level does not increase the possible estimates of capacity beyond our previous maximum. If the Parliament chamber was used, with stage and galleries proportioned as at the Fortune, the seating capacity could have been little more than 800.

In financing, the coterie theatres were in no way comparable with the public theatres. The cost to Richard Farrant for tearing down partitions, blocking windows, and providing stage and seats at the first Blackfriars in 1576–1577 would have been inconsiderable as compared with the £666 or thereabouts spent in building Burbage's Theatre about the same time. The owners of the Theatre received as a net rental at least £100 yearly (see above, p. 23), their mere ground rent of £14 exactly equaling the total rent paid by Farrant. Farrant and his associates had difficulty in paying even the £14. In the second Blackfriars, James Burbage had invested £900; yet, at a time when rentals of over £300 a year were received by owners of public theatres housing the popular troupes (see above, p. 23), this theatre was put at the disposal of the Chapel children for only £40 a year. Evidently their competition was not feared, and the transaction was viewed as a bit of salvaging. Again there was difficulty among members of the syndicate in paying the rent and in meeting the cost of repairs as small as £10 (see Rastell and Kirkham *versus* Hawkins, in Hillebrand, *Child Actors*, pp. 180–185).

The shares in the coterie companies had a lower cash value than those in the public companies, even though they were fewer and the operating expenses lower. John Marston may have succeeded in selling his one of the six shares in the Blackfriars company, acquired about 1603, to Robert Keysar for £100 about 1608 (Keysar *versus* Burbage *et al.*, in Wallace, *Shakespeare and His London Associates*, p. 76), but the £600 named by Keysar as the total value of the enterprise, while not in itself utterly inconsistent with gross receipts of £1,000 a year, is an inflated figure. Edward Kirkham claimed that the ownership of the lease of Blackfriars was worth £200 a year until about 1606, and £300 a year thereafter (Kirkham *versus* Painton, in Fleay, *Chronicle History of the London Stage*, p. 249); but his claim was properly dismissed (*ibid.*, p. 251) on the ground that he was identifying the earnings of a theatrical company with those of the theatre it occupied. Nowhere in the proceedings is it stated that the sums Kirkham mentioned were one-half gallery receipts, or that the Blackfriars company, either before or after Keysar's appearance on the scene, used the system of rental payments employed at the public theatres. T. W. Baldwin (*Organization and Personnel of the Shakespearean Company*, pp. 349–350) makes this assumption, over and above his assumption that Kirkham and Keysar were "two experts" whose statements are "approximately correct," and concludes that £1,000 had been earned regularly just before 1608. This deduction implies that the boys made as much from their weekly performances as the King's Men made from their daily performances, and that Evans, in yielding up his interest in this wonderfully profitable organization for a one-seventh share of the rental payments of the King's Men, cheated not only Kirkham but himself. Actually Kirkham was bringing a nuisance suit fraudulent on the face of it. His figures, if they mean anything—and there is a certain consistency about them—mean that the total net earnings of the boys at Blackfriars were between £200 and £300 a year.

The Repertories

(For explanation, see above, p. 85.)

1560–1582

POPULAR

DUDLEY-LEICESTER'S MEN

Preston, *Cambyses*, T, c. 1560; Preston(?), *Sir Clyomon and Sir Clamydes*, C, c. 1570; Wilson, *The Three Ladies of London*, M, 1581.

RICH'S MEN

Pikering, *Horestes*, T, c. 1567.

DERBY'S MEN

Anon. *The Rare Triumphs of Love and Fortune*, C, 1582.

SELECT

CHAPEL BOYS

Edwardes, *Damon and Pythias*, C, 1565; Anon., *Liberality and Prodigality*, M, c. 1567, rev. c. 1600?; Peele, *The Arraignment of Paris*, C, c. 1581.

COMPANY UNKNOWN

Phillip, *Patient and Meek Grissill*, C, c. 1560; W. Wager, *The Longer Thou Livest the More Fool Thou Art*, M, c. 1560; Ingelend, *The Disobedient Child*, M, c. 1560; W. Wager, *Enough Is As Good As a Feast*, M, c. 1560; Anon., *Play of Robin Hood*, C, c. 1560; Anon., *Tom Tyler and His Wife*, C, c. 1560; Anon., *The Pedlar's Prophecy*, M, c. 1561; Anon., *New Custom*, M, c. 1563; Anon., *Appius and Virginia*, T, c. 1564; Jeffere (?), *Bugbears*, C, c. 1564; Anon.,

343

King Darius, M, c. 1565; Anon., *The Trial of Treasure*, M, c. 1567; Fulwell, *Like Will to Like*, M, c. 1568; Anon., *Marriage of Wit and Science*, M, c. 1568; Garter, *The Most Virtuous and Godly Susanna*, M, c. 1569; Anon., *Juli and Julian*, C, c. 1570; Woodes, *The Conflict of Conscience*, M, c. 1572; Wapull, *The Tide Tarrieth No Man*, M, c. 1576; Anon., *Common Conditions*, C, c. 1576; Lupton, *All for Money*, M, c. 1577; Merbury, *The Marriage Between Wit and Wisdom*, M, c. 1579.

1583–1594

POPULAR

QUEEN ELIZABETH'S MEN

Anon., *The Famous Victories of Henry V*, H; Anon., *The Troublesome Reign of King John*, H; Anon., *King Leir*, C; Anon., *The True Tragedy of Richard III*, H; Greene, *Friar Bacon and Friar Bungay*, C; Greene, *James IV*, C; Greene, *Orlando Furioso*, C; Greene (?), *Selimus*, T; Greene and Lodge, *A Looking Glass for London and England*, M; Peele, *The Old Wives' Tale*, C; Wilson, *Three Lords and Three Ladies of London*, M.

STRANGE'S AND ADMIRAL'S MEN

Anon., *Fair Em*, C; Anon., *A Knack to Know a Knave*, C; Anon., *A Knack to Know an Honest Man*, C; Anon., *Jeronimo*, T; Kyd, *The Spanish Tragedy*, T; Lodge, *The Wounds of Civil War*, T; Marlowe, *I Tamburlaine*, T; Marlowe, *II Tamburlaine*, T; Marlowe, *Doctor Faustus*, T; Marlowe, *The Jew of Malta*, T; Marlowe, *The Massacre at Paris*, T; Munday, *John a Kent and John a Cumber*, C; Peele, *The Battle of Alcazar*, T.

SUSSEX'S MEN AND PEMBROKE'S MEN
(*with plays later taken over by the Chamberlain's Men*)

Anon., *Mucedorus*, C; Anon., *The Taming of a Shrew*, C; Greene (?), *George a Greene*, C; Marlowe, *Edward II*, H; Shakespeare, *II Henry VI*, H; Shakespeare, *III Henry VI*, H; Shakespeare, *I Henry VI*, H; Shakespeare, *The Comedy of Errors*, C; Shakespeare, *Love's Labour's Lost*, C; Shakespeare, *The Two Gentlemen of Ve-*

rona, C; Shakespeare, *Richard III*, H; Shakespeare, *Titus Androni-cus*, T; Shakespeare, *The Taming of the Shrew*, C.

SELECT

CHAPEL AND PAUL'S BOYS

Lyly, *Campaspe*, C; Lyly, *Sapho and Phao*, C.

CHAPEL BOYS

Anon., *Wars of Cyrus*, T; Marlowe and Nashe, *Tragedy of Dido*, T.

PAUL'S BOYS

Lyly, *Endymion*, C; Lyly, *Love's Metamorphosis*, C; Lyly, *Midas*, C; Lyly, *Mother Bombie*, C; *Gallathea*, C.

COMPANY UNKNOWN

Anon., *Two Italian Gentlemen*, C, c. 1584; Greene, *Alphonsus King of Aragon*, C, c. 1587; Peele, *David and Bethsabe*, T, c. 1587; Wilson, *The Cobbler's Prophecy*, C, c. 1590; Anon., *Edward III*, H, c. 1590; Anon., *Soliman and Perseda*, T, c. 1590; Anon., *Arden of Feversham*, T, c. 1591; Peele, *Edward I*, H, c. 1591; Anon., *Locrine*, T, c. 1591; Anon., *Jack Straw*, H, c. 1591; Nashe, *Summer's Last Will and Testament*, M, c. 1592; Greene (?), *John of Bordeaux*, C, c. 1592; Anon., *Richard II or Thomas of Woodstock*, H, c. 1592; Lyly, *The Woman in the Moon*, C, c. 1593; Yarington, *Two Lamentable Tragedies*, T, c. 1594; Anon., *Alphonsus Emperor of Germany*, T, c. 1594.

1595–1598

POPULAR

ADMIRAL'S MEN

Anon., *Captain Thomas Stukeley*, H; Chapman, *The Blind Beggar of Alexandria*, C; Chapman, *An Humorous Day's Mirth*, C; Chettle and Munday, *The Downfall of Robert Earl of Huntington*, C; Chettle and Munday, *The Death of Robert Earl of Huntington*, T; Haughton, *Englishmen for My Money*, C; Porter, *The Two Angry Women of Abingdon*, C.

CHAMBERLAIN'S MEN

Jonson, *Every Man in His Humor*, C; Shakespeare, *Romeo and Juliet*, T; Shakespeare, *Richard II*, H; Shakespeare, *A Midsummer Night's Dream*, C; Shakespeare, *King John*, H; Shakespeare, *The Merchant of Venice*, C; Shakespeare, *I Henry IV*, H; Shakespeare, *II Henry IV*, H; Shakespeare, *Much Ado About Nothing*, C.

SELECT

BOTH COMPANIES DORMANT

COMPANY UNKNOWN

Anon., *Edmond Ironside*, H, c. 1595; Anon., *Thorney Abbey*, C, c. 1595; Jonson, *A Tale of a Tub*, C, first version c. 1596–1598?; Munday, Chettle, Dekker, Heywood (?), Shakespeare (?), *Sir Thomas More*, H, c. 1595–1599.

1599–1603

POPULAR

ADMIRAL'S MEN
(*Moved in 1600 from Rose to Fortune*)

Anon., *Look About You*, C; Chettle, *Hoffman*, T; Dekker, *Old Fortunatus*, C; Dekker, *The Shoemaker's Holiday*, C; Chettle and Day, *The Blind Beggar of Bednal Green*, C; Chettle, Dekker (and Haughton?), *Patient Grissill*, C; Drayton, Hathway, Munday, and Wilson *Sir John Oldcastle*, H.

CHAMBERLAIN'S MEN
(*Moved in 1599 from Shoreditch theatres to Globe*)

Anon., *Alarum for London*, T; Anon., *Warning for Fair Woman*, T; Anon., *Thomas Lord Cromwell*, H; Anon., *The Merry Devil of Edmonton*, C; Dekker, *Satiromastix*, C (for Marston's and the Paul's Boys' interest in the play, see above, p. 108); Jonson, *Every Man Out of His Humor*, C; Jonson, *Sejanus*, T; Shakespeare, *Henry V*, H; Shakespeare, *Julius Caesar*, T; Shakespeare, *As You Like It*, C; Shakespeare, *The Merry Wives of Windsor*, C; Shakespeare, *Twelfth Night*, C; Shakespeare, *Hamlet*, T; Shakespeare, *Troilus and Cressida*, T; Shakespeare, *All's Well That Ends Well*, C.

DERBY'S, OXFORD'S, AND WORCESTER'S MEN
(*Chiefly at Boar's Head and Rose*)

Anon., *Trial of Chivalry*, C; Anon., *The Weakest Goeth to the Wall*, H; Heywood, *The Four Prentices of London*, C; Heywood (?), *I Edward IV*, H; Heywood, *II Edward IV*, H; Heywood (?), *How a Man May Choose a Good Wife from a Bad*, C; Heywood (and W. Smith?), *The Royal King and the Loyal Subject*, C; Heywood, *A Woman Killed with Kindness*, T.

SELECT

PAUL'S BOYS

Anon., *The Maid's Metamorphosis*, C; Anon., *The Wisdom of Doctor Dodypoll*, C; Anon., *Blurt Master Constable*, C; Marston, *Histriomastix*, C; Marston, *Antonio and Mellida*, C; Marston, *Antonio's Revenge*, T; Marston, *Jack Drum's Entertainment*, C; Marston, *What You Will*, C; Middleton (and Dekker?), *The Family of Love*, C.

CHAPEL BOYS
(*At Blackfriars*)

Jonson, *Cynthia's Revels*, C; Jonson, *Poetaster*, C; Chapman, *The Gentleman Usher*, C; Chapman, *May-Day*, C; Chapman, *Sir Giles Goosecap*, C.

COMPANY UNKNOWN

W. Rowley (?), *The Thracian Wonder*, C, c. 1599; Anon., *Charlemagne or the Distracted Emperor*, T, c. 1599; Heywood (?), *Devil and His Dame*, C, c. 1600; Anon., *Lust's Dominion*, T, c. 1600; Heywood (?), *The Fair Maid of the Exchange*, C, c. 1602; Dekker (with Day and S. Rowley?), *The Noble Soldier*, C, c. 1602; Anon., *Wily Beguiled*, C, c. 1602.

1604–1608

POPULAR

PRINCE HENRY'S–FORMERLY ADMIRAL'S–MEN
(*At the Fortune*)

Dekker and Middleton, *I The Honest Whore*, C; Dekker, *II The*

Honest Whore, C; Dekker, *The Whore of Babylon*, H; S. Rowley, *When You See Me You Know Me*, H.

KING'S—FORMERLY CHAMBERLAIN'S—MEN
(*At the Globe*)

Anon., *The Fair Maid of Bristowe*, C; Anon., *The London Prodigal*, C; Anon., *A Yorkshire Tragedy*, T; Barnes, *The Devil's Charter*, T; Jonson, *Volpone*, C; Middleton (?), *The Revenger's Tragedy*, T; Shakespeare, *Measure for Measure*, C; Shakespeare, *Othello*, T; Shakespeare, *King Lear*, T; Shakespeare, *Macbeth*, T; Shakespeare, *Antony and Cleopatra*, T; Shakespeare, *Timon of Athens*, T; Shakespeare, *Coriolanus*, T; Shakespeare (and Wilkins?), *Pericles*, C; Wilkins, *The Miseries of Enforced Marriage*, C.

QUEEN ANNE'S—FORMERLY WORCESTER'S—MEN
(*Moved in 1605 from Rose to Red Bull*)

Anon., *Nobody and Somebody*, C; Day, W. Rowley, and Wilkins, *The Travels of the Three English Brothers*, H; Dekker and Webster, *Sir Thomas Wyatt*, H; Heywood, *I If You Know Not Me You Know Nobody*, H; Heywood, *II If You Know Not Me You Know Nobody*, H; Heywood, *The Wise Woman of Hogsdon*, C; Heywood, *The Rape of Lucrece*, T; W. Rowley, *A Shoemaker a Gentleman*, C.

SELECT

PAUL'S BOYS

Beaumont (with Fletcher?), *The Woman Hater*, C; Chapman, *Bussy D'Ambois*, T; Dekker and Webster, *Westward Ho*, C; Dekker and Webster, *Northward Ho*, C; Middleton, *The Phoenix*, C; Middleton, *A Trick to Catch the Old One*, C; Middleton, *A Mad World My Masters*, C; Middleton, *Michaelmas Term*, C; Middleton (?), *The Puritan*, C.

QUEEN'S REVELS—FORMERLY CHAPEL BOYS
(*At Blackfriars*)

Beaumont, *The Knight of the Burning Pestle*, C; Chapman, *All Fools but the Fool*, C; Chapman, *Monsieur D'Olive*, C; Chapman, *The Widow's Tears*, C; Chapman, *I Charles Duke of Byron*, T; *II Charles Duke of Byron*, T; Daniel, *Philotas*, T; Day, *The Isle of Gulls*, C;

Fletcher, *The Faithful Shepherdess*, C; Fletcher (with Beaumont?), *Cupid's Revenge*, T; Jonson, *The Case Is Altered*, C; Jonson, Marston, and Chapman, *Eastward Ho*, C; Marston, *The Dutch Courtesan*, C; Marston, *The Malcontent*, C; Marston, *The Fawn*, C; Marston, *Sophonisba*, T; Middleton, *Your Five Gallants*, C; Sharpham, *The Fleire*, C.

KING'S REVELS
(At Whitefriars)

Armin, *The Two Maids of Moreclack*, C; Barry, *Ram-Alley*, C; Day, *Humor Out of Breath*, C; Day, *Law-Tricks*, C; Machin and Markham, *The Dumb Knight*, C; Mason, *The Turk*, C; Sharpham, *Cupid's Whirligig*, C.

COMPANY UNKNOWN

Anon., *The Wit of a Woman*, C, c. 1604; Brewer, *The Lovesick King*, T, c. 1607; Machin (?), *Every Woman in Her Humor*, C, c. 1607; Anon., *The Tragedy of Nero*, T, c. 1607.

1609–1613

POPULAR

PRINCE HENRY'S–LATER PALSGRAVE'S–MEN
(At the Fortune)

Dekker and Middleton, *The Roaring Girl*, C; R. A., *The Valiant Welshman*, H.

QUEEN ANNE'S MEN
(At the Red Bull)

Cooke, *Greene's Tu Quoque*, C; Dekker, *If It Be Not Good the Devil Is in It*, C; Dekker, *Match Me in London*, C; Heywood and W. Rowley, *Fortune by Land and Sea*, C; Heywood, *1 The Fair Maid of the West*, C; Heywood, *The Golden Age*, C; Heywood, *The Silver Age*, C; Heywood, *The Brazen Age*, T; Heywood, *1 The Iron Age*, T; Heywood, *II The Iron Age*, T; Webster, *The White Devil*, T; Webster and Heywood, *Appius and Virginia*, T.

SELECT

QUEEN'S REVELS
(At Whitefriars)

Chapman, *The Revenge of Bussy D'Ambois*, T; Field, *A Woman Is a Weathercock*, C; Field, *Amends for Ladies*, C; Fletcher (with Beaumont?), *The Coxcomb*, C; Fletcher (with Beaumont?), *The Scornful Lady*, C; Jonson, *Epicoene*, C; Marston and Barkstead, *The Insatiate Countess*, T.

POPULAR OR SELECT

KING'S MEN
(At Globe and Blackfriars)

Anon., *The Second Maiden's Tragedy*, T; Beaumont and Fletcher, *Philaster*, C; Beaumont and Fletcher, *The Maid's Tragedy*, T; Beaumont and Fletcher, *A King and No King*, C; Fletcher (with Beaumont?), *The Captain*, C; Fletcher, *Bonduca*, T; Daborne, *A Christian Turned Turk*, T; Chapman, *Caesar and Pompey*, T; Jonson, *The Alchemist*, C; Jonson, *Catiline*, T; Shakespeare, *Cymbeline*, C; Shakespeare, *The Winter's Tale*, C; Shakespeare, *The Tempest*, C; Shakespeare and Fletcher, *The Two Noble Kinsmen*, C; Shakespeare and Fletcher, *Henry VIII*, H.

LADY ELIZABETH'S MEN
(By 1613 at Whitefriars and Hope)

Fletcher (with Field and Massinger?), *The Honest Man's Fortune*, C; Middleton, *A Chaste Maid in Cheapside*, C. (Jonson's *Bartholomew Fair* was performed by this company in 1614.)

COMPANY UNKNOWN

W. Rowley, *The Birth of Merlin*, C, c. 1608; Fletcher (with Beaumont), *Wit at Several Weapons*, C, c. 1609; Tourneur, *The Atheist's Tragedy*, T, c. 1609; W. Rowley, *A New Wonder or a Woman Never Vexed*, C, c. 1609; Fletcher, *The Woman's Prize*, C, c. 1611; Beaumont, Fletcher (and Field?), *Four Plays in One*, M, c. 1612.

Shakespeare As Expurgator

As noted above (p. 207) Shakespeare, in line with popular practice but with greater consistency, tends to eliminate from his plays acts of illicit love found in his sources, and rarely invents any of his own. Transgression is more often suspected than real and, when real, is more often alluded to briefly than emphasized. The phenomenon will be recognized as evidence of a working principle if the plays are surveyed in series, with source materials, analogous plays, and alternate possibilities of plot development in mind. What follows is only the sketch of such a survey. Unless otherwise noted, no act of fornication or adultery occurs among the characters as they figure in the plays.

In *I Henry VI* Joan of Arc tries to save her life by feigning pregnancy; but in Shakespeare (V, iv, 1–93) as in Holinshed (*Chronicles*, III, 171) her actual immorality remains only a matter of suspicion. In *II Henry VI* the guilty relations of Queen Margaret and the Duke of Suffolk also remain in Shakespeare (IV, i, 75, iv, 1–25, *et passim*) as in Holinshed (III, 212, 220, 236) a suspicion. In *III Henry VI* Edward IV is called "lascivious" (V, v, 34), and his propensities are mentioned by his brothers (III, ii); but his criminal attempts upon the daughter or niece of Warwick, as described in Holinshed (III, 284), are not dramatized, nor are his other amours.

In Plautus, Menaechmus of Epidamnum is an unabashed lecher, robbing his wife to supply his mistress. In *The Comedy of Errors*, the corresponding character, Antipholus of Ephesus, is a faithful husband. His visit to the courtesan (III, i, 107–121) for the purpose of spiting his wife is chaperoned by Balthazar (V, i, 223). No ribald capital is made of the wife's mistaking the twin from Syracuse as her husband although the opportunities are obvious and formed the sole source of humor in the modern musical comedy suggested by the play, *The Boys from Syracuse*. In *The Two Gentlemen of Verona*, Proteus's conduct remains at the level of bad intentions, and the purity of the Titus and Gisippus story of Boccaccio, and the Felismena story of Montemayor's *Diana*, if these be the sources, is retained. Contrary to what might seem to be the comic demands of the situation in *Love's Labour's Lost*, Jaquenetta, the country wench, goes through the play unscathed so far as we know, and Costard's charge that she has been seduced by Don Armada seems to be a canard.

Jane Shore, most famous of English paramours, is excluded as a character in *Richard III*, and the allusions to her are fleeting and none too friendly (I, i, 73, 93–94, 98, 100, III, i, 185, v, 30–31, 50–51). Her career was treated in the narrative verse of the period whenever opportunity offered, and was dramatized in Legge's *Richardus Tertius*, the anonymous *True Tragedy of Richard the Third*, Heywood's *Edward IV*, and, at last, by Nicholas Rowe in what he mistakenly thought the manner of Shakespeare. The account of her career incorporated in Holinshed's *Chronicles* was written by Sir Thomas More, who portrays her as beautiful, witty, cheerful, well mannered, and even modest. More even apologizes for her betrayal of her husband: ". . . forsomuch as they were coupled ere she were well ripe, she not very fervently loved him . . . which was haply the thing that the more easily made her incline unto the king's appetite" (*Chronicles*, III, 384). Her charitable deeds and bitter end won her the sympathy of the Londoners who had stiffly persisted in calling her "Shore's wife," and Heywood's treatment is homiletic but tender. Shakespeare, although following the *Chronicles* closely in dramatizing the events of these years (III, 386–388), takes the widow Anne but leaves the mistress Jane, refusing to feature an adulteress who, because of the peculiar nature of her personality, experience, and end, with their attendant tradition, could be presented only sympathetically.

In *Titus Andronicus* adultery and rape are conspicuous, among a series of additional (nonsexual) themes ordinarily avoided by Shakespeare (see the present author's *As They Liked It*, pp. 13–15). In developing the subplot of *The Taming of the Shrew*, Shakespeare, whatever the relation of his play to *The Taming of a Shrew*, had direct recourse to Gascoigne's *The Supposes*; but he departed from Gascoigne by eliminating the bawd Balia, and by transforming

Polinesta and Erostrato, who gets Polinesta with child, into Bianca and Lucentio, a pair of pure lovers./

In *Richard II* Shakespeare presents all the offenses of the King except the sexual ones, in spite of Holinshed's "there reigned abundantly the filthy sin of lechery and fornication, with abominable adultery, specially in the king" (*Chronicles*, II, 868). *King John*, although otherwise following closely the action of the older *Troublesome Reign of King John*, eliminates the comic pictures of sexual license among nuns and friars.

In *A Midsummer Night's Dream*, which appears to be almost purely Shakespearean invention, nothing suggestive attends the episodes of the lovers' wandering and sleeping together in the wood, or even of Titania's infatuation with Bottom while under the influence of the love charm. In *Romeo and Juliet*, despite the ardor of the lovers and the earthiness of their familiars, the action is chaste; there is not, as in Broke's *Romeus and Juliet*, any tendency to luxuriate over the lovers' night of "pleasant sport" (*Shakespeare's Library*, ed. W. C. Hazlitt, Part I, Vol. I, pp. 113–114). The irreproachable Portia in *The Merchant of Venice* is fashioned out of the Widow of Belmonte in Fiorentino's *Il Pecorone*, and the Widow of Belmonte is a genteel harpy who uses her beauty as carnal bait for a succession of men in order to cheat them of their fortunes.

In *I Henry IV* the wild Prince Hal speaks of maidenheads being available "by the hundreds" in time of war (II, iv, 399), but his escapades take no amatory form, and neither, for the time being, do Falstaff's. In *II Henry IV* Falstaff consorts with Doll Tearsheet and Mistress Quickly. The latter, who had a husband in Part One (III, iii, 62–68, 135–138) has become a widow in Part Two (II, i, 75–90), and adultery is thus averted!

Among the sources and analogues of *Much Ado About Nothing*, Dalinda in the story of Ginevra and Ariodante in Book V of Ariosto's *Orlando Furioso*, and Pryene in Book V, Canto IV, of Spenser's *Faerie Queene*, are the characters equivalent to Shakespeare's Margaret. Dalinda certainly, and Pryene almost as certainly, have guilty sexual relations with the characters equivalent to Shakespeare's Borachio, but Margaret's misdemeanor consists solely of conversing with Borachio from a window while wearing Hero's clothes. Since she has no good reason for remaining silent when Hero is falsely accused of a liaison with Borachio, Shakespeare meets the difficulty simply by suppressing her as a character in the relevant scenes. Her role is ambiguous, and her virtue is preserved at the expense of plausibility. (See II, ii, 40–41, III, ii, 115, iii, 153–161, V, i, 235–251, 311.) The diatribes against Hero's supposed offense are more strident than anything in the sources (IV, i, 31–62, 121–144), and the cruel exposure at the altar occurs only in Shakespeare. There is nothing to indicate that it would have been considered damnable had Hero really been guilty; Don Pedro is party to the action, and after its supposed deadly effect, he shows no compunction, while Claudio feels that he has sinned only "in mistaking" (V, i, 283–284).

In *As You Like It*, Audrey is a poor thing, like Armado's Jaquenetta; but she is not made poorer by the loss of her virtue, Touchstone's intentions being reasonably honorable. Rosalind, Celia, Phebe, and Audrey—ladies, shepherdess, and village wench—are all led to the altar.

In composing *Julius Caesar*, Shakespeare ignored the suggestion in Plutarch that Caesar had formerly been the lover of Brutus's mother and was possibly Brutus's true father. The dramatic possibilities in the situation are obvious, and were utilized by Voltaire. In *Henry V* illicit love affairs do not occur and, in view of the subject matter, could scarcely be expected.

The frustration of all amours in *The Merry Wives of Windsor* is contrary to the traditional requirements of the situation. When, in antecedent literature, a trusting husband like Page and a jealous one like Ford are contrasted, the latter is predestined to be cuckolded. Ford is equivalent to Maestro Raimondo in the story of Nerino of Portugal in Straparola's *Le Tredeci Piacevoli Notti*, IV, 4 (1550–1553). Raimondo had been naturalized in England as old Mutio in the tale of the two lovers of Pisa in Tarleton's *News Out of Purgatory*, 1590. Ford is also equivalent to the husband of Madonna Giovanni in the story of Buccinola and Pietro Paola in Fiorentino's *Il Pecorone*, 1558. This character was naturalized in England as the Doctor in the story of Lucius and Camillus in *The Fortunate, the Deceived, and the Unfortunate Lovers*, some time before 1632. The question is this: If Raimondo, Mutio, Giovanni, and the Doctor, like dozens of similarly suspicious husbands in fabliau, farce, and novella, should be cuckolded, why not Master Ford? It seems as if certain popular ballads, in which would-be lovers instead of husbands are discomfited (see *The Friar in the Well*, Adam of Cobsam's *The*

Wright's Chaste Wife, etc.), have crossed with the cuckoldry tales. The popular dramatist declined to treat adultery in a comic vein even in order to punish a jealous husband and to effect a neat didactic contrast.

In *Twelfth Night* the character of Olivia has been refined like Portia's. There are a dozen Italian, French, Spanish, and English plays and stories all apparently stemming from *Gli Ingannati,* 1537, and in those otherwise most similar in plot to Shakespeare's play, the character equivalent to Olivia is made pregnant by the character equivalent to Sebastian. As in the case of *The Merry Wives of Windsor,* the change effected by Shakespeare cannot be considered broadly as an "English" change: the Anglo-Latin comedy of *Laelia,* acted at Cambridge about 1595, and Barnabe Riche's story of Apolonius and Silla in *Farewell to Military Profession,* 1581 (probably Shakespeare's immediate source), are both "unexpurgated."

In *Hamlet* sexual transgression, save for the doubtful item of what has occurred before the action begins, is confined to the technically incestuous marital relations of Claudius and Gertrude. In Saxo Grammaticus and in Belleforest, the character equivalent to Ophelia is employed as a seductress of the Prince. In the former (Gollancz, *The Sources of Hamlet,* p. 108), the cleverness of the Prince is manifested in his enjoying the lady and yet escaping the trap; and in the latter (*ibid.,* p. 202), although the treatment is more ambiguous, the Prince would obviously enjoy the lady if safety permitted. The only survival of this motif in Shakespeare's play is the solicitude for Ophelia's chastity displayed by her father and brother, and the suspicions of Hamlet himself. Disgust at sexual laxity is not prominent in Saxo Grammaticus and Belleforest, and is probably Shakespeare's addition to any antecedent dramatic version of the legend.

Fornication and adultery do occur in *Troilus and Cressida* and asperse the military aims of Greeks and Trojans alike. Shakespeare's spirit is not blithe in the treatment, and his Troilus, unlike Chaucer's, does not offer Pandarus any of his sisters in return for Cressida's favors. In *All's Well That Ends Well* Bertram's sin of adultery is in intention only; yet it is surrounded by an atmosphere of moral condemnation, and Bertram's character is written down to the level of an adulterer's (see W. W. Lawrence, *Shakespeare's Problem Comedies,* p. 62). No stigma attaches to the equivalent character of

Beltramo de Rossiglione in Boccaccio's *Decameron*, III, 9, as rendered in Painter's *Palace of Pleasure*.

In *Measure for Measure* fornication occurs but is followed in each case by marriage, in line with the tragicomic pattern of the play. The offenses of Julietta and Mariana are only technical, and even Kate Keepdown, who is mentioned but does not appear, is made an honest woman in the end! Lucio is forced to marry this girl whom he seduced with false promises (III, ii, 210–215, V, i, 524–526). Epitia in Cinthio's *Hecatommithi*, VIII, v, and Cassandra in Whetstone's *Promos and Cassandra*, 1578, and *Heptameron of Civil Discourses*, 1582, are equivalent to Shakespeare's Isabella; but, unlike Isabella, they yield their bodies to the unjust deputy. Shakespeare does not permit Angelo to use certain formidable arguments against Isabella's refusal—to wit, that her virtue, as he admits about his own (II, iv, 10), may be mostly only pride, that she demonstrate her contention that Claudio's sin is venal by committing it herself, and that the saintly stand ready to do *more* for others than for themselves—although the fashion in which he skirts such arguments suggests that they were in the dramatist's mind. Isabella's arguments, too, in extenuating her brother's offense, although bitterly regretted by her later, are more inhibited than those in Cinthio (see Raleigh, *Shakespeare*, pp. 168–169). Whetstone's heroine, like Cinthio's, is freer in extenuating the offense. We hear in Shakespeare that the Duke has seen "corruption boil and bubble" in Vienna (V, i, 320–324); but in Whetstone more corruption is displayed. In Whetstone the wicked deputy is attended by lecherous Phallax, in Shakespeare by virtuous Escalus. In place of Whetstone's courtesan Lamia and her enticements, Shakespeare gives us Mistress Overdone.

In *Othello* Cassius frequents the house of a courtesan as does the Moro's lieutenant in Cinthio's *Hecatommithi*, III, 7, and less is made of the fault than of the character's drunkenness; but the note of admonition, slight as it is (V, i, 115–123), represents an addition to the source. In *King Lear* Goneril's adulterous passion for Edmund is Shakespeare's invention. She is defeated of her desires, unlike Tamora in *Titus Andronicus*, the only other woman of the kind in Shakespeare. In *Macbeth* the sex motif is excluded and, as noted by Professor Stoll ("Shakespeare Forbears," *M.L.N.*, LIV (1939), 332–339), Lady Macbeth is a wife, not a tempting siren. In *Antony and Cleopatra* adultery is treated but, as noted above (p. 198), without the traditional palliation. In *Timon of Athens* the mistresses of Alcibiades appear but only to provide a text for the misanthrope. The betrayals which he has experienced have been exclusively by men. In *Coriolanus*, as in *Henry V*, the absence of a sex-motif may be considered as owing to the nature of the story.

To what has been noted earlier about the brothel in *Pericles* may be added a curious detail about Marina's lover Lysimachus. In Gower's story of Apollonius of Tyre (*Confessio Amantis*, VIII, 271–2008) the equivalent character has no contact with the brothel. In Twine's *Pattern of Painful Adventures*, c. 1576, he is an unabashed patron, only reforming in time to make an eligible suitor for the virgin. In Shakespeare he frequents the brothel, but for ambiguous reasons. In George Wilkins's *The Painful Adventures of Pericles Prince of Tyre*, 1608, which seems to have been based largely on the play, he is still a reformed patron, but the dramatic text (IV, vi, 111–117) renders the point doubtful:

> Had I brought hither a corrupted mind,
> Thy speech had altered it . . .
> . . . I came with no ill intent; for to me
> The very doors and windows savour vilely.

It is impossible to say whether Shakespeare has given Lysimachus virtue or a becoming hypocrisy.

In *Cymbeline* the episode of the wager over the wife's chastity is conducted with none of the cynicism of the corresponding episode in Boccaccio's *Decameron*, II, 9, where unfaithful wives are assumed to be the rule. Boccaccio's Bernabo, unlike Shakespeare's Posthumus, does not insist upon a duel in the event that his wife's questioned chastity be vindicated. The exclusion from *The Winter's Tale* of the incest motif in Greene's *Pandosto* has been illustrated above (p. 210). In *The Tempest* the opportunities for the salacious offered by the presence of a maid who has never seen a young man are not grasped, although they were to be recognized and exploited in the adaptation of Dryden and Davenant. In *Henry VIII*, for reasons irrelevant to the present sketch, the king is not a lecher; the Queens Katherine and Anne are equally admirable.

The portions of *The Two Noble Kinsmen* assigned severally to Shakespeare and Fletcher are as distinct in their sexual emphasis as in their versification. The jailor's daughter is disrespectfully used only while under Fletcher's manipulation. (Compare IV, i, and V, ii, usually assigned to Fletcher on stylistic grounds, with Shakespeare's V, iv, and with IV, iii, which is probably his. An amusing distinction is also observable between Palamon's prayer to Venus as it appears in Chaucer's *Knight's Tale* (lines 2234–2236, Globe ed.)—

> I shal for evermoore,
> Emforth my myght, thy trewe servant be,
> And holden werre alwey with chastitee—

and the prayer as rendered by Shakespeare (V, i, 97–107):

> [I] Have never been foul-mouth'd against thy law;
> Nev'r reveal'd secret, for I knew none—would not,
> Had I kenn'd all that were. I never practis'd
> Upon man's wife, nor would the libels read
> Of liberal wits. I never at great feasts
> Sought to betray a beauty, but have blush'd
> At simp'ring sirs that did. I have been harsh
> To large confessors, and have hotly ask'd them
> If they had mothers. I had one, a woman,
> And women 'twere they wrong'd.

It is difficult to see what Venus could have done with this client except refer him to Diana.

List of Works Cited

Acts of the Privy Council of England, new series, ed. John R. Dasent, Vols. VI (1556–1558), IX–X (1575–1578). London, 1892, 1894–1895.

Adams, Henry H., *English Domestic or Homiletic Tragedy, 1575–1642*, New York, 1943.

Adams, Joseph Q., *Shakespearean Playhouses*. Boston, 1917.

——, ed. *Chief Pre-Shakespearean Dramas*. Boston, 1924.

Adkins, Mary G. M., "Puritanism in the Plays and Pamphlets of Thomas Dekker," *Univ. Texas Studies in English*, XIX (1940), 86–113.

Allen, Don C., "The Degeneration of Man and Renaissance Pessimism," *Studies in Philology*, XXXV (1938), 202–227.

Allen, Morse S., *The Satire of John Marston*. Columbus, Ohio, 1920.

Andreas Capellanus, *The Art of Courtly Love*, trans. and ed. John J. Parry. New York, 1941.

Ariosto, Lodovico, *Orlando Furioso*, trans. William S. Rose. New York, 1907.

Armin, Robert, *Works*, ed. Alexander B. Grosart. Manchester, 1880.

Babb, Lawrence, "Melancholy and the Elizabethan Man of Letters," *Huntington Library Quarterly*, IV (1941), 247–261. (See also *The Elizabethan Malady*, East Lansing, Mich., 1951.)

—— "The Physiological Conception of Love in the Elizabethan and Early Stuart Drama," *PMLA*, LVI (1941), 1020–1035.

Baker, Oliver, *In Shakespeare's Warwickshire and the Unknown Years*. London, 1937.

Baldwin, Thomas W., *The Organization and Personnel of the Shakespearean Company*. Princeton, 1927.

Bandello, Matteo, *The Novels*, trans. J. Payne. 6 vols. London, 1890.

Barnes, Barnabe, *The Devil's Charter*, ed. R. B. McKerrow (in *Materialien zur Kunde des älteren englischen Dramas*, Vol. VI, 1904).

Barnfield, Richard, *Complete Poems*, ed. Alexander B. Grosart. Roxburghe Club, 1876.

Barry, David, *Ram-Alley or Merry Tricks*. In Dodsley (*q.v.*), Vol. X.

Baskervill, Charles R., *English Elements in Jonson's Early Comedy*. (*Bulletin of the Univ. of Texas, Humanistic Series No. 12, Studies in English No. 1*, 1911).

Battenhouse, Roy W., "Chapman and the Nature of Man," *ELH*, XII (1945), 87–107.

Beaumont, Francis, and John Fletcher, *Works*, ed. Arnold Glover and A. R. Walker. 10 vols. Cambridge, 1905–1912.

Becon, Thomas, *The Boke of Matrimony* (in *Works*, 3 vols., London, 1560–1564).

Beeching, Henry C., "On the Religion of Shakespeare," in *The Works of William Shakespeare*, ed. A. H. Bullen (10 vols., Stratford-on-Avon, 1904–1907), Vol. X.

Belleforest, Francois de, *Histoires tragiques*, Vol. V (1570), ed. Sir Israel Gollancz (in *The Sources of Hamlet, with Essay on the Legend*, London, 1926).

Bennett, Josephine W., "Oxford and Endymion," *PMLA*, LVII (1942), 354–369.

Bentley, Gerald E., *The Jacobean and Caroline Stage*. 2 vols. Oxford, 1941.

Bethell, S. L., *Shakespeare and the Popular Dramatic Tradition*. Durham, N.C., 1945.

"Blackfriars Records," ed. A. Feuillerat, *Malone Society Collections*, Vol. II, Part I (1931).

Bliss, William, *The Real Shakespeare: A Counterblast to Commentators*. New York, 1949.

Blurt Master-Constable. In Middleton (*q.v.*), *Works*, Vol. I.

Boaistuau, Pierre, *Théâtre du Monde*, trans. John Alday. London, 1603.

Book of Homilies. See *Certain Sermons or Homilies*.

Bredvold, Louis I., "The Naturalism of Donne in Relation to Some Renaissance Traditions," *Journal of English and Germanic Philology*, XXII (1923), 471–502.

Bridges, Robert, "On the Influence of the Audience," in *The Works of William Shakespeare*, ed. A. H. Bullen (10 vols., Stratford-upon-Avon, 1904–1907), Vol. X.

Broke, Arthur, *Romeus and Juliet* (1562), ed. W. C. Hazlitt, in *Shakespeare's Library* (6 vols., London, 1875), Part I, Vol. 1.

Brooke, C. F. Tucker, *The Life of Marlowe*. London, 1930.

——, *Shakespeare of Stratford*. New Haven, 1926.

——, ed. *The Shakespeare Apocrypha*. Oxford, 1918.

Browne, Edward H., *An Exposition of the Thirty-nine Articles*, ed. J. Williams. New York, 1887.

Buckley, George T., *Atheism in the English Renaissance*. Chicago, 1932.

Bush, Douglas, *The Renaissance and English Humanism*. Toronto, 1939.

Byrne, M. St. Clare, ed. *The Elizabethan Home, Discovered in Two Dialogues by Claudius Hollyband and Peter Erondell*. London, 1930.

Calendar of State Papers, Domestic Series, of the Reign of Elizabeth, ed. Mary A. Green, Vols. II (1581–1590), V (1598–1601). London, 1865, 1869.

Campbell, Lily B., *Shakespeare's "Histories": Mirrors of Elizabethan Policy*. San Marino, Calif., 1947.

——, *Shakespeare's Tragic Heroes: Slaves of Passion*. Cambridge, 1930.

Campbell, Oscar J., *Comicall Satyre and Shakespeare's Troilus and Cressida*. San Marino, Calif., 1938.

Captain Thomas Stukeley, in Richard Simpson, ed., *The School of Shakspere* (2 vols., New York, 1878), Vol. I.

Castelvetro, Lodovico, *Poetics of Aristotle*, trans. Allan H. Gilbert (in *Literary Criticism: Plato to Dryden*, New York, 1940).

Castiglione, Baldassare, *The Book of the Courtier*, trans. Leonard E. Opdycke. Immortal Classics, n.d.

Certain Sermons or Homilies, Appointed by the King's Majesty to Be Declared and Read by All Parsons, Vicars and Curates, Every Sunday in Their Churches Where They Have Cure, 1547. *The Second Tome of Homilies*, 1563. *Homily of Rebellion*, 1571. Edition of 1623 collated with above. Oxford, 1840.

Chambers, Sir Edmund K., *The Elizabethan Stage*. 4 vols. Oxford, 1923.

——, *The Mediaeval Stage*. 2 vols. Oxford, 1903.

——, *Shakespearean Gleanings*. Oxford, 1944.

——, *William Shakespeare: A Study of Facts and Problems*. 2 vols. Oxford, 1930.

Chambers, Raymond W., *The Jacobean Shakespeare and Measure for Measure* (Annual Shakespeare Lecture of the British Academy, 1937). London, 1938.

Chapman, George, *The Comedies*, ed. Thomas M. Parrott. London, 1914.

——, *The Tragedies*, ed. Thomas M. Parrott. London, 1910.

——, *The Poems*, ed. Phyllis B. Bartlett (Modern Language Association of America, General Series, No. 12). New York, 1941.

"Chapman," *Times Literary Supplement* (London), May 10, 1934, pp. 329–330.

Charlton, H. B., *Shakespeare, Politics, and Politicians*, Oxford, 1929.

Chaucer, Geoffrey, *Works*, ed. Alfred W. Pollard et al. (Globe ed.) London, 1925.

Chettle, Henry, *Kind-Hartes Dream* (1592), ed. G. B. Harrison, (Bodley Head Quartos, No. 4). London, 1923.

——, *The Tragedy of Hoffman, or A Revenge for a Father*, ed. A. F. Hopkinson. London, 1917.

——, and Anthony Munday, *The Downfall of Robert Earl of Huntington*. In Dodsley (*q.v.*), Vol. VIII.

——, and Anthony Munday, *The Death of Robert Earl of Huntington*. In Dodsley (*q.v.*), Vol. VIII.

Child, Francis J., *The English and Scottish Popular Ballads*. 5 vols. Boston, 1883–1898.

Cinthio (Giovanni Battista Giraldi), *Hecatommithi*, III, 7 (1565), ed. W. C. Hazlitt, *Shakespeare's Library* (6 vols., London, 1875), Part I, Vol. II.

Clark, A., "Malden Records and the Drama," *Notes and Queries*, 10 Series, Vol. VII (1907), 181–183, 422–423.

Clode, Charles M., *The Early History of the Guild of Merchant Taylors*. 2 vols. London, 1888.

Coleridge, Samuel T., *Coleridge's Shakespearean Criticism*, ed. Thomas M. Raysor. 2 vols. Cambridge, Mass., 1931.

Collier, Jeremy, *A Short View of the Immorality and Profaneness of the English Stage*. 3rd ed., London, 1698.

Collier, John P., *The History of English Dramatic Poetry to the Time of Shakespeare and Annals of the Stage to the Restoration*. 3 vols. London, 1831.

"Commissions for the Chapel," ed. E. K. Chambers, *Malone Society Collections*, Vol. I, Parts IV and V (1911).

Cooke, Jo., *Greene's Tu Quoque, or, The City Gallant*. In Dodsley (*q.v.*) Vol. XI.

Corbin, John, "Shakespeare and the Plastic Stage," *Atlantic Monthly*, XCVII (1906), 369–383.

Coulton, G. G., *Medieval Panorama: The English Scene from Conquest to Reformation*. New York, 1939.

Craig, Hardin, *The Enchanted Glass: The Elizabethan Mind in Literature*. New York, 1936.

——, "Ethics in the Jacobean Drama: The Case of Chapman," in *Essays in Dramatic Literature*, ed. Hardin Craig. Princeton, 1935.

Creizenach, Wilhelm M. A., *The English Drama in the Age of Shakespeare*. Philadelphia, 1916.

Crosby, Ernest, "Shakespeare's Attitude to the Working Classes." See Tolstoy, below.

Daniel, Samuel, *Complete Works in Verse and Prose*, ed. Alexander B. Grosart. 5 vols. London, 1885–1896.

Davenant, Sir William, *Dramatic Works*, ed. J. Maidment and W. H. Logan. 5 vols. Edinburgh, 1872–1874.

Davenport, A., "The Quarrel of the Satirists," *Modern Language Review*, XXXVII (1942), 123–130.

Day, John, *Complete Works*, ed. A. H. Bullen. London, 1881.

Dekker, Thomas, *Dramatic Works*, reprinted by John Pearson. 4 vols. London, 1873.

——, *Non-Dramatic Works*, ed. Alexander B. Grosart. 5 vols. London, 1884–1886. (Vol. V contains *Patient Grissill*.)

Derby. *The Derby Household Books*, ed. F. R. Raines, *Chetham Society Publications*, Vol. XXXI (1853).

Dickson, M. J., "William Trevell and the Whitefriars Theatre," *Review of English Studies*, VI (1930), 309–312.

Dodsley, Robert, *A Select Collection of Old English Plays*, ed. W. Carew Hazlitt. 15 vols. London, 1874–1876.

Donne, John, *Complete Poetry and Selected Prose*, ed. John Hayward. New York, 1929.

Dowling, Margaret, "Further Notes on William Trevell," *Review of English Studies*, VI (1930), 443–446.

"Dramatic Records from the Lansdowne Manuscripts," ed. E. K. Chambers and W. W. Greg, *Malone Society Collections*, Vol. I, Part II (1908).

"Dramatic Records of the City of London," ed. Anna J. Mill and E. K. Chambers, *Malone Society Collections*, Vol. II, Part III (1931).

"Dramatic Records of the City of London: The Remembrancia," ed. E. K. Chambers and W. W. Greg, *Malone Society Collections*, Vol. I, Part I (1907).

Eccles, Mark, "Middleton's Birth and Education," *Review of English Studies*, VII (1931), 531–541.

Edwardes, Richard, *Damon and Pythias*. See J. Q. Adams, ed., *Chief Pre-Shakespearean Dramas*.

Eliot, T. S., *Selected Essays, 1917–1932*. New York, 1932.

Ellis-Fermor, Una M., *The Jacobean Drama: An Interpretation*. London, 1936.

Ellison, Lee M., *The Early Romantic Drama at the English Court*. Menasha, Wis., 1917.

Erasmus. *Desiderius Erasmus Concerning the Aim and Method of Education*, ed. William H. Woodward. Boston, 1904.

——, *The Praise of Folly*, trans. Leonard F. Dean. Chicago, 1946.

Fair Em. See C. F. T. Brooke, *The Shakespeare Apocrypha*.

Fair Maid of Bristowe, ed. Arthur H. Quinn (Publications of the Univ. of Pennsylvania, Series on Philology and Literature, Vol. VIII, 1902).

Famous Victories of Henry the Fifth, The. See J. Q. Adams, ed., *Chief Pre-Shakespearean Dramas*.

Farnham, Willard, *The Medieval Heritage of Elizabethan Tragedy*. Berkeley, Calif., 1936.

——, *Shakespeare's Tragic Frontier: The World of His Final Tragedies*. Berkeley, Calif., 1950.

Feuillerat, Albert, *Documents Relating to the Revels at Court in the Time of King Edward VI and Queen Mary, Materialien zur Kunde des älteren englischen Dramas*, Vol. XLIV (1914).

——, *Documents Relating to the Office of the Revels in the Time of Queen Elizabeth, Materialien zur Kunde des älteren englischen Dramas*, Vol. XXI (1908).

Field, Nathan, *The Plays*, ed. William Peery. Austin, Texas, 1950.

Firzgeffrey, H., "Notes from Blackfriars" (in *Certain Elegies Done by Sundry Excellent Wits with Satires and Epigrams*, 1620, reprinted by G. E. Palmer for Edward Utterson, Beldornie Press, 1843).

Fleay, Frederick G., *A Chronicle History of the London Stage, 1559–1642*. London, 1890 (New York reprint, 1909).

Fletcher, John. See Beaumont.

"Four Letters on Theatrical Affairs," ed. E. K. Chambers, *Malone Society Collections*, Vol. II, Part II (1923).

Foxe, John, *The Acts and Monuments*, ed. Stephen R. Cattley, Vol. VIII. London, 1839.

Freud, Sigmund, *Civilization and Its Discontents*, trans. Joan Rivière (International Psycho-Analytical Library, No. 17). London, 1930.

Gascoigne, George, *Supposes and Jocasta*, ed. John W. Cunliffe. Boston, 1906.
——, *Complete Works*, ed. John W. Cunliffe. 2 vols. Boston, 1907–1910.
Gentleness and Nobility, ed. Kenneth W. Cameron. Raleigh, N.C., 1941.
George a Greene, the Pinner of Wakefield, in J. Q. Adams, *Chief Pre-Shakespearean Dramas* (q.v.).
Gosson, Stephen, *Plays Confuted in Five Actions* (1582) (in W. C. Hazlitt, *The English Drama and Stage, 1543–1664*, London, 1869, pp. 159–218).
——, *The School of Abuse* (1579), ed. John P. Collier for Shakespeare Society. London, 1841.
Gower, John, *Complete Works*, ed. G. C. Macaulay. 4 vols. Oxford, 1899–1902.
Grace, William J., "The Cosmic Sense in Shakespearean Tragedy," *Sewanee Review*, L (1942), 433–445.
Gray, H. David, "The Chamberlain's Men and the 'Poetaster,'" *M.L.R.*, XLII (1942), 173–179. Comment by P. Simpson and rejoinder, *Ibid.*, XLV (1950), 148–152.
Greene, Robert, *The Life and Complete Works in Prose and Verse*, ed. Alexander B. Grosart. 15 vols., London, 1881–1886.
——, *The Plays and Poems*, ed. J. Churton Collins. 2 vols. Oxford, 1905.
Greg, Sir Walter W., *Dramatic Documents from the Elizabethan Playhouses*. 2 vols. Oxford, 1931.
Griffin, William J., "Notes on Early Tudor Control of the Stage," *Modern Language Notes*, LVIII (1943), 50–54.
Guilpin, Everard, *Skialetheia; or, A Shadow of Truth in Certain Epigrams and Satyres* (1598) (Shakespeare Association Facsimiles, No. 2). Oxford, 1931.
Hall, Edward, *Chronicle.* (1548). London, 1809.
Hall, Hubert, *Society in the Elizabethan Age.* London, 1892.
Hall, Joseph, *Complete Poems*, ed. Alexander B. Grosart. Manchester, 1879.
Haller, William, "Hail Wedded Love," *ELH*, XIII (1946), 79–97.
——, and Malleville Haller, "The Puritan Art of Love," *Huntington Library Quarterly*, V (1941–1942), 235–272.
Harbage, Alfred, *As They Liked It: An Essay on Shakespeare and Morality.* New York, 1947.
——, *Cavalier Drama.* (Modern Language Association of America, General Series.) New York, 1936.
——, *Shakespeare's Audience.* New York, 1941.
——, *Sir William Davenant.* Philadelphia, 1935.
Harington, Sir John, *A Brief Apology for Poetry* (1591) (in *Elizabethan Critical Essays*, ed. G. Gregory Smith, 2 vols., Oxford, 1904).
——, *The Epigrams*, ed. Norman E. McClure. Philadelphia, 1926.
Harmon, Alice, "How Great Was Shakespeare's Debt to Montaigne?" *PMLA*, LVII (1942), 988–1008.
Harris, Frank, *The Man Shakespeare and His Tragic Life Story.* New York, 1909.
Hart, Alfred, *Shakespeare and the Homilies, and Other Pieces of Research into the Elizabethan Drama.* Melbourne, 1934.

Harvey, Gabriel, *The Letter-Book*, ed. Edward J. L. Scott, *Camden Society Publications*, Vol. XXXIII (1884).

Haughton, William, *Englishmen for My Money; or, A Woman Will Have Her Will*, ed. Albert C. Baugh. Philadelphia, 1917.

Haydn, Hiram, *The Counter-Renaissance*. New York, 1950.

Hazlitt, William, *Characters of Shakespeare's Plays* (1817) (in *Collected Works*, ed. A. R. Waller and Arnold Glover, 12 vols., London, 1902–1904, Vol. I).

Henslowe, Philip, *Diary*, ed. W. W. Greg. 2 vols. London, 1904–1908.

——, *Papers*, ed. W. W. Greg. London, 1907.

Heywood, Thomas, *An Apology for Actors* (1612), ed. Richard H. Perkinson (Scholars' Facsimiles and Reprints). New York, 1941.

——, *Dramatic Works*, reprinted by John Pearson. 6 vols. London, 1874.

Higgins, Michael, "The Convention of the Stoic Hero As Handled by Marston," *Modern Language Review*, XXXIX (1944), 338–346.

Hillebrand, Harold N., *The Child Actors: A Chapter in Elizabethan Stage History* (Univ. of Illinois Studies in Language and Literature, Vol. XI, Nos. 1, 2). Urbana, Ill., 1926.

——, "Thomas Middleton's 'The Viper's Brood,'" *Modern Language Notes*, XLII (1927), 35–38.

Holinshed, Raphael, *Chronicles of England, Scotland, and Ireland*. 6 vols. London, 1807–1808.

Hooker, Richard, *Works*, ed. John Keble. 3 vols. Oxford, 1888.

Hotson, Leslie, *The Commonwealth and Restoration Stage*. Cambridge, Mass., 1928.

How a Man May Choose a Good Wife from a Bad. In Dodsley (*q.v.*), Vol. IX.

Hundred Merry Tales (1525), ed. W. C. Hazlitt in *Shakespeare Jest-Books* (3 vols., London, 1864), Vol. I.

Jackson, William A., "The Lamport Hall-Britwell Court Books," in *Joseph Quincy Adams Memorial Studies*, pp. 587–599. Washington, D.C., 1948.

Jeronimo. In Dodsley (*q.v.*), Vol. IV.

Johnson, Francis R., *Astronomical Thought in Renaissance England*. Baltimore, 1937.

Johnson, Samuel, "Preface," in *The Plays of William Shakespeare*, ed. I. Reed 5th ed.; 21 vols., London, 1803), I, 245–311.

Jonson, Ben, *Dramatic Works*, ed. C. H. Herford and Percy Simpson. 11 vols. Oxford, 1925–1950.

Kennedy, Charles W., "Political Theory in the Plays of George Chapman," in *Essays in Dramatic Literature*, ed. Hardin Craig, pp. 73–86. Princeton, 1935.

Keynes, John M., *A Treatise on Money*. 2 vols. London, 1930.

King, Gregory, *Two Tracts by Gregory King*, ed. George E. Barnett. Baltimore, 1936.

King Leir, ed. W. W. Greg. Malone Society Reprints, 1907.

Knack to Know a Knave, A (in John P. Collier, *Five Old Plays*, London, 1851).

Knack to Know an Honest Man, A, ed. H. de Vocht and W. W. Greg. Malone Society Reprints, 1910.

Knights, L. C., *Drama and Society in the Age of Jonson.* London, 1937.

Laelia: A Comedy Acted at Queen's College, Cambridge, ed. G. C. Moore Smith. Cambridge, 1910.

Laing, David, "A Brief Account of the Hawthornden Manuscripts," *Archaeologia Scotia,* IV (1857), 57–116.

Lawrence, W. J., *The Elizabethan Playhouse and Other Studies.* Philadelphia, 1912.

——, "The Elizabethan Private Playhouse," *Criterion,* IX (1929–1930), 420–429.

——, *Pre-Restoration Stage Studies.* Cambridge, Mass., 1927.

——, "The Site of the Whitefriars Theatre." *Review of English Studies,* XI (1935), 186.

Lawrence, William W., *Shakespeare's Problem Comedies.* New York, 1931.

Leech, Clifford, *Shakespeare's Tragedies, and Other Studies in Seventeenth Century Drama.* London, 1950.

Legge, Thomas, *Richardus Tertius* (in W. C. Hazlitt, *Shakespeare's Library,* Part II, Vol. I, London, 1875).

Legouis, Émile, "The Bacchic Element in Shakespeare's Plays." In *Aspects of Shakespeare* (British Academy Shakespeare Lectures), Oxford, 1933.

Letters and Papers Foreign and Domestic of the Reign of Henry VIII, ed. J. Gairdner and R. H. Brodie, Vol. XIV, Part II (1539). London, 1895.

Levin, Harry, Introduction to Ben Jonson, *Selected Works.* New York, 1938.

Lewis, C. S., *The Allegory of Love: A Study in Medieval Tradition.* Oxford, 1936.

Leycester's Commonwealth: conceived, spoken and published with most earnest protestation of all dutiful good will . . . (1584). London, 1641.

Liberality and Prodigality, Contention Between. In Dodsley (*q.v.*), Vol. VIII.

Lodge, Thomas, *Complete Works,* ed. Edmund Gosse. 4 vols. Glasgow, 1883.

——, *Defence of Poetry* (in Vol. I, *Elizabethan Critical Essays,* ed. G. Gregory Smith, 2 vols. Oxford, 1904).

The London Prodigal, in C. F. Tucker Brooke, ed., *The Shakespeare Apocrypha* (*q.v.*).

Look About You, ed. W. W. Greg. Malone Society Reprints, 1913.

Lovejoy, A. O., *The Great Chain of Being.* Cambridge, Mass., 1936.

Lust's Dominion. In Dodsley (*q.v.*), Vol. XIV.

Lyly, John, *Complete Works,* ed. R. Warwick Bond, 3 vols. Oxford, 1902.

MacCallum, M. W., *Shakespeare's Roman Plays and Their Background.* London, 1910.

Machin, Lewis, and Gervase Markham, *The Dumb Knight.* In Dodsley (*q.v.*), Vol. X.

Maid's Metamorphosis, in Lyly (*q.v.*), *Works,* Vol. III.

Mankind (c. 1475) in J. Q. Adams, *Chief Pre-Shakespearean Dramas* (*q.v.*).

Manningham, Sir John, *Diary,* ed. John Bruce, *Camden Society Publications,* XCIX (1868).

Marston, John, *Plays,* ed. H. Harvey Wood. 3 vols. London, 1934–1939.

——, *Poems,* ed. Alexander B. Grosart. Occasional Issues. Manchester, 1879.

Marx, Karl, and Friedrich Engels, *Manifesto of the Communist Party*, Authorized English Trans. 8th Printing. New York, 1937.

Mason, John, *The Turk*, ed. Joseph Q. Adams, *Materialien zur Kunde des älteren englischen Dramas*, Vol. XXXVII (1913).

Medwall, Henry, *Fulgens and Lucrece* (c. 1497) (in Frederick S. Boas, *Five Pre-Shakespearean Comedies*, London, 1934).

Meres, Francis. *Francis Meres's Treatise "Poetrie"* (from *Palladis Tamia, 1598*), ed. Don C. Allen, Urbana, Ill., 1933.

Merry Conceited Jests of George Peele, in Peele, *Works* (*q.v.*).

Merry Devil of Edmonton, in C. F. Tucker Brooke, ed., *The Shakespeare Apocrypha* (*q.v.*).

Merry Tales, Witty Questions and Quick Answers (1567), ed. W. C. Hazlitt, *Shakespeare Jest-Books* (3 vols., London, 1864), Vol. I.

Middleton, Thomas, *Works*, ed. A. H. Bullen. 8 vols. London, 1885–1886.

Milton, John, *Works*, ed. Frank A. Patterson et al. 20 vols. New York, 1931–1940.

Montaigne, Seigneur Michel de, *Essayes*, trans. John Florio, ed. J. I. M. Stewart. New York, 1933.

Montemayor, Jorge de, *Diana*, trans. Bartholomew Yong. London, 1598.

Morrow, Donald, *Where Shakespeare Stood: His Part in the Crucial Struggles of His Day*. Milwaukee, 1935.

Motter, T. H. Vail, *The School Drama in England*. New York, 1929.

Mucedorus (in C. F. Tucker Brooke, ed., *The Shakespeare Apocrypha* [*q.v.*]).

Munday, Anthony, *John a Kent and John a Cumber*, ed. M. St. Clare Byrne and W. W. Greg. Malone Society Reprints, 1923.

Murray, John T., *English Dramatic Companies, 1558–1642*. 2 vols. London, 1910.

Nashe, Thomas, *Works*, ed. Ronald B. McKerrow. 5 vols. London, 1904–1910.

Nichols, John, *The Progresses and Public Processions of Queen Elizabeth*. 3 vols. London, 1823.

Nicolson, Marjorie H., *The Breaking of the Circle: Studies in the Effect of the "New Science" upon Seventeenth Century Poetry*. Evanston, Ill., 1950.

Noble, Richmond, *Shakespeare's Biblical Knowledge and Use of the Book of Common Prayer*. London, 1935.

Nobody and Somebody (in Richard Simpson, *The School of Shakspere*, Vol. I, New York, 1878).

Otto, Prince von Hessen-Cassel, "Itinerarium einer Reiss auss Cassell in Engeland A.D. 1611," extracts by Karl Feyerbend, *Englische Studien*, XIV (1890), 437–452.

Overend, G. H., "On the Dispute Between George Maller, Glazier, and Trainer of Players to Henry VIII, and Thomas Arthur, Tailor, His Pupil," *New Shakspere Society Transactions*, Series I, Part 3 (1877–1879).

Owst, G. R., *Literature and Pulpit in Medieval England*. Cambridge, 1933.

Painter, William, *The Palace of Pleasure*, ed. Joseph Jacobs. 3 vols. London, 1890.

Palmer, John L., *Political Characters of Shakespeare*. London, 1946.

Parnassus Plays, The Three, ed. J. B. Leishman. London, 1949.

Partridge, Eric, *Shakespeare's Bawdy: A Literary and Psychological Essay, and a Comprehensive Glossary*. London, 1947.

Paston Letters, 1422-1509, ed. James Gairdner. 3 vols. London, 1872-1875.

Peele, George, *Works*, ed. A. H. Bullen. 2 vols. London, 1888.

Penniman, Josiah H., ed., *"Poetaster," by Ben Jonson, and "Satiromastix," by Thomas Dekker*. Boston, 1913. (Introduction.)

Penshurst Papers. Report on the Manuscripts of Lord De L'Isle and Dudley Preserved at Penshurst Place, ed. C. L. Kingsford. 4 vols. *Historical Manuscripts Commission*. London, 1925-1942.

Percy, Henry Algernon, Fifth Earl of Northumberland. *The Regulations and Establishment of the Household*, ed. Thomas Percy. London, 1827.

Perkinson, Richard H., "Nature and the Tragic Hero in Chapman's Bussy Plays," *Modern Language Quarterly*, III (1942), 263-285.

Philip Julius, Duke of Stettin-Pomerania. "Diary of the Journey . . . Through England in the Year 1602," ed. G. von Bülow and W. Powell, *Transactions of the Royal Historical Society*, New Series, Vol. VI (1892).

Phillips, James E., *The State in Shakespeare's Greek and Roman Plays*. New York, 1940.

Pikering, John, *Horestes*, ed. Alois Brandl, *Quellen und Forschungen zur Sprach- und Kulturgeschichte*, Vol. LXXX (1898).

Platter, Thomas, *Travels in England, 1599*, trans. Clare Williams. London, 1937.

Plautus, *Works* (Loeb Classical Library). 5 vols. London and New York, 1916-1938.

Plomer, H. R., "New Documents on English Printers and Booksellers of the Sixteenth Century," *Transactions of the Bibliographical Society*, Vol. IV (1896-1898), 153-183.

Plutarch. *Shakespeare's Plutarch*, trans. T. North, C. F. Tucker Brooke. 2 vols. New York, 1909.

Porter, Henry, *Two Angry Women of Abingdon*, ed. W. W. Greg. Malone Society Reprints, 1912.

Powell, Chilton L., *English Domestic Relations, 1487-1653*. New York, 1917.

Power, Eileen, "The Position of Women," in *The Legacy of the Middle Ages*, ed. C. G. Crump and E. F. Jacob, pp. 401-433. Oxford, 1926.

Pratt, Norman T., Jr., "The Stoic Base of Senecan Drama," *Transactions of the American Philological Association*, Vol. LXXIX (1948), 1-11.

Preston, Thomas, *Cambyses*, in J. Q. Adams, *Chief Pre-Shakespearean Dramas* (*q.v.*).

Primrose, Lady Diana, *A Chain of Pearl* (1603), in John Nichols, *The Progresses, and Public Processions, of Queen Elizabeth* (3 vols., London, 1823), Vol. III.

Puritan, The, or The Widow of Watling-Street, in Brooke, ed., *The Shakespeare Apocrypha* (*q.v.*).

Raleigh, Sir Walter, *Shakespeare* (English Men of Letters Series). London, 1907, 1928.

Randolph, M. C., "The Medical Concept in English Renaissance Satiric Theory: Its Possible Relationships and Implications," *Studies in Philology*, XXXVIII (1941).

Rare Triumphs of Love and Fortune, The, ed. W. W. Greg. Malone Society Reprints, 1930.

Ratsey's Ghost (1606), ed. G. B. Harrison, *The Life and Death of Gamaliel Ratsey*, Shakespeare Association Facsimiles, No. 10. Oxford, 1935.

Reed, A. W., *Early Tudor Drama*. London, 1926.

Rennert, Hugo A., *The Spanish Stage in the Time of Lope de Vega*. New York, 1909.

Revenger's Tragedy, ed. Allardyce Nicoll, in Cyril Tourneur, *Works* (London, 1930).

Rich, John, *Apolonius and Silla*, ed. Morton Luce. London, 1912.

Ringler, William A., "The First Phase of the Elizabethan Attack on the Stage, 1558–1579," *Huntington Library Quarterly*, V (1942), 391–418.

——, *Stephen Gosson: A Biographical and Critical Study*. Princeton, 1942.

Rogers, James E. Thorold, *A History of Agriculture and Prices in England, 1259–1793*. 7 vols. Oxford, 1866–1902.

Rollins, Hyder E., "The Black-Letter Broadside Ballads," *PMLA*, XXXIV (1919), 258–339.

——, "The Troilus-Cressida Story from Chaucer to Shakespeare," *PMLA*, XXXII (1917), 383–429.

Rowlands, Samuel, *Complete Works*. 3 vols. Printed for the Hunterian Club, 1872–1880.

Rowley, Samuel, *When You See Me You Know Me*, reproduced by J. S. Farmer, Student's Facsimile Edition, 1912.

Rowley, William, *A Shoemaker a Gentleman*, ed. Charles W. Stork (Publications of the Univ. of Pennsylvania, Series in Philology and Literature, Vol. XIII). New York, 1910.

Saxo Grammaticus, *Historia Danica* (in Sir Israel Gollancz, *The Sources of Hamlet, with Essay on the Legend*, London, 1926).

Schoell, F. L., "George Chapman and the Italian Neo-Latinists of the Quattrocento," *Modern Philology*, XIII (1916), 215–238.

Second and Third Blast of Retreat from Plays and Theatres, A (1580) (in W. C. Hazlitt, *The English Drama and Stage, 1543–1664*, London, 1869).

Seebohm, Frederic, *The Oxford Reformers*, rev. ed. 1869 (Everyman's Library). London, 1914.

Shakespeare, William, *Complete Works*, ed. George L. Kittredge. Boston, 1936.

——, *The Plays of William Shakespeare*, ed. Isaac Reed. 21 vols. London, 1803.

——, *Measure for Measure*, ed. Sir Arthur Quiller-Couch and J. Dover Wilson. Cambridge, 1922.

Shapiro, I. A., "The Mermaid Club," *Modern Language Review*, XLV (1950), 6–17.

Sharpe, Robert B., *The Real War of the Theatres: Shakespeare's Fellows in Rivalry with the Admiral's Men, 1594–1603, Repertories, Devices, and Types* (The Modern Language Association Monograph Series, Vol V). New York, 1935.

Sharpham, Edward, *Cupid's Whirligig*, ed. Allardyce Nicoll. London, 1926.

——, *The Fleire*, ed. Hunold Nibbe, *Materialien zur Kunde des älteren englischen Dramas*, Vol. XXXVI (1912).

Sheavyn, Phoebe A. B., *The Literary Profession in the Elizabethan Age*. Manchester, 1909.

Sherbo, Arthur, *English Sentimental Drama*. MS. dissertation, Columbia Univ., 1950.

Sidney, Sir Philip, *The Countess of Pembroke's Arcadia* (1590), ed. in Vol. I of *The Complete Works*, ed. A. Feuillerat (4 vols., Cambridge, 1912–1926).

——, *An Apology for Poetry*, in G. Gregory Smith, *Elizabethan Critical Essays* (2 vols. Oxford, 1904), Vol. I.

Sir Clyomon and Sir Clamydes, ed. W. W. Greg. Malone Society Reprints, 1913.

Sir John Oldcastle (by Drayton, Hathway, Munday, Wilson), in C. F. Tucker Brooke, ed., *The Shakespeare Apocrypha (q.v.)*.

Sir Thomas More (by Munday, Chettle, Dekker, *et al.*), in C. F. Tucker Brooke, ed., *The Shakespeare Apocrypha (q.v.)*.

Sisson, C. J., *Lost Plays of Shakespeare's Age*. Cambridge, 1936.

——, "Mr and Mrs Browne of the Boar's Head," *Life and Letters Today*, Vol. XV, No. 6 (Winter, 1936), 99–107.

——, "Notes on Early Stuart Stage History," *Modern Language Review*, XXXVII (1942), 25–36.

Small, R. A., *The Stage-Quarrel Between Ben Jonson and the So-Called Poetasters*. Breslau, 1899.

Smirnov, A. A., *Shakespeare: A Marxist Interpretation*, trans. from the Russian, 3rd ed. rev. New York, 1936.

Smith, D. Nichol, "Authors and Patrons," Chap. XXII in Vol. II of *Shakespeare's England*, ed. Sir Walter Raleigh, Sir Sidney Lee, and C. T. Onions (2 vols., Oxford, 1916).

——, "Warton's History of English Poetry," *Proceedings of the British Academy*, Vol. XV (1929), pp. 73–99.

Smith, Logan Pearsall, *On Reading Shakespeare*. New York, 1933.

Spencer, Hazelton, ed., *Elizabethan Plays*. Boston, 1933. (Introductory Note to *The Knight of the Burning Pestle*.)

Spencer, Theodore, "The Elizabethan Malcontent," *Joseph Quincy Adams Memorial Studies*, pp. 523–536.

——, *Shakespeare and the Nature of Man*. New York, 1942.

Spenser, Edmund, *Poetical Works*, ed. J. C. Smith and E. De Sélincourt, London, 1929.

Starkey, Thomas, *A Dialogue Between Cardinal Pole and Thomas Lupset, Lecturer in Rhetoric at Oxford,* ed. J. M. Cowper, Early English Text Society, Extra Series 12, Vol. XXXII (1878).

Stirling, Brents, "Daniel's *Philotas* and the Essex Case," *Modern Language Quarterly,* III (1942), 583-594.

——, *The Populace in Shakespeare.* New York, 1949.

Stoll, Elmer E., "Modesty in the Audience," *Modern Language Notes,* LV (1940), 570-576.

——, "Shakespeare Forbears," *Modern Language Notes,* LIV (1939), 332-339.

Stone, Lawrence, "State Control in Sixteenth-Century England," *Economic History Review,* XVII (1947), 103-120.

Strathmann, Ernest A., *Sir Walter Raleigh: A Study in Elizabethan Skepticism.* New York, 1951.

Strype, John. *The History of the Life and Acts of the Most Reverend Father in God, Edmund Grindal.* Oxford, 1821.

Stubbes, Philip, *The Anatomy of Abuses* (1583) (in W. C. Hazlitt, *English Drama and Stage, 1543-1664,* London, 1869).

Taming of a Shrew, The, ed. F. S. Boas. London, 1908.

Tawney, R. H., *Religion and the Rise of Capitalism* (1926), new ed. New York, 1947.

Thaler, Alwin, "The Travelling Players in Shakespeare's England," *Modern Philology,* XVII (1920), 489-514. (Reprinted in *Shakespeare and Democracy.*)

——, *Shakespeare and Democracy.* Knoxville, Tenn., 1941.

Thomas Lord Cromwell, in C. F. Tucker Brooke, *The Shakespeare Apocrypha* (*q.v.*).

Tillyard, E. M. W. *The Elizabethan World Picture.* New York, 1944.

——, *Shakespeare's History Plays.* New York, 1946.

Tolman, A. H., "Is Shakespeare Aristocratic?" *PMLA,* XXIX (1914), 277-298.

Tolstoy, Leo, *Tolstoy on Shakespeare,* trans. V. Tchertkoff and I. F. M., followed by "Shakespeare's Attitude to the Working Classes," by Ernest Crosby. New York, 1906.

Transcript of the Register of the Company of Stationers of London, 1554-1640, ed. Edward Arber. 5 vols. London and Birmingham, 1875-1894.

Trevelyan, G. M. *Illustrated English Social History,* Vol. II: *The Age of Shakespeare and the Stuart Period.* London, 1950.

Trial of Chivalry, The (in Vol. III of A. H. Bullen, *A Collection of Old English Plays,* 4 vols., London, 1882-1885).

Troublesome Reign of King John, The, ed. F. J. Furnivall and John Munro. London, 1913.

True Tragedy of Richard the Third, The, ed. W. W. Greg. Malone Society Reprints, 1929.

Tupper, Frederick, "The Shakespearean Mob," *PMLA,* XXVII (1912), 486-523.

Twine, Laurence, *The Pattern of Painful Adventures* (c. 1576) (in W. C. Hazlitt, *Shakespeare Library,* Part I, Vol. I, London, 1875).

"Two Early Play-Lists," ed. E. K. Chambers, *Malone Society Collections*, Vol. I, Parts IV–V (1911), 348–356.

Upton, Albert W., "Allusions to James I and His Court in Marston's *Fawn* and Beaumont's *Woman Hater*," *PMLA*, XLIV (1929), 1048–1065.

Utley, Francis L., *The Crooked Rib: An Analytical Index to the Argument About Women . . . to the End of the Year 1568*. Columbus, Ohio, 1944.

The Valiant Welshman (by R. A.), reproduced by J. S. Farmer. Students Facsimile Ed., 1913.

Vives, Juan Luis, *On Education*, trans. Foster Watson. Cambridge, 1913.

Walker, A., "The Reading of an Elizabethan," *Review of English Studies*, VIII (1932), 264–281.

Wallace, Charles W., "The Children of the Chapel at Blackfriars, 1597–1603" (*University Studies, pub. by the Univ. of Nebraska*, Vol. VIII, Nos. 2–3, April-July, 1908).

——, "The Evolution of the English Drama Up to Shakespeare, with a History of the First Blackfriars Theatre" (*Schriften der Deutschen Shakespeare-Gesellschaft*, Vol. IV, 1912).

——, "The First London Theatre: Materials for a History" (*University Studies, Pub. by the Univ. of Nebraska*, Vol. XIII, Nos. 1–3, Jan.-July, 1913).

——, "Shakespeare and His London Associates As Revealed in Recently Discovered Documents" (*University Studies, pub. by the Univ. of Nebraska*, Vol. X, No. 4, Oct., 1910).

Warburton, William, Preface to Shakespeare, *Plays*, ed. I. Reed (*q.v.*), I, 226–245.

Ward, B. M., "The Chamberlain's Men in 1597," *Review of English Studies*, IX (1933), 55–58.

Warning for Fair Women, A (in Richard Simpson, *The School of Shakspere*, Vol. II, London, 1878).

Wars of Cyrus, ed. James P. Brawner (Illinois Studies in Language and Literature, Vol. XXVIII, Nos. 3–4). Urbana, Ill., 1942.

Warton, Thomas, *History of English Poetry*, ed. W. C. Hazlitt. 4 vols. London, 1871.

Weakest Goeth to the Wall, The, ed. W. W. Greg. Malone Society Reprints, 1912.

Webster, John, *Complete Works*, ed. F. L. Lucas. 4 vols. London, 1928.

Whetstone, George, Promos and Cassandra (in W. C. Hazlitt, *Shakespeare's Library*, Part II. London, 1875).

Whitehead, Alfred North. *Science and the Modern World*. New York, 1949.

Whitelocke, Sir James. *Liber Famelicus*, ed. John Bruce, *Camden Society Publications*, LXX (1858).

Wilkins, George, *The Miseries of Enforced Marriage*. In Dodsley, Vol. IX (*q.v.*).

——, *The Painful Adventures of Pericles*, ed. Tycho Mommsen. Oldenburg, 1857.

Williams, Arnold L., "A Note on Pessimism in the Renaissance," *Studies in Philology*, XXXVI (1939), 243–246.

Wilson, Edmund, *The Triple Thinkers: Twelve Essays on Literary Subjects.* Rev. and enlarged ed. New York, 1948.

Wilson, F. P., *Elizabethan and Jacobean.* Oxford, 1945.

——, "Some Notes on Authors and Patrons in Tudor and Stuart Times" (in *Joseph Quincy Adams Memorial Studies*, 1948, pp. 553–561).

Wilson, J. Dover, "The Elizabethan Shakespeare" (in *Aspects of Shakespeare*, British Academy Lectures, Oxford, 1933).

Wilson, Robert, *The Three Ladies of London.* In Dodsley, Vol. VI (*q.v.*).

——, *Three Lords and Three Ladies of London.* In Dodsley, Vol. VI (*q.v.*).

Wisdom of Doctor Dodypoll (in Vol. III, A. H. Bullen, *A Collection of Old English Plays*, 4 vols., London, 1882–1885).

Wright, Louis B., *Middle-Class Culture in Elizabethan England.* Chapel Hill, N.C., 1935.

Wyclif, John, *Select English Writings*, ed. Herbert E. Winn. Oxford, 1929.

Yorkshire Tragedy, A (in C. F. Tucker Brooke, *The Shakespeare Apocrypha* [*q.v.*]).

Zeeveld, W. Gordon, *Foundations of Tudor Policy.* Cambridge, Mass., 1948.

Index